"Kiss Your Elbow – A Kentucky Memoir"

---*Memoir of a young girl, growing up as the oldest child in a large family of 13, facing the challenges of farm living on the suburban edge of Louisville, Kentucky during the 1940' and '50's.*

Explanation of the title,
"Kiss Your Elbow,"
an old southern saying

"When I was a little girl, I quickly discovered that my three younger brothers enjoyed many privileges that I, the only girl, did not have. While they were outside being part of the world, it seemed I was stuck in the house doing 'women's work'. I asked Grandma Anna, who lived with us until I was six, "When am I going to get to be a boy?"

Her answer seemed very reasonable to me then, and I tried nightly to make it come true, so desperate was my wish. Smiling at me, as I was all snuggled into my winter bedding, Grandma said...

"All you have to do is kiss your elbow before you go to sleep at night, Deanna, and by morning you will be a boy."

"Kiss Your Elbow" —
A Kentucky Memoir

Deanna O'Daniel

authorHOUSE®

AuthorHouse™
1663 Liberty Drive
Bloomington, IN 47403
www.authorhouse.com
Phone: 1-800-839-8640

First published by AuthorHouse 7/9/2010

ISBN: 978-1-4520-4179-7 (e)
ISBN: 978-1-4520-4178-0 (sc)

Library of Congress Control Number: 2010909245

Printed in the United States of America
Bloomington, Indiana

This book is printed on acid-free paper.

This is a book of creative, historical, non-fiction. Many names of people and locations have been changed to protect the innocent. References such as these are intended to provide a sense of authenticity and are used fictitiously. Incidents and dialogue are drawn from the author's memory and imagination and not to be construed as real.

Front cover:
O'Daniel Siblings-1954-taken on Hunsinger Lane
Back left: Johnny, Marcellus, Deanna
Front left: Margaret Jane, Jimmy, Tony, Mary Ann, Theresa
Phillip (pulling wagon) Pat, dog-Snowball, Billy

Dedication Page

I dedicate this book, *Kiss Your Elbow – A Kentucky Memoir* to all the good neighbors, good times, and hard times which augmented my life during this incredible period of America's history – the time after World War II. I also wish to acknowledge the wonderful help I received from my many writer friends who encouraged me to publish this memoir, as an act of demonstrating the love in my family and of preserving this time period of the mid-twentieth century.

I particularly wish to thank all the superb helpers I had during the proof reading process, especially John Boyd, Mary Popham, Ruth Merriam and Bob Korn. Particular gratitude goes to my brother Jim for computer help, without which the book would have never happened.

Kiss Your Elbow – A Kentucky Memoir

Gethsemane:

  Poem – Lessons from My Mother's Heart xi

Introduction: Everybody Has a Past xiii

Goldsmith Lane:

  Poem – Frozen Moments... xxix
  1. – If Only I'd Listened to Mama 1

Lexington Indiana:

  2. – Lexington and the Loftus Mansion 15

Hunsinger Lane:

  3. – The Price of Getting an Ice Cream Cone 37
    Poem – Winter Mornings 49
  4. – Christmas Comes, Slow as Molasses........................51
  5. – Here Comes the Easter Bunny 69
    Poem – Our Elbows Sticking to the Oilcloth 79
  6. – A Vacation at Last! 81
  7. – Shopping in Downtown Louisville 97
    Poem – Frozen Moments......................................115
  8. – The Ranger's Club 117
  9. – Hogkillin' Days..129
  10. – Risen From the Dead 149
  11. – Pepsi Cola Days at Fontaine Ferry Park 157
  12. – First Time in Charge 195
  13. – Eighth Grade Summer Days 221
    Poem – My Orange Blossom Cookie Canister......247

Moving On:

14. – Flashlight Dance 249
15. – Snails, Snails, and More Snails…...............................259
16. – Supper at Aunt Ida's..281
17. – "Roll Me up Some More Vanilla".......................................289
18. – Teaching is Enchanting 307

Alta Ave:

19. – "Where is Pat?"...339
    Poem – Daddy's Expectations..353
20. – Epilogue 355

Preface:

I have always fought for women to have a better life. As I made my way out into the world, I knew I wanted a different life than the one my mother lived. I respected the lessons of independence, discipline and resourcefulness that I learned on the farm, but I knew I wanted more. The influences of television and my suburban neighbors convinced me to experience more of the world than what my family referred to as "women's work."

The period after World War II was a time of prosperity and upward mobility for the middle class. Social morés changed as this slower juncture bridged our agrarian past into the complexities that now comprise our modern, technological world.

My purpose in writing this memoir is to celebrate this hope-filled period by loosely using my family and our simple life experiences to reflect the values, strengths, and comfortable realities that came from this unique era of the American Quilt.

Lessons from My Mother's Heart

I watched my mother grow and stretch
into life. Moving into strength
from the innocence
of a young farm girl,
straddled with responsibilities,
of pregnancies and children

to a woman of courage.
A guiding force in the
lives of many.
As her oldest daughter,
ours was the partnership
that made our family strong.

From working at her side
I imbibed her spirit, and absorbed
lessons that could
come from nowhere else.

She guided me into a
power of endurance, showing me
the ability that carried her through
thirteen pregnancies and the
constant chores that
filled our country life.

I worked along with her
through the growing, picking,
canning, the feeding, the plucking
and freezing required to
fill our winter larder.

I learned resourcefulness
from watching her magic fingers
make dresses from feed sacks,
and full wardrobes from
cousins' and neighbors' discards.

I helped her resurrect Aunt Bertha's
discarded furniture from
the `37 flood, that we proudly
claimed as part of our
living room suite.

Reveling in the abandon
of her laughter, we snapped
beans while listening to the radio,
or played cards in the evening.
Joy in the simple things was
her constant companion,
and our delight.

Mama's heart was always open,
her faith strong. Her innocent
dependence on God being the most
important virtue she showed me.

No matter how little we had
with the burdens of eleven children,
her reminders of, "God will take
Care of us," were always true.

Never desiring material wealth,
instead, elated by the contentment
that comes from knowing
how to trust God, and be grateful
for gifts already given.

I watched her spirit soar
as she made do with very little
but the love she had for us,
and the hope of a better day
residing inside.

My mother's heart showed
us siblings how to find
peace among each other, as
childhood battles gave way
to adult support and friendship

These are the very simple
but powerful gifts. And,
in a world that is frantic
for satisfaction – I know
what is real...

Thanks to my mother's heart

Introduction

Everybody Has a Past

"O'Daniel? Why, that's a Nelson County name," my new boyfriend told me when we met. He had grown up in Lebanon, Kentucky.

"In fact," he continued, "we have some O'Daniels back in our family tree. I bet we're related. Almost everybody in that area *is* related, you know."

I knew that from my own relatives in Nelson County where I was kin to almost everybody in Howardstown, Gethsemane/Gethsemani, New Haven, and New Hope.

After he'd asked a few questions from his family members, my new boyfriend found out that he was right, we were distant cousins. He told me about the "Maryland League." This name was given to the migration of the original groups of Catholics that came over from Maryland in the 1780's and settled, along with many other religious affiliations, in several areas of Kentucky. The families chose areas along the creeks in Marion, Nelson, and Washington Counties. Today, these counties in Kentucky are known as part of America's Holy Land.

Both my mother's and my father's ancestors were part of the Maryland League. For some reason my parents never spoke of this migration. Until the late 1960's, Nelson County remained a fairly closed community with most of the inhabitants being direct descendants of these, and other original settlers.

Almost 150 years before they met, both my parents' ancestors decided to settle in these counties in Kentucky's heartland. The end of the Revolutionary War opened up the land west of the Allegheny Mountains for settlement. My family's ancestors settled within ten miles of each other. What brought them to this area of sprawling valleys and gentle knobs? The answer was easy, the soil was fertile, the knobs (small mountains) were filled with wild game and hardwoods, and there were deep rivers and streams. They could tell that life here would be successful.

Also, around the time that America's Revolutionary War ended, Europe was undergoing a religious upheaval called the "Great Awakening." Members of several religious groups suffered persecution as heretics. This unrest pushed them to leave Europe and come to our shores. At play too, was the French Revolution, which caused many French Catholics to escape to the New World. The beliefs that these groups held were not well accepted in America, either. Baltimore, Maryland, was designated as a place of religious tolerance. Many groups took refuge there as they awaited the end of the war.

In 1785, a group of several Catholic families of Scottish, Irish and English descent, agreed to migrate across the Allegany Mountains for a new life in Kentucky. Called 'Maryland League,' their purpose was to establish a large enough community to be given a priest of their own. Encouraged by their success in the move, additional groups of Catholic families came to join them. The League's first settlement was along a creek in Nelson, County, in an area called Pottinger's Creek.

Many of the Catholics who settled in these counties (Nelson, Marion, and Washington), were accused of a type of heresy called Jansenism. The Jansenists were overly strict in their interpretation of Catholic rules. Their austere beliefs brought them into conflict with the Church of Rome. These zealous Catholics showed their devotion to God by building many beautiful churches with parish schools, convents for the religious Sisters of Loretto, Sisters of Charity, and the Dominican Sisters. They also built Catholic hospitals and orphanages.

****

French Trappist Monks joined the Maryland League in the location of Pottinger's Creek in Nelson County, in order to increase the strength of the Catholic faith in America. There, they built the famous monastery, the Abbey of Gethsemani, in 1848. The settlement's name was then changed to Gethsemani or Gethsemane. This was the area where my father was from, where I was born and where I lived until I was five years old.

Later, as a child growing up in Louisville, I never knew how to spell the name of my birthplace and tended to just put Nelson County. I noticed that Gethsemani sometimes ended in "e" and sometimes with an "i." My parents didn't seem to know about the reason for the difference, and just said, "Spell it either way – it all goes to the same place." When I went to the Abbey on retreat as an adult, I asked one of the monks for the proper spelling of the area. His answer was very clear, "Our monastery was built here first. We arrived in 1848. This Abbey was named after the biblical story of the The Garden of Gethsemani. The area soon became built up with several distilleries. There was never really a town here, only a train depot and a post office that were both used to support the needs of the distilleries. We did *not* want our Abbey to be confused with whiskey, so when the post office came in, we insisted that the end of the area's name be changed to an 'e' instead of an 'i.' Only the monastery ends with an 'i.'" His explanation cleared up a lifetime of confusion for me.

****

The history of my parents is part of the history of the area. My mother came from Howardstown and my father came from Gethsemane. Both of these locations are in close proximity to Bardstown, the major hub of the Catholic Church during its early days in America. My mother, Josephine Boone, descended from the Boones and the Howards. These were both notable families in the settlement of the Maryland League in Kentucky during the time of the 1780's. The Howard's were members of the first group of settlers in the League, and were instrumental in its success to establish the faith in the wilderness.

When we were children, Mama told us that our fifth great uncle, Thomas Howard, and his wife, Anne Goff, donated 300 acres just south of Bardstown, Kentucky, to the Catholic Church in 1810. The donation of the land also contained a large, well-built cabin. Due to the central location of this land, it became the first headquarters for the Catholic Church (called the Holy See) west of the Allegheny Mountains. In celebration, a church patterned after the famous cathedral in Baltimore, Maryland was built on this property. It was named St. Thomas after their benefactor, Thomas Howard.

From the land that Uncle Thomas donated, the first bishop, Bishop Flaget, became overseer of the new territory. This headquarters was also the site of the ordination of America's first priest, Father Stephen Badin, who was sent to lead the Catholic Church from the small, nearby town of Loretto, Kentucky.

Mama was proud of her Catholic faith and told us of her family's heritage in the early days here. "Bishop Flaget lived at one end of the cabin that Uncle Thomas and Aunt Anne built, and Aunt Anne lived at the other end. Both of them shared that cabin until she died a few years later. The cabin is still there today." The land that Uncle Thomas donated to the church was also used for the first convent of the Sisters of Charity, before they moved to larger quarters on the northern side of Bardstown. Though it is no longer in use as the Holy See, this land is still used by the church today, and now simply called St. Thomas.

Eventually, Mama's people settled in a large valley south of Bardstown. The farmers were so productive that a mill was soon built on Rolling Fork River there. Able to see a need for even more material goods, my great-grandfather, Samuel Howard, and his five brothers added an enormous general store to the site, along with the mill. The brothers hauled cedar and poplar trees by wagonload down from the plentiful supply in the knobs. The strong smell of the cedar wood discouraged termites and was still evident when I went into the store as a child. Farmers came from miles around to have their corn and wheat ground into meal and flour by the huge millstone that was turned by the river's rushing waters. The area was first known as Howard's Mill, but the name was eventually changed to Howardstown.

The Howard brothers ran a profitable business at the mill/general store for many years. This was the only store around and it sold everything. While the farmers had their wagons in the long line for the mill, their wives shopped for dry goods and necessities inside the store. Shopping was available on three immense floors.

Mama told me several recollections about the Howardstown Store. "When your father was courting me, we used to skate in a roller rink on the third floor of that store. It was so big that we had plenty of room to do dances and circles."

As a child, I noticed that the store sold everything from aspirins to coffins. I liked to look at the toys, especially the dolls with their pretty carriages. Grandpa Emanuel Boone's farm was down the road from the store, and was called the Boone Brothers Farm. This was the place where Mama grew up. My brothers and I walked up to this store when we were down visiting Grandpa from Louisville. On a hot summer day we bought popsicles, in the winter we went inside to warm our hands by the roaring fire in the potbelly stove. There was always a crowd of men gathered in the store talking about the weather, or most likely, the local gossip. In the summer, they were on the store's long front porch trying to catch the breeze coming down out of the knobs. Winter found them, like us, huddled inside around the stove. I enjoyed listening to their tales as they passed the time, talking, slapping their knees in laughter, and whittling twigs into toys with their pocketknives.

When machines became more dependable for grinding grains, and the millstone no longer needed the river to turn it, this store was moved forward, up from the aggravating floodwaters of the Rolling Fork, to its final location by the State Highway that goes through Howardstown.

Mama said, "It took my uncles two weeks, sixteen mules, and about a hundred oak tree trunks to roll that big store up there, but they never had to close their doors to business. It was open for customers the whole time." She continued, "The farmers had to watch out that their livestock didn't run off, though, because my uncles had to cut down most of their 'bob-wire' fences in order ta' get that big store through the fields." My eyes widened, the first time she told me this story, I was amazed that something that size could be moved by any means. Extra storage areas were added to the store when it reached its final location. (The store was unfortunately, recently lost, due to neglect in 2003).

Mama was the oldest of ten children and loved growing up in this close-knit community of Howardstown. She told me stories of her hard working father, Emanuel, and his jovial brother, her Uncle Charlie, who ran the Boone Brothers Farm with him. Charlie was a great musician. He played his fiddle on the front porch at night after chores and supper. Everybody came and gathered around to pick their banjos or guitars and sing country music. On Saturdays they square-danced most of the night away in his front yard.

"When I was growin' up, the priest didn't allow any round-dancing," Mama said. "That's where you just dance with one partner like in a waltz," she smiled as she reminisced. Mama told all of the stories about her family. She told of her mother, Lucy, who died before I was born during delivery of the tenth child in the family, my Aunt Saloma. With all the farm work, all the kids, and the fact that Lucy was frail anyway, she worked herself into a state of exhaustion. Her sister Cora was her mid-wife and said that the baby didn't kill her. "She was just too tired," Mama said, her eyes misting, "Aunt Cory told Daddy that Grandma Lucy (her mother) died of kidney failure."

This tragedy left my mother and her sister, Mary Cora, to take over the many tasks their mother performed, as well as their own chores. Mama was twenty and Mary Cora was only fourteen. Of the ten children, four were still under age six. The little ones just didn't understand why their mother wouldn't get up. "When's Mama gonna' stop sleepin' in the parlor?" Aunt Aurelia, who was only three, wanted to know.

Grandpa had to explain to her that Grandma was not sleeping, that she was laid out for visitors to see her one last time before she would be buried in St. Ann's Cemetery on the side of the hill above the church. "From there Mama will join God in heaven," he told his anxious children

Mama and Aunt Mary Cora had to boil cow's milk for the new baby, and break the ice on the water bucket in the mornings before they could make coffee for Grandpa Emanuel. The siblings learned to work together by doing the chores in the house and the fields without complaining. They had to help their grieving father get through this painful period of losing his life partner. He and Grandma Lucy had been sweethearts since childhood. He never remarried even though he was still a young man. "Grandpa said, when anybody asked him why he didn't remarry," Mama explained to me about her father, 'Why, who'd want a man with ten kids to raise!' But Mama knew he would never love anybody but Grandma Lucy. He loved her so much that he married her even though she was on her sickbed with pneumonia on their wedding day. The traveling priest had to perform the ceremony at Lucy's parent's house on the Howard Farm.

"We had to stop fightin' and help each other out. Daddy had enough to worry about." Mama's eyes misted again as she continued, "We were all crying, we missed Mama so much, but, after we made it through that, we never fought about anything anymore. It pulled us together."

I noticed that at the many family gatherings of my aunts and uncles and their families, they didn't have arguments like my brothers and I did. They always laughed and cut up and really had fun with each other. I wondered if we would be like them when we got older.

When I was growing up, Mama and I passed the time with stories while we did the farm chores necessary to keep our family fed and clothed. She told me about the days when she was young in Howardstown. She and I were best companions. Since we were both oldest girls of large farm families, we had a lot in common.

The funniest story that Mama ever told me was one that happened to her when she was twelve, in 1926. Her Uncle Virgil, one of her mother's (Grandma Lucy) eight brothers, (out of a family of ten siblings by Sam and Sudie Howard), and his wife, Ruby, took Mama and her cousin Margaret to Chicago with them. Both the girls were only twelve years old, and had never even been to Louisville before. The trip was hastily put together. After their parents talked for a few minutes, Mama and Margaret found themselves riding in the rumble seat of Uncle Virgil's roadster and on their way to the "Windy City."

The next day, after their arrival, Aunt Ruby and Uncle Virgil left the girls in their hotel room when they went out to take care of some business. Returning to the room, they found the door unlocked and the girls gone. They were horrified! The girls had never locked a door before in their lives. They didn't know how to lock the hotel door, so they left it unlocked.

Unbeknownst to them, Uncle Virgil had hundreds of dollars hidden in one of his suits in the closet. Mama and Margaret had gotten bored after they tried on all of Aunt Ruby's clothes. Looking for something to do, they went to the hotel's lobby fountain to buy a soda. The soda jerk gave them soda straws with their drinks. They had never seen these before, but noticed other fountain patrons using them. Being too shy to ask the clerk how the straws were to be used, the girls put them in the bubbly drink and lifted the glass as usual. Naturally, the syrupy soda went all down the front of their dresses. They returned to the hotel room a sticky mess!

When they were older, Mama and Margaret found out about the real reason for the hasty trip. The `20's was the time of alcohol prohibition. Uncle Virgil and Aunt Ruby were making a bootleg whiskey run for the hotel, bringing in moonshine that several families had made up in the knobs of Howardstown. "The knobs were full of stills," Mama chuckled.

Uncle Virgil and Aunt Ruby took the girls along so they would look like a regular family to the police. The big bucks they had hidden in the closet were to be divided among the contributing families when they got back to Howardstown. Fortunately, Ruby found that the money was all there, right where it had been hidden, but the girls got a strong talkin' to about how different things were in the big city.

"There's a lot of bootleg stories," Mama laughed, shaking her dark curls as she spoke. "If wasn't for moonshine, we'd a' starved on the farm. The `20's may `a been the 'Jazz-Age,' for city folks, but life was a struggle for farmers."

My father, John Hegenauer O'Daniel's family descended from the Heads and the O'Daniels and had moved in the 1920's to the Gethsemane area from Loretto, Kentucky. My grandfather Demetrius' farm was about eight miles north of Howardstown, and about two miles down the road from the famous monastery, the Abbey of Gethsemani. Again, all these locations are less than twenty miles from Bardstown.

Daddy's father, Demetrius Phamphlaus O'Daniel brought a new element into the family and to the area. During the winter months when things were slow on the farm, he went to Louisville to find work. He met and married a German girl named Anna Hegenauer, whose family came from Alsace Lorraine. They met at St. Martin de Tours Catholic Church where they later married in 1904. My Grandmother (Grandma Anna), brought an urban influence to our family that my country cousins did not have.

Anna came from a wealthy family. Her father, John Hegenauer was a carpenter by trade. Because of his superior skill, he was hired to be the supervising foreman for the rebuilding of Louisville's famous Galt House Hotel after it burned 1869. He also supervised the construction of several large buildings in the heart of downtown Louisville and many of the mansions in what is now called Old Louisville.

John Hegenauer thought it was very important to establish the Hegenauer name in America, and tried desperately to do so by having ten children of his own. He and his wife had six girls and four boys. Unfortunately for John, my great grandfather, his only male grandchild, John Vernon Hegenauer, became a priest. However, having a priest in the family was a great honor in those days, so this was bittersweet. My grandmother, Anna, in order to console her father, named my father John Hegenauer O'Daniel to carry on the name for one more generation. To include Great-Grandfather in his name, Daddy was called J.H., never just John.

At twelve years old Daddy almost drowned when the ice broke in the dangerous waters of Pottinger's Creek, a deep, swift running stream near the O'Daniel farm in Gethsemane. Amazingly, a train was coming into the Gethsemane Depot located close by the water's edge. The conductor and the brakeman ran through the snow and saved my father's life.

When my siblings and I went through our parent's effects after Mama's death in 2001, we found two letters, one from each of these two men. These letters described this event more clearly for us. Daddy had never really talked about it except to tell us not to ice skate on farm ponds.

Grandpa Demetrius had sent each of these men money for their efforts in saving Daddy's life. They had both written letters back to him thanking Grandpa Demetrius for the ten-dollar check that he sent to each of them. Both of the men declined the money, each saying in his own way, "I only did what anybody would do in that situation. Who would ignore a young boy a' drownin'?" Twenty dollars was a fortune for a farmer in 1923.

After my parents married in 1939, they moved into Grandma Anna's house to help take care of the farm. Grandma told Mama what a hard time she had getting used to rural life after Demetrius brought her, a city girl, to live on the farm. She told Mama how she, being a resourceful woman, got used to living in the country. Mama told me that Grandma Anna had said to her, "I declare, Josephine, I used to hate it here. I was so lonely. The people around here looked on me as some kind a' curiosity. Well, things changed when I found out how much my own family enjoyed getting away to the country. I always loved cookin', and entertainin'. After I learned how to go out in the chicken yard, chase down a chicken and ring its neck, I had no trouble fixing the rest of the meal. Word got around about my good cookin', and that's all it took for me to fit in. I got real popular for church picnics and socials," Mama's blue eyes shined as she remembered Grandma's story.

Then she continued the story for me: "Grandma was no spring chicken when I entered the family, so I helped her get things ready for company. Sometimes we'd cook for the picnics and the church socials, but mostly we cooked for family gatherings. Grandma's kin were always so much fun, and they loved to play with you and your brothers while we got dinner on," Mama told me this story while did the washin' one Monday. She continued, "Your grandma and I got the house all cleaned up on Friday and cooked all day Saturday. Then on Sunday, Daddy drove down the hill to the train depot and picked up some of Grandma's brothers and sisters or cousins after Mass. Sometimes, as many as a dozen." Mama smiled, "We sure had a good time. Demetrius met them there with a horse and buggy when he was alive."

Coming to the country was an easy trip for Grandma's relatives. They caught the train at Union Station, on Broadway in Louisville, and got to the Gethsemane Depot in about an hour.

Mama continued: "They liked our farm-fresh food. And, when they went home, they carried dried cow and horse manure wrapped in newspaper on the train with 'em, for their rose gardens back in the city." Then Mama and I both laughed thinking about the smell of manure with everybody dressed in their fine travelin' clothes on the train.

My parents, John Hegenauer O'Daniel and Josephine Boone, were unusual for farm kids growing up in the 1920's. They were both lucky enough to have graduated from high school at a time when most farm kids had to quit school in the early grades in order to work on the family farm. To be able to make this sacrifice of their labor, their parents must have strongly believed in the value of education. John and Josephine met each other at the Lincoln Tavern near Hodgenville, which was located next to the Lincoln Memorial Cabin. In the 1930's it was a popular restaurant where young folks went for lunch and dancing on Sunday afternoons after Mass. Now, it is part of the Lincoln Museum Complex.

They married at St. Ann's in Howardstown. Mama was pretty and energetic. Grandma Anna was delighted when they moved into the O'Daniel Farm. Because of Grandpa Demetrius' untimely death, she could use the extra help, and Mama's being a farm girl, meant that she was used to hard work. Demetrius had been killed a couple of years earlier, in 1937, when rising floodwaters somehow spooked his team of horses and they dragged him to his death. This happened during the time that floodwaters from the Ohio River devastated Louisville in that same year.

Daddy's only other sibling, Marcellus (we later called him Uncle Mac), yearned for the bright lights of the big city. He left the farm at age fifteen and moved in with some of Grandma Anna's people who had already left Louisville to live in Chicago. He loved the farm, however, and visited frequently, with his wife, Aunt Gen, a pretty, dark haired farm girl from Peoria, Illinois.

Since Demetrius' death, Daddy and Grandma took in boarders. There were many teenage orphans who did farm work free in exchange for room and board. However, much more manpower than their contribution was needed to run this big farm, and hiring help was expensive. Even though I was only five, I remembered Mama ringing the dinner bell during harvest time and over a dozen men coming in from the fields to wash up at the hand pump on the back porch. This was more than we could afford, but the harvest could not be left to rot on the ground.

****

The house on the O'Daniel Farm in which I was born has had an interesting history of its own. My family lived in this house and owned this farm from 1918 to the late 1940's. As a large ten-room clapboard farmhouse it was unique because of the generous wrap-around front porch. There were two houses of this type built in Gethsemane around the turn of twentieth century, most likely by the owners of the prosperous distilleries located there. Except for the houses in the city of Bardstown, these homes were considered among the finest in Nelson County. Without Grandpa Demetrius, life was too hard and lonely for Grandma on the farm. After her many years in the country, she was finally ready to re-join her relatives and go back home to Louisville. At her urging, Daddy sold the farm after World War II to J. W. Dant Distillery. Our house was used for their office. They filled in a lake down the hill in the back of the house in the pasture where I used to chase the calves into the barn.

Over the years, the property was sold several times. The house was rented and therefore fell into disrepair. In 1972, twenty-six years after we left it, it was discovered vacant and covered with choker vines by Sister Madeline, a member of the Sisters of Charity. Her convent, located north of nearby Bardstown was interested in establishing a retreat center for women in the vicinity of the Abbey of Gethsemani. The Abbey was used as a popular retreat house for men, but women were not allowed to enter for retreat there until the 1990's. With the help of local donated labor, most of it from the monks at the Abbey, the house was repaired and updated. Dividing the large rooms into separate bedrooms, the house was able to handle ten to twelve retreatants at a time. A few years later, two other retreat structures were added to the back of the property.

In 2008 the Sisters sold our former home, that they had named Bethany Springs, to the Thomas Merton Society. Still open for public retreat, the house is now maintained by the group that honors Gethsemani's most renowned citizen, Thomas Merton. He became a world famous intellectual, religious scholar, and noted author. Merton arrived in Gethsemani (the Abbey), the same year I arrived in Gethsemane (the area), 1941. But I beat him – I came in February, and he arrived in December. Unfortunately, he died young, in an accidental death while on a peace mission in 1968.

When we lived in that house, it had electricity, which was unusual for most farm homes in Nelson County back then. However, there was only one plug-in because the electric company charged a large fee to run the wires to the farm from the highway, and a separate fee for each plug installed. Daddy could only afford one plug and Grandma used it for her Westinghouse refrigerator. This machine was the envy of all the local farmers' wives. Grandma used it mostly to store her fancy, cooked food for social occasions. Our milk and butter were stored in the cool springhouse at the bottom of the hill where we got most of our water. Our meat was cured and kept in the smokehouse.

Kerosene lanterns provided our indoor lighting. Two coal stoves gave us the heat we needed and the cooking in the kitchen was done in a cast-iron wood-fired stove. Grandma kept a small hatchet in the wood box by the stove so she could chip the logs down to the size that fit into the stove's fire chamber. She had her own indoor bathroom, (another asset that made her the envy of everyone around), using water that came from a cistern, but my family and I used the outhouse out back.

****

After leaving the farm in 1946, we moved Grandma with us to the outskirts of Louisville, on Goldsmith Lane, between Hikes Point and Buechel. Daddy took a job at Sealtest Dairy. In his heart, Daddy never gave up his love of farming and spent much of my childhood looking for "just the right place." Our family moved several times, settling for most of my youth in Hikes Point, another farm community on the edge of Louisville but a bit farther out from town than where we were on our first move away from Gethsemane, on Goldsmith Lane.

We missed living in the country so much that we drove back to Nelson County almost every Sunday for several years. Daddy kept us involved in the ways of farming by commenting on the farms we saw as we drove along the highway. Passing the freshly plowed furrows, he'd say to us kids as he pointed out the window, "See, looky there! That black dirt is the best kinda' dirt for growin' things."

I was proud of my father. To me he was magic. He could read the soil for nutrients, and read the sky for weather. I recall him looking up at sky in the evening and forecasting the day ahead. He used country sayings like, "Red skies at night, sailors delight… red skies in the morning, sailors take warning." Daddy could make anything grow, and he could build almost everything we needed.

When we left Gethsemane, Mama already had three children: Johnny, Marcellus, and me. I was five, Johnny four, and Marcellus three. As the oldest, I was an only child for less than a year; Johnny and I were only fifty-one weeks apart. Soon after we moved to Goldsmith Lane, my next brother, Jimmy, was born. Altogether, Mama had twelve full term pregnancies – seven boys, five girls. However, one of girls, Josephine Ann, was stillborn. Mama also had a partial pregnancy before I was born.

As a child, I had no choice except to become a tomboy since my sisters were so much younger than me. The boys and I were very competitive due to the closeness in our ages. As we grew up, fortunately, all of us took on the energy of Mama's family and learned to laugh and have fun together, instead of arguing and fighting like we did plenty of as kids. Childhood squabbles gave way to adult friendships. I'm proud of my family's history and the time period of the 1940's and '50's when I grew up. Leaving the country saddened me. Even as a young child, I was attached to the beauty of the farmland. My family struggled to be accepted in the suburban area where my parents chose to live. Bringing America into the cities from the farms was not an easy task for those involved. We didn't feel like we really belonged in either place. For most of my childhood I felt split in half, and longed for a sense of belonging somewhere. I enjoyed the feeling I had when I was among my country relatives who lived in the loving community of Howardstown. They spoke the way I did and wore clothes like mine. I felt at home, a feeling I struggled to find during most of my childhood.

Nelson County, Kentucky – Vicinity of Gethsemani/e

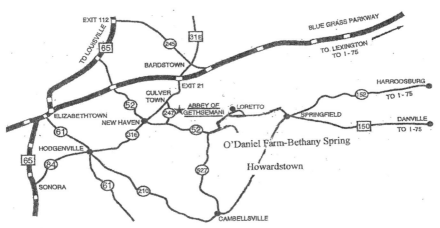

Area of Nelson County referred to in this book

Dee O'Daniel, Age 63, Fatally Injured By Run-A-Way Team

Mr. Dee O'Daniel, age 63, was fatally injured Tuesday morning at his farm at Gethsemane. A team of horses ran away, threw him from the wagon containing baled hay. He was injured when he struck the ground and hay fell on him. He was carried to the Baute Infirmary Lebanon, Ky., in the Charles J. Coyle ambulance and died one hour after reaching there. He is survived by his wife Mrs. Anna O'Daniel and two sons Marcellus and J. H. He was a high class gentleman and one of the prominent farmers of his community. His funeral took place Thursday at St. Vincent's Church at New Hope and was conducted by Rev. A. L. O'Shea.

Obituary of Demetrius O'Daniel-1937

JOHN HEGENANER DEAD.

Carpenter Foreman Who Had Worked on Many Large Buildings.

John Hegenaner, a retired carpenter foreman, who superintended the work on the Galt House, Custom-houses and other large buildings in this city, died this morning at 6:15 o'clock of diabetes at his home, 534 East Lampton street. He had been ill several months.

Mr. Hegenaner was born in 1836 in Germany, coming to this city forty-two years ago. He led a successful career as a carpenter foreman, retiring from that occupation some years ago.

Mr. Hegenaner is survived by his wife, ten children and six grandchildren. The children are: John and William Hegenaner, of New York; Mrs. Nora Klaisher, of Indianapolis; Mrs. Anna O'Daniels, of Gethsemane, Ky.; Edward, Adolph, Mrs. Maggie Brown, Mrs. Rosa Kantlener, Mrs. Ida Brakmeyer and Miss Bertha Hegenaner, of Louisville.

Obituary of John Hegenauer-1915

xxvii

Frozen Moments

Gethsemane
Rambling white farmhouse
With wrap-around porch,
We race on our "stick-horses,"
Always falling off the end

Coal oil lamp
I watch it flicker
And flame, its wick dangling
In an amber glass bowl

In from the fields
Running down to meet Daddy
Finish plowin' at
The end of the day – we
Ride 'old Jack' up to the barn

Noon meal
Grandma rings the dinner bell
Farmhands file in for dinner –
The day's biggest meal

Bedtime stories
Into the cornshuck bed
We leap with faces shined –
Time for Grandma's stories

'Lace' curtains
Delicate crystal curtains
Sparkle the window panes
On cold frosty mornings

Churning butter
"It's your turn now,"
He tosses it to me.
Cream becomes butter
Soooo slowly!

Summer storm
"Don't stand by the screendoor!"
Mama screams as I watch the show
Of heat lightening
Fill the summer sky

Fetching water
Grabbing her buckets,
Grandma scrambles down the hill
To the cool springhouse

Basket picnics
A bushel basket filled
With fried chicken and lemonade
Ready for a hot summer Sunday!

Lightning bugs
Here they come, there they go
Making our yard twinkle
Like Christmas tree

Aunt Ida
Quiet and elegant
Smelling of sweet perfume
Grandma's sister

Aunt Bertha
Your laughter rolled up from
Deep in your belly, your
Love came straight from your heart

Picnic games
Marshmallows on strings
Tug of war, sack races
Laughing kids and parents

Calling in the cows
At day's end, Mama
Calls the cows up to the barn
From the pasture behind our house

Abe Lincoln
Born near Howardstown
On a poorer farm that we –
Greatness that inspired us

Summer night noises
Amidst kadydids, locusts and
Whippoorwills, a bob white
Calls out... I listen

Chapter One:

If Only I'd Listened to Mama

It was 1946 and we lived in the outskirts of Louisville. I was going on six and not yet in school. Only rich kids went to kindergarten, and our new parish, St. Bartholomew's, didn't even have one. Johnny was almost five, Marcellus almost four, and Jimmy was the baby. In January, Mama was expecting her fifth child. Grandma Anna who still lived with us, and I were hoping for another girl – I wanted a sister.

Daddy liked the stability of his delivery job for Sealtest Dairy, but he wanted to feed the family from the farm. While looking for a farm of his own – the one he called "the perfect place" – he rented a small farm on Goldsmith Lane. This area was filled with beautiful rolling pasture land and the white split rail fences of horse farms. One of the things Daddy did to make extra money was to sell hay to those horse farms. To me, the horses were so beautiful, I just wanted to pet them. Daddy showed us how to give them carrots by holding them on our flat hands so the horses wouldn't nibble our fingers.

****

The air smelled sweet after Daddy cut the timothy and alfalfa grasses several nights ago, when he got home from his job at the dairy. These grasses became hay, but first they had to lie in the field for days and dry in the sun. Johnny, Marcellus and I played in them, tossing the stalks into the air and throwing them at each other. When they were thoroughly dry, we helped Daddy rake the hay into piles. Then Daddy tied it into three-foot bales, the best size to sell to the horse farms. Then, the three of us had fun jumping from bale to bale, and pushing each other off to the ground, before some of our neighbors came by to help him hoist the heavy bales into the hayloft.

In the cool of the evening, Daddy took Johnny, Marcellus and me along with him to sell some bales to one of the farmers down Goldsmith near Hikes Lane. My brothers and I lay back on the itchy haybales and stared up into the trees that lined both sides of Goldsmith Lane as we bumped our way along on the back of Daddy's farm truck. Goldsmith Lane was a gravel road at the time. It was fall and the crisp weather had us in our sweaters. This was one of the things we liked about our move out of Gethsemane, Daddy was always driving somewhere and taking us along. It was great adventure and we tried to be good so he would take us again the next time. Being an almost only child himself, he never really adjusted to noisy children.

****

On the day after our ride on the haybales, Mama, Grandma and I were outside enjoying some of last few days of 'Indian Summer' weather. It was warm and sunny, not chilly like the night before. It was a perfect day for cleaning Grandma's curtains. Grandma's lace curtains had to be hand washed and stretched in order get the winter coal soot from our potbelly stove out of them.

I knew why Grandma wanted to clean the curtains – Uncle Mac and Aunt Gen were coming down from Chicago to spend the weekend with us. The whole family was excited. Grandma, especially. She wanted everything to look perfect for them, now that we had moved to the area around Louisville. I thought about Uncle Mac, his jolly laugh, and how much fun the whole family had when he visited. He loved the Irish folksongs of his father's side of the family. I knew that in no time after his arrival he would pick up Grandpa Demetrius' squeezebox (an old instrument similar to an accordion) and have us singing, *McNamara's Band, My Wild Irish Rose* and *When Irish Eyes Are Smilin,'* while his wavy blond head moved side to side in the rhythm of the Irish melodies. If Daddy was in the mood, he would play his harmonica or guitar. Otherwise, he would just sing with along Grandma and Mama, while we kids kept up as best we could.

I looked over the stiff, lacy material as Mama and Grandma carefully removed them from the windows. Grandma exclaimed, the lines in her round face tightening, "I declare, these curtains are filthy." Mama and Grandma called this part of their spring-cleaning, but the past year had been too busy with our farm auction and moving to Louisville to get them done in the spring. Grandma was very cranky about the care of her curtains because they were so delicate.

They could never be ironed. The heavy flat irons we heated against the stove would tear them to pieces. Instead, they were put on stretching frames. These frames were made of wood and each one was as large as the curtain that fit on it. Tiny nails were all around the edges. She and Mama had to be careful not to prick their fingers and bleed on the lace as they pushed the edges of the material down over the nails. I watched them work across from each other, stretching each inch at the same time so they could keep the pattern straight as the curtain dried. My job was to look after Jimmy, the baby, as I sat with him on the pallet that I threw down into the grass for us nearby.

Grandma was very proud of these curtains and loved to work with them. Taking time to push the stray ends of her gray hair up into the bun at the back of her head, she looked over at me and said, "Deanna, your grandfather Demetrius gave me these curtains for our tenth wedding anniversary." Then her voice saddened. "He died before you were born. They're over thirty years old, and fooling with them reminds me of him," she went on, smoothing them as she stretched. "He was called Dee, and that's where your name, Deanna, comes from. I told your mama to name you after me and him, Dee, and Anna. Josephine had her heart set on calling you Mary Ann, but I talked her into saving that name for the next girl. I'm an old woman and I wanted a child named after me before I died." She continued to look over at me, her plump little belly leaning against the wood, her hands working smoothly, while she waited for my smile. I had heard this story before, but Grandma liked to tell it, and I loved Grandma. So I smiled and said, "I wish I knew Grandpa Dee, too. Your curtains sure are purdy', Grandma." The light from the sun made my eyes squint and my light brown hair glisten as I looked at the curtains.

She turned to Mama and said of the curtains, "You be careful now, Josephine." Mama chuckled and said, "Grandma, you say that ever' time we take 'ese curtains off the windas'. You know I love 'em, too." The two women had several frames to work through. They laid each frame, as they worked on it, on top of the sawhorses Daddy used for his carpentry work. When they finished with each one, they carried it over to the back of the house where they leaned it to dry, next to the fragrant sweet pea vines Mama loved so much. Then they jumped back quickly because the bees liked the sweet pea vines, too. The aroma of the pink flowers filled the air and I sniffed in as much of it as I could while I played with Jimmy and settled into the beautiful autumn day.

"I knew this was the right place for us when I saw those sweet peas growin' by the house," Mama said as they worked. "We had 'em by our house in Howardstown, and my father said they meant good luck."

I gave Jimmy his rattler. He gurgled and cooed as he shook it, then dropped it and rolled onto his back. I giggled as he pulled his toes down into his mouth, then I pushed his blond curls back out of his eyes. Mama turned the radio on to our favorite old time country music show, "Georgie Wildcats." The fast pickin' banjo and guitar music tickled our ears. Jimmy pulled himself up into a crawling position and rocked his little body to the rhythm of the fiddle. He looked real cute to me, going back and forth like a little motor.

"I can get a lot of work done when Georgie's on," Mama laughed to Grandma as her foot started to tap on the grass beneath the sawhorse to the sounds of, *There's a bright and a sunny side of life,* from the Carter Family. "I'm glad he's on every day," Grandma agreed. Soon the fiddle music of "Turkey in the Straw," started up and encouraged her own foot to move. The music made it easier to continue working with the lace.

While we women were busy with the curtains and the baby, Johnny and Marcellus were gathering the apples from under the three trees of yellow apples growing in the orchard. Daddy called them Golden Delicious. I peeked around the corner of the chicken house and watched them throw as many apples at each other as they threw in the bushel basket. Their job looked like a lot more fun than mine, and I wished I could have been over there throwing apples, too. Grandma and Mama would be canning these apples into applesauce in the afternoon.

With the curtains done, and the Georgie Wildcats program ended, it was time for lunch. We called it dinner back then because that is what we called it on the farm. We called the evening meal supper, and it was a lighter meal. Farmers always ate their heartiest meal in the middle of the day when they were working at their hardest in the fields. Mama fixed cottage cheese and sauerkraut, and Grandma got out the bacon and biscuits that were left over from breakfast. Jimmy sat in his high chair and smashed his food on its tray with his hands before he put it into his mouth. We laughed watching him and he giggled along with us, enjoying the extra attention.

It was Johnny's turn to help me with the dishes while Mama and Grandma busied themselves getting jars and lids ready for the afternoon canning. After the dishes, we three kids ran for the front porch where we pumped our legs back and forth sitting on the wooden swing. The porch went all the way across the front of our old, white farmhouse.

Glancing into the sky, I noticed it was the same color as the blue cornflowers that grew along the side of the highway that we took when Daddy drove us back to Howardstown on Sundays. Fluffy clouds, as full as the cotton candy puffs we'd seen at Fontaine Ferry Park, filled the blue sky. The leaves on the maple trees in our front yard were so pretty, showing ruby reds and golden yellows. I felt so peaceful, just looking through it all.

Our long front yard stretched all the way down to the road. The part of it by the lane was planted in corn that grew so tall we couldn't see the road from the house. We kids liked living on Goldsmith Lane because we had other kids to play with – the Allens and the Philpots. Dad was happy with his steady job. He and Mama didn't seem so worried about money anymore, and that felt good to us.

As we sat in the swing, we heard Grandma go upstairs for her afternoon nap. Mama took Jimmy into her bedroom for his bottle. This room was located right behind the window where we were sitting on the porch swing. The baby's crib was next to my parent's bed. She sang as she rocked him in the creaky rocker that had once belonged to my grandfather, Demetrius. We heard Jimmy's sucking sounds on the bottle as she rocked. When his bottle was done, Mama patted him on his back, and we heard him belch. Putting him down to sleep, she leaned over and spoke through the window screen to us on the swing, "Deanna, after the canning gets done this afternoon, I want you and the boys to take the jars down into the cellar."

I shivered a little thinking about the dirt-floored cellar under the kitchen floor, with the rickety steps and the cobwebs. It scared me. When winter got here Mama would be sending me down there every Sunday to get a jar of applesauce for our Sunday dinner, just like she did at Gethsemane. Mama made it taste real good by grating nutmeg and cinnamon on top. I liked the way it smelled, and always asked to grate the little brown nut that sprinkled into nutmeg. It was about the size of a walnut. "We'll cross that bridge when we get to it," she said. "You're fingers aren't strong enough yet."

Mama broke into our peaceful afternoon by saying, "Time for you kids to get on upstairs and take yur' naps. Ya' better get some rest, so you can help out later today." We were prickling for something interesting to do, like visiting the Allen kids or the Philpots. Napping was never something on our list, but we wanted to keep Mama happy so we unhappily trudged up the steps to our bedroom. All three of us slept in the same large bed. Its mattress was made of corn shucks. Grandma shook it up every morning when she helped us make up the bed, leaning down and rubbing the pain in her back as she did so. "Oh, I got the misery," she'd said. Then her strong arms took over, and she shook the devil out of the shucks, making them fluffy again, after out night of smashing them 'flatter than a flitter.' When we left the room in the morning the mattress was pretty and plump under its colorful quilt.

As soon as we three got to the bedroom, we jumped into the mattress and immediately started wrestling and kicking, causing the shucks to go flat. We kept our squeals of laughter down because we didn't want to wake up Grandma who was sleeping in the room across the hall. After we had just had all the fun we were going to have, we felt rested quickly enough.

"I hate naps," I said, pulling my long brown hair back out of my mouth and eyes.

"Why do we have to take a nap? I'm not tired," Johnny agreed. We kids didn't realize that this was a break time for Mama and Grandma. "I know what," Johnny sat up on the flattened mattress shucks, lifted his dark head and said, "Let's go down to the Allen's."

I spoke up, "You know Mama won't let us do that." Marcellus listened to our discussion and was willing to try whatever we older ones could figure out.

"Deanna, yur' just a dumb girl. If you had a brain you'd run backwards!" Johnny shot back at me, copying one of Daddy's country sayings. "She's not gonna' see us leave." Then I kicked him and we started wrestling all over again.

Our bedroom was above our parents' and also faced the front of the house. Its tall window was only about a foot above the porch roof. We climbed out on the roof to figure out how we were going to get out of the house. We frequently climbed out on the roof when we didn't want to take our naps. If Mama found out we did this she would probably make Daddy nail the window shut. I felt like a king on a hill as I stared into the trees and over the rolling countryside. I would be happy just sitting up here watching the chestnut horses chew the pasture grass and go to the creek for drinks of water. We walked back and forth on the porch roof holding onto the house for safety. Butterflies tickled my stomach, I didn't care, it was thrilling to be so high up in the air.

"We can't get down from here. You're the dummy," I whispered back to Johnny. Thinking we could shimmy down off the edge of the porch roof and slide down the porch column didn't work. We soon lost our nerve and changed our minds. An opportunity to sneak down the back stairwell that led into the kitchen came fast enough, with the way our busy Mama scrambled around the house, working from one room to the next. Making our move, we snuck out the back door.

The Allens were the neighbors who owned the farm across the road from our house. They had eight kids. The bigger ones were at school, but the ones our age would be home and want to play with us. Something was always going on over at their busy house.

We took off for the cornfield in the front part of our yard by the road. If we used the gravel driveway, Mama would see us. Our Border collie, Blackie, followed alongside us. I was so glad we had Blackie back again. Daddy gave him to neighbors in Gethsemane because he didn't think Blackie would do well in the city. Blackie missed us so much, he sniffed his way all the way up here to find us at Goldsmith Lane. He came over seventy-five miles and it took him several weeks. Daddy was shocked to see him, but I was delighted. His fur was caked with mud and full of cockle-burrs. When we heard him whimpering on the front porch, the whole family, even Grandma, ran out to greet him and give him big hugs.

Suddenly Blackie took off from us to chase a chipmunk. He started sniffing around the old boarded-up well in the side yard where the chipmunk disappeared. Marcellus toddled over to check things out, his blond curls bouncing. Remembering the little girl in the news story who had drowned in an old well the week before, I ran over and pulled him back. There were always stories of farm kids falling into wells, particularly, abandoned ones like this one. They scared me. I didn't speak because I didn't want Mama to hear us outside.

In our bare feet, we tiptoed quickly across the hot gravel on Goldsmith Lane. We climbed through the split rail fence bordering the Allen's front yard and noticed Mr. Allen, a tall dark haired man with a busy expression, in the large garden in front of their house. Several men were in the garden with him. It was harvest time, and they were collecting the freshly plowed potatoes into gunnysacks and bushel baskets.

"Can we play with Billy and Dorothy?" we yelled to him from across the field.

"Not now," he called back to us, "they're taking their naps. Does your mama know you're over here?" He asked, casting us a suspicious glance.

"She told us to go out and play," Johnny answered him so fast that I had to admire his quickness. Blackie trotted over and found the shade of a peach tree to enjoy while he waited for us.

"Nobody's got time ta' play 'round here today. If you kids wanna' to stick around, ya' can help pick potatoes," he said, handing me one bag for all three of us. We looked at each other. If we went home, we would be spanked for being disobedient. Disobedience was a crime unforgivable by both Mama and Grandma. Taking the scratchy burlap bag, we walked over to the row Mr. Allen pointed out for us. The furrow was filled with a "million" potatoes. In no time the bag was too heavy for us to pull along with us. Then, we had to run the potatoes back to the bag. We did this over and over until the bag was full.

"Can we have another bag, Mr. Allen?" we asked, about fifteen minutes later.

"By God, you kids work fast!" Mr. Allen slapped his dirty overalls in amazement, letting the dust fly all over our faces. He grabbed the heavy bag from the row and took it over to the changing table. There was a fat man in a straw hat sitting at this makeshift table who was in charge of passing out burlap bags and money. He gave us a new bag and surprised each of us with a shiny new dime! It was harvest time, and Mr. Allen paid the extra help he had hired to bring in the crop for the market.

"Can we keep this money, Mr. Allen?" I asked him, afraid to hear the answer.

"Don't see why not," he declared. "You earned it." All the other workers are gettin' paid." Wow! We couldn't believe our good luck. Now we worked even faster.

While working, we noticed that the field hands were laughing and sprinkling their words with a lot of colorful language. Naughty words and curse words we hadn't heard before. Not knowing it was cursing, we thought it sounded like big people talk, and we felt pretty big making all this money. So, while we worked, we tried it out.

"This feels_____good to be talkin' like men!" Johnny said.

"It sure as _____does!" I agreed. We felt important, and using these big words proved it.

When we had a whole dollar between us, we quit. We were just too tired to go on. Mama was right, kids need naps. By now, Billy and Dorothy were up from theirs and standing on the front porch. Dorothy rubbed the sleep out of her pretty blue eyes, her blonde hair blowing in the breeze, as she said, "Come on, Deanna, let's play with my tea set. Bring your dolly. Usually, I would love to do this. Dorothy was my best friend next to my cousin Mary Jane, and we always had fun. But, today was different

Oh,_____I sure as _____ don't wanna' play dollys now, I thought, *I'm makin'a _____of a lot a' money today. I don't have time for silly games, now!* I smirked to myself, feeling my new importance.

"We're workin," I called out as I ran over to her leaning against a column on their front porch. Then I then ran back to join the boys. Suddenly, Marcellus spoke up, "I'm tired, I miss Mama and I wanna' go home." His blond curls were now full of field dirt.

Making up a plan, we decided to go home, take a little rest and come back to make some more money. Even though we were exhausted, the hot sun had our bare feet dancing quickly across the sizzling gravel of Goldsmith Lane. After jumping into our cornfield, we crawled back up on the front porch, pooped. The pleasant aroma of the bubbling applesauce wafted through the screen door as we passed it to get to the swing.

"We'll rest up here, so Mama won't see us," Johnny said, lying down on the swing and leaving the concrete floor for Marcellus and me. However, with money jingling in our pockets, we rested pretty fast, being really taken with ourselves. Before we knew it, we forgot that we had to be quiet and started laughing, singing, and shouting the words that we picked up from the men in the potato field. Johnny told some of the bawdy jokes he heard, and we all chimed in with what we remembered.

"Marcellus, come in here," Mama whispered through the screen of her bedroom window behind the swing. We paid no attention to this at all. When she repeated it, Marcellus waddled slowly into the house. Johnny and I got louder and louder. We were too preoccupied to care what happened to Marcellus. Soon, Mama was behind the screened window again. This time she called for Johnny. "Johnny! Johnny, come in here a minute," was all she said. It was not much fun using these great words on myself, and I was soon bored. Neither Marcellus nor Johnny returned. *They musta' had to take their naps,* I thought. I heard some noises but I was too preoccupied to care. It would never do for a little girl who was so full of herself to be as bored as I was. Getting up off the swing, I started to go down our driveway, having in mind to impress young Tommy and Jimmy Philpot with my new words. Their ears were saved by Mama's third visit to the window screen.

"Deanna, I need you in the house," was all she said. She seemed calm enough. I figured it was time for me to take the jars of applesauce down to the cellar. Regretting that the afternoon's fun was over, I trudged into the cool darkness of our wallpapered front hall. *Where's Johnny and Marcellus?* I wondered, letting my eyes adjust as I looked through the dimness.

"Come out back with me," Mama requested, motioning with her hand. I caught a glance at the serious look in her eyes. When we arrived behind the woodshed I knew what that look meant, and my heart started pounding. She rubbed her stomach, which meant that the baby must have been paining her. Moaning, she did not have the pleasant face of earlier in the day when she was singing and laughing with Grandma. "Deanna, I've talked to you until I'm blue in the face about the way you behave!" Now, I knew things were bad. My parents loved using the country sayings from Nelson County when they lost their temper.

Mama continued, "Who do you think you are using language like that on our front porch?" She demanded. Her harsh words made my eyes sting with tears and my stomach tremble. *I'm always gettn' myself inta' trouble,* I thought, hanging my head so she wouldn't see my guilty face.

"We're just lucky that we live far enough from everybody that none of our neighbors could hear you kids," she went on. "What would they think, a *young* lady talking like that? My daughter?" Mama always had a fear of what others would think of us. Since moving up here from Nelson County, my parents worked hard to be accepted. Parents reputation were set by how well mannered their kids behaved. Unruly children meant uneducated and unsuccessful parents. And this was very bad behavior indeed!

With that, Mama grabbed the strong, snappy willow switch she kept stored by the corner of the woodshed. Lifting her arm, she let me have it. *Where's Grandma?* I whimpered to myself. Grandma used to come to my aid when we lived on the farm, but she wasn't here now when I needed her. Having grown up on a farm herself, Mama had the muscles of any wrestler. I jumped around and squealed as she used one of her strong hands to hold my hand in a tight grip. I couldn't believe that Johnny and Marcellus were quiet when they got their licks, but then she explained.

"I only gave the boys one swat, they're too young to know what they are doing, but you! You should know better, you'll be in school next year. You're the oldest. It's your job to set the example for your little brothers."

"I never thought of that," I said, hoping Mama would take pity on me. I couldn't fool her, Mama told me of this 'first-born' obligation almost everyday of my life. "Don't lie ta' me," she said through tight lips, her aggravation increasing.

After the spanking, she gave me the same treatment she gave to the boys. Marching me up the stairs and into the bathroom, I found Johnny and Marcellus. They were kneeling down and spitting into the toilet. *No wonder I didn't hear 'em*, I thought. Mama took a wet washrag and put some soap on it. Because we were farmers we made our own soap. Daddy made it out of boiling hog fat with lye and it was called lye soap. I couldn't imagine having to taste the smelly stuff.

"I'm going to clean those dirty words right out a' yur' mouth, just like I did with the boys," she said, spinning the rag around on my tongue. This didn't sound like much to me after the switchin' I'd just gotten. My legs still stinging, I leaned obediently over the edge of the sink as she continued. "Yuk!" I yelled to show Mama that this was really awful. The disgusting taste of the lye made my stomach wretch. I hated throwing up; it made me feel like such a baby. *I shoulda' done what Mama told me in the first place and taken my nap.* However, the truth was that I knew I deserved my punishment and didn't mind taking it because the adventure I had today was worth it. Joining my brothers at the toilet, I spit out the lye suds. *It's over, at last,* I thought, but then I heard the words we always hated to hear Mama or Grandma say:

"Wait until I tell your father when he gets home!" We kids looked at each other and sighed.

****

Daddy stood before us, his arms folded on his tall frame, his wavy brown hair shining under the kitchen lamp over table. He looked pretty scary to us. But, he surprised us, when he found out how much money we made at Mr. Allen's, he was delighted. "My goodness, Josephine, these children are getting big enough to make money. Bring the piggy bank! Why, they made a whole dollar today." Money always excited Daddy. Mama and Grandma didn't agree with him. They didn't move and stood on the other side of the kitchen with their arms folded across their chests.

"They were just playing with those words," he continued to show us a big smile. This time when we looked at each other, we started to feel at ease. But suddenly, his tone changed and he got serious. Turning his smile into a frown, he suddenly pointed his finger at the three of us. "Don't you let me ever hear of you kids usin' those words

again!" he bellowed. "You're not gonna' embarrass me in public."
More worries about what the neighbors would think.

We went to bed happy that night with one less spanking than we
planned on for the day. It seemed we usually got at least two every
day, it was just part of being a kid. I stretched my legs after we
climbed into the bed, kicking Johnny in the behind. He moved over
to give me some more room, and in his sleep, kicked me back. Daddy
had shaken the corn shucks up fluffy again. No wrestling tonight like
we usually did when we were sent to bed, the potatoes wore us out.

Chapter Two:

Lexington and the Loftus Mansion

A rooster crowed from the fence next door, screaming in my ear. "Er-er-er-er-er!" I opened my eyes as the Saturday morning broke. Being chilly, I pulled my part of the blanket that I shared with my brothers Johnny and Marcellus up around my neck. It was May of 1949, I was eight years old. Daddy had finally found the farm he wanted, and we had just spent our first night in our new home in Lexington, Indiana. It took all of the day before and part of the night to make the big move. Lying on the plank floor of our sleeping porch, I was too excited to get back to sleep. Glancing up, I stared through the long windows and on up into the trees of our new backyard. My mind wandered over our latest situation, I thought, excitedly, *we're livin' town*! Daddy's farm was down the road about a mile out of town.

I noticed that the porch windows were pulled up and closed, and guessed that Mama had tiptoed in and done it when the house cooled off during the night. Our new house was built in 1890 in what was called, "Steamboat Gothic" design. This is what Daddy told us when we got here last night. He pulled his tall body up from his task of putting his and Mama's bed together, and said that a steamboat captain could have built this house since many of them came into Madison, Indiana, a ship building town about ten miles up the river from Lexington. "Some of them settled here," he said. "These are the type a'windows you find on riverboats. They pull up from the bottom instead of down from the top, that way the water doesn't get into the boat," he explained to us when we had trouble figuring them out.

I thought back to Friday, the day before this, and the long process of moving here. Arriving after dark, we were the last things Daddy delivered and stumbled in, exhausted. Everything was brought up from the house and outbuildings at our small farm on Goldsmith Lane. My mother's brothers, Uncles Leon and Garland, came to Louisville from Howardstown, in Nelson County, Kentucky, with their flatbed farm truck to help us with the move. Uncle Bud, Mama's brother who lived in Louisville, was there, too. He arrived at our house, a strong, tall man with a shock of black hair falling out from underneath his straw work hat, in the extra delivery truck he had on hand for his garbage pickup business. Mama was horrified when she saw Uncle Bud's garbage truck in our driveway.

"Don't worry, Josephine, he assured Mama, who came over to check out the truck, the sun shining through her dark curls, with her mouth open. She was Uncle Bud's older sister. When he saw the look on her face, he explained, "This truck is clean – I only use it for paper drives." His ready smile and laughter told her he was telling the truth. As her brother, he delighted in teasing her.

It took more than one trip to bring all our farm equipment, tools, and furniture the fifty miles from Louisville to Lexington, Indiana. The men went back and forth all day loading stuff and tying ropes while Mama and I packed and sorted the things in the house.

Finally, near dark, Daddy had brought us up in the family car. Mama held the new baby, Tony, who was born April fifth, on her lap. He gurgled and sucked his fingers as Daddy drove along. They named him Anthony Ignatius after Uncle Bud whose real name was Ignatius Alphonsis. It seems Uncle Bud was always helping us out with his trucks, his laughter, and his physical strength. Tony was our fourth boy.

At this time, there were seven of us brothers and sisters. After me, there was Johnny, age seven, Marcellus, age six, Jimmy, age three, Margaret Jane, age two, and Theresa one. Grandma was no longer with us, having passed away in 1947. I missed her very much and wanted Mama's new baby to be another girl, knowing Grandma would want that, too if she were still alive.

"You're havin' way too many boys, Josephine," she used to tease Mama, her blue eyes twinkling – as if Mama could do anything about it. When I asked God to give us a girl, it didn't occur to me that this girl baby wouldn't be ready to help me with my chores for years to come.

Daddy was proud of his decision to move. This was the second time he had moved us since we left Gethsemane, but he only rented the farm on Goldsmith Lane. He bought this new one, now Daddy had his own farm – his "perfect place."

Lexington was an old town established in 1778, but it was a typical American small town of the 1940's. Except for the storekeepers who lived there, many of the other homes were occupied by the farmers in the area who wanted to live in town. No one drove very far to work.

****

My siblings snored as Daddy drove us along in our old Chevy in the move to Lexington from Louisville. It had been a busy day for all of us. As we sped along Indiana's Highway 56, I forced my eyes to stay open, being too curious about our new life for sleep, and feeling the excitement in his voice as he described our new situation to Mama.

"And, Josephine, Daddy began, "We're gonna' be livin' in a much bigger house. You'll be in town, not stuck out in the country." Mama's smile widened as he went on. From the back seat, I smiled, too. "Our new farm's a big one," he continued, "over a hundred acres, and it's about a mile from our house in town." It seemed an unusual situation to me, but I was sure Daddy knew what he was doing. Mama and I were both thrilled to be living in town, and enjoyed the thought of being around other people and close to stores. Daddy was glad to get back to the farm life he loved. He did, however, cautiously decide to keep his Louisville job. By this time, he had left the dairy and now worked at Fehr's Brewery. "A better payin' position," he explained when we complained about losing the surplus ice cream he sometimes brought home from Sealtest.

His plan was to stay at Aunt Bertha's (Grandma's sister), in Louisville, by Shawnee Park, during the week to save on time and gasoline. He kept the tenant farmer, Mr. Able, from the former owner to tend the land. Mr. Able and his family lived in a small tenant house out on the farm and near the highway. Soon, Daddy planned for the farm to be successful enough to quit his Louisville job and become a full time farmer. His dream of returning to farm life was finally coming true. Mama knew this made him happy, though she hated farm life; this was different, we would be living in town.

****

Rising up on my elbows, and continuing to stare into the trees from my pallet on the porch floor, I remembered my glimpse of the house from the night before when I first saw it. As we climbed out of the car it looked huge and mysterious under the shine of the moon. I noticed that it had a tower room, a wrap-around porch, and two sleeping porches. I thought of the castle in Cinderella, *I wanna' to see the house, now,* my stomach started tingling. Too scared to see it alone, impatience made me kick Johnny, who was sleeping next to me.

"Come on, let's see the house before Mama and Daddy get up," I suggested.

"Stop picking on me," he said shivering and pulling his eyes open. "I get to slide down the banister first," I told him before he was fully awake. "Hurry," I pleaded, pushing on his shoulder, "when Mama gets up, I haf' ta help with the biscuits."

Johnny grunted and we wiggled out from under our blanket as Marcellus snuggled into a better sleeping position. Carefully, we stepped over the sleeping forms of our younger brothers and sisters. All my siblings, except for the baby, had spent the first night here on the plank floor of the downstairs sleeping porch. As Johnny and I came into the house from the porch, my head swiveled, slinging my brown pigtails from side to side. We looked for the staircase. Still sleeping, our parents snored peacefully in the parlor. The sounds of their steady rhythm had comforted me during the night. Daddy had slung their bed together when we got here from our long drive. Johnny held the flashlight for him while I helped Mama put down the sleeping pallets on the other side of the parlor wall for us kids.

Johnny and I continued to sneak through the downstairs as quietly as we could, and tiptoed up the creaky winding staircase. Looking out the windows on all three of the floors as we went up the steps, we stared at the street view below, and felt like giants by the time we reached the attic.

"What if somebody is hiding up here? I'm gettin' scared!" I admitted, my voice trembling. "You're just a girl – scardey cat,"

Johnny bragged, but his lip quivered, too. The ceilings were eleven feet high downstairs and ten high feet upstairs. Most of the rooms had peeling wallpaper with large flower prints, the kind that was popular years ago, in the twenties. I feared ghosts popping out of the closets or from behind the heavy draperies. We ran through at least five of the eight bedrooms and found four of the baths. Unfortunately, we also found out that none of the bathrooms worked, and we ended up going outside to use the outhouse in the back of the yard.

"This is just like Gethsemane. Hurry up, Deanna," Johnny yelled, pounding on the wooden outhouse door. I had to admit, I sure got used to the indoor bathroom on Goldsmith Lane. I hated the wasps that fly around outhouses, and I hated the way they stunk in the summer. "Phew!" My nose pinched, *this outhouse stinks!* I thought, and wondered how long it had been since anybody had lived in the Loftus to sweeten it with lime. Loftus was the name of our new home.

Johnny chased me back into the house. This time Marcellus joined us and we checked out the downstairs. All the rooms had window seats, but none of them had treasures inside. *Darn!* Ornate, wooden gingerbread hung from the ceiling that separated the parlor from the dining room. This was another reminder of the steamboat gothic design of the house.

Fascinated, we rolled the pocket doors back and forth that were between many of the rooms. The regular doors were so tall that we grabbed the knobs, lifted our knees and swung on some of them. We knew we couldn't get by with this if Daddy was up. This house was so much more exciting than our farmhouse on Goldsmith Lane and our big house in Gethsemane.

When we went outside on the large, columned front porch, a small, dark-haired boy in a striped tee shirt surprised us.

"Hi," he chirped. "My Mama said it'd be okay ta' come over and meet ya'll. My Daddy got killed in the war. I live next door, my name is Bradley Bernard, and I'm seven years old." He pointed to the gray stucco house on the left side of ours. It was arts and crafts style, with a big porch stretching across the front of it. Johnny and I looked at each other. No doubt about it, we were thrilled to have a playmate next door. We already missed the Allen's across the road from us on Goldsmith Lane. I especially missed Dorothy who was my age.

Immediately I asked, "Do you have a sister?"

"I'm an only child," he said, smiling with self-satisfaction, like he could tell that I would love to be an only child. *How'd he know that,* I wondered? Then he said, "Naw, there ain't many girls 'round here, but dere's plenty of 'em in Lexington School," he continued, looking over his shoulder at the large brick building across the street from both our houses. *It's a school,* my excitement built again.

Johnny, the first grader, interrupted us, "Aw, but, we haf' ta go to the Catholic school," he whined. Daddy came out to see what was going on. The sun shone on his wavy brown hair as he pulled up and fastened the strap on his bib overalls. I could tell he was ready to get to work on our new house.

Daddy shook his head and wrinkled his brow, "No, Johnny," he said, "the closest Catholic school is ten miles away in Scottsburg and there's no school bus. You'll be going across the street, too." "Yay!" all three of us kids yelled. Johnny and I clapped our hands and jumped up and down. Now, we could go across the street to school instead of walking two miles to wait for a school bus, like we did on Goldsmith Lane. Then he added, "Deanna, your mother wants you in the kitchen." I groaned at having to leave our new friend. My shoulders slumped as I went back in the house to help Mama make the breakfast biscuits, grumbling, "Why do I have to be a girl?" Johnny snickered, watching me turn down the hall toward the kitchen at the back of the house.

Finally, I finished rolling out the biscuit dough, dusting it with flour so it wouldn't stick to the rolling pin or the glass that I used to cut them out. I filled the baking pans with our daily supply of four dozen. Mama had fixed the dough for me. Humming, she was mixing the baby formula as the bacon sizzled in the skillet. I whistled, stood on a chair and slammed the biscuits into the hot oven of the coal-oil cook stove. It stood on tall metal legs beside the copper-lined kitchen sink. Daddy called it a "zinc," because in the country they were lined with zinc and not copper. Long windows that almost reached the floor let lots of light into the sunny room. The kitchen looked very pleasant, and I felt good being in there, despite my chore. Balmy May breezes came through the screens bringing in delicious aromas of fresh baked apple pies. Bradley's busy mother already had several cooling on her kitchen windowsill. Mrs. Bernard told Mama later on that she made extra money to help out with the government pension that she got for her husband's death, by selling pies to the Lexington Bakery, which was located on the town square.

The electricity in the house was another matter. Like the plumbing, it needed to be fixed. Several of the fancy brass chandeliers in the front rooms were equipped with gas at the turn of the century, but that was cut off during the depression. This didn't bother either Mama or me. "I grew up without electricity and I don't care if we have it or not," I heard her tell Daddy, "Just so we get to live in town." I felt the same way. *I'm happy if Mama's happy,* I thought.

Soon the kitchen smelled like breakfast, with the coffee perking, the bacon frying, and the biscuits browning. I knew I was pushing my luck but I begged anyway.

"Mama, when can I go outside and explore? I want to see everything, the school, the park, and all the stores."

"Well, I'll swan! So do I, Missy," she said, adjusting her print housedress, her dark hair shining from the sun coming in the side window. "You can go as soon as you all get the dishes done." I sighed, resigned. My brothers took turns helping me with the meals. Marcellus was setting the table from the special box of breakfast things Mama had packed just for this morning.

There was no milk this morning, so he poured each kid a glass of water and put out the coffee cups for Mama and Daddy. I hurried him along. Jumping up and down with the motion of the hand-crank at the sink, I pumped enough cold water to do the dishes in a large pan. The water had to be heated on the stove. With no electricity, we had no hot water heater, either. Pushing my chair over to the sink, I hoped that, in standing over the pan, I would have more strength to lift it. Getting this meal out of the way was my only goal. Mama seemed able to read my mind and said, "Deanna, you're always trying to hurry up our meals, now stop it! If you pick that pan up, you'll have that water all over the floor. Then you'll never get outside." I knew she was right.

Pushing the coffee pot to the back burner, she took the water to the stove herself. We could get along without a hot water heater, nothing was going to discourage Mama and me from our new home.

In Gethsemane, we took baths in a galvanized washtub in the middle of the kitchen floor every Saturday. As the oldest, I got to use the water first. The rest of the kids followed me, all using the same water. *This is a good thing about being the oldest,* I recalled, smirking to myself.

While we ate breakfast, the man who owned the rooster and chickens next door, Mr. Sanders, came over to welcome us to Lexington. An older man, he and his family lived in back of his barbershop on the other side of our house. Knocking on our screened door, he introduced himself, saying, "I'll be glad to run an extension cord over from my shop, Mr. O'Daniel, pointing to the barbershop sign next door. "So's ya' all can have 'lectricity 'till ya' get yours fixed," he continued.

"That's mighty nice a' ya', Mr. Sanders," Daddy smiled, "but we have plenty of coal oil lamps from our farm in Gethsemane – we'll do fine." Of course, Daddy didn't think about us, he would be in Louisville most of the time. Inviting Mr. Sanders in, Daddy pulled up a chair from the disheveled heap of furniture that still needed to be arranged. Before he left, Mr. Sanders told Mama that his wife, Ruth, would be over later on and help her get settled in the town.

I overheard Mama tell Daddy, "J.H., I think we're gonna' like it here, these people seem real nice." I smiled when she said that and felt the same way. I washed the dishes while Marcellus dried. We were both eager to find Johnny and Bradley, who were already out exploring the town. Finally, we crossed the street, and Marcellus and I stood in the schoolyard where we gazed back at the size of our new house. Daddy was telling the truth last night – *wow, this is a big place!* I thought. A white frame, it had thirteen rooms and three porches, a veranda and a tower room. Known as a Victorian Queen Anne style, locally it was called the "Loftus Mansion." There were two, five-foot stone pillars at the head of the sidewalk that lead from the street to our stained glass front door. I was impressed.

"Are we rich now?" Marcellus asked, our blue eyes widening as we took it all in. I knew better than that. I did know that Grandma left Daddy some money when she died two years ago. I overheard Daddy and Uncle Mac talking about it when Mama and Aunt Gen were cooking supper on the night Grandma was buried. Maybe more than I thought. I never thought much about money, always being told there was enough, and that it was none of my business.

When Johnny and Bradley found us, a couple of other boys were with them. They were brothers named Larry and David Brown, and they lived across the schoolyard from our house. Most of Lexington was built around the schoolyard. The schoolyard was several acres large and also served as the town square. All the businesses and most of the houses faced it. The yard was filled with shady trees and it was also used as a city park. There were slides, seesaws, swings and a big sandbox there, too. It separated itself from the sidewalk by a two-foot stonewall that surrounded the whole school yard.

Always competitive, Johnny and I decided to use this opportunity to show off, since Mama wasn't there to stop us. We refused to remember her usual complaints of, "You kids are always embarrassing me, nobody likes a show-off." Jumping up on the schoolyard wall, we chased each other on its flat top, hoping Bradley and his friends envied our balancing skill. Then we shoved each other off the wall in a game of "King of the Hill," to see which one of us was left standing on the wall. Marcellus joined us. It took both Marcellus and I, but we managed to push Johnny off the wall. Soon, the other boys jumped up and joined us in the fun.

I skinned my knees from the many times I got pushed off to the ground. My dress gave my knees no protection and the blood flowing down my legs embarrassed me. Running for the swings, I swung until my bloody knees scabbed over. *We're so lucky to get to live across from a city park.* Closing my eyes, I smiled at our new life, completely contented.

"Come on, Deanna," I heard Bradley and the Brown brothers calling for me to join them and my brothers. Treating us like some newfound treasure, they took us into all the stores and introduced us to everyone we could find there.

"Aren't you a nice young lady?" a dime store clerk told me. "I'm so glad you have a large family, the Loftus place needs a large family." All the people we met were friendly and complimented us on our good manners. I knew this would make Mama proud, so I smoothed my dusty dress and pulled my shoulders back. Always wanting me to look nice, Mama would tell me to do this if she were standing beside me.

This town was far away from Louisville, but the stores reminded me of ones I knew back home. We checked them all out. Following the aromas of fresh fruits and vegetables, we pushed through the double screen doors of the Food-Liner Grocery. The bell attached to the top of the door tinkled as we went through it. A painting of a lovely young girl with blue eyes and blonde curls, advertising Sunbeam Bread, was printed on the screens. A mixture of smells – produce, spices, and coffee greeted our noses, smelling so good, that I almost forgot that I had just finished breakfast. There were large, pyramid-stacks of oranges and apples, and bushel baskets of green beans and cabbages beside the coffee grinder and the spice rack. *This is just like the food in Scotty's Market on Bardstown Road, and the Piggly Wiggly in Buechel,* I thought.

The Murphy's Dime Store next door displayed sets of china dishes in the front windows like the Woolworth's Five and Dime did on Fourth Street in downtown Louisville. Hope's Drugstore decorated their front window with a glass apothecary jar that was filled with red colored water and sealed tight. A tiny Bressler's Ice Cream Parlor was tucked into the corner of the square. Peeking in, I saw a counter and several twirling stools in front of large mirrors. I looked at the posters of milkshakes, sodas, and banana splits covering the walls and knew I wanted to come back there. We stumbled around the lawn tables and chairs in front of the furniture store and the rack of yard tools in front of Elmer's Hardware on the other side of the square. On that corner by Highway 56, where the truckers passed, there was Texaco Filling Station. Like I had seen in Louisville, the station had shelves of glass Depression-ware dishes they used for gas premiums. Men in green, drill-cloth uniforms with matching hats ran around the cars as people pulled in for a fill-up. Of course, next to our house was Sander's Barbershop. My eyes followed its red, white, and blue stripes spiral up and down, up and down the tube-shaped sign.

Everything bustled on this Saturday morning. We met other kids. Many kids from the country came to town today because it was Saturday and they helped with the family shopping. Tomorrow, Sunday, all the stores, even the filling station, would be closed. Sunday was a day of rest.

Before long we returned home to help rearrange the pile of furnishings stacked in the parlor. Mama and Daddy had a lot to talk about and get done before he left for Aunt Bertha's on Monday morning. It was time for dinner (lunch) when we returned, but quickly found things were too busy for cooking today, so we snacked on leftovers from breakfast.

"You kids take these chairs and all the clothes upstairs," Daddy caught us as we entered from the kitchen. In trip after trip, we toted everything up the steps that we were able to carry. My parents were too busy to care that we slid down the banister instead of using the steps. We also found a back stairwell that was shorter and faster than the front staircase. It was so exciting to help get us settled into our new life that we raced to do our share and helped our parents work hard all afternoon.

Daddy let the boys continue to help him carry stuff to all the rooms both upstairs and down. Mama called for me to help her in the kitchen. I fed and diapered the baby, and took care of the little ones, so Mama could think about the way she wanted things situated. Then we organized the huge room and its pantry. Johnny and Marcellus brought the pots and pans into the room for us to pile into the glass-fronted cabinets. I followed Mama's directions, taking things to where she pointed. I climbed the baby's high chair to reach the counter where I could then walk from one cabinet to the next, loading the upper shelves. I got Margaret Jane (age two) to help carry things to me. Laughing, she was enjoying helping out, as well. Bradley came over to play but we put him to work, also. He thought it was fun. Suppertime came at last. Now, it was Johnny's turn to help me with the meal.

After finishing with the dishes, Daddy walked us older kids up our winding staircase under the glow of an amber glass coal oil lantern. The light cast our shadows against the peeling wallpaper. They seemed to lengthen as we continued up the squeaky staircase. This made Marcellus cling close to me and me cling close to Daddy. Nothing scared Johnny until Daddy took the lantern back down the steps. The old house yawned and creaked but we were too tired to care.

The streetlight from the sidewalk outside our window filled the bedroom we all shared with long patterns of the trees in our front yard, making it look ghostly. We wished we were sleeping downstairs on the back porch again with the little kids, listening to Mama and Daddy snore on the other side of the wall like we had the night before. But, exhaustion put us to sleep before we gave it too much consideration.

Sunday morning we dressed up in what clothes we could put together, climbed into our black 1934 Chevy, and Daddy drove the ten miles to the Catholic Church in Scottsburg, Indiana. On the way to get there, we noticed several round-shaped barns as we drove through the farmland. Some of them also had small, round, red and blue paintings of birds and flowers over their haylofts.

"All right, you kids, those are Hex signs. Farmers put them there to keep bad luck away from their farm. I think this area was settled a long time ago, by a religious group called the Mennonites," Daddy explained to our constant questions. "They're people who keep on doing things the old fashioned way. They use horses and buggies and don't even go to doctors." All this unusual information made everything about our move to Lexington seem even more exotic.

After church, he took us to our new farm and we met the tenant, Mr. Able, and his family. Mr. Able showed a toothless smile as he shook Daddy's hand. His slender wife was a slinking shadow behind him. Their house was full of kids, including a girl my age, named Mary. Now, I wished we lived closer to the farm. "Well, I declare, that daughter o' mine's never satisfied," Mama chuckled to Mrs. Able as she nodded hello. The women shared an understanding smile about the mysteries of raising children.

When we got back home, we found Sunday to be a quiet day, just like it was in Louisville. All the stores were closed and families stayed pretty much to themselves. After eating the large noon meal, they relaxed on their front porches, or sat under the trees in their yards, reading the paper and nodding to the passers-by. While our parents relaxed on the front porch, it was a great time for us kids to continue exploring our "mansion."

Opening a strange "half-door" in the bedroom above the kitchen, we found a traveling cabinet. "What is this?" Johnny, Marcellus and I looked at each other in confusion. Johnny wanted to experiment, so we put Jimmy, who was only three, inside the little cabinet and began to lower him down to the kitchen. Mama ran into the house screaming when she heard Jimmy laughing through the wall. "I get to go next," Marcellus yelled down the chute, as he watched the cabinet descend through the wall

"You kids stop playing with that Dumb Waiter," she called out as she returned to her chair on the porch. Johnny and I were jealous because we were both too big to fit inside the little cabinet. "There must have been an invalid in that room at one time," Mama told us. We found a laundry chute up there, too. We were smart enough not to go down that, but we did let some marbles fall down just to hear them bounce on the kitchen floor.

****

Even with all the problems we already knew about in our beautiful home, life there turned out to be a bit harder than we planned. Soon, we noticed that the water from our cistern tasted funny. Lexington didn't have city water; all the homeowners were responsible for their own supply. The county health inspector came out to check ours.

"Yes, Mrs. O'Daniel, you have pigeons roosting in your gutters," he said. "All their business is rained down into the water in your cistern. You need to boil it for fifteen minutes every time you use it."

"What a nuisance," Mama told him, "We had the same problem at Goldsmith Lane, and I hated it! We never had to boil water in the country," she complained. I remembered that problem on Goldsmith Lane and didn't like it either. Boiled water tasted flat, and it was never cooling to me on a hot day. Sadly, when I heard the way Mama said this, I felt betrayed. For the first time, I feared maybe things weren't going to work out in our wonderful new home, no matter how much I wanted to stay here. I had trusted my parents to figure things out and make them okay for us. Now, I was scared they weren't going to be able to.

Luckily, Daddy wasn't fed up. Mama told him the bad news when he returned from Louisville on Friday, and he reminded her, "Josephine, don't look a gift horse in the mouth. In Gethsemane we had a spring at the bottom of the hill, you had to carry the water up the hill. I think you should count your blessings." He wanted no complaints, and I breathed a sigh of relief. At least he was still on my side. *If he didn't stay at Aunt Bertha's most of the time, he'd be as aggravated as Mama is,* I realized.

In Lexington, our neighbors were very important to us. Mr. Sanders told Mama about a well in the basement, that the former resident used. "It gets its water from the water table, so there's no trouble with pigeons." He told her.

On the next Saturday, Daddy took Johnny and me down there to find it. The basement looked more like a dungeon than part of a house to me. The walls were thick limestone, and the dirt floor showed occasional stepping stones. The darkness felt spooky. Cobwebs hung from the rafters above us. There were steep, wooden steps going down, with a wobbly banister along side. This scary place made the root cellar at Goldsmith Lane look like a playpen. Johnny and I were the only ones big enough to take turns going down there and bring up the buckets of water that Mama needed in the kitchen.

Daddy wouldn't let us use the flashlight, which was only kept for emergency use. He didn't consider this an emergency. "Your eyes will adjust," he said. "Pretty soon you'll know the path by heart." He only turned on his flashlight when we reached the dirt floor. I had to wait for my eyes to adjust and I didn't like what I saw. Not far from the bottom of the steps, was a stream that ran through the dirt of the basement floor. It came from a spring and always flowed, depending on how much rain we had. Daddy shined his flashlight on the water, as he searched through the cavern for the well that Mr. Sanders had described.

The water was black and looked like some writhing monster. "This water is alive!" I screamed, pointing. There were so many salamanders living in it that it bounced and churned as they whipped and thrashed over each other. I caught my breath, watching them twist and turn. "Don't be a scardey-cat, Deanna," Daddy said calmly, crouching down to see what I was screaming about. "They're not going to hurt you. Salamanders don't bite humans. They're just water-puppies," he smiled, trying to make me find them adorable. *Impossible,* I cringed.

"Deanna is a chicken! Deanna is a chicken!" Johnny chanted. I guess I was and I didn't care. Knowing that I would hate this job, I wished with all my might that I didn't have to do it.

Being stronger than me, Johnny ran through the stream when it was his turn to carry the water buckets. The salamanders never bothered him. But, I found the buckets heavy and moved slower. They swam around and between my legs. In the darkness, their long tails felt just like snakes. Screaming, I found this job terrifying, and it almost had me discouraged. Not wanting to let Mama down, and not wanting to move from our mansion, I did it and prayed to St. Christopher like Mama told me to, every time I descended the steps.

During a game of Frozen Catchers at recess, I noticed a hand pump in the schoolyard. Even though it was more work to carry the water buckets from that distance, when it was my turn to get the water, I did it gladly, proud of being able to help Mama. Bringing water into the kitchen was an important job. *Now, I'm as good as Johnny,* I bristled, straightening my shoulders, and smiling to myself.

Lexington Graded School was a great experience for me. Mama loved it that Johnny and I got to come home for lunch. The school had no cafeteria. Since some of the country kids had to walk pretty far, we got a whole hour off. I loved seeing Mama during the day, and the progress she was continuing to make on our "mansion." Happy to see us too, she really depended on our help since Daddy was gone all week.

We gobbled down our peanut butter and molasses sandwiches, then went to work. When we finished what Mama had in mind, we ran back to play in the schoolyard. Marcellus, who would be a first grader next year, came along with us. When the principal rang the big brass bell that she held high over her head, Marcellus scampered back home.

I liked jumping rope and loved the funny jump rope rhymes that were different than the ones we had in Louisville. The funniest one was:

"Lincoln, Lincoln,

What in the world have you been drinkin'?

Is it whisky, is it wine?

Oh, good lord, it's turpentine...

How many bottles did he drink?"

Two girls turned the long rope, one on each end. It floated over my head, then smacked the asphalt with a cracking sound, my feet jumping over it with a side to side rhythm, as the rest of the girls counted aloud along with my jumps: "One, two, three..."until I missed and it was somebody else's turn.

At St. Bartholomew's I was considered a daydreamer and a slacker who was always forgetting to do her homework. Sister Lawrence Ann gave me many paddlings over these problems. Some of the girls from the well-to-do subdivisions around Buechel made life hard on me at St. Bartholomew's. They thought they were more sophisticated than we farm children and called us names. I always hated school.

Up here I was miraculously called a genius. The girls here didn't tease me for being a hick because all these girls were from the country. I was actually looked up to because *I* lived in the Loftus Mansion. Everybody wanted to meet me. Nobody seemed to know about the interior condition of the Loftus, and I *was not* about to tell them. I was picked first for all the teams and the girls fought to sit by me. We didn't have to wear ugly uniforms, either. I wore my Sunday dresses to school and felt pretty. I actually looked forward to going to school.

"What a difference," Mama said, as she brushed my unruly brown hair and braided my pigtails.

Since we arrived late in the year, I had already completed the lessons they were still learning at Lexington Graded School. Their school year was two weeks longer. Even though we were done for the year, Daddy made us go because he could get into trouble if he didn't have his school age kids enrolled in school. We were now under Indiana law. The teacher, Miss Grace, had me work with the slower students. These kids were happy to have my help. Mary Able, our tenant farmer's daughter was in this group. My face beamed when Miss Grace told me how good I was at helping the others. She made me feel so important, that from that time, in the second grade in Lexington, I decided to be a teacher when I grew up.

After school and chores, my brothers played in the schoolyard with Bradley, Larry and David. I got to join them if Mama could spare me. Being a girl was not easy in the 1940's. Girls were busy helping mothers with the large families that were born during that time after the war. Plus, girls always had to wear dresses, no matter where they went or what they did. It was not customary for girls to *ever* wear pants. Daddy insisted on my need for dresses – I didn't even own any pants. The only girls who wore pants were the ones who had to work in the fields.

"I don't want my daughter ta' look like a field hand," he told me when I begged to dress like my brothers. My everyday dresses were tough enough to work and play in, but I longed for the freedom the boys had when they jumped, climbed, and hung from the monkey bars in the schoolyard. Also, I was sick of hearing Mama say things like, "Keep your legs together, Deanna, you don't look ladylike." I didn't care to be ladylike. I wanted to be a tomboy and keep up with the boys.

After a few weeks, Johnny and Marcellus, who were always exploring, discovered a large set of woods down on Highway 56 across from the town cemetery. There wasn't much traffic on the road, so Daddy let us play there if we promised to be careful crossing the highway. Having woods to play in made life even more perfect for us here in Lexington. It was just like going to Howardstown and playing on Boones Brother's Farm. Howardstown was our favorite place to visit. Now, we didn't have to wait for Daddy to be in the mood to drive us there. Since our move to Indiana, we didn't drive to Nelson County every weekend, anymore. Here in the woods, we had our own monkey vines to swing on, creek to swim in, and crawdads to chase through the creek moss. My brothers and I looked at being in the woods like most kids looked at going to an amusement park. After a while, the town kids missed playing with us and finally decided to join us and play in the woods, too.

"My Mama never lets me come here. She said the woods are full of wild animals and mad dogs, but she said I could come down here with y'all. Ain't you scared of snakes biting us underwater?" Bradley shivered as we waded, knee-deep through the creek.

"Naw," I told him, "they can't do that. If they open their mouths in the water they'll drown, silly," thinking I had this problem figured out.

I was especially happy because Mama let me wear a pair of Johnny's old pants when I went swimming. And, I didn't have to wear a shirt. Mama always said, "Girls look rude without a shirt,"

31

whenever I begged for the freedom to dress like the boys. It seemed that clothes were always an issue between us.

Then, Johnny and the Brown brothers started splashing at Bradley and me when we got over to the swimming hole, where the water was up to our shoulders. Suddenly, Marcellus interrupted our play by swinging over us on a monkey vine and dropped in the middle of our swimming circle.

We kids found life was so much easier in Lexington because Daddy was only home on the weekends. Like many fathers in the 1940's, he ruled the household like a sergeant. Daddy could be so bossy and demanding. We were always exhausted when he left for Louisville on Monday mornings. Now, he just gave Mama a list of chores he wanted the boys to do during the week. After they finished, they were free to play. My chores came from Mama and centered around laundry, cooking, cleaning, and helping with the baby and the younger kids, Jimmy, Margaret Jane, and Theresa.

When I got a few minutes to myself, I snuck off to the tower room where I kept my books to read, my scrap paper for drawing, and my embroidery materials – patterns, needles and threads. This was my special room, my secret hiding place. I felt cozy in my sunny little space. Sitting on lumpy pillows, I surveyed the town from its tall, skinny windows. Comforting breezes and the aromas of Mrs. Bernard's many apple and cherry pies wafted up through the tiny room. The screens were old and rusty and sometimes let wasps come through their gaping holes, but I was fast with my flyswatter. Mama let me off when she could, realizing I was a kid too, and knowing how much I loved to read and draw. She also wanted me to get better at my embroidery skills saying, "All refined young women are good at embroidery, you need to start working right now for your Hope Chest. You'll need to have it full of pretty things by the time you're ready to get married." Our dressers and chests-of-drawers were protected by embroidered runners and doilies she had started embroidering when she was a young girl of my age. I already had one doily done. It was made in many colors of cross-stitch, which Mama told me was the simplest stitch.

At Goldsmith Lane, she liked to have me around to have somebody to talk to. I loved the funny stories she told me when we worked side by side, about her cousins and growing up with her large family of brothers and sisters in Howardstown. However, I had more freedom here in town, because ladies were always coming by to visit Mama and play with the baby. There weren't any chickens or a cow to take care of, and no crops to gather, so there was less work for all of us to do here in town. Mr. Able and his family took care of all of that.

Sometimes the boys made the mistake of putting off their chores and didn't have them done by Friday. They weren't afraid of only getting one big spanking a week. Daddy gave us a nickel a week allowance if we got our chores done. That was enough of a bribe for me. I used mine to buy treats at the ice cream parlor and trinkets at the dime store. The boys hardly ever got anything but a whipping because they usually didn't have their chores done. Daddy used the long leather razor strap that he shared between his whiskers and our hides.

I loved going to the store for Mama. This was the only time in our lives that we didn't have a cow so Mama sent me to the Food Liner frequently for milk. I liked the taste of city milk, but I found the butter funny. It was called Oleo Margarine, and came like white lard in a waxed paper package. Mama made it turn yellow so it looked like butter, by letting it soften and then mixing in an envelope of red coloring. Somehow, the red coloring made the white lard turn yellow. Then she rounded it into a large patty on a saucer and decorated its sides and top with designs made by the back of a teaspoon that she kept dipping in water to keep the butter from sticking to it.

I sometimes stepped into Murphy's Dime Store for a quick look around before I got the milk home, dreaming about how I would spend my weekly nickel. One hot day in June, the bottle was so slippery, and I was so sweaty, that it slipped from my arms and broke on the sidewalk before I could get it home. Grocery clerks never wasted a whole paper bag on the purchase of only one item.

Without thinking, I let out a scream. Both Mama and Mrs. Sanders heard the noise and came running out to see what it was all about. My dress was drenched with milk. Holding Tony, I could see that Mama was upset, "Why can't you be more careful, Deanna. I need that milk for the baby. Now I'm out of money 'till your father gets home." She turned on her heel and went back to the house. Seeing Mama unhappy made tears come to my eyes. Sobbing, I began picking up the broken glass.

Ms. Sanders came back out with a broom and a dustpan and helped me clean up the mess. She took a quarter out of the pocket in her gingham apron and pressed it into my hand. She didn't say anything, she just looked right into my eyes. I knew what it was for and ran back to the Food Liner, in my smelly, milk-soaked dress and bought another quart. I don't think I ever loved anybody as much as I loved Mrs. Sanders that day.

Mama wasn't as proud as Daddy. Being alone all week with seven children, she accepted the help our neighbors gladly gave us and was grateful for it. After fixing the baby formula, she called Mrs. Sanders on Mrs. Bernard's wooden box-telephone, thanked her for the money, which she promised to repay when Daddy returned. Mrs. Bernard's phone was old-fashioned and had to be cranked like the one we had on Goldsmith Lane. There, we were on a party line with the three other people. Our ring back then was two short bursts and a long. Here we didn't have a phone. If Daddy needed to call Mama during the week, he called either one of our two neighbors and they called her over to take the message.

Friday nights in Lexington were really special. Our neighbors, and people from all around the countryside, gathered in the schoolyard, right in front of our house, for movies. The men of the town council put up a screen and rented an old movie from one of the local drive-ins for everyone's enjoyment. There was no cost. We brought our blankets and lots of popcorn to share. Some people brought cookies or fudge. Bradley's mother made the best brownies and fudge. There was a big black walnut tree in their back yard and she filled her treats with nuts. Her goodies always disappeared first. Some of the movies I saw were, "Blondie and Dagwood," "Abbott and Costello," and the "Boy with Green Hair." There was always a Woody Woodpecker or a Bugs Bunny cartoon feature to begin the show.

Daddy was usually too tired after working all week to join us. He stayed home with the baby who still spent most of his time sleeping in his bassinet. This was a break for Mama, at last. She was laughing as she laid out our blanket near the ones of Mrs. Bernard and Mrs. Sanders.

Playing with Jimmy, Margaret Jane, and Theresa, at the sandbox and the seesaws, I waited for the feature to start. Some of the other girls from around Lexington showed up with their younger siblings, too. The little ones played together while we girls talked and swung, pumping our legs back and forth from the wooden seats, trying to see who could fly the highest. After the show started, all of us took our little ones back to our blankets and enjoyed the picture show with our families.

During the movie, I looked above my head, through the leafy canopy of maple trees in the school yard, at the stars twinkling high up in the dark sky. I thanked God for letting me get to live here in Lexington, Indiana. Glancing over, I saw the bodies of my younger brothers and sisters heaving, sound asleep on our blanket, and snuggled around either Mama or me. Johnny and Marcellus were hanging out with Bradley and the other boys of the town. They seemed to require more action than I did.

****

The worst fears for me finally happened after only two months of our stay here in Lexington. Sadly, things didn't work out with the farm. Daddy found it too much work to have a job in town and keep a big farm going at the same time. Besides, it was obvious that our mansion needed a lot of work to be livable enough for the baby and the little ones before winter came.

It turned out that Daddy only had an option to buy on the house and farm. He lost money on the deal, but at least we got to have this wonderful experience. We moved out in late July. While Daddy spent time at Aunt Bertha's, he asked his cousin, Edna, a real estate agent, to help him find a small farm on the east end of Louisville. We moved to Hikes Point, a farm community about ten miles out from the city. It was very close to where we used to live on Goldsmith Lane. St.Bartholomew's would be our parish again.

We would be moving from our wonderful Loftus Mansion to a drafty old tenant house with only one electrical outlet, but at least, it did work. We wouldn't have to have ice brought over for our icebox anymore. We could use Grandma's Westinghouse Refrigerator again and Mama would love that. We would be on well water, of course. *More trouble with pigeons?* I wondered. Again, we would have another outhouse... *sigh.*

The farm was just a little over five acres but had enough land for a cow, some pigs, and chickens. Also we would be able to raise enough food for our growing family. Daddy would keep his job at Fehr's Brewery. Mama and I were sad that our city days were over. It was back to unending farm chores for us and no stores. Saddest of all for me, was that I had to leave Miss Grace and the Lexington Graded School where I was so eager to enter the third grade in the fall

.

The day we moved out, the whole town came over to say goodbye to us. I felt they really would miss us, like they said they would. "Don't forget to write and tell us about your new place," both Mrs. Sanders and Mrs. Bernard urged Mama. Holding Tony in her arms, Mama tried to conceal the tears in her eyes. She was so happy here and so was I. Johnny, and Marcellus, who didn't seem much concerned, were playing, "Got you last," and "no touch backs," with Bradley and the Brown brothers, Larry and David. They chased each other back and forth from the house to the car. I wanted to join them in our last bit of fun here, but I knew I needed to say good-bye to the house.

My heart was breaking. I would miss all these nice people, the town, and especially the beautiful Loftus Mansion. While my uncles and Daddy got everything packed up on their trucks, I secretly ran from room to room, kissing each one goodbye. I even kissed the fluted columns on the front porches.

I didn't care to go into the basement though. The salamanders didn't get any of my regret. They were the only things I was glad to leave behind in Lexington, Indiana.

"Come on, you kids! Stop playin' and get in the car." I heard Daddy calling for us. I slowly moved away from the house and bid farewell to the best two months of my busy childhood.

Chapter 3:

The Price of Getting an Ice Cream Cone

"Deanna, find those little kids so we can get in the car," Mama called out through the screen of the kitchen window in the dilapidated farmhouse that was our new home. Having left Lexington, Indiana, we now lived on Hunsinger Lane in Hikes Point. She turned and went back into her bedroom to continue getting herself and the baby, Tony, ready to leave. It was the summer of 1949. I was eight years old and like the rest of my brothers and sisters, not happy about us living here. Mama was unhappy about the new move, too. All of us missed the excitement and friendships we had in Lexington. We'd only been living here for a few weeks. Hikes Point was not really a town at all but just the intersecting point of four roads that were named after the farmers who founded the area over two hundred years ago: Hikes Lane, Taylorsville Road, Hunsinger Lane, and Browns Lane. The only business establishments in Hikes Point were Bauer's Restaurant and Beer Garden, and a combination blacksmith shop and filling station called Jack Finn's Conoco Gas and Blacksmith Shop. Daddy found time to stop in at Bauer's Beer Garden and have a drink with the local farmers on his way home from work at Fehr's Brewery whenever he could.

"Got to meet the neighbors," he told Mama, who kept asking why he got home late with all the work there was to do on this run-down farm. It had been owned by an elderly widow for the last twenty years and showed the neglect of that situation. We were only three miles from the place where we used to live on Goldsmith Lane before we had moved to Lexington. All this moving took place in just four short months.

In Hikes Point the farmers were old, and their kids were married and gone. The homes were too far away for the wives (the ones who were still alive) to come by for a visit. I was lonely and so was Mama. We were each other's only companions, working the farm chores together. Even though I loved the stories she told me as we worked, we had both been spoiled by the social life we had had in Lexington. No longer lackadaisical, the boys were now back to working hard again out in the fields with Daddy, or doing the chores he had on the list for them when he was not home. Nobody was having any fun at this place.

The drafty old house was full of black widow spider's nests. I saw the red hourglass on the belly of several. "Just stay away from them and they won't bother ya'," Daddy told me.

Easy for you to say, I thought. He walked away before I could tell him there were nests in the corner of my bedroom. I laughed when I remembered how scared I was of the salamanders in the basement at Lexington. They were nothing. Now, I had to pay much closer attention when I watched after my little brothers and sisters. It was obvious that my parents were too busy for all the problems this new place presented.

Hikes Point was in a beautiful area, however, and I admired that. There were waving seas of wheat, deep woods, and rolling pastureland surrounding our little farm. Our closest neighbor was the Stiedenberger Farm across the road from us. Mr. Stiedenberger was a widower. All of his children were gone but his son, Paul. Daddy met them in the beer garden at Bauer's shortly after we moved in during July. The farmers here were called truck farmers. They raised produce and took it to the Haymarket in downtown Louisville to sell off the back of their farm truck. We didn't do that, we only raised enough food to feed our family. Daddy worked a full time job at Fehr's during the week. Even though it was small, this little farm kept the whole family busy, constantly dealing with food in some way.

****

On this particular day we were taking a break from our usual tasks. We loved to have a day off from farm chores, but we weren't happy about where we were going on this day. Usually, we eagerly jumped into the car. But not this day, today we had a reason to be slow. It was our annual visit to the dentist, Dr. Campbell. His office was a good distance away, and we did love to ride in the car. Buechel was the closest town to us, being four miles down Hikes Lane. But, Dr. Campbell's Office was on past there, closer to Fern Creek. It took a serious reason for Daddy to leave the car at home because that meant he had to walk a quarter mile down Hunsinger Lane to the bus stop, which was in front of Bauer's, at the corner of Hunsinger and Hikes Lanes. But, he considered going to the dentist serious enough. "Thank God, this happens only once a year," he told Mama as he finished his coffee before leaving the house that morning. We felt that it was serious, too.

****

Disgruntled, I went about Mama's orders, slowly searching the house and yard for my younger siblings —Jimmy age three, Margaret Jane age two, and Theresa age one. Margaret Jane and Jimmy were chasing through the evergreens in the side yard and Theresa was rocking in Grandpa Dee's creaky rocking chair. I lead them slowly around the back of the house to the orchard where I had them each visit the outhouse. Their hands and faces were still sticky from the molasses of breakfast. Next, we went to the hand-crank pump in the side-yard where I washed them off. Then I took the three into the house to dress them in nicer clothes, and brought them back out again. Both Mama and Daddy insisted that we look neat and clean before we left the place.

"Deanna," Mama's voice came again from inside the house, "I'll swan, you kids are slower than molasses. Now, start gettin' those kids inta' the car or we are gonna' be late." Settling Margaret Jane and Theresa in the car was easy. They loved to go riding. However, I had no information as to how to get my brothers to do anything. I started pushing and shoving just like them, knowing this was the only fun we were going to have today. Maybe it was just Dr. Campbell we didn't like. All of us worked to delay this trip as long as we could. When I managed to get the boys near the driveway, we started fighting over the seats.

"I get the front seat." My brother Marcellus yelled as he whizzed in front of me.

"I want a window." Jimmy followed.

"I'll take the front seat; get out of my way!" Johnny said flatly, as he proceeded to take the prize. He wasn't the oldest, but being the biggest and the strongest, he usually got what he wanted.

"You're just a girl, girls don't count," he said, as he pushed me aside. Finally we were all packed in the car. Jimmy, Margaret Jane, Theresa, and I were crammed into the backseat. Johnny and Marcellus sat smirking at us from the front seat.

At last, Mama appeared carrying the baby, the black baby satchel, and her purse. "You boys get in the backseat and let Deanna up here," she stated, ready to slide Tony into my arms. I threw up my shoulder to them as we traded places in our two-door '34 Chevrolet sedan. Watching Johnny and Marcellus bristle tickled me pink. Jimmy beamed when Mama called for him to join us up front.

I loved sitting in the privileged front seat and being close to Mama. Tony cooed and laughed, enjoying the bounce of the car as we drove along the gravel of Hunsinger Lane. Mama was a nervous driver and drove very slowly. She wasn't used to driving because she didn't do it often. Luckily, there were just a few other cars on the road on this day. Sometimes we had to wait behind a farm tractor that was going down the road to plow a field in another location on the farmer's property. We loved to ride in the car and soon fell into the enjoyment of the trip. On Hikes Lane, we passed orchards and dairy farms. Smells of different farm animals and crops wafted through the car as we passed corn, alfalfa, dairy cows, and horse and pig farms. Pigs and silage smelled the worst. Mama drove past a skunk that was killed by another car. "Pheeew!" we all said and rolled up the windows quickly.

"That corn's tasseling out pretty good," Johnny remarked as we passed Edinger's fields, trying to take Daddy's place of authority in the car. The sun was warming up and, even though it was a beautiful day, as we got closer to Buechel, nothing looked good because Dr. Campbell's office was getting closer.

Slowly, the farm fields gave way to the buildings of Buechel. I loved Buechel. Though it was a small town, there were several churches, offices, garages, stores, and a stoplight. I almost felt like I was in Lexington again except instead of being built around a town square, Buechel was built along the side of the railroad track. Now that we had moved back into the east end area again, we took up the same life that we had when we lived on Goldsmith Lane, going to the same doctors, stores, and school.

What I liked most about Buechel was the stores: The Buechel Five & Dime, the Piggly Wiggly Grocery, Buechel's Taylor's Drugs with an ice cream fountain, and Fanelli's Ice Cream Bar. Cathy Fanelli was in my class at St. Bartholomew's. Buechel was almost as exciting as Lexington except that we didn't get to live there.

I saw some of the girls from my class at St. Bartholomew's jumping rope on the sidewalks in Stieger Villa, one of the richer subdivisions. I knew lots of kids in Buechel, as St. Bartholomew's was located just down the road on Buechel Bank Lane. Mama saw the sign for Fanelli's as we passed it and remembered her usual bribe, "If you kids don't put up too much of a fit at the dentist, we'll go to Fanelli's when we get done."

We had hoped she would remember that. "Yay!" we shouted all together. Suddenly, the attitude of the day changed. Now we were on a mission. We seldom got away from home, and the only way we ever got an ice cream cone was to suffer through some kind of pain from either Dr. Campbell or our family doctor, Dr. Duncan. We began to laugh and punch at each other again.

Continuing to drive on, Mama passed Buechel Bank Lane, all the stores, and Dr. Duncan's office. Sadly for us, we soon reached our destination. Mama slowed the car and cautiously turned into Dr. Campbell's driveway. Our shiny black Chevy crunched onto the gravel circle in front of his tiny two-room brick office building. We quieted as we remembered where we were and got ready to enter the torture chamber. Slowly, we climbed out of the car. Our eyes began to widen, and we stared at each other, because of the screams we heard coming from inside the building. They came from the unfortunate occupant of his ugly spinach-colored-naugahyde dentist chair. I swallowed when I realized just how hard it was going to be to earn my ice cream cone.

A memory popped into my head as I recalled my secret fear – that beneath that friendly veneer, Dr. Campbell really enjoyed our painful yells and hollers. Indeed, despite his comments to the contrary, I thought he even did things to cause them. Perhaps I was wrong, but this is what comes out of the mind of an eight year old. I thought this gave him a strange control over his two-room world.

"Don't you kids walk so stoop-shouldered –stand up straight," Mama said as we moved glumly toward the door, hunched over, and wishing we could run back to the car, again.

"Good morning, Mrs. O'Daniel. I see you got the whole family with you today," Dr. Campbell greeted us with a big smile. We didn't have a phone to call ahead; Mama just hoped he could work us in today. He spoke to us as he leaned around the corner, continuing to drill the teeth of the woman sitting in the chair as he did so. He didn't look so scary. He was tall and muscular with deep red hair and horn-rimmed glasses. He wore his hair standing straight up in a flattop. Being a jovial Scotsman, he had a hearty laugh and always seemed to be in a good mood.

However, his good mood had no effect on us at all. We lumbered into his small waiting room, trying to ignore the screaming coming from inside, that was getting louder. Rubbing alcohol and dental cleaning paste stung our noses as we lunged for the chairs without broken springs. Mama took the most comfortable chair and gave Tony his bottle. Next, we distracted ourselves by going through Dr. Campbell's collection of magazines, doing as much pushing and shoving as we thought we could get by with in public, before Mama told us to settle down. Dr. Campbell's magazines were never as good as Dr. Duncan's, our family doctor. Dr. Duncan was a grandfatherly old gentleman who made you feel good even when you had to get a shot. Needing to get a shot was about the only reason we ever went to the doctor. We got flu shots in the winter and tetanus shot every summer. We were always stepping on rusty nails or glass in our bare feet.

Dr. Duncan had *National Geographic* magazines. When we were at his place, we looked for the ones that showed actual bare chests and naked bottoms of some tribal peoples. Nothing like that here, only farm implement catalogues and hunting magazines. Nonetheless, we all found something. Anything would do to keep our minds off the groans coming from the dreaded naugahyde chair and the constant "whirr, whirr" of the dental drill.

My stomach tightened, *I'm never gonna' get my ice cream cone,* I despaired, and didn't have much faith in my strength over pain. *I'll be screaming just like that lady.* I thought. Looking up to heaven,

I prayed, "Oh, God, please help me when my turn comes. *How can I be a good example to my little brothers and sisters?* I knew Mama expected me to do this, as she constantly reminded me of my responsibilities as the oldest child. These responsibilities both challenged and scared me. I knew if I screamed like a baby, Mama would be disappointed in me. I never wanted to disappoint Mama. My prayers didn't seem to bring me the courage I needed. *I'm such a coward,* I complained to myself.

I did notice my fervor strengthen when I had smart-alecky thoughts of showing up to the boys. *What's a little pain? That's not gonna' bother me, I'm the oldest. Mama will be proud of me,* I beamed at the thought. Pleasing Mama was my greatest desire. Soon the screaming stopped and terror shot down my spine, making me sit up straight. *Who's gonna' be next?* My mind scrambled as I looked from one of us to the next. Our family members were the only people in the waiting room. The lady left the office gripping her chin, her mouth stuffed with cotton, her eyes filled with relief. Dr. Campbell appeared in the door between the dental chair and the waiting room.

"Who's going to be next?" he smiled his sardonic smile, speaking my thoughts aloud. I panicked until I heard Mama speak up.

"Here, Deanna, take this baby," she said, again sliding Tony into my arms. *I'm glad I'm a girl!* I was so happy that I clutched Tony for dear life, letting his little body absorb some of my fears.

"I'm going in next," she smiled at us. We looked up from our magazines relieved. "I want you kids to notice that I'm not going to be screaming." Then, with the grin of a cat that had just caught a canary, Mama shared her biggest secret with us, "Besides, if you don't think about it, going to the dentist doesn't hurt a bit!" That all sounded good, but how could I stop thinking about it? I'd heard her say this before about other things, but it never seemed to help me.

"Don't think about it, Deanna," is what she said every time she rubbed alcohol on one of my flesh wounds, but just the smell of the stinky liquid made my cut sting like fire. It didn't occur to me then, but she had just delivered her seventh child in April. She was an expert on pain and knew what she was talking about. Mama was in the chair so long, Tony grew heavy in my arms. Sure enough, Dr. Campbell drilled "whirr, whirr," incessantly, but all we heard coming from Mama's mouth, when she got a chance to speak, was pleasant conversation. *How does she do that?* I thought Mama was the bravest woman in the world.

"Please let me be like Mama," I prayed, looking heavenward from Tony, who was giggling and shaking his rattle. I stared up at the ceiling, and noticed the crumbly plaster of Dr. Campbell's waiting room. That distracted my concentration, and reminded me of our new home on Hunsinger Lane.

Johnny took his turn next. He thought he was a big man and that he would show me a thing or two. Because of his first name, he had a John Wayne complex. He would rather die than cry. I envied him. When it came to going to the dentist, Johnny, was really a lucky guy. Having inherited the hard enamel of Mama's family, he never had a cavity. No drills for him, all he ever had was a cleaning. He thought we were all wimps – his turn was over in no time.

"No problem!" He bragged as he swaggered back into the waiting room where the rest of us were sweating out our turns. Jealously, I thought, *that smart-alec's already done!* I waited for Marcellus, Jimmy, and the girls to finish before I gave in. I wanted to see what my competition was like. Of course, they all squealed like pigs the whole time. I was relieved! But, I remembered they were all younger than me and didn't have the responsibility of being a good example. I continued to pray for strength. More than just making Mama proud of me, I wanted to show Johnny that I was as strong as he was. We were only fifty-one weeks apart in our ages and were competitive about everything.

It was almost mealtime when my turn finally came. "You have three cavities, young lady," Dr. Campbell chimed as his sardonic look caught my gaze. Again, I was reminded of my secret fear about him. I crumpled – I expected no cavities.

"I really have been brushing my teeth, Dr. Campbell. Twice a day like you told us to," I explained trying to get him off his usual lecture about the importance of brushing, brushing, and brushing. It didn't work. He ignored my comment and proceeded to rattle on like I had never touched a brush to my teeth.

Sadly, I had inherited the softer enamel of Daddy's side of the family – Daddy, who was in false teeth by the time he married

Mama at age twenty-seven. All of a sudden I was knocked out of my daydream as Dr. Campbell presented the needle for the Novocain shot. "It will only feel like a mosquito bite," he lied to me, cheerfully. *I never feel mosquito bites, but this shot feels like a railroad spike!* I stifled my breath, and sucked in my stomach. My jaw quickly hardened, and my mouth began to drool.

"Go ahead and spit," he instructed. I took my small break and leaned over and spit into the little green glass tureen located on the pole of the dental chair. This helped me to clear my mind. When I raised my head up from the tureen, suddenly, for some reason, I imagined an immediate happiness. In my mind's eye our new tan and white collie/spitz-mix dog, Bullet and I run through the back pasture toward Judge Jeffrey's' wheat field. We went down the dusty road and on to the creek for a hot afternoon swim in the creek's cool waters. Miraculously, it worked. The pain of the shot was not felt by me. At last I got Mama's message – *It's just like she said, don't think about pain and you won't feel it.* This is my big day. I was thrilled, finally understanding what Mama was talking about.

My celebration disappeared when I saw Dr. Campbell adjust the drill. My body stiffened as the bit entered my mouth. My fingers clutched the green arms of the naugahyde so hard that my knuckles turned white. I noticed the glint in his eye as he ground away on my tender teeth. The smell of burned enamel hovered in the air and filled the little room. He seemed to enjoy the look of terror on my face. Dr. Campbell's carrot red flattop and his horn-rimmed glasses were all I could see as he bent over me. Humming, he put all his effort into my tiny mouth. His old slow drill bit felt like a jackhammer. The pleasant thoughts of Bullet and the swimming hole evaporated. *Who cares about an ice cream cone, anyway?*

With a scream forming on my lips, I was surprisingly rescued by my vanity. The memory of Johnny swaggering back into the waiting room and bragging, "Nothing to it," in front of the rest of us future sufferers crossed my mind in time to save me from embarrassing myself. Using sheer determination, I managed to go back to my happy thoughts and made it through the first cavity with no tears. Bursting with pride, I congratulated myself by thinking of Mama's words, "If you don't think about it, it doesn't hurt at all."

Shocked, Dr. Campbell's tone got serious and he said, "Well, young lady, we must not be drilling deep enough today!" My fear of his sardonic attitude gave me the courage to make it through all the rest of the work. Not about to beg for his mercy, I didn't even muffle a sound. That ice cream cone was mine!

At last we were all done with the dentist for another year. It was no trouble getting the kids back into the car while Mama paid the bill. Johnny and Marcellus even willingly climbed into the backseat without complaint. I had the baby. Fanelli's was in our minds. Mama came out and we were off.

"I have to stop at the grocery before we go to Fanelli's," Mama announced as she carefully pulled the car out onto the busy highway. We were so relieved that we would not see Dr. Campbell again until 1950. The new decade made it seem like another century.

Mama remembered her promise. The thought of the ice cream cones made our energies explode and we shouted about our favorite flavors.

"Hope they have orange sherbet."

"No, I want pineapple!"

"You're stupid, peach is the best!"

Before we knew it, we started fighting – big families fall into fighting easily. Mama, surprisingly enough, didn't seem to notice. She was too busy concentrating on the road to care. She only matter-of-factly told us, "You kids hush up, don't you know we're in public. Act like you have some manners!" Then she pulled the car in front of the Piggly Wiggly.

Wanting to join her, I struggled to get up with Tony on my lap. "No, Deanna, you can't come into the store with me," Mama said, ignoring the disappointment on my face. "You stay out here and keep these kids quiet." This was one of those times I hated being the oldest. I wanted to look at all the colorful packages and enjoy the great smells of the grocery store. Almost all of our food was home grown and I found groceries stores to be delightful. However, I didn't complain because I realized that Mama would get back much faster without us tagging along and getting in her way.

I sat back down and tried to make Johnny and Marcellus stop yelling. That was impossible. After a while, Jimmy clung close to me and the girls started to cry, "When is Mama coming back? We want our ice cream cone." I wanted her back more than they did, fearing that this situation was definitely out of my control. I was not at all successful in keeping the noise level down. In fact, I did my share of making it.

Finally, Mama returned with a bag of groceries and a different mood. The racket from our car had reached a fever pitch. She was embarrassed that her kids were the ones that the women in the store had been talking about. We kids failed to see the reality of Mama's new mood, even though it was spoken plainly on her face. My mother, a gentle soul and a genteel lady, was furious by our demands of, "Hurry up, Mama, and get us to Fanelli's!" She didn't care for our complaints of, "It's about time you got back!" What she saw was a car full of kids who were noisy and rude, and it humiliated her as our mother.

"Who do you think you are talking to? You kids have made of fool of me in front of the ladies in the store. I will not have my children shouting out in public like a bunch of savages. I'm not raising you all to be show-offs!" She meant it, too. She punctuated her resolve by turning the car around from the direction of Fanelli's and pointed it in the direction of Hikes Point. We groaned and pleaded, but it was too late. We knew better than to act like we did, but we hadn't thought. It was just another part of being a kid.

This was quite a day. Not only did I learn how to control pain, I learned, again, to take my mother's expectations for good behavior seriously. I did get to show Johnny up, and that meant more to me than ice cream, anyway. So, it was a good day after all.

Winter Mornings

Ice crystal swirls
Decorate windows
Warm breath hides
Waking faces

Tripping down the steps
In our night clothes, we
Hurry to the beckoning
Blaze in our potbelly stove
And shiver around its warmth

Roaring orange glow that
Snaps and crackles
We surround it with
Outstretched hands

Shadows slant
Across willowy forms
As we become
A writhing dance…

Pushing unwilling bodies
Into school uniforms and
Getting ready another
December day

Chapter 4

Christmas Comes, Slow as Molasses

I was eight years old – this was our first Christmas at Hikes Point. It seemed Christmas would never get here. We started talking about it early in the fall when the thick *Sears and Roebuck Catalogue* crammed our mailbox. The colorful pictures showed us the world of city children. Slick photos of dolls and cowboy guns beamed out at us and oiled our imaginations. Grabbing the book from each other's grasp, we chased through our drafty farmhouse. The noise exasperated Mama. "If you kids aren't careful with that book, Santy won't even know what your toy looks like! You all haven't been worth two cents since we left Lexington, Indiana. All you wanna do is fight and run through the house!" Her dark curls shook in disbelief as she stirred the bubbling tomatoes on our coal oil cooking stove. "Last year you got along so much better and you were more help to me," she sighed. Mama's words stung. At eight years old I knew that I should know how to behave. *Darn-it, I'm always lettin' Johnny get my goat,* I thought, disgusted at my gullibility.

Daddy was practical. He wished he could buy us all the toys we wanted, but he couldn't. Raising our family of seven kids and trying to keep the farm going already had him working in town at Fehr's Brewery. But, Daddy could help us enjoy the catalogue more easily. With his ruddy farmer's hands, he ripped out the toy section. The other 450 pages went to the outhouse where we used it for toilet paper. We liked the soft thin pages better than the scratchy *Courier-Journal* and *The Louisville Times*.

Johnny, Marcellus, and I left the house and took our fights outside – away from Mama's ears. We ended up standing in the back yard looking out over our wilting harvest cornfields where we had an earnest talk. Marcellus, the blond headed first grader said, his blue eyes widening, "Santa Claus must be like God. He must be everywhere."

I leaned into Marcellus and whispered, "Maybe we should pray to Santa, too."

Johnny's bossiness settled down and he agreed with us. Getting serious, he said, "Mama's right. No more fightin' 'til after Christmas." He saw himself as our leader. We looked into each other's blue eyes and promised. Both our parents had blue eyes and all of us children did, too. We feared our promise would only last a few days, but, at least we hoped Santa noticed our good intentions.

****

Weeks later, sitting on the scratchy wool blanket that covered the loose springs on the old couch that Aunt Bertha gave us, we made our Christmas lists over and over again. "You kids sure are wasting a lot of time deciding on one toy," Daddy laughed, bending his tall frame to throw another lump of coal into the blaze of our potbelly stove. When we were finally satisfied with our selections, we sat squirming around our long kitchen table. With the oilcloth sticking to our elbows, each of us wrote Santa a letter and told him what we wanted. We also reminded him of how much work we did on the farm, and that we hadn't fought with each other for several days. Mama helped us get our spelling right while Daddy, with his feet propped up on the fenders of the stove, enjoyed a Lucky Strike cigarette, and listened to the radio. Marcellus couldn't write yet, so Mama wrote a letter for him. Then he watched Johnny and me take turns addressing the big brown envelope into which Mama dropped all three letters.

"When Daddy goes to work in the morning, he'll put the stamp on this when he mails it at the post office," she assured us. Our eager eyes watched her hands close the envelope and her tongue trace over the glue that held it shut. Of course, we trusted Daddy to do this.

****

At St. Bartholomew's we learned about Advent and chanted, *O Come, O Come, Emmanuel*, every morning while we lit the pink and purple Advent candles. Our anticipation of the season grew. I daydreamed about Santa during arithmetic class. Feeling sorry for this poor man who worked so hard for children, I asked Mama later

that night, "Why does he have to live in such a frozen land?" Mama
settled my worries when she said, "Oh, both Santa and Mrs. Claus
really like it there. Besides, that's the only place that the elves and the
reindeer want to live." Right then my guilt about Santa's hard work
disappeared. I always envied Santa for his beautiful reindeer. *If I
could have some pretty reindeer, I'd live there, too,* I thought.

The excitement mounted around Thanksgiving. On the Friday
after, we received a huge box in the mail. Our Christmas gifts from
Uncle Mac and Aunt Gen had arrived. The postman knocked on the
screen door of our front porch and delivered a big package protected
in brown wrapping paper. It held several gifts, and Mama had to
sign for it.

"Wow!" Johnny exclaimed. "The Santa in Detroit must be rich!"
Uncle Mac and Aunt Gen had just moved from Chicago to Detroit
last summer.

"Well, the one in Hikes Point is just like we are – as poor as
Job's turkey." Mama answered him quickly before he could get any
ideas.

We loved Uncle Mac and Aunt Gen. They didn't come down as
much as they did before Grandma died, and we missed them. He
was Daddy's only sibling. They had no children, and it made us feel
warm inside when Mama told us how we made Christmas special
for them. Uncle Mac was a sales manager at Swift and Company. It
was a meat packing plant. They gave us great gifts, but they were the
only relatives who could afford to do that.

Mama was the oldest of ten brothers and sisters. She and her other
siblings had at least six kids apiece. They only sent Christmas cards,
but we loved them, too. The cards also increased the hope of the season.
Every day between Thanksgiving holidays and Christmas break we
raced from Bauer's Restaurant, where the school bus dropped us off,
to our farm about a quarter-mile down Hunsinger Lane. Some days I
tripped on the gravel and came home with skinned knees and blood
on my navy blue uniform skirt. The first one home yanked open our
aluminum mailbox. It sat on top of a cedar post across the country
road from our front yard. The cards came in so-o-o slowly. As they
arrived we helped Mama hang them on a long string-clothesline
Daddy put up for us at one end of the dining room. We used this

room for our family room. Most of the cards showed jolly Santas and manger scenes. *The Christmas tree's gonna' be standing in front of those shiny Christmas cards,* I thought, my eagerness increasing.

Mama usually stashed the Detroit treasure behind the baby bed in my parent's bedroom. Her thought was, "Out of sight, out of mind." But not to me. As the oldest, I knew where everything was in the house, and I didn't rest 'til I found it. When changing the baby's diaper, I pushed that box from side to side and tried to shake it. Not making any sounds, I gave up, sighing, *Aunt Gen sure is a great packer!*

There'd be a separate gift for each of us, even the baby. *I hope she didn't buy any more of that sissy, girl stuff for me.* In the last letter I wrote to her, I hinted of my need for a Roy Rogers gun belt to hold the cap pistols I got from sending in twenty-five cents and three Post-Toasties cereal box-tops last summer. But Aunt Gen, being a former clothing model, had her own ideas of what a young girl needed.

The Friday after Thanksgiving was also special because Santa Claus came to Louisville for a big Christmas Parade. As evening settled in, we couldn't wait to get downtown. When Daddy came home from Fehr's he was usually tired after delivering heavy cases of beer all day, and always ready to relax after he milked the cow and ate his supper. Mama kept it warm for him on the hotplate, which was a special tightly closed steam-plate. Every year we feared he wouldn't take us to the parade.

But tonight, his quick walk and big smile told us he wanted to go downtown and enjoy the parade almost as much as we did. Grandma used to tell us that Christmas had happy memories for Daddy. She said sometimes they came to Louisville by train from Gethsemane and spent part of the season with Aunt Bertha and her family, just to enjoy the excitement of being in the city at this time.

Daddy hurried out to the pasture field. We heard him call for the cow, "Hey cow, suu, cow, suu cow..." Calfie came running for the barn, the bell around her neck clanging as her stride quickened. Johnny and Marcellus finished their evening chores, watering her and feeding the pigs. "Here, pig! heeere pig, pig, pig, pig....," they called. Jimmy quickly took care of the chickens. I got the little kid's clothes ready and then helped Mama fix supper. Anxious to get to the parade, we helped each other out like any kids would do if they expected Christmas gifts. Also, we were smart enough to keep Daddy in a good mood.

The parade took place downtown around Broadway and Fourth Street. We loved to go down Broadway at night with all its lights shining. To us, Broadway was as bright as a Christmas tree all year round. Sensational neon action signs made of tubes of fluorescent lights called attention from rooftops and inside business windows.

"Ooo, look at that!" we said sliding from one end of the backseat to the other in order to watch the lights move. I was glad the traffic was thick because even though he complained, Daddy had to drive slowly. We saw drops of water fall in neon from a drippy florescent faucet sign on a plumbing company. Red cats chased white neon mice at the Sturgeon Pest Control Company, and bubbles fizzed from glasses of beer in the windows of taverns dotted here and there along the street. The L&N (Louisville and Nashville Railroad) sign over their national headquarters on down Broadway by the Union Station Train Depot at Tenth Street lit up slowly from left to right, and then back again from right to left. We were mesmerized.

Daddy took time to point out the sign representing his company on the huge brick side of the OK Storage Building at Broadway and Barrett. In neon colors of reds, blues and yellows, their famous jingle danced the words, "It's Always Fehr Weather, When Good Fellows Get Together." The refrain flashed off and on, and fluorescent beer bubbles bounced up and down. Golden beams, like an enormous morning sun radiated from the back of a large, frothy mug of beer. We were proud that our Daddy delivered Fehr's Beer. We sang the jingle as the lights bounced it up and down

The big department stores downtown put on the parade. This was Louisville's only large shopping area at the time. Santa rode from Fourth and Broadway all the way down to Market Street. People lined the sidewalks to see him. Many came from Union Station Depot, where shoppers continually arrived by train. Next door to the depot was Sears and Roebuck's Department store. After Sears was the L&N headquarters, the tall building that held the neon sign we liked to watch go forward and back.

Daddy found a spot for us to stand near Fourth and Broadway. What a crowd! While we waited for Santa to arrive, we older kids wanted to go down and explore Fourth Street. Daddy let us do it last year, and that's where we were eager to go. We asked if we could walk around through the crowd and meet back with the family later, right before Santa came. The thrill of the decorated store windows was on Fourth Street and pulling us in that direction.

"Wait for me at Stewart's," Mama said, as we got ready to leave. She would join us in a little bit. I was glad to hear Mama say that, I enjoyed looking at the store windows even more when she came along. First, she had to get the little ones settled before Daddy was willing to watch them.

"You all stay together and don't get lost," Daddy called out as we hurried away. Excitement had us moving quickly and we were soon out of earshot.

We knew from the years past that when Santa arrived, he would be resting on top of a float that looked like a mountain of snow. Daddy looked at the parade with the innocence of a child and lifted each of the little ones for a turn on his shoulders. When I was smaller I got a turn, too, and so did my brothers. We, along with Mama, would be sure to come back and be with Daddy for Santa's arrival.

But now, we were in a hurry to see the mechanical Christmas displays in the department store windows. The bigger stores like Stewart's, Kaufman-Strauss, Sutcliff's, and Bacon's had their fanciest decorations for the season. Mama and I thought that Stewart's windows were the prettiest. The boys liked the ones at Sutcliff's best because they showed layer upon layer of Lionel electric trains racing through tiny towns.

"Don't get so close," older kids yelled out, "your breath is steaming up the windows!" The thick crowd, several rows deep, pressed us up against the glass. Our eyes widened as we watched the magical show take place inside. The holiday music made my tummy tingle as I watched the jerky mechanical actions of the Christmas figures.

"This is my favorite," we heard Mama's voice come up behind us. Carrying Tony, the baby, she finally caught up with us as we stood at the Stewart's window. *Old Time Christmas,* was the title displayed in the corner of the window. The characters enchanted us. Mama's eyes sparkled as a smile opened up her face. I was as happy to see that as I was to see the windows. Children rocked on mechanical horses, mothers served turkey, a horse-drawn sleigh filled with singing carolers moved back and forth over a mechanical track. In the back of the huge window, Christmas trees twinkled as they bulged with shiny presents. Stewart's had music from the window scene piped out into the street using a loudspeaker.

****

Part of my enjoyment of Christmas was that it reminded me of Grandma Anna. She loved all the special foods that went with Christmas. These foods were too expensive for any other time of the year. Daddy insisted we keep her traditions and we had dates, figs, tangerines, Brazil nuts, and marzipan candy. Grandma's baking reflected her German background. She baked kuchens and streusels and Christmas cookies like Lebkuchens, Springerles, and Pfeffernusse that were unusual for Gethsemane, Kentucky when Daddy was a child. When she was alive, the kitchen buzzed with her singing and quickness. She let us watch her sift the flour and sugar, and measure out the goodies of raisins, nuts and candied fruit. If she caught us nibbling, she kicked us out. Grandma had no patience with sneaky fingers. She laced her fruitcake with bourbon every three days until Christmas.

After Grandma died, Mama and I did the baking. I dreamed about coconut, prunes, citron, and piles of black walnuts during my afternoon classes at St. Bartholomew's. Getting the nuts ready was a job for the whole family. Daddy brought in bushels of walnuts from our huge walnut tree that stood near the muddy, and stinky, hog "waller "out in the pasture field.

After supper dishes and homework, we cracked them while we listened to the radio. The dark nuts turned our hands brown if we didn't immediately wash them with lye soap after we finished handling them. Our enthusiasm grew as we all did our daily share to get everything ready for the big day.

I mixed the dough for our Christmas cookies by squishing it between my fingers, then used Grandma's cookie cutters to turn it into Santas and angels. These, I decorated with red sugar and nonpareils. Sometimes temptation was too strong, and I pinched here and there. Just like Grandma, Mama said, "Stop nibbling, Deanna, or I'll let the boys help me do the baking – then you can go outside with Daddy and slop the hogs." Enough said. I had waited all year for this, and wasn't about to let one of my brothers take my place!

Three weeks before Christmas we celebrated the Feast of St. Nicholas on December 5th. This special day was sometimes called Little Christmas. It was important because it gave a signal to us. Now, we knew that Christmas was just around the corner. Usually, when Mama called up the steps for us to get up in the mornings, we groaned and had a hard time pulling ourselves out of our warm beds. The upstairs was unheated and so cold we could see our breath. Lacy patterns of ice crystals stayed on the windowpanes until spring. None of this bothered us on St. Nicholas Day. We grabbed our school uniforms, scrambled down the steps, and spilled into the dining room. With the dusty smell of coal smoke rising up our stovepipe and assaulting our noses, we jumped in front of the crackling fire in the potbelly stove and quickly got dressed. Daddy stoked it up every morning before he went out to milk Calfie. On St. Nicholas day, we found one of our shoes stuffed with popcorn and a piece of divinity fudge (a particular type of white fudge with black walnuts). At school there would be a small celebration in St. Nick's honor. We would sing a song for him and color in a picture of the jolly man with the long coat and the big smile.

The Saturday before Christmas was special because we went back downtown again. I dressed Jimmy, Margaret Jane, and Theresa in their finest clothes. Today, we were going to visit Santa Claus. We piled into the Chevy and sang Christmas carols while Daddy drove the fifteen miles from Hikes Point to Sears and Roebuck's. The car had no radio or heater, so we snuggled under the scratchy horsehair blanket Mama put in there for us. Driving into Sears' back parking lot, we entered the store's back door. Delicious smells came at us from the candy counter, the baked nut counter, and the popcorn machine, almost causing us to swoon. These glass counters were strategically placed on either side of the back door. You couldn't help but be distracted by them.

Asking Daddy for money always brought a frown to his face, "No candy! We didn't come down here to eat candy. Do you kids want to see Santy or don't you?" But Sears had another plan for stiff customers like Daddy. The air brought in heavenly Christmas carols over the loudspeaker. When *Silent Night*, his favorite, played, he gave in and became part of the Christmas mood. "Here," he said, "take this quarter, and get a half-pound of licorice to divide between you." We looked through the glass case at all the other candies we would rather have than licorice – like the green gumdrop Christmas trees and colorful pieces of almond marzipan shaped like Santas, angels, and ornaments. But we knew better than to complain. We knew we were lucky to get the licorice.

Mama pulled us back from thinking about candy by reminding us of why we came to town. "Let's go to the toy department!" she said. Following the signs we ended up in the basement, which, for the season, was completely taken up by the toy department. Now, we saw the pictures from the Sears' Catalogue come to life! The clerks did a lot of work before the children arrived. They had the toys out of their boxes, assembled and ready for children to try them out. With their parents, children went from toy to toy, winding them, rocking them, or riding them. Plenty of salespeople were on hand to help everyone.

The Sears' brand of electric trains, The American Flyer, covered several tables. Johnny and Marcellus ran from one table to the next to watch them lace through snowy villages like a shoestring runs through a shoe. They chugged up wooded hillsides, and slid down through mountain tunnels. Their stacks smoked and their whistles screamed. I thought it was more realistic than the display we had seen in the Sutcliff Christmas window on Fourth Street. Looking at the boy's smiles, I could tell they *almost* agreed with me.

"Mama, do you think Santy will bring us a train set?" they begged.

"I don't know if he thinks you've been that good," she answered, shaking her dark head.

The tall dolls, whose eyes opened and shut had ringlet curls and wore little velvet coats over their silk dresses, fascinated me, even though I was a tomboy.

"Aren't they beautiful, Mama?" I asked wistfully.

"Too expensive, Deanna. You better look at the Betsy Wetsy Dolls," she said. When you gave Betsy her bottle, she wet the bed. For me, this was too much like the real babies I had to change. Instead, I hoped for one of the dollhouses that was made of metal and had a brick facade with shutters at the windows stenciled on its front. I took some time playing with one that was already filled with a make believe family and lots of tiny furniture. I knew I couldn't have all this at one Christmas; maybe I could talk Jimmy into asking Santy for the furniture and the little doll family to go with the house. We could make up all kinds of stories.

Rows of shiny red and white lead soldiers did battle on shelves of glass. Jimmy, who was three, played with these. He liked little figurines. The clerks helped him reach some of the ones on a higher shelf. Along the back wall wagons, scooters, and tricycles were parked diagonally. If you were willing to wait your turn, there was room to try them out for a ride. I helped Margaret Jane, age two, onto a tricycle. Jimmy jumped on one without any help. I rolled Theresa, age one, around in a Sears' brand red wagon. Being cowboy fans, we tried out cowboy hats, gun belts, and cap pistols. We played with model ranch sets and their animal figurines. For some reason Mama seemed to be checking out the prices, and I wondered why.

Some countertops were filled with furry mechanical dogs that barked and wagged their tails – and fuzzy ducks that quacked and waddled. Margaret Jane and Theresa were fascinated with them. Smiling clerks continually wound them up with big silver keys. We were in the Toy Department for more than an hour. Finally, Mama suggested, "Are you kids ready to see Santy now? I want to join your father." Daddy had told us he was going to check out the farm implements, and I couldn't imagine why Mama would want to see that ugly stuff. I believed her though, because I had seen from the catalogue that Sears sold everything, even tractors for the farm.

We wished she didn't have to go and begged, "Oh, Mama, stay with us. Pleeese!"

As we came up the escalator from the toy department, Johnny asked, raising all our doubts about the Christmas story, "How can Santa be sitting in that chair when he is supposed to be up in the North Pole making our Christmas toys?"

Mama was quick and ready with a story of her own "That man is only one of Santy's helpers, dear. He's just dressed to look like

Santy, but he's careful to tell Santy exactly what you ask for. And he also tells him how good you're acting in this store! Besides, it's really the elves that make most of the toys." This last piece of information made it so fanciful that we just had to believe her. I breathed a sigh of relief, and thought, *I've been better than Johnny and Marcellus. I hope Santa saw them fighting in the pasture yesterday, when I was in the house giving the baby the bottle.* Grabbing my sisters' hands, I, along with Jimmy, ran for the Santa line. Johnny and Marcellus went exploring and would join us later as we got closer to our great benefactor with the jolly "ho-ho-ho!" My parents used this time to get the toy shopping done for us. We had no idea they were doing that. We just thought they liked looking at farm tools.

Carrying Tony, Mama took off up the escalator saying, "You kids behave. Remember, Santy sees you every minute. Don't be an embarrassment to your father and me."

As we waited in the long line, Jimmy and I rehearsed what we wanted. Margaret Jane and Theresa were always ready with their gift ideas. Remembering my plan, I said, "Jimmy, if you get the little family and tiny furniture for the dollhouse that I get, we can use it all together." He agreed that it was a good idea and seemed to have some information I didn't.

"I know Johnny and Marcellus are going to ask for a train set," he said. "We can let our little family ride on the train, and make up all kinds a' games." I was glad to see that he was excited about our plans. Santa sometimes surprised me with a doll besides the gift I asked for. Like Mama and Aunt Gen, I guess Santa also figured I needed to act more like a girl.

We were careful not to ask for something too expensive because we knew the Santa in Hikes Point was poor. Somehow I didn't connect this fact with Mama checking the prices in the toy department. We didn't realize this store hired Santa was directed to push more expensive toys and would never say, "No, you can't have that. It's too expensive!"

****

A few days before Christmas, we strained at our front windows to hear the old Chevy crunching down the gravel of our driveway. Finally, we heard Daddy call from the car. "You kids come on out here and help me bring this stuff inta' the house." We were there before he got the words out of his mouth. Fehr's Brewery, where Daddy worked, gave each worker a turkey and a large fruitcake to share with their families for their Christmas dinner.

Johnny and Marcellus grabbed the turkey. About twenty pounds, it was frozen solid and in a cardboard box. They reached for the corners and lugged it up the back steps to our kitchen. I carried the fruitcake and couldn't stop sniffing around the edges of the cardboard box where its flavors escaped the cellophane. Daddy brought in bushel baskets of groceries. The turkey was placed in the refrigerator to thaw out. When it was half thawed out Daddy would be taking a sharp hacksaw and cut it in half. Mama would bake the other half on New Year's Day. Running back to the car several more times, we got everything he had packed in the trunk. Daddy bought our groceries at the Haymarket downtown on Jefferson Street near Fehr's Brewery. This was the same place where the truck farmers at Hikes Point took their vegetables to sell. He liked the prices down there and he could get produce by the bushel. This time of year there were lots of different kinds of fruit for Christmas. Bananas were our favorite, but we also loved oranges, tangerines, and apples. We didn't see him sneak in the dates and figs and Christmas nuts. Santa would put these in our Christmas Stockings.

Three days before Christmas, we helped Mama put up the Christmas Crib. Johnny and Marcellus climbed up into the attic on a ladder to bring it down. She would not allow us to put the Baby Jesus figure in his little straw cradle. "The Christ Child doesn't arrive until Christmas Day," she told us. He would magically arrive, right in his little cradle, on Christmas morning before we got up. We figured Baby Jesus got there before Santa came because, after all, it was His birthday!

Mama won this crib set many years before by having the highest grades in her fourth grade class at St. Ann's School in Howardstown. She was very proud of it. I touched the little figurines and enjoyed their bright colors. We took them out of the white tissue paper into which we had lovingly wrapped them the year before. Mama used that same paper since the year she won it in 1924. I shuddered to think of how old it was.

The boys ran outside and gathered tiny pinecones, twigs, and bits of evergreen. When they came in with their treasures, we took turns putting the scene in place. Mama put on the finishing touch – the snow on the roof. From the last roll of tissue paper, she fashioned the "snow." It was a piece of cotton bunting that she shaped and reshaped every year and put on top of the manger to make it look like a snowy roof. On its peak, she placed a pink Christmas angel with silver wings. "It's so pretty, Mama," I said as she smiled.

When supper was finished on Christmas Eve, we gathered around Daddy on the lumpy couch for the annual reading of *The Night Before Christmas.* We loved the part about the "bowl full of jelly." Daddy read that part again and again and watched us roll over each other in laughter.

This year there was fresh snow outside. Johnny and Marcellus gathered some of it in a large pan. Mama made snow cream by skimming fresh cream off the top of our crock of Calfie's milk, and adding sugar and vanilla to it. Many people in the country made it, and we loved it. It was about the only ice cream farm people had in the winter. After this treat, it was time for the little ones to go to bed. Mama and I took care of this while Johnny and Marcellus helped Daddy gather what was needed to decorate the Christmas tree. Earlier in the day, they had brought in a cedar tree that they found growing around the edge of our pasture field fence. The fresh evergreen scent swirled through the house – now it really smelled like Christmas.

Getting the lights to work was always hard. Johnny, Marcellus and I searched for that one dead bulb which caused the whole string to go bad. This job took forever. At last, with the lights working, the tree looked like it was filled with colorful stars. "Yay!" we shouted as we jumped up and down, hardly able to contain our excitement. Then we decorated it with all our pretty ornaments and that was the most fun. We unwrapped and handed our parents the shiny glass ornaments. Daddy stood on a ladder and reached way back into the tree to place some of them. Most of the glass balls came from Woolworth's Five and Dime, but some came from Daddy's childhood Christmas trees, and were priceless to him.

Because Grandma Anna was German, they had more elaborate Christmas decorations than Mama's family. Her family decorated their tree with colored paper cutouts from the Sunday funny papers, and strings of popcorn. Mama told us some years they didn't have a tree if the crops were bad. "There wasn't anything to celebrate, but my mama (Grandma Lucy), always made sure we had a great big coconut cake every year." Mama's voice was always tearful when she talked about her mother. "And besides, God always gave us what we needed. We didn't need ta'wait for Christmas." At that thought, she smiled, beginning to cheer up

Daddy took out a worn cigar box. When he opened it, the aroma filled the room. I loved that smell. The box was filled with about twenty small-toothed decorative clamps that fit on the tree limbs. These clamps still held fragrant pieces of old Christmas candles. "Here, you kids help me put these up," he said handing several to Johnny, Marcellus and me. Thrilled, we loved to handle these clips and smell them. Scrambling, we stretched all over the branches that we could reach, he and Mama took care of the rest. "When I was a kid in Gethsemane, we didn't have electricity," Daddy explained. "We used these candles to light up our tree. You could only let it burn for a few minutes, or it would catch fire. That's why we didn't cut the tree till Christmas Eve." Daddy liked that idea, of putting the tree up on Christmas Eve. But I wished we would put it up before then, like the other kids at school. However, I had to admit, there was something magical about not seeing the tree until Christmas morning when it sat on top of the gifts. We imagined Daddy's story about the candles, but we were glad to have the colorful bulbs of reds, yellows, blues, and greens peeking out from behind the branches and their tiny bit of heat making the tree smell even better.

Finally, Johnny, Marcellus, and I stumbled up the stairs to our cold bedrooms and joined our younger siblings who were already fast asleep on their own side of the bed, all of us shared our bed with another sibling. The spirit of Christmas had kept us working together with no fighting over anything. I was proud of us and hoped Santy noticed this. A contented exhaustion caught us in its grip, and we settled into slumber.

****

Silently, Mama got up on Christmas morning around five o'clock and put the turkey in to bake. Every half hour or so she returned to the oven and basted it with our home churned butter. The delicious smell of the roasting turkey wafted upstairs and pulled us out of our warm beds. The whole house smelled good enough to eat. We were ready to celebrate!

With a yelp, "It's Christmas!" we bounded down the stairs, all of us managing to cram through the single doorway at the bottom of the steps, and spilled into the dining room where the tree was located. We saw a glorious sight. In the corner, my parents had the lights on the tree turned on, it glowed, stuffed with presents. They were wrapped in the Sunday comics and colored pages from the Sunday Magazine that the *Courier-Journal* called the *Roto Gravure.*

The individual gifts from Uncle Mac and Aunt Gen, removed from their brown protective wrapping, always stood out, being wrapped in shiny red or green foil, with big gold bows. Across the room heat radiated from our potbelly stove and the red glow reflected in the glass ornaments, setting the scene.

As eager as we were to tear into these gifts, we respected the ritual that our parents wanted. First, we had to check for the arrival of the figure of the Christ Child in the manger set. It was there! "It's Jesus' birthday," Mama reminded us. "Now, go upstairs and get dressed for Mass," she said. "We'll open presents when we get home."

"Aw..." we sighed in disappointment. But we did as we were told. Then Daddy called to us as we went up the steps to get dressed for church, "And don't forget to thank God for your Christmas. Ya' know, some kids don't get a Christmas." I couldn't imagine that. Those kids must really be bad for Santa Claus to ignore them. Of course, I had no idea that money had anything to do with Christmas.

It was hard to concentrate on prayer during Christmas Mass. The choir sang, *Away in a Manger,* and *O Come All Ye Faithful,* but my mind returned again and again to the tree in our dining room. My heart filled with joy and I did remember to thank God many times. I knew we had a Christmas!

After church, and breakfast, the whole family settled around the Christmas tree. Santa taped each kid's name to their present. The way we did the gifts was that we took turns to go to the tree and collect the ones bearing our name. Because I was the oldest, I got to go first! Every year I got what I asked for. I usually asked for something to add to my cowboy gear – like cap pistols or cowboy hats. Sometimes I also got a doll. This year I got the Betsy Wetsy doll Mama admired at Sears along with my metal dollhouse. This meant Santa *had* noticed the extra work I did as the oldest. For that reason, I cherished my doll.

The gift from Uncle Mac and Aunt Gen was usually also something to remind me that I was really a girl. Aunt Gen told me, "I wish I had a little girl like you to dress up," when she and Uncle Mac spent Christmas with us last year. They gave me things like dresses, necklaces, or bracelets. These gifts made Mama a lot happier than they made me. My brothers teased me to death every time I ever wore any of that stuff. So usually, I only wore it for Mass on Sunday morning.

Mountains of ripped Sunday comics and Christmas wrapping paper soon filled the room. Johnny and Marcellus rolled up the papers and stuffed them into the potbelly. The glow flickered around the room, and we settled into its cozy contentment.

Mama and I went into the kitchen and put our noontime Christmas dinner together while the rest of the kids played with their toys. The boys ran out to the pasture and played with the new set of noisy caps for the cap pistols they got last year. Daddy sliced the turkey for us. This was the only time he ever helped out in the kitchen. "Cooking's woman's work," he declared flatly. But I watched him enjoy nibbling at the crunchy pieces of skin he pulled off the bird.

Next to hogkillin' time, when we fed eight to ten hungry men, this was the best meal of the year. Mama's dressing (stuffing) was made from the pieces of stale bread we stored for months in an air tight tin so the mice couldn't get at them. It was baked separately in a large pan, and Mama poured giblet gravy over it when she put it on the table.

I opened the can of jellied cranberries and pushed them out with our wooden potato masher. Mama carefully sliced the exact same-sized piece of the delicious berries for each of us. Nobody trusted me to be fair about this division. Cranberries tasted like candy, and we liked them as much as the turkey.

We had mashed potatoes and gravy to go with the turkey. I opened jars of green beans and corn from last summer's canning and Mama cooked them together with some ham grease for succotash.

I brought some sweet potatoes up from the root cellar under the kitchen, just like we had on Goldsmith Lane. Mama topped these with caramelized brown sugar and cinnamon, and I grated fresh nutmeg over the top before they went into the oven. By now my fingers were strong enough to hold on to the slippery brown nut that I hand-grated. The Fehr's fruitcake was for dessert, and we savored every morsel. The fruitcake was really the part of the meal we all waited for.

After dinner, each of us scrambled around the downstairs of our house and found the Christmas stocking that Santy had hidden the night before after he put the toys under the tree. We didn't have a mantle, so they could be anywhere. He filled them with Christmas cookies, figs, dates, and several pieces of colorfully striped hard candy. We snacked from these stockings for the rest of the week.

The boys and I took the Erector Sets and Tinker Toys that we got last year to the living room at the other end of the house. There was less furniture in there and we had more room to build. We put on our winter coats because this room was far away from the warmth of the potbelly. I took my metal dollhouse in there with me. Here, in the living room, we had room to stretch out and create community projects. We built a little village for the electric train set that Johnny and Marcellus got from Uncle Mac. *And, just how did Jimmy know about this?* I wondered, when I recalled his remark in the Santa line. Santa brought Jimmy a little family of figurines that we could use for the dollhouse and for the train. He also got a set of soldiers. I could make the dollhouse furniture out of scraps of things I found around the house. I would have a great time thinking about how I could do it.

Christmas evening came too soon. After supper we put our coats back on and gathered again in the living room around Mama's old upright piano for one of our favorite Christmas activities. The piano was out of tune, but we didn't care. Mama played all the Christmas carols, and we sang to our heart's content. We loved to show off in front of each other, and to Mama. Since the beginning of Advent, we had been singing the carols at school, and we heard them on the radio. Unlike most of the other kids at school, we didn't spend enough time in stores to get tired of them.

Daddy enjoyed an evening smoke by the glow of the tree with his feet propped up on the fenders of the stove. When we got tired of singing, we finished the evening with another Christmas treat – a drink called Orange Christmas float. I helped Mama make it the day before on Christmas Eve. We made it from thin custard just like we made our eggnog. But instead of the nutmeg flavoring, Mama boiled some orange rinds in a bit of sugar water and poured the flavor into the custard with some more sugar and vanilla. I put in orange rinds and watched them float to the top. After sitting overnight, the flavors were outstanding.

Regretfully, the day was over and it was soon time to put everything away and go back to our beds up under the eaves. We didn't care too much because we were off from school for a full week. After we finished our chores, our time off school would be filled by making up stories and acting them out. Most of them were about children getting lost or about cowboys and Indians. When our play was perfected through many rehearsals, we begged Mama to take time from her busy schedule and watch it. Being a good mother, she did so and always told us our plays were very good. Beaming, we went back to make up the next one. If the weather wasn't too cold we would go down to the woods to explore, or if there was snow, we would slide down Judge Jeffery's hill by the creek.

****

Fehr's had one more special event for their employee's families during Christmas week. A party was held for all the children of the workers in the famous Rookwood Pottery paneled room located in the basement of the Seelbach Hotel on Fourth Street, called the Rathskeller. The room glowed with Christmas lights and flickering candles. One of the mothers played the piano for us, and we again sang Christmas carols, drank glasses of punch and got a piece of sheet cake. Santa called each child by name to come up to sit on his generous lap, where he gave each of us a small gift and a stocking stuffed with nuts and more colorful hard candy. For this elegant event, I wore the nice dress and jewelry given to me by Aunt Gen and Uncle Mac, and felt as pretty as any of the city girls. *I guess Aunt Gen knew what she was talkin' about*, I thought, but, I knew I'd go back to being a tomboy tomorrow.

However, on this night I thought that celebrating Christmas in a beautiful downtown hotel was just about the fanciest thing I could imagine!

Chapter 5

Here Comes the Easter Bunny

Darn-it, is Lent ever gonna' get over with? I wondered, sitting at my desk during Catechism class. My mind kept returning to this thought and the anticipation for my Easter Basket grew. It was the spring of 1950, and I was nine years old. We had been living at Hikes Point for several months, but still complained to Daddy that we missed Lexington, Indiana.

Deciding to enjoy what we could of our new location, we kids realized that Hikes Point was beautiful farm country, that spring was a great time of year, so we delighted in the new surprises we found at home almost every day when we returned from school. Our new milk cow, Calfie, had just presented us with a beautiful brown calf. Soon we would have baby chicks, and the old sow had just charmed us with her new litter of piglets. She delivered them in the special little house Daddy made for her – and got finished just in time!

We kids thought this little house would make a fine clubhouse for the new club we formed among ourselves. "Stay away from there!" Daddy shouted as we tried to check it out. As he plowed the fields for the spring planting, Daddy ran his tractor over many rabbits' nests hidden in the winter grasses. This was a sad time for me – tears stung at my eyes as I watched the tiny bunnies run down the rows of upturned dirt looking for shelter. Chasing after them in vain, I begged Daddy to let me keep some of them. His answer was always the same, "Stop cryin' over spilled milk, Deanna. You ought a' know we can't make pets outa' everything." Drying my tears, but not comforted, I went back to work with the rest of the family on the spring planting.

The sight of the little rabbits increased my eagerness for the Easter Bunny's arrival. As innocent country kids, we still believed

69

in his magic. Sister Lawrence Ann, my teacher at St. Bartholomew's Grade School, reminded us daily that this important religious feast day was coming up, and warned: "It's a long time before Easter, Boys and Girls, so don't you be thinking about your Easter baskets. You need to cleanse your souls by sacrifice in order to get ready for the sorrow of Christ's crucifixion. Lent comes before Easter and it is to teach you how to do this. Learning how to sacrifice is important because it gets you to heaven. And, you have to do your part to make up for the sinfulness of mankind," she continued. I thought, *getting to heaven must be hard,* and bowed my head.

When Lent started a few weeks before this, the Nuns at St. Bartholomew's encouraged the children in all the grades to give up candy as their Lenten sacrifice. My fellow classmates grumbled, barely under their breath, "No candy for six weeks!" Sister Lawrence Ann ignored their complaints. It seemed the Nuns feared candy was some evil force that put children on the wrong path, steering them away from salvation.

In our family giving up candy was no sacrifice because Daddy wouldn't let candy come into the house if it wasn't Christmas or Easter. This gave Mama a better plan for our Lenten intention. Instead, she made us give up arguing and fighting with each other. "Now," she said, her face beaming with relief, "maybe, I can have some peace!" She was right; her plan was going to be tough for Johnny, Marcellus, Jimmy and me.

Always feeling like I needed more of God's attention for the problems of my life – like my brothers, the chores, the babies, and mostly the teasing from the kids at school, I made another sacrifice as well. I gave up telling lies on my brothers, Johnny and Marcellus – that was even harder to do. Because of this extra effort, I knew I would have God's grace, whenever I needed it. At the beginning of Lent my classmates and I were actually excited to show God how capable we were.

The Nuns prepared us for Lent by making use of special holy days designed to form the necessary attitude for this serious religious period. They prepared us for the feast day of St. Blaise on February third. This caused me to again fall into daydreams. This time it was about birthdays – February third was Johnny's birthday. Mine was

February tenth, a week later. *Every year we're the same age for a whole week,* I daydreamed, *why did God let us be born during such sad time of the year?* Then my mind wandered to the kind of cake Johnny would request for his birthday. He usually asked Mama to give him a white coconut. I knew I wanted chocolate when mine came. I realized that my extra sacrifice should have been to give up daydreaming – but I knew that would be impossible.

"February third is the feast day of St. Blaise, the patron saint of the throat." I heard Sister Lawrence Ann explain, over my inattention. "This day is where you young people are reminded to tell the truth. Our priest, Father Leo, will take the lies that you have told before today, off your soul with St. Blaise's help." She went on as we sat listening, with our hands folded on the wooden lids of our desks. "Father will place two candles, one crossed over the other, under your throats and gives you a special blessing when you come up to kneel at the communion rail. This blessing erases all your old lies." Thinking of how hard it was to get to heaven and of my desire to get there, I thought, *this is a good time for St. Blaise to help me stop lying on my brothers.*

Two weeks after the feast of St. Blaise, we were told of the particular day that opened the Lenten Season, called Ash Wednesday. "Children, this is a very serious day – the most severe day of the church calendar, next to Good Friday," Sister Lawrence Ann explained, "Father Leo will use real ashes to draw a cross right in the middle of your foreheads. While he does this, he will chant in Latin, 'From dust thou cometh, and to dust thou shalt return.'" With our hands folded as usual on our desk lids, our eyes widened and our mouths fell open. *Death?* I thought. She went on further, "The whole purpose of your life here on earth, children, is to make sure your soul is pure enough to enter the Kingdom of Heaven when you die. The sacrifices you make during Lent help to purify your soul. God knows if your soul is clean or not." I sighed, thinking, smugly, *I'm glad I'm making two sacrifices.*

Our school day began everyday with Mass. All during Lent, the church, which was usually bright and colorful, looked dark and gloomy. Every statue and crucifix was draped in a shadowy purple cloth. No flowers or candles were at any of the three altars. A few years later the church would look this same, sad way at an occasion when it was *not* Lent. This was to be in 1953, after a visit from the Vice-President under President Harry Truman. Senator Alban Barkley was his former title, and he was actually from Kentucky. Being a friend of Father Leo's, he came to St. Bartholomew's from Washington, D.C., to help Father Leo celebrate his twenty-fifth anniversary in the priesthood. The Nuns had us making thorough preparations for this important occasion for weeks ahead of time. The whole parish felt quite honored by the presence of such a significant person. Our little church was packed.

Unfortunately, Vice President Barkley had a heart attack while he was giving his congratulations to Father Leo. My class was sitting right in front of him in the first row, and I felt every pang as Vice President Barkley gripped the podium, looked at us, wide-eyed, gasped and then crumpled to the floor. The whole congregation was shaken-up for quite some time. He did not die that day, but the somber purple cloth went up the day after, while he was in the hospital, and it stayed there for weeks in reverence for him.

Lent meant that our Friday art classes became limited to mimeographed sheets (old fashioned type of zerox) of Paschal Lambs and the risen Christ holding his arm in the air with his index finger pointed toward the heavens. He carried large banners showing a ship of the faithful cast about on the dangerous waters of life. "These pictures are to remind us of the seas of temptation," Father Leo told us when he visited our classroom on one of the Lenten Fridays. We conscientiously filled in the designs with our crayons and colored pencils.

The Nuns hung our artwork in the halls all over the school. "As a reminder to keep your sacrifice," they explained in grim tones with their lips pursed and their eyes downcast. The atmosphere was heavy – I felt like I was caught in a mud hole, deeper than our hog waller.

Is Lent ever gonna' stop? I continued to wonder. Every Friday we spent the morning before lunch in the church where we prayed and chanted the "Stations of the Cross," crossing our foreheads and genuflecting many times. During this ritual we begged to be forgiven for our sins while we stared at the twelve colorful, ceramic sculptures of Jesus' suffering during His journey toward the crucifixion. These depictions were the only things in the church that were not covered in the purple drapes.

With our bare knees resting on the hard wooden kneelers behind the church pews, we listened as the school principal, Sister Robert Harriet, reminded the whole student body, "Christ did this suffering in order to save your souls from burning in Hell for all eternity. You need to show your gratitude by being faithful in keeping your Lenten sacrifice."

Holy Thursday was the last day of school before Easter Vacation, celebrating the feast of the Last Supper. Sister Lawrence Ann spent the afternoon reading the story of how St. Peter betrayed Christ three times in the Garden of Gethsemani. This cast me again into daydreams of self-importance because of being born in the area of Gethsemane, Kentucky, near the famous Abbey of Gethsemani Monastery. *If my classmates only knew that,* I thought, *they'd stop calling me names.* Then I got mad at myself because of the sin of vanity, one of the seven deadly sins, and despaired; *now I'll never get to heaven.*

The next day, Good Friday, was a somber day and would be a day off from school. Before she let us go to our busses on the afternoon of Holy Thursday, Sister Robert Harriet had us stand in long lines on the playground, wanting to make an impact on us because of the strictness of tomorrow's holy day before we left. "Each family is to observe this sacred day in their own special way," she cautioned us. It was chilly; we stood bundled tightly in our winter coats and leggings (girls' long woolen leg coverings that zipped up the sides), as she spoke, standing above us on the landing of the school's second floor. Our eyes winced at sharp sun-glint as we stared up at her, pointing her index finger sternly down at us.

"Tomorrow is not a free day," she warned. "God will know how well you spend the day. The day should be spent without talking, and in prayer." Then she made the sign of the cross, as we joined her, and dismissed us to our busses.

Mama took this requirement for silence seriously, and no talking was allowed on Good Friday from the time we got out of bed that morning. We followed this rule with as much reverence as we could because we didn't want to mess up our chances for a good Easter basket (like Santa, we knew the Easter Bunny was watching us all the time). The silence also made it easier for us to keep our no-arguments sacrifice, and for me to keep my secret no-lying promise.

In helping Mama get things ready for Easter, the only talk we heard came from the orders she gave us. Johnny, Marcellus, Jimmy, and I went to the chicken house and gathered all the eggs our Rhode Island Red hens had laid. The hens pecked our hands plenty as we took away their future little children. Our hope was to find enough eggs for the Bunny to give each one of us three dyed eggs in our Easter basket.

Before he left for work that morning, Daddy climbed up into the rafters of our smokehouse, and took down the plumpest country ham he could find from our winter hog killing. This meat would be fixed in a special way because it was our Easter ham. Mama baked it instead of frying it with red-eye gravy like she usually did. Also, in order to make it an Easter ham we put kale greens inside of it. Mama boiled some of the kale that we put into the freezer during last fall's harvest. We carefully re-examined the curly leaves for the elusive green kale slugs that hid so well in them. The worms were easier to see now, because the freezing had turned them white. After the ham cooled to touch, Mama used her sharpest butcher knife to open several deep crevices into the body of the ham. She told me to stuff the freshly boiled greens into these holes. I pushed them down to the bone in each one. The ham was prepared two days before Easter so the flavor of the kale would be all through the meat for our feast on Sunday. This ham was a traditional ham for the Easter Season out in the country, and it made us feel good to eat it.

Mama allowed me to help her dye the eggs that we hard-boiled for the baskets. She explained it to me like this, "The Easter Bunny is very busy this year, Deanna, and he asked me to give 'im a hand. You can help 'im, too. If ya' very carefully follow the directions he told me ta' do." Her eyes widened to increase the mystery of it all. I was delighted to get a chance to prove myself.

The dye came in little colored tablets that were about the size of the sulpher-drug pills Dr. Duncan gave us when we had the flu. Mama dissolved the tablets in separate cups of boiling water, and put a tablespoon of vinegar in each cup to "fix" the color. When the water cooled down I lowered the eggs into the cups on their little wire guide-rings. For some of the eggs, I put each of the two ends into different colors, so they really looked elegant. *When the Easter Bunny sees how smart I am, he'll want my help again next year,* I boasted to myself. Again, I had to remind myself that God did not like show-offs.

After the other kids went to bed, I helped Mama arrange all the green Easter grass we had saved from last year into the seven baskets. There wasn't enough grass, so I went to the barn and borrowed some clean straw from the hayloft. After placing the colorful hard-boiled eggs into the grass, I added the shiny, sugarcoated candy eggs and jellybeans that Daddy brought home from the Haymarket. He also got each one of us a small chocolate cross, covered in pink foil. Of course, I had no idea how we got these things, so I had no trouble believing Mama's story:

"The Easter Bunny dropped off these supplies last night when he came through Hikes Point. He was in such a hurry, I hope he remembered everybody," she told me, clucking her tongue and shaking her head when she gave me these goodies, "be sure to count 'em out carefully." The cross in pink foil was a perfect accent to complete each basket. I was proud of the way they looked. When Mama came back in from her work in the kitchen to look at them, she said that the Easter Bunny himself couldn't have done a better job. I looked up at her and smiled.

Although Mama let me help her make the baskets, only the Easter bunny told Mama and Daddy where to hide them. Following his instructions, my parents hid them all over the house, never in the yard or the cellar. The Easter bunny didn't want the rats and mice to be the ones to find them. When we got up on Easter morning, the household tingled with expectation. Nobody spoke. Each of us set about looking for our own Easter basket.

Some were lucky enough to find the basket before we left for church. Johnny usually found his first. Mine was generally behind the piano in the living room. No matter if we found our basket before Mass or not, none of the baskets could be gotten into until we came home from church. The Catholic rules at that time said that no one was allowed to eat or drink anything, not even water, before going to communion, under pain of mortal sin (this was the sin that could send you right to Hell if you were not lucky enough to get to confession first, and have the priest take it off your soul before you died). By the time Mama and I got all the kids cleaned and dressed, it was time for the last Sunday morning Mass at nine o'clock.

Before this big day, I had been helping Mama for weeks to repair the finery my brothers and sisters wore to church today. She used her old treadle powered sewing machine to stitch in the new seams of the dresses and pants for us. I used one of Daddy's castaway razor blades to rip out the old threads. Together, we toiled to make our set of clothes work its way down the line of the family members. Besides taking in and letting out seams, we patched, replaced buttons, and put in hems. Mama taught me how to make a new embroidery stitch called a French-knot. I was excited – I always loved it when she showed me how to do new things. I used the French-knot and flower-petal stitches to decorate the collar of one of the girl's dresses. Then we added the new paper flowers that we bought at Woolworth's Five and Dime store to the Easter bonnets cast off from our neighbors, the Hemlings, who lived down the road from us.

Before we left the house for Mass, Mama and I checked over the kids, and looked at each other, smiling. We were proud of the way the family looked in their new clothes with their faces washed and their hair combed. "You all look good enough for the Easter Parade," Mama said, speaking to me as well. Beaming back at her, we thought we looked pretty good, too. Today, we wouldn't be pushing and shoving like we usually did in the car on the way to church.

St. Bartholomew's Catholic Church was a big part of our lives. "Easter Mass is the most important Mass of the year – even more important than Christmas," Father Leo reminded the congregation when he started his sermon. The church looked beautiful again. Today, the somber purple Lenten drapes were removed from all the statues. The three altars, the Blessed Mother's, St. Joseph's, and the main altar, were decorated in white Easter lilies, and had candles burning. Sunshine streamed in all the windows. "This is a day of celebration!" Father Leo continued, with a big smile replacing his solemn Lenten expression.

The Easter Parade at St. Bartholomew's was simply going up to the communion rail as a family. Those who were old enough took communion. "Deanna, hold your shoulders back, and stop walking like you're walking behind a plow," Mama reminded me before we started to go down the aisle. She said this to me every time I left the house and had on a Sunday dress. Disappointed, I thought I was swaggering like a cowboy, and was really impressed with myself, but Mama wanted me to walk more like a lady. Daddy usually never noticed how we looked as long as we were clean, but I saw the pride in his eyes on this Easter Sunday.

After Mass there was an egg hunt for the schoolchildren. The PTA Members who went to the earlier Mass at seven o'clock hid the eggs for us. When we got to the playground, Mr. Chase, the president of the PTA announced to us, "Children, the Easter Bunny hid these eggs for you on his way through Buechel during the night. Now, hurry up and see if you can find them all." Even though there were hard boiled eggs at home, we kids loved to see how many more we could get. Scrambling and chasing each other in our good clothes, we ran all over the playground and into the woods behind it.

The prize for finding the most eggs was a new rosary. Marcellus won it one year and gave it to Mama on Mother's Day. She prized it so highly that she used it even during her last days at St. Anthony's Hospital. It was buried with her.

When our fine Easter clothes were carefully put away, we sat down for our delicious Easter dinner. Joyfully, we feasted on our chilled stuffed ham, mashed potatoes with ham gravy, green beans, a jar of canned beets, and stewed tomatoes. Our special Easter cake was white cake with coconut sprinkled all over the boiled, white icing. Mama sacrificed a few jellybeans from our baskets to help decorate its top. This feast was as big as Christmas or Thanksgiving.

After the meal Mama gave me my holiday reward, "You have worked so hard helping to get everything ready, Deanna, you can go on out and play. I'll do the dishes." These seldom heard words were music to my ears, and I ran out the door as soon as I could get my coat on, afraid she would change her mind. Actually, I found out later, that she did the dishes because on special days we always used Grandma's beautiful set of dishes. She inherited these from her family in Alsace Lorraine, and Daddy didn't want any kids touching them. *"Yay!"* I thought when I found out. This was when I realized that some of Daddy's stiff rules actually helped me.

All afternoon, we stuffed ourselves on Easter basket goodies. After tiring of playing outside, we listened to Fred Astair and Judy Garland sing, *Easter Parade* and other Easter songs, like *Here Comes Peter Cotton-Tail*, on the radio. Somehow it didn't really feel like Easter until we heard these songs.

Our knowing that we didn't have to go back to school 'til Tuesday let us enjoy the day even more. The Catholic schools were off on both Good Friday and Easter Monday. Because of the holy days and feast days we celebrated, the Catholic schools got a lot more days off than the public schools. That always made us happy when the Nuns told us that, even though we didn't know any kids who went to the public schools.

On Easter Monday, Johnny, Marcellus, Jimmy and I played down in the woods and had the first meeting of our new club that we called The Rangers Club. Since there were no other kids around our neighborhood to play with, we made an adventure out of exploring all the areas of Hikes Point for the best places to hike, explore, and swim. We set up the Ranger's Club for this purpose. The day was warmer as springtime became stronger and winter released its grip. We huddled together on logs near the creek's bank, and under the monkey vine we had just used to swing out over the water, and made plans – increasing our anticipation of the summer fun that would come in a few weeks.

Easter Break disappeared quickly, but that was okay because Lent was over for another year. *Let the fights begin!*

Our Elbows Sticking to the Oilcloth

Patterns of red and yellow flowers
On a background of blue
Hints of a thousand meals,
Shiny with grease, sticky with syrup

I trace a daffodil, waiting my turn
For mashed potatoes, sauerkraut
And a platter of back bones

Johnny's elbow jabs my ribs.
I kick his leg and everybody moves
"No fighting at the table!"

Mama stops the platter
To catch our attention, as
Theresa's spilled milk
Drips off an oilcloth rose
And on to my lap

Chapter 6

A Vacation at Last!

"But Mama, how come Deanna gets to go to Aunt Lena's for a whole week?" Johnny complained, his fists poking into the sides of his ribs. He also voiced the disappointment of two of my other brothers, Marcellus and Jimmy, both of them standing behind him. *All* of us loved to visit our favorite relatives, Uncle Bud, Aunt Lena and all our cousins. Because of where they lived and all the great stuff they had to play with, getting to go to their house was as much fun as going to St. Bartholomew's summer picnic.

Mama's answer was immediate and simple. "Johnny – you have a lot 'a brothers you can play with – Deanna has nobody. She needs to spend some time doing girl things with her cousins, Mary Jane and Lucy. So, stop complaining!"

I smirked at the boys, wrinkling up my nose and sticking out my tongue – they joined me in doing the same thing. It felt good to hear Mama take up for me. I didn't care what my brothers said, because I was too busy packing up my everyday clothes, books, embroidery materials, and sketchpads. I was getting out of here! A week away from doing chores and taking care of babies – I couldn't wait.

By this time, our family had lived here at Hikes Point for over a year. Ever since we left Lexington, Indiana, the year before, I'd been moaning about my loneliness. Getting tired of listening to my bellyaching, Mama set up this trip for me. I was so excited I couldn't think, I just kept running around the house and grabbing things.

"Deanna, stop runnin' 'round like a chicken with its head cut off! Yur' not gonna' need all that stuff," Mama said, looking up from over the top of her ironing board, at my two grocery bags and a suitcase. "Now, finish getting' yur' stuff together," she continued. "Aunt Lena'll be here to get 'cha pretty soon."

My mind was way ahead of me. *Oh Boy, I get to spend a whole week with my favorite aunt and uncle, and Mary Jane, my favorite cousin.* Mama and Daddy would come to get me, at their house next Sunday when our family came over for a Sunday afternoon visit. Our two families visited each other at one house or the other almost every weekend.

Being from the country, our two families had a lot of fun together. Aunt Lena and Uncle Bud had a bunch of kids like we did, and their ages were almost the same as ours. Both Uncle Bud and Aunt Lena laughed all the time, and all of us kids loved them. Mary Jane was nine years old like me, but I was a few weeks older than she was. As my closest cousin in age, I considered her to be my best friend.

"I'm gonna' miss ya' this week, Deanna." Mama told me, turning me around and tying the bow on the back of my dress. I knew what she meant. She'd miss all the work I did as the oldest girl. The next girl under me, Margaret Jane, was only three. Mama would have to make the boys stay in the house and help her. This in itself would be a struggle, hardly worth the effort. Knowing what a sacrifice Mama was making for me made me appreciate the trip even more.

One more thing, I thought, feeling the discomfort in my bladder, and I ran to the orchard for one last trip to the outhouse. Sitting on the rough wooden seat and hearing the wasps buzzing around and bumping into the metal roof over my head, I smiled because I remembered that my cousins had an indoor bathroom. *I get to use a bathroom inside at Mary Jane's house, like the one we had on Goldsmith Lane,* I thought, remembering how easy life was then. Suddenly, I stopped daydreaming and whacked a blue wasp on the bench beside me, using a rolled up section of *The Louisville Times* newspaper. Then, hearing Aunt Lena's Buick crunch down our gravel driveway, I raced back to the house.

****

Uncle Bud (Mama's brother) and Aunt Lena also grew up in Howardstown. They moved to Louisville around the same time our family did in the 1940's. Daddy helped Uncle Bud build his new home out of concrete blocks several miles from us. The area where they lived was great fun to visit because a creek ran through their property, and there were woods all around where we kids could play.

82

Also, I would get to see Uncle Ed. He was the absolute favorite uncle in the whole family. Uncle Ed and his pretty wife Lila lived close to Uncle Bud and came by to visit them all the time. Uncle Ed had an interesting story. After doing a very dangerous job during World War II, he managed to come back with no injuries. He was home only two months when a drunken driver struck his car, rolling it over three times. Uncle Ed's neck was broken, and sadly, he became wheelchair bound. A hard working farm boy all his life, he wasn't about to let these circumstances get him down. He found his sense of humor, and this saved him from a life of misery. His funny bone is what brought his beautiful, VA (Veterans' Administration) nurse, Aunt Lila into his life. Unable to resist his happy, positive attitude, she sacrificed her life in Chicago, married him and moved to Louisville. Everybody loved Uncle Ed, from the smallest cousin to the oldest relative. A cluster of people always surrounded his wheelchair, to hear his laughter, his jokes and his songs. He was the pied piper of the whole family.

Mary Jane and I were like sisters when we got together. Her older sister, my cousin, Lucy was very pretty, and old enough to go out on dates. She had lots of friends, and I probably wouldn't see much of her this week. I fell into a different world when I was around them. Mary Jane and Lucy showed me another way to live. For example, at reunions we found our own kind of fun.

These were huge events when Mama's brothers and sister's families were all in Howardstown together. The men stayed out under the shady trees in the front yard, enjoying the breeze that came off the knobs that were across the creek from Grandpa's house. They were drinking beer, laughing and gossiping. The women were inside the house getting the meal together, sweat rolling down their necks, and they were laughing and gossiping. When any kids passed through the house, they couldn't understand a word the women were saying, because they were all talking "a mile a minute," and seemingly at the same time. Every sentence was followed by a loud outburst of laughter from the whole group. Children were not really allowed around them unless there was an emergency. The parent of any child that might show up near the adults, would stop and immediately tell that child, "You get on outta' here, an' outside and play, we'll call ya' when dinner gets ready!"

So, all the other cousins, most of them younger than us three girls, were running around splashing in the creek, chasing, swinging on monkey vines, or climbing the knobs.

"Baby stuff," we three smirked, wanting more sophisticated things to do besides chase chickens or play in the creek. We snuck off to the cool wash shed behind Grandpa Emanuel's house. This was our private space where we hid from the boys and the little kids. There, we lay on piles of dirty farm clothes, read the movie magazines Lucy brought along, and dreamed about being one of the beautiful people.

When I got to Aunt Lena's, I was saddened to find out that Uncle Bud considered my fun loving, twelve-year-old cousin Bob, big enough to help him with the garbage business. Bob liked to tell jokes and also kept everybody laughing. I was disappointed that he would be spending his days on the truck with my uncle and his helper Gus Ferris. Uncle Bud's company picked up garbage from all the new subdivisions that were not serviced by the city of Louisville. This gave him a successful business.

To me, it was obvious that my cousin's family was rich – I could tell from the way they did things. For example, in the summer, Aunt Lena kept her fans on all the time, and they had a fan in *every* room. We just had *one* fan and it was in the living room. We turned it on only on Sunday when we had company, otherwise, it stayed off. She burned her light bulbs during the day. Daddy never allowed lights to go on before it was almost dark. Also, Aunt Lena had new furniture, not the hand-me downs from relatives like we had.

Uncle Bud's garbage pick-up business was very successful. Sometimes his clients would give him nice things they didn't want anymore and didn't know what to do with. "This is too good to throw away, can you use it?" They'd ask. Uncle Bud channeled these items to his neighbors and to his church, sometimes even to us if Aunt Lena didn't want them. We were always grateful. She did keep the sparkly cut-glass bonbon dish that she proudly displayed on her coffee table. This, along with the beautiful painting of pink carnations hanging over their sofa, made their living room look elegant. I thought of Aunt

Bertha's and Aunt Ida's fancy living rooms down in the West End when I first saw it.

The sleeping arrangement for the children was dormitory style. Girls were in a large dormer on one side of the upstairs hall, and the boys in the other dormer on the other side of the hall. As soon as we got there, Mary Jane and I put our sleeping pallets on the wooden floor out in the hall so we could sleep together. A window fan that ran all day kept the upstairs cool. "We'll have more room out here. And besides, it's cooler in the hall, too," she told me as we worked. I didn't really care because I was used to hot nights. Daddy told us to stop complaining – that we didn't need a window fan.

Aunt Lena was dark haired and skinny. She wore her curly brown hair pinned back in a pretty barrette. Like Mama, she also wore a smock because she was expecting another child, too. She served us a lunch of sliced baloney sandwiches and Jell-O salad with Kool-Aid to drink. Again, I thought they must be rich. *All these foods are store-bought.* Daddy called foods like these unnecessary and named them 'monkey foods.' He never allowed any monkey foods to come into our house. I was glad Aunt Lena liked them because I thought they were tasty. The only time I ever got to eat anything that Daddy considered a monkey food, was when somebody else's family brought it to a family picnic.

After lunch, Aunt Lena made Lucy do the dishes so Mary Jane and I could have more time to play. Like any sister, Lucy protested, of course, but finally gave in. Lucy was a good sport, and put up with us playing dress-up with her clothes and make-up. Being a tomboy like I was, I thought all this stuff was sissy, but I would do anything to get away from my house for a while, and I wanted to be a good guest.

Later, I saw Mary Jane and Lucy smirk at each other as we left the house. They were the closest sisters in age and I could see they got along about like Johnny and me.

Walking across my cousins' front yard we stopped to talk to Mrs. Jordan, their nice next-door neighbor. She was hanging up her washin' on a clothesline stretched between two skinny trees. Her family lived in a strange house that was made out of about thirty-five doors. Mr. Jordan and some friends were building their new home in back of this temporary place that they had been living in for about three years. A lot of people were building their own homes after the war (World War II). The Jordan's had five kids in that house of doors, and I thought they must get really cold in the wintertime. Her kids were all playing in a sandbox and were too little to join us. I liked to talk to neighbors, and enjoyed meeting her. While Mrs. Jordan and I chatted, I noticed that my cousin disappeared.

Soon I heard Mary Jane calling me, "Come on, Deanna," she beckoned, running over to the Jordan's yard from one of Uncle Bud's many out-buildings, her blond pigtails flying. She carried a bunch of comic books. This excited me because I loved comic books. "Good-bye, Mrs. Jordan," we called as we took off for the road in front of both Mary Jane's, and the Jordan's houses.

"I know where we can read these. It's nice an' cool and nobody'll bother us," she laughed, her blue eyes twinkling. She was excited to get away from chores, herself. Wearing our everyday dresses, we could go anywhere. It didn't matter if we got them dirty, everyday dresses were never changed until the end of the week. "This is it," Mary Jane told me as we reached the road, but quite a ways down from her house. I didn't see anything there but the gravel rocks. *The road? Read on the road? There's no chairs 'round here.* I was confused. "What is she talking about?" I mumbled, saying nothing aloud because I didn't want to be a bad guest.

"Oh, you'll like it," she laughed again, seeing my doubtful face. I just had to trust her so I followed her along the road until we found a shady spot where the ruts were more deeply gouged into its surface from the heavy trucks that used this road. As the road went around the bend to go deeper into the woods, we climbed down into these holes and read our comic books. Mary Jane was right. After I wiggled and squirmed around the rocks that poked me in the back, the deep ruts were cool and as comfortable as reclining chairs. We kept an ear out for the rumble of on-coming trucks. Luckily, that didn't happen too frequently. After the trucks geared past us, we jumped right back down into our holes, re-arranged our dresses, and went back to our comic books. Happily, we read without aggravation from any little kids for most of the afternoon.

During supper that night I got another special treat. Aunt Lena fixed fried chicken. It was *just* Monday night, at our house we only had fried chicken on Sunday. All the kids gathered around a long kitchen table on assigned chairs just like we did at my house. There were Lucy, Hugh, Paul, Carol, and Tommy (in the highchair by Aunt Lena's place), plus Mary Jane and I. Uncle Bud was working, and Bob was with him. They would eat later with Mr. Ferris, who lived alone, but always ate supper with them before he went home.

When Aunt Lena brought the platter to the table, she said, "Deanna, you're our guest. You can have the first choice of the chicken." My eyes were as big as saucers – at our house all the pieces were assigned, and I'd never even tasted any piece but the thigh. Without another thought, I grabbed the breast. *Wow! Now I know they're rich!* Aunt Lena had fried *two* chickens. The delicious white meat was so juicy that I wiped my chin with the back of my hand as it rolled out of my mouth.

Like us, my cousins raised their own pigs and chickens. Daddy and my brothers helped them with hog killing just like they helped us. I noticed a scrap bucket in the corner of the kitchen for pig food, sort of like we had – but it was neater. However, Uncle Bud was not a farmer like Daddy. He was too busy with his business to raise crops. He made enough money for his family to buy most of their food in the grocery store.

After supper and dishes were done, all us girls, Lucy, Mary Jane and I gathered in the living room with Aunt Lena and worked on our embroidery patterns. Mine was a long dresser runner showing daisies and twines of ivy. I was excited because Aunt Lena showed me a new stitch, called a satin stitch, for making the flower petals. *Aunt Lena can do everything,* I thought, looking at my piece with new appreciation at the perfect flower petals. Then we all went outdoors for fun in the yard as the evening turned into night.

The next day, Mary Jane handed me an extra swimming suit from their collection, and we went for a swim in the creek in the woods across the gravel road in front of my cousins' house. Other kids in the neighborhood came to the creek to join us. We swung on monkey vines and jumped in the deepest part of the swimming hole. I was shy and stuck close to Mary Jane. Lucy, who thought she was too big for little kids, went swimming at a friend's house that had a pool in their back yard. After swimming for a while, all the girls sat in a circle on the creek's rocky bottom, at the shallow end and talked while the boys showed off to us. What clowns! We laughed at them and ignored them at the same time, trying to act refined.

When we got tired of swimming, we spent the rest of the day riding bikes. My cousins had several to choose from. Mary Jane and I went up and down their bumpy gravel road, and even out to the asphalt of Indian Trail. I was beginning to feel pretty brave. Hunsinger Lane was gravel, too, and never had much traffic. But, with all my chores, I didn't have much time to ride a bike, and didn't consider myself very good at it, either.

Tonight, after supper, Mary Jane whispered to me, "I think Lucy snuck off with that boy named Wayne that Mama does *not* want her to see." Her blue eyes met mine. "I want to go and catch her, and I know how we can find out," she continued in a serious tone.

Lucy was picked up over an hour ago by some girlfriends. They said they were going to Preston Highway Drive-In.

Then Mary Jane went on, "We'll ride our bikes to the drive-in and find them. Then I'm gonna' tell Mama, and is Lucy gonna' get it! She thinks she's so pretty that she can get by with anything." I had to agree with her that Lucy, with her long blonde pageboy hairdo and big brown eyes, was indeed pretty.

This idea scared me and I really didn't want to go. Even though it was July and we were in Daylight Savings Time, I could read the sky enough to know that it would be dark before we got back home. I didn't know where the Preston Highway Drive-in was, and I was shocked to find out that is was at least eight miles away. Besides, Uncle Ed and Aunt Lila were coming over for a visit tonight, and I was eager to see them. Also, I looked forward to hearing some more of Aunt Lena's stories and roasting marshmallows on a little bonfire in the backyard like we did the night before. I never knew much about Aunt Lena's family, and liked it when she talked about their life growing up in Howardstown with Mama's brothers and sisters. They all went to St. Ann's grade school together in Howardstown.

But, Mary Jane kept begging, so I did what she wanted against my better judgment – again. I didn't want to be a bad guest. Going down Indian Trail to Preston Highway was long, but easy. We got to ride alongside each other – we laughed and talked. It seemed that

Lucy got Mary Jane in trouble for something the week before, and now Mary Jane was taking up for herself. This was like the stuff that went on between my brothers and me. When we got to Preston Highway, the biking was another story. The cars were bumper to bumper on this busy street. Drivers blew their horns at us, and that made me nervous. It was quite a ways to get to the drive-in. Mary Jane, who was a much more skillful biker rider, was on a mission and didn't pay any attention to my suggestions to turn back.

Finally, we reached the drive-in. Because we were on bikes, the drive-in attendant accepted our story that we had to give a message to our older sister inside. We rolled our bikes over to the car that had picked Lucy up earlier. Mary Jane was right. We found her sitting on a blanket that the teens had thrown out on the gravel next to the car. She was with some other teens, *but she was holding Wayne's hand.* She and Mary Jane had some heated words, and Lucy's pretty face didn't look so good as she twisted it out of shape. I was embarrassed to be there and cast my eyes down to the ground. I felt like I was in the middle of their fight. Lucy had always been nice to me and I didn't want to get on her bad side.

"I'm gonna' tell Mama on you!" Mary Jane threatened, as we turned our bikes to leave. "You do and I'll tear up all your stuff," Lucy yelled after us. All I could think of was, *Thank God, we're gettin' outta' here.* Going back to Aunt Lena's was even worse than I thought it would be. I prayed the whole time. Now, it was twilight and it much harder for the drivers to see us. Several times I almost got hit. Horns blew and drivers cursed at us. "Get the _____ off the road, you _____, _____ stupid kids!" they shouted. I was so nervous, my heart pounded and my body shook. I wasn't a good bike rider anyway. I feared that I would lose my balance and fall into the path of a car as I skidded again and again in the gravel on the side of the highway.

Just as I suspected it was very dark before we got home. I was so grateful to finally turn my bike into the grass of Aunt Lena's front yard that I didn't notice she was sitting, rocking back and forth in the front porch glider, and *holding a big switch.* Uncle Ed and Aunt Lila had already gone home. *Darn! I missed them,* was all I thought. Mary Jane didn't even get to tell Aunt Lena the juicy news about Lucy until after she got her licks from the switch. Then Uncle Bud, a mountain of a man, got his turn. "I swear, Mary Jane, sometimes you act like you don't have enough sense to come in out 'a the rain," his voice growled. "I've talked to you kids till I'm blue in the face about how dangerous it is to rides bikes on Preston Highway!" This sounded like my father when he was upset. "Don't you know you all coulda' been killed!" he continued. I had never seen Uncle Bud or Aunt Lena, who were always so pleasant, upset before, and I was scared.

Then they started in on me. "Deanna, you're the oldest. We thought you had more sense. Don't you know your parents expect us to take better care of you then to let you ride bikes on a busy highway, especially at night?" Now I *really* felt bad and wished I was back home with the simple fights I got into with my brothers.

This was the most complicated thing that had ever happened to me. I was considered disobedient by my favorite aunt and uncle, and I didn't even realize I might hurt them. I just wanted to please Mary Jane as her guest. "I'm sorry," was all I could say. I didn't want to get Mary Jane in any more trouble than she was already in. They sent us right to bed and didn't seem to care about Mary Jane's big story. There was no chasing lightening bugs and roasting marshmallows in the backyard like we did the night before.

I tossed and turned on my pallet that I had laid out, with Mary Jane yesterday, on the hard wooden floor of the upstairs hall. I had slept like a baby there on this pallet the night before. Tonight my stomach churned with guilt. It was almost enough to make me wish I was back home. *Is Aunt Lena gonna' take me home tomorrow? She probly' hates me now.* I worried about this all night. *I hope I don't hav' ta' give up my vacation.* My mind shifted back and forth. The next morning couldn't come too soon.

****

Stumbling down the steps for breakfast, we heard Aunt Lena's cheerful voice again, and I sighed with relief. "Today we're going to Howardstown! Hurry up and eat," she announced. Before he left for work that morning, Uncle Bud had helped her pack up the car for the trip. Howardstown! There couldn't have been better news. I guess they thought it best to get me out of temptation's way – and to separate Lucy from Wayne.

Mary Jane's smile widened as she whispered in my ear, "Bob told me that Lucy got a good spanking when she came in last night, for lying to Mama and Daddy. I was relieved that Mary Jane was out of trouble – maybe that meant that I was, too.

I loved to go to Howardstown, but, this time, instead of going to Grandpa Emanuel's place where we usually went, we visited Great-Grandma Sudie Howard's place. The drive was long and took about two hours. When we got there, a gaggle of Great-Grandma's big old gray geese came honking and running at the car as Aunt Lena turned it off the highway and pulled it into the parking space in the front of their yard. Hissing and snapping, the geese circled the car and pecked at the doors. We couldn't get out, they made quite a racket. Mary Jane, Lucy and I held our ears. The Howard farm used them for guard animals like the beagles that Grandpa Emanuel used. Both were trained to keep the farm safe from intruders.

"My Lordy, what is goin' on out here?" We heard Aunt Elizabeth's booming voice coming from the front porch. She came on out into the yard, beating a mixing spoon on the bottom of her metal dishpan, to run them off. Honking even louder, the gaggle scooted together, like a big gray cloud, back into the field. Nobody had phones out here, so she was both surprised and delighted to have company.

"Well, I'll swan," she laughed, "if this don't beat all! It sure is good ta' see ya!" She welcomed us as we pulled our cramped bodies out of the hot, stuffy car.

Aunt Elizabeth was Aunt Lena's younger sister, and like her, had a never-ending laugh. Instead of being tall and skinny like Aunt Lena, she was plump and wore her long brown hair on her head in a bun. She was my cousins' aunt due to being Aunt Lena's sister, but she was my aunt in a different way, so I called her Aunt Elizabeth, too. She was married to Great-Grandma Sudie's youngest son, Linn, and he was my great uncle. Everybody in Howardstown was related to each other in some way. When they got married, Aunt Elizabeth and Uncle Linn moved in with Great Grandma Sudie to help take care of her, because as old as she was, she was in ill health. They also helped her manage the Howard's farm.

Great Grandma Sudie was born during the Civil War and was a very interesting person. Her oldest grandchild was my mother,

Josephine. Great Grandma Sudie (she had ten children) was also the mother of Virgil Howard. He and his wife Ruby were the ones who made the bootleg run back in the `20's, taking Mama and her cousin Margaret along as twelve year olds, to Chicago during the prohibition days. Over the years, Mama had told me many wonderful stories about Great Grandma's generosity and kindness. (In later years, she would be written up in the "Kentucky Standard" newspaper as the oldest self-employed farm woman in the United States, and able to receive a monthly social security check, though she waited until age 96 to do so. Uncle Linn was her partner in the workings of the farm.

Not able to walk very well anymore, she called me over to her rocking chair. A tiny lady wearing a flowered housedress, Great-Grandma also wore her thinning gray hair pulled up into a bun on the top of her head like Aunt Elizabeth fixed hers. Picking up her black "ear-trumpet," with the violet mother-of-pearl inlays, she showed me a big smile and took my hand with her bony fingers. Looking directly into my eyes she said, "Why, Deanna, I do declare! You are growing like a weed, and you're almost as pretty as your mother. How is Josephine?" Inserting the trumpet into her left ear, she waited for my answer. The softness of her touch, her bright eyes, and loving smile made me feel better. I had been feeling pretty unhappy since Mary Jane and I pulled our blunder last night.

After we ate, Aunt Elizabeth soon said, "I'm sure you kids would like to go for a swim after that long ride down here. Why don't ya' all go on down ta' the river." Swimming was always a good idea in the July heat. Besides, we had to get in all the swimming we could before the 'dog days of August' came upon us. Daddy said the stagnant water in the creeks during those hot August days made dogs go mad (get rabies), and it might make us kids get polio. We were never allowed in the water during dog-days.

With the toughened hide on our summer barefeet, we walked through the fields to the Rolling Fork River, avoiding the stingy thorns of jimson weed that grew in the pastures, and ducking away from the grasshoppers whirring around us. They flew from plant to plant, exposing their black and yellow wings, to chew on the tobacco leaves as we cut through the tobacco crops. Even though no one in town had a telephone, somehow news got out that we were there. The swimming hole soon filled up with our country cousins. We found a riverbank with a nice gentle slope that we could use for a slide. It was filled with ragweed and brilliant flowered orange jewelweed. Electric-blue-colored-snake doctors darted in and out all around the mud at the river's bank, telling us to beware of the snakes that lived there. Tall mud holes of crawdaddys' stood plentifully around the side of the water. The older boys kept pouring water down the bank and made it muddy enough for us to slide over the weeds. A log full of turtles warming themselves in the sun was across the water on the other side of the river. They all plopped in at the same time when they heard our screams. This slide was fun, and a lot better than swimming in the creek on Hunsinger Lane where the water only came up to my waist.

We spent the rest of the week in Howardstown and had a great time doing all the country stuff we liked to do. The country cousins were always daring us to play "chicken" over something. We collected wiry-legged June Bugs and played chicken by seeing who could hold them in their hands the longest. The city kids always lost that battle, not having the tough hide of those who worked on the farms. They also dared us to swing on the long ropes that hung from the haylofts in the barns and went across the deep, wide openings separating one side of the loft from the other. The country kids won that contest, too, until we got up the courage to try it. We turned out to be stronger than they thought. Mary Jane and I captured field toads that were no bigger than our thumb nails because we thought they were so cute. We made little houses for them out of grass and twigs before they escaped. The country kids thought this was real sissy and they laughed at us. We climbed the highest knobs, chased crawdads in the creek moss, and walked all over the town visiting our other relatives. In the afternoons we walked down to the gigantic Howardstown Store (the old Howard's Mill) and got popsicles. Then it was called "F.M. Head's Howardstown Store" because he owned it. F.M. was Daddy's second cousin.

When we needed to use the bathroom, the boys found a tree, but we girls walked up to any house in Howardstown and asked to use their bathroom, they were all related to us. Most of the time it was just an outhouse with a Sears and Roebuck Catalogue and wasps, like I had at home.

When the dinner bell rang we ran back to Great-Grandma Sudie's for the best meals I had ever had. Both Aunt Lena and Aunt Elizabeth were great cooks and because it was summer harvest time, they were fixing extra food for the hired hands. In the mornings, we jumped out of bed at the rooster's first crowing and ran out to play before breakfast. We had sliding contests in our bare feet on the dewy grass. When we heard the squeal of the teapot for Great Grandma's sassafras tea, we knew it was time for breakfast, and we scooted back into the house.

Assembling at her long kitchen table, we found the breakfasts impossible to beat. There were biscuits, bacon, eggs, pancakes with maple syrup, cantaloupe, and fresh blackberries with cream. This was the first time I had ever tasted cream before because Mama saved all of ours for making butter at the end of the week. I rolled its smoothness over my tongue as I crunched the sweet berries. The food seemed never ending. The farm workers ate and ate, and so did we. Aunt Lena and Aunt Elizabeth kept refilling the bowls that the men passed from one end of the table to the other. The men were dressed for work in the hot fields. They wore straw hats (which they removed in the house) bib overalls and clodhopper shoes. We thought they were funny and laughed when they teased us. Knowing I would never see the likes of food like this again, I ate until I almost popped.

Because of all the work it took to run the farm, we kids helped Aunt Elizabeth and Aunt Lena in the afternoons when we were not visiting relatives or swimming. We picked blackberries in the knobs in back of their barn. Timidly, we poked our hands into the thorny briers avoiding the green snakes that liked the berries, too. Churning butter was boring to do alone, but it wasn't so bad when we did it together and took turns. Even the boys helped turn the crank on the ice cream churn. Aunt Elizabeth made homemade strawberry or peach ice cream for evening dessert.

One afternoon Uncle Linn brought up a cold watermelon he had stored in the springhouse. I had never spent much time getting to know Uncle Linn before, because my family always went down to visit Grandpa Emanuel's farm, but I found him to be very nice to us.

Like most farmers, he was serious and always in a hurry to get back to the fields. We took the melon out in the side yard with a saltshaker. It was so cool and sweet that we pushed our faces all the way down into the rind. Enjoying its sticky juiciness, we spat the seeds at each other while we ate it, and even Lucy didn't consider herself too grown up to join in this fight.

It was four days of feasting and fun. As much as I could, I sat by Great Grandma Sudie's rocker and listened to her stories of the old days. She was very entertaining and funny. Sitting by Great Grandma Sudie made me feel close to my grandma, Daddy's mother, again. Grandma Anna had died three years before, and I missed her constant companionship and loving smile.

There weren't any bikes out here or any of the other fun stuff like there was around Uncle Bud's house, but staying in Howardstown was the best part of my vacation week with my cousins. Lucy did bring along plenty of movie magazines, and Mary Jane toted several comic books. We walked down the hot, dusty road from Great Grandma's farm to read them in the cool washhouse at Grandpa Emanuel's. Our Aunt Saloma, Mama's youngest sister, still lived with Grandpa. She was a teenager, not much older than Lucy. Many times she joined us, when she could get a break from her chores. We had lots of girl talk. For the first time I had a feeling of what it must be like to have sisters my own age.

All in all, it was quite a week, and I hated to see it come to an end. *These people think like we do, and they act like us. Why did we hav' ta' move from Nelson County?* I wondered, wistfully. In Louisville, it seemed to me that we were treated like we didn't really belong there. My parents worked very hard, and made many demands on us kids, in hopes of us being accepted in our new location. I liked what I saw of life out here from my country relatives, and wished we could move back to our old farm in Gethsemane, which was located only a few miles up the road from Howardstown. But sadly to me, my parents had other plans.

Chapter 7

Shopping in Downtown Louisville

As the oldest girl in our big family I felt like I had way too much work to do. But there was one chore I really loved, and that one couldn't come fast enough. I loved helping Mama shop for clothes for me and my school-age brothers, Johnny, and Marcellus. In 1950, at nine years old, I was the only girl in the family old enough to be in school. We went downtown to shop because that was Louisville's only big shopping area. From 1949 until 1955, when we got our own shopping center in Hikes Point, Mama and I made this pilgrimage every summer. Going to our local stores was never the adventure of shopping downtown.

Mama waited for the "Before School Sales" in late summer. School started on the Tuesday after Labor Day. We did our shopping on Saturday, so Daddy could watch the other kids. In 1950 there were seven kids in our family. He would rather have plowed a field with a mule than watch kids.

For me, getting time alone with Mama was almost enough of a treat all by itself. It was a big occasion to go to town and we dressed up in our finest outfits. I was so eager to go I could hardly get the buttons together on the back of my polka dot "Sunday" dress. It was called a Sunday dress because I wore it only for church and special visiting occasions. Mama twirled me around and tied the long sash, fluffing up the bow and my sleeves as she did so. I poked my feet into my shiny black patent leather Mary Jane shoes while she tamed my bushy, disobedient brown hair, pulling it back and cramming it into her prized tortoise-shell hair barrette. I no longer wore pigtails, Mama didn't have time to braid them anymore. Frowning, I peered at my freckles in the mirror located over my parent's waterfall veneer bedroom dresser. Mama told me that this was a very popular furniture finish when she got married in 1939. In fact, she said that she told Daddy he didn't have enough money to marry her until he could afford to buy her a bedroom set like this.

These freckles make me look ugly, I thought as I pondered over my reflection.

"When are these freckles gonna' go away?" I asked Mama.

"Don't look a gift horse in the mouth, Deanna," she said. "Freckles are a sign you're healthy. Now, stop lolly-gaggin' around, we don't wanna' to be late for the bus."

Mama topped off her homemade smock top and navy skirt with walking heels, white gloves, and her navy straw hat. She was expecting a baby in January. Everybody wanted to look the best they could when they went downtown. Most likely, you would run into somebody you knew. Also, the dress code was strict. Aunt Bertha once told us, "I saw a policeman telling two girls to shop somewhere else because they were wearing shorts." Most importantly, Mama didn't want anyone, whether they knew us or not, to think that we didn't know how to dress, when we went out in public.

Mama was excited, too, and she couldn't stop humming – I loved it when she felt this way. We were meeting her sister, Aunt Aurelia from Howardstown, at Union Station train depot on Broadway. She was coming in from the tiny train depot in Gethsemane, where we used to live. Howardstown was eight miles from Gethsemane and Grandpa was dropping her off there in his Model T Ford. *I bet she's standin' there waitin' for the train right now,* I thought. Trains made travel from Nelson County to Louisville easy. I loved it when Aunt Aurelia came to visit us. Always looking for a chance to come to Louisville, she would be spending the whole weekend with us.

Ready to catch the earliest Saturday morning bus that left Hikes Point at 7:15, we first had to hear Daddy give Mama his usual lecture. But, we never let Daddy's worries dampen our spirits. To us, the only thing that mattered was that we were leaving the farm and going to enjoy the glamour of the big city. Daddy's forehead wrinkled and his eyes narrowed, "Josephine," he started in, "ya' better watch out for all those pickpockets downtown. They have all kinds of schemes. Ya' know there is ever' kind of people in the world down there. And don't cha' let that Deanna talk ya' into buying anything foolish!" No doubt about it, Daddy sure hated to part with his money.

My envious brothers and sisters lined up at our screendoor to watch us leave. Johnny put his hands on his hips and complained, "Deanna gets to ride the bus *all the way* downtown, and we have to stay home." Riding in busses and cars was something we kids always enjoyed.

"Yeah, and I get to wear my best clothes, too," I smirked. We stuck our tongues out at each other as I bounced out of the house with Mama.

"Come on," she said pulling my hand as we crossed over our long front yard, "it's a good-ways before we get ta' the bus." Johnny's bottom lip curled as we started off for the bus stop at Bauer's Restaurant. The only bus that served Hikes Point was the Blue Motor Coach Bus Line. It came in from Jeffersontown, about five miles east of Hikes Point. We took this bus everywhere we went. I jumped up the bus steps and noticed how good John, our usual driver smelled, with his "Old Spice" aftershave and "Brill Crème" hair gel. *Why doesn't Daddy smell good like that?* I wondered. Daddy thought these city products made a man smell sissy, and only wore them to church on Sunday. John was ready for the busy Saturday shopping crowd, looking sharp in his navy uniform and matching bill cap.

It was hard staying in my seat because I wanted to cross from one side of the bus to the other for the best views. Mama's sense of decorum kept that from happening by giving me the window seat and sitting on the outside seat beside me. I settled in and watched the crops of the countryside disappear, as the buildings of the city took their place. My imagination filled with the way that the people we passed lived their lives, doing the ordinary things that people do naturally, like hanging clothes on the line, mowing the grass with push mowers, or kids playing hopscotch on the sidewalks. *What would Hunsinger Lane be like with sidewalks?* I pondered.

We passed by "fillin'" stations with the racks of used tires. Many of them displayed Depression-ware glass dish sets like we used to see at the gas stations in Lexington, Indiana. The dishes stood in front of clean, white, damask tablecloths thrown over tall shelves. The pink glass sparkled in the morning sunshine. Mama noticed me staring and explained, "When you buy gas, you get different pieces as a gift, depending on how much gas you buy." Then she wistfully recalled her own unfinished green set with irises etched into the glass.

"I wish Daddy got his gas in town instead of going to Jack Finn's Station in Hikes Point, so you could get some more of your pretty green dishes," I sympathized with her.

She laughed and nodded as she said, "Yes, and you know the only reason he goes there is to get a beer at Bauer's before he comes home." Jack's business was diagonally across the street from Bauer's. Jack split his business into two parts. There was a Conoco gas station on the front part of his lot, and a blacksmith shop on the back part. Some of the old farmers in Hikes Point still used mules for plowing. Jack's station had no deals on glassware or anything else.

John pulled the bus over at the bus stop in front of a Texaco Station to let on some more riders. I watched the spiffy looking gas station attendants in their dark green drill cloth uniforms and matching caps work very hard on the cars as they drove in. In just a few minutes they had scrambled around the cars filling the gas, checking the oil and washing the windows on all sides. *How da they stay clean, doin' such dirty work?* I pondered. Besides Texaco, we passed Standard Oil, Marathon, and Conoco stations. We were on Bardstown Road – and Bardstown Road was a busy place. Jack Finn's Station back home was nothing like these service stations. Not only did Jack have no premiums, he wore bib overalls, which were usually black from the sooty, smithy forge at the back of his lot. His hands and face usually matched his pants. *But Jack sells the only candy bars at Hikes Point,* I reminded myself, and my thoughts about his place softened.

As we continued up Bardstown Road, John pulled the bus over many times to pick up other passengers. Soon, all the seats were taken and the new passengers had to stand up, holding on to the long rail high above our heads. They lurched back and forth and swung in and out against us as the bus moved along. I stretched my neck to see the special Marathon gas station with the two six-foot polar bear statues standing out front by the street. Their concrete right paws were lifted in a friendly hello for the customers. This was a landmark for Mama. "Now," she said, "we're almost halfway to town." The butterflies in my stomach danced around again. We would be seeing Aunt Aurelia soon – and stores!

Continuing down Bardstown Road until it turned into Baxter Avenue, we felt the bus make a stop at the red light in front of Cave Hill Cemetery. I got a good look at the cemetery's beautiful entrance, this was where Broadway started on the left. My head turned almost completely around to take it all in before John finished making the sharp turn. There were colorful gardens planted in front of the entrance's stone pillars that held wide iron gates. The Resurrection Angel on top of the clock tower looked down on us as John spun the bus to the left to go down Broadway. The seated passengers swung out to the right and held onto the rails at the top of their seats to keep their balance. The standing passengers now grabbed onto the rail with both hands, letting the handles on their purses slide down to their shoulders as their bodies swung into each other in the aisle. Broadway took us right into the heart of the city. "Gong... gong... gong..." the cemetery clock's heavy toll rang eight times as we passed it.

"That means its eight o'clock," Mama said, "We're right on time."

"Is Fourth Street getting close now?" I asked, but Mama was busy talking to another shopper in the seat in front of us.

Ten minutes later, John called out "Next stop, Fourth and Broadway." Almost everyone seated on the bus jumped up, and I joined them.

"Sit down, Deanna," Mama reminded me. "We're going to Union Station first, to meet Aunt Aurelia, and that is six more blocks." The anxious shoppers adjusted their hats, grabbed their purses with their white-gloved hands, and scrambled down the steps at the bus stop in front of the Brown Hotel.

The train depot was at Tenth and Broadway. We said good-bye to John as the bus stopped in front of Sear and Roebuck's next to the train station. "Remember, the last bus back to Hikes Point is five o'clock this een'ing," he called to us as we hurried down the steps.

Louisville was known as the "Gateway to the South." Daddy had showed us the big sign that said this, down by the river one Sunday when we were out for a Sunday drive. This meant that the Union Station Depot was huge and busy. It was beautiful and looked like a temple with marble walls, mosaic tile floors, and stained-glass windows. Before we crossed the street, I stood in front of the gigantic stone building and tried to take it all in.

Mama brought me back to attention when she said, "Help me find Aurelia in this mob." My head still went "ever-which-a-way," turning from one activity to the next as we walked up the front steps and entered the station. I saw people standing in line to buy tickets, men in business suits reading newspapers, and young women with bouncy hair sitting on swivel stools at the luncheonette counter. They ordered cups of "Jo," and seemed to like it.

"What is a cup of Jo?" I asked.

"Your Uncle Mac told me they called coffee 'Jo' in the army," Mama said. I remembered some of his stories of when he fought in the Pacific during World War II, and smiled. Children clung to mothers' hands, and soldiers from Fort Knox were everywhere. Sticking close to Mama, my eyes glazed over in trying to see everything.

"Gosh, Louisville sure is a big-city," I said, but Mama wasn't listening. I was brought back to reality when I heard, "Move back out of the way, please, Miss," one of the porters in a white coat and black bill cap requested as he wheeled a cart stacked high with luggage past me. I hadn't seen so many things happening at once since we went to Fontaine Ferry Park, in July.

Young boys approached strangers in the bustling crowd. "Shine for a dime, mister?" *If these boys can make money just for shining shoes, so can I,* I thought, and pondered a prosperous future. I watched the youngster prop his customer's foot on his wooden shine-crate. The air smelled like the same oily polish we used to shine our potbelly stove. There were also professional shoeshine men – usually colored men in their white coats and black pants. (Colored was the name that Black People preferred to be called in the mid- twentieth century. To have called them anything else would have been considered an insult). They performed their business in padded, red leather shoeshine stalls. These tall, wooden chairs had a rung for the customers to prop up their feet so they could read the morning newspaper. The customers were well-dressed men and they looked relaxed while the shiners snapped their flannel cloths on the tops of the men's wingtip shoes. The chairs were located against the back marble walls of the train station. "Get a good shine! My shine lasts five days," they each sang out, in effort to pull the crowd away from the cheaper shine of the shoe-shine boys. "And, it only costs twenty-five cents."

"That's a lot of money for something I can do for free," I told Mama, who was too busy looking for Aunt Aurelia to hear me. "Help me find your Aunt," she reminded me again.

Looking up, I tried daydreaming again, trying to figure out the patterns of the gigantic round stained glass windows in the peaks of both the north and the south station walls. These impressive windows sprayed sunlight over the crowds below and danced across the mosaic tile floor. Realizing I was not paying attention, I made another grab for Mama's dress, so I wouldn't get lost in all this activity. Checking the large clock that could be seen from three sides, I saw that it was already 8:30. *Why isn't Aunt Aurelia here? I wanna' get to Fourth Street and the stores,* I winced, getting impatient.

Suddenly, Aunt Aurelia ran to us from the crowd. She gave both Mama and me a big hug. At eighteen, she was a tall, skinny brunette and wore bright red lipstick and fingernail polish. She smelled so good. "It's White Shoulders perfume," she said, seeing me sniff the air. This was stuff Mama didn't have time for, but I thought it was nice. I smiled at Aunt Aurelia to let her know I thought she was as pretty as the women we saw in the picture shows.

"Let's hurry," she prodded us, "I want to see the Clark Gable double feature at the Rialto." *Oh, boy,* I thought, *we're gonna' see a picture show.* We turned around and took off for Fourth Street. Besides shopping, Fourth Street was also Louisville's major entertainment center. Several theaters dotted the street. The most popular ones were the Rialto, Ohio, Kentucky, Mary Anderson, Brown, and the Loew's. They competed for the early morning Saturday shoppers with an early-bird special. If you got there by nine thirty, you could see a double feature for a dime.

I liked Roy Rogers, "The King of the Cowboys," and was hoping for a cowboy show, but Mama loved Clark Gable, too, and agreed with Aunt Aurelia. Almost running, we made it just in time. We hurried over the lush, flowered carpet of the lobby. I breathed in deep, pulling in as much of the heavy popcorn scent as my lungs could hold. "We'll eat later, Deanna," Mama said, noticing me lingering at the concession stand.

Last year when we came to town there was a vaudeville theater at Fifth and Walnut called The National Theater. I watched a clown on stage throw a pie into the face of another clown. I couldn't believe such a waste of good dessert – it made me hungry for custard pie. Now, all the vaudeville theaters were gone, and there were only movie houses. I liked the picture shows better than silly clowns and pies.

Two hours later, we left the dark theater. I thought all that gushy kissing in the picture was sissy, but I liked the story. Mama and Aunt Aurelia went on and on about Clark Gable. We entered the busy shopping crowd. Shoppers crammed the sidewalks on both sides of the street. No doubt about it, Fourth Street was the busiest street in town. The buildings were tall and serious. Department stores stretched all the way from Broadway to Main Street. They also crossed Fourth Street from Third Street to Fifth Street at the intersections of Market Street and Jefferson Street. Two of our favorites were on Market Street and Jefferson Street: Jefferson Dry Goods and Ben Snyder's. These two stores called themselves stores for the workingman. Daddy said that that was who we were – the workingman, and according to him, "the salt of the earth."

Several other large department stores lined Fourth Street itself. Stewart's Dry Goods was the most elegant and expensive. It was the favorite of most Louisvillians. Daddy didn't know we ever went in there. "That place is too expensive," he said. "Stay out of it." Kaufman-Strauss, Byck's, Selmen's, Bacon's, and J.C. Penny's were nice stores that we explored, too; but, according to Daddy, they were also too expensive. I felt high class when we went downtown. The buildings were big, the stores were beautiful, and everybody dressed up. I thought the people in Louisville looked just as good as the people I saw in the picture shows about New York City. *And,* I thought, *Mama, Aunt Aurelia and I look as good as anybody else in this crowd. Nobody'd guess we're from the country.*

We did most of our shopping in the dime stores. First, we went to Woolworth's because Aunt Aurelia wanted a new lipstick color. I loved dime stores because they were good for so many things. They even had exotic pets located on their back walls.

"Josephine, I'm ready for a banana split," Aunt Aurelia suddenly announced. I liked the way Aunt Aurelia pushed things along. I was always ready for ice cream. Off to the lunch counters we went. All the dime stores and most of the drugstores had them. There were fancier ones in the department stores and hotels, but we seldom saw the insides of those. Part of the fun of our shopping experience was to forget about nourishing food. We got that every day on the farm. It was our rule, when we went downtown that we each had a banana split. The waitresses at the lunch counters almost looked like the nurses did at St. Anthony's Hospital when I got my tonsils taken out three years before. They wore white dresses and little white caps over their hairnets. They decorated their uniform with a frilly white apron and a colorful print handkerchief in their shoulder pocket. They were efficient and moved like machines.

We looked for a counter that ran a banana split special. We found one at W.T. Grant's Dime Store. The challenge of getting a good deal made our ice cream taste even better. Pale blue tinted mirrors backed most lunch counters and went all the way up to the ceiling. Lunch specials were painted on them in tempera paint. During the banana split sales, a string clothesline was taped to the mirrors as well. Bright balloons were tied to this string. Inside each balloon was a tiny folded piece of paper with a price on it. The price would be anywhere from one cent to twenty-nine cents. The full price for the split was twenty-nine cents and most of the papers were marked with that price. We didn't care. Mama's price was two cents, mine was a nickel and Aunt Aurelia's was eight cents. This meant we could afford another treat before we got home. That was, if we finished shopping in time.

With our stomachs crammed, we crunched ourselves back into the shopping crowd, going from one dime store to the next. We went to Woolworth's, Kresge's, and McCrory's. As we walked over the mosaic tile entrance of McCrory's, I noticed that the street window display in most of the dime stores was sets of pretty china dishes on lace tablecloths. The roses painted on these dishes made them prettier than the glass depression-ware sets at the fillin' stations. Bowls of colorful waxed fruit and tall dinner candles called tapers were also displayed.

"Our dining room would look so pretty with those candles," I told Mama as we walked through McCrory's door.

"Deanna, remember Daddy told ya' not to talk me inta' buying anything foolish," she laughed, her blue eyes twinkling. I followed Mama over to another aisle to look at McCrory's large selection of embroidery thread colors and hoops while Aunt Aurelia shopped for some pretty things. Mama found a color we could both use and she bought a new skein of thread for us.

When Aunt Aurelia joined us at the door, we saw that she had some new treasures stuffed into her shopping bag. "For my future," Aunt Aurelia smiled and winked at us.

I liked the way the dime stores smelled, and noticed that the expensive stores smelled like perfume when you came in, and the dime stores smelled more like food. The popcorn machine in the ten cent stores smelled as good as the one did in the Rialto Theater. We pushed through the crowds at the roasted nut machine in order to get over to the fragrant chocolate aroma of the candy counter. Candy was sold by the pound and you could get something for as little as a few pennies. Aunt Aurelia gave me two cents. "Here," she said, "help yourself." I got some saltwater taffy because it always lasts for a long time. The clerks in the dime stores were easy to find because they all wore long-sleeved smocks over their street clothes. Each store's clerks had a different color smock – Woolworth's had blue, Kresge's and Grant's had green and McCrory's had pink.

While we were in Kresge's, we heard a piano playing a popular song that we had heard on the radio many times, "Put another nickel in, in the nickelodeon, all I want is loving you and music, music, music." Aunt Aurelia and I started singing along because we knew it by heart. The store hired a piano player to hawk the latest new tune in sheet music. People gathered around the piano making other requests. Mama asked for her favorite, *The Black Hawk Waltz*. She learned to play this when she was a child from her Aunt Cora, who taught all the piano lessons in Howardstown.

"An old favorite," the piano player smiled up at Mama as his fingers slid across the keys for the jaunty waltz.

I tried on the cowboy hats and the gun and holster sets while they shopped for clothes. "Deanna, don't you know you're a girl?" Aunt Aurelia asked, seeming exasperated.

"She's a tomboy," Mama said, rolling her eyes. I ignored them. Didn't they realize that if I ever wanted anybody to play with, I had to be like one of the boys? Margaret Jane, my closest sister in age, was only three, and there were no other kids at Hikes Point.

After I tried on the Roy Rogers, Gene Autry, Lone Ranger and the Hopalong Cassidy gear, I did what I really loved, and ran to the back of the store. This area was alive with small pets. I watched as the frilly-finned goldfish swam in small glass fish bowls while the elegant angelfish swam in large tanks with many other tropical fish. I was surprised at the pet mice. *Who'd to buy a mouse?* I thought, remembering the ones we caught in the mousetraps under our kitchen sink. I chuckled at the blue and green colored parakeets as they sidled nervously back and forth in their cages. Canaries chirped melodies, and gray and red lovebirds peeked out from their tiny straw houses. I remembered the pretty birds we had in the fields at Hikes Point, the yellow Meadowlarks, blue Indigo Buntings, and striped Killdeer, and the beautiful songs these birds sang for us all day long.

There were saucers holding tiny turtles with brightly painted shells, some had flower doilies transferred onto their backs. They were so much cuter than the snapping turtles we saw on the banks of the creek where we swam in the woods by Hunsinger Lane Quarry. I let one crawl on my finger. "Get your hands out of the turtle dish, Miss." The clerk said. Embarrassed to be caught doing something I wasn't supposed to do, I backed away and looked around for Mama. Finding her in the area of boys' school socks, I tried my hand at begging for one of these pets. Except for the mice, they all looked cute to me.

"Please, can I have a pet? Something, just for me? I'll take good care of it," I pleaded. I wanted a pet that was *not* going to end up on our dinner table like, Rocky, the fat Plymouth Rock hen that I used to cuddle, ended up last year. "Don't be such a cry-baby, Deanna," Mama had said to me on that day that I begged her not to wring my favorite chicken's neck. "She's old, we have to use her before she gets sick and makes us all die." I could hear the necessity in Mama's explanation, but it didn't make me feel any better about losing Rocky. I watched my other family members eat their Sunday fried chicken, but I couldn't imagine eating my friend, and refused the platter as it passed by me – Jimmy got the thigh, my usually assigned piece, that day. I sadly watched his smile and delight as he munched the juicy meat.

Mama had a cooler head than me and said, "All these pets have to have special food and equipment, Deanna. They can't just run in the pasture field like our other animals." I sighed and went to look at the comic books. Maybe she would get me a Roy Rogers comic book. Usually, if there was some money left over, she let me get something special just for myself. One year I got an eraser shaped like a cat, complete with whiskers and a curly tail. It cost a fortune, fifteen cents, which was the price of three ice cream cones. *I feel special when I use it at St. Bartholomew's*, I smiled.

Besides clothes, we also bought the pencils and tablets we needed to start school. Hikes Point didn't have any stores and St. Bartholomew's didn't sell these things. The Nuns expected us to have them on the first day of school so we could get to work. Like Daddy, they hated to see time wasted. Daddy realized that school clothes cost money, so he actually gave us some, though, naturally, not nearly enough. This meant we had to walk all over this huge shopping area looking for the best bargains. We went from one end of Fourth Street to the other several times. If we overheard some other shoppers talking about a "Blue Light Special" markdown on the price of socks or shirts, even if it was just a nickel cheaper at a previous store, we hurried back. My job was to help remember the prices and be a packhorse. "For a girl, you're pretty strong," Aunt Aurelia complimented me. I beamed her smile.

Mama agreed, "I depend on her a lot." My shoulders went back as I took in this extra attention. *This must be what it's like to be an only child*, I thought.

When it came to buying school clothes, we actually got off easy. St. Bartholomew's wore uniforms. Blue pants and white shirts for the boys and a navy skirt and white blouses for me. Mama usually got the skirts and pants at the used uniform sale on the day of school registration, so we didn't buy those today. Today we shopped for shirts for the boys, blouses for me, and socks, underwear, and sweaters. Hats, gloves, and scarves were usually saved from the year before and went down the family line for the best fit.

Sometimes we bought a new coat for Johnny. The other boys got it later as a hand-me-down. I got my coats from my city cousins, Pat and Alice. They were child-clothing models for Bacon's Department Store and had beautiful clothes, though sometimes a little unusual for St. Bartholomew's. My mind went back to the deep purple coat that caused me to be called "Grape juice" by my classmates. Daddy never noticed all the money Mama saved him. He didn't think spending money on clothes was nearly as important as spending it on feed for Calfie, our Guernsey cow, or for the hogs that we killed for meat late in the fall.

When we got to Jefferson Dry Goods, sometimes Mama and Aunt Aurelia tried on the dresses. My job then was to run back and forth fetching different sizes and styles for them as they yelled out from the fitting room. They laughed and joked while they tried on outfit after outfit. It was like the time Mary Jane and I played dress up with Lucy's clothes when I visited their house earlier in the summer.

"I wouldn't wear this to a dog fight," Mama frowned as she looked into the mirror at the three-quarter length sleeves. Aunt Aurelia came out, looked at her, and said,

"Yes, Josephine, that dress makes you look as ugly as a mud fence!" They laughed again and called for me.

"Deanna, do you remember that blue one with the white collar? Get it for your mama, and bring me the green one in size ten," Aunt Aurelia said, calling out from behind the curtain. Helping these adults made me feel important. I was always happy when I found exactly what they were looking for. They liked to try things on so they knew what looked good on them, but they never bought any of these store-made clothes. Both Daddy and Grandpa Emanuel expected them to make their own clothes. After they finished in the fitting room, we went to Ben Snyder's where Aunt Aurelia bought the material to make what she wanted. "I think Ben Snyder's has a better quality of yard goods when I want to make a really nice dress," Aunt Aurelia said.

"I use feed sacks, or empty flour sacks to make most of the things I sew," Mama told her. "JH would never settle for lettin' me buy yard goods if we have any a' those around".

"Me too," Aunt Aurelia agreed. "Some of those sacks are really pretty, but I want something real special this time." They had both been sewing for so long, they didn't need to buy sewing patterns. When they got to the dry goods counter, the clerks measured Aunt Aurelia and helped her decide on how much material she needed to buy for the outfit she wanted. "You'll need another yard and a half if you make it with a pleated skirt," I heard the clerk tell her. Mama had some checked feed sacks she'd been collecting in mind to make her dress – Daddy had just brought in another one from Calfie's stall last week. But she did buy some blue rick-rack to add to the collar.

Finally, all three of us were heavily burdened with bags of purchases. Luck was with us, and we finished in plenty of time before the last Blue Motor Coach bus back to Hikes Point at five o'clock. We had time to go into the higher-priced stores like Stewart's just to look around and see the nicer things. Stewart's had hired a beautiful model seated on a rope swing to swoop back and forth over the cosmetic counter. The ropes on the swing were covered with fresh flowers. Everything smelled really good. I was so moved that I wanted some cosmetics, but my brothers would tease me to death if they even knew I had a thought like this. Kaufman Strauss and Burdorff's had the best furniture. Byck's and Selman's had the prettiest gowns. For some reason Aunt Aurelia wanted to look at these.

"Oooo," Aunt Aurelia said, as she leafed through the rack of white ones, examining each one and pushing it along in order to see the next behind. I thought they looked like whipped cream, delicious and frothy enough to eat.

In Bacon's, I noticed the sound of the women's high heels changed from "thump, thump, thump," on the wooden floors as they entered on the Fourth Street side to, "click, click, click," they made as they struck the terrazzo floor when they exited on the Market Street side. This difference in the sound of the same shoes puzzled me.

Mama was patient with my desire to ride up and down the elevator in these expensive stores. She and Aunt Aurelia busied themselves at the cosmetics counter while I enjoyed the elevators. The attendant wore a smart uniform that looked something like that of a member of a marching band. Some of them were complete with brass buttons and shoulder fringes. He grabbed the big brass handle, pulled it down to the left, and the ratcheted door closed all of us inside. The ride tickled my tummy. Most of these operators were skillful enough to stop the elevator car completely level with the approaching floor. For others, it was a matter of lots of "jockeying" the brass handle back and forth. Then, our stomachs were jolted up and down. Some of the customers rudely complained out loud, but I was just happy for the ride. It almost felt like the Ferris wheel at Fontaine Ferry Park.

Besides stores and theaters, several elegant hotels were located up and down Fourth Street. I snuck peaks through the tall glass doors as we walked past them. The doormen were polite, always tipping their hat and saying, "Good afternoon, young lady." In my pretty polka-dot dress and Mary Jane shoes, they probably thought I was from the city.

I used my best manners and answered, "Fine, thank you, Sir." They wore top hats, long-tailed suits, and white gloves. I begged Mama to let us take the time to go inside and see the lobbies of the Seelbach and the Brown Hotels. These two had the most handsomely dressed doormen. On the days had time to do this, Mama always chose the Brown because it was closer to our bus stop at Fourth and Broadway.

Having Aunt Aurelia along made our shopping go faster, and we ended our day by having iced tea in the Tea Room of the Brown Hotel. Just being inside there made me feel special. It was so elegant – my heart almost stopped when I saw the white lace tablecloths with linen napkins rolled into little silver rings. Each table had a crystal vase holding a fragrant pink rose. We felt a bit awkward with all our packages, but the waiter smiled at us and helped us arrange them under the table. I guess he could tell by our drawn faces that we were pooped!

All the waiters in the Brown's Tea Room were required to be Colored men. They wore white cotton coats and gloves with dark pants. Swift and skillful, they were able to carry food around all day on huge trays and never get their gloves dirty. They were very friendly and treated me like I was somebody who mattered. *It helps when I dress up in my Sunday best,* I thought, and wished the girls from school, who always teased me, could see me now here at the Brown.

Soon, it was time for the long bus ride back out to Hikes Point. We crossed Broadway for the bus stop in front of the Heyburn Building.

Again, I was looking forward to the ride. We greeted John, who was still energetic enough to give us a big smile, as we climbed back up the steps of the bus. With all the stops and starts, it took about an hour to get home. This was plenty of time to rest our tired legs and sore feet.

I remembered to sit on the same side of the bus so I could see what I missed hours ago when we came into town. Aunt Aurelia chatted with Mama, but I got to meet some pretty interesting strangers. I didn't care as long as I got to have a window seat. No matter how tired the shoppers were, nobody ever slept on the bus. Sleeping in public places was considered common. Besides, everybody used bus travel as an opportunity to meet strangers and talk to friends and neighbors. People sat down and pushed their packages under their seats. Except for people like us, most people traveled light. The better stores home delivered anything you bought, even something as small as make-up.

The scene inside the bus was lively, chirping with conversation and bubbling with laughter from the exhausted, but contented shoppers. I didn't talk to the nice lady beside me because I was too busy concentrating on our trip back home, so she talked to the man across the aisle. I welcomed the sight of the brick mansions and stone churches that lined Broadway, many peeking out from their leafy lawns as the bus lurched ahead. It was kind of a sad good-bye to our adventure until next year.

Finally John, yelled out, "Hikes Point," just as I pulled the cord. I wanted to hear the bell ring. As we got off the bus at Bauer's, we heard laughter coming from their Beer Garden under the trees in the backyard of the restaurant. We used Bauer's long shady porch to rearrange our packages for the walk home. Sometimes we were lucky enough to be picked up by a neighbor on his way home from Buechel, Jeffersontown, or St. Matthews. Hunsinger Lane was a gravel road at the time, and walking with our tired feet and these packages was a struggle. It was almost painful for Mama and Aunt Aurelia in their high heel shoes. I was too contented to care.

Johnny, Marcellus, and Jimmy were watching at the side window of our house for our return. They knew we would catch that last bus home, and they ran down the gravel and grabbed our load. They couldn't wait to see what we bought. We were happy to see them and gave them everything. Mama and Aunt Aurelia even let them carry their purses.

I couldn't believe the commotion we stirred up when we came in the house. "What did you get me? What did you get me?" they all wanted to know, swarming around us.

Daddy, who had been watching the kids all day, greeted us with the usual, "Well, it's about time you-all got home!" The look of relief on his face at our arrival was definitely noticed by Mama. Every item was taken out of the bags, examined, and exclaimed about. What a noisy racket!

Everything of course, except my special gift from Mama. I kept my Roy Rogers comic book to myself. I didn't want to start a fight. My brothers thought I was lucky enough just to get to go downtown, and I had to agree with them.

Aunt Aurelia helped Mama get supper on while I kept the little ones out of the way. I got to have a big sister for two days. She talked me into putting away my cowboy gear for the rest of the weekend. I liked trying on her dresses and playing with her make-up including all the new stuff she bought today.

I didn't know it was so much fun to be a girl. She showed me the beautiful lace tablecloth she got at Ben Snyder's and the candles from McCrory's Dimestore. "These are for my Hope Chest," she said. Then she told me about her special boyfriend named Earl. "We're getting married soon," she had told Mama the big news during the Clark Gable picture show this morning. I was very happy about this because I thought Earl was the most handsome man in the world, and that she better not let him get away.

While we talked, I practiced my embroidery stitches, pushing the wooden hoop over the part of the design that I wanted to work on. I was eager to try out the new turquoise skein Mama bought for us at McCrory's that morning, and put some in my flower designs.

"Keep your stitches looser, Deanna," Aunt Aurelia advised, looking over at the chain stitches on my doily that showed a morning glory design. After putting the baby to bed, Mama joined us with her own embroidery work, and showed us her progress on the pattern of a cross with a big sun radiating behind it. Relaxing with our embroidery and talking, Mama and I spent the rest of the evening finding out all we could about the details of Aunt Aurelia's wedding plans.

Before we went to bed that night, Aunt Aurelia rolled up my hair in bobby socks. "Now, your hair won't be so bushy for Mass tomorrow," she said.

"I wish Mama would stop giving me permanents," I told her before we went to sleep. We slept in the tall Lincoln bed that I usually shared with my sister Theresa. It was hard sleeping on the knots of those socks, though. I squirmed most of the night, but I woke up beautiful!

****

On Monday morning Daddy dropped Aunt Aurelia off at Union Station on his way to Fehr's Brewery. He took Mama and all us kids along in the car with him. I stayed in the car and watched the kids so Mama and Daddy could wait for the train with Aunt Aurelia. Afterward, Daddy drove on to work at Fehr's. Mama, along with us kids took the Blue Motor Coach home, and we got to see our driver, John, and his big smile again.

"Will Aunt Aurelia get to come and spend the weekend with us after she marries Earl?" I asked Mama.

"Even better than that," Mama said, "after they get married, they're moving to Louisville. Earl already has a job at Reynolds Metals on Eastern Parkway. We'll see them all the time!" I hoped so. I felt lucky to share in the good news about Aunt Aurelia's wedding. These were the times I was happy to be the oldest girl!

Frozen Moments

Picking vegetables
Entering the garden
At dawn's break
Sunlight glistens on the
Spiderweb's dew

Before school
Daddy brings the milk inside
Coffee and biscuits
Aromas that fill the air –
Morning stirs

Scene from the kitchen window
Golden daylight streams
Through the orchard
And down the pasture field

Hog killin' Day
Neighbors come to help
Six hogs soon hang
On silver rods –
Butcher knives fly

Wintry memory
Snow tipped pines
Beckon me to enter the little
Woods behind the chicken coop

Chicken coop
Early to bed, with muffled
Sounds, heads rest deep in
Fluffy chests – roosting time

Creeks of the forties
Flowing crystal clear
Filled with minnows,
Moss, crawdads, snakes
And splashing kids

Playing in the creek
Slipping, sliding, and letting
The water roll over us,
Laughing with glee

Summer creeks
Waist deep water
In the bend of our babbling
Creek, cooled us
On hot summer days

Happy creek
"Snake doctors and water
Striders prove the creek
Is alive," Daddy explained

Summer comforts
Sitting on the grass under
A full moon, I watch
Silver clouds drift
Through a pewter sky

Drive-in movies
Dollar a car-load with
Ten kids packed in –
"Don't forget to bring
the popcorn!

My dog Bullet
Big brown eyes, flouncy fur
My heart wraps around
Your smiling face

Bullet's Disappearance
After weeks of tears
Jimmy and I knock on
Farmer's doors, searching
For our dog.

Rusty
My handsome rust-colored
Pig is so smart, he
Follows me like a dog

Progress?
Bulldozers crunching
Farmhouses to death
I cry bitter tears…

Chapter 8

The Ranger's Club

By 1951, I was ten years old, Johnny nine, Marcellus eight, Jimmy five. We had been living at Hikes Point for almost two years. Getting used to this completely childless area took an adjustment from us complaining kids. A situation like this should have improved the way we got along with each other, but we loved to fight, and fell into it so easily. When we were able to get along, we did lots of fun things together. Our favorite activities were playing cowboys and Indians, hiking in the woods down Hunsinger Lane by the huge rock quarry, or swimming in the creek. There was even a cave we could explore not far from the creek.

Still longing for the adventure we had in Lexington, Indiana, we wanted to have some adventure here, too. Using the open countryside as our guide, we pretended to be the cowboys we saw on the western movies at the Skyway Drive-In located in Buechel where Mama sometimes took us. With this thinking in mind, we had a reason to explore our new area like cowboys explored the open range. To help organize our explorations we formed a club that we called the Rangers' Club. As the oldest, I was the club president, but in truth, Johnny was still the boss. Treating Hikes Point like a state park, we called every trip away from our farm "exploring,' like the cowboys. Daddy had diligently made friends with the local farmers by joining them frequently for a beer at Bauer's, so they knew him well, and trusted him to keep us in line and out of their crops.

He certainly did. One time we came in from school and Daddy met us at the door with a switch. It seemed that a neighbor saw us walk home from our bus stop at Bauer's and cut through his field of wheat. Thinking that we had found a good shortcut, we were careless about where we put our feet, and stomped on several of the precious plants as we ran through the field. The news got home before we did, and a visit with the switch was our reward. As long as we kept our feet out of the crops the farmers didn't care about us walking through their fields

Our Rangers' Club met once a week under the pear tree in the back corner of the orchard. Johnny and I wanted a nicer place to hold our meetings so they felt official. More importantly, we wanted a place to keep what we called our *valuable club stuff* so the little kids, Margaret Jane four years old, Theresa three, and Tony two couldn't mess with it. Mama had a new baby, Mary Ann, who would be into our stuff, too, before long. For months we begged Daddy to build us a small house out in the pasture field like the one he had built for the sow.

He answered our begging by giving us a lecture on sows. Wrinkling his forehead and scratching the bristly whiskers on his chin, he looked directly at us and said, "You kids gotta' realize how important a house is to a sow. Now, a sow is a contributing member to a farm and needs special treatment. She produces pigs that we eat or sell. I built her that little house to keep her happy. You have to make a sow feel safe, and that means she has to be away from the rest of the animals when she has her litter, and nurses it."

Looking at all four of us at the same time, he continued, "Sows can get very dangerous if they feel threatened. Many a farmer has been attacked by a scared sow! Old Widow Watson, who lived down the road from us in Gethsemane, lost her arm to one when she came upon a nursing sow without warning her first. And the widow was even comin' to give the sow her slops!" We kids looked at each other. Now, we knew when to stay away from the little house. Luckily, the sow had already delivered six weeks ago and was out of the house for the rest of this year.

Having a clubhouse was important to us, so, we continued to beg Daddy for a solution. As a busy farmer who also worked in town, he didn't seem to have much compassion for our cause. Suddenly he stood up, pushed back the straw hat covering his wavy brown hair, and wiped the sweat off his brow. A smile spread across his face as his eyes lit up. "All right, you kids," he said, "I can make ya' a deal. Ya'all can use the sow's house when she's not usin' it. She only needs it about two months out of the year. But chu' kids have to clean it good and get it ready for her when it's time for the next litter."

"We will! We will!" The four of us spoke up at once smiling, and knuckling each other on the arms by giving 'hambones' (sharp taps on the upper arms, with the knuckles of our hands).

A clubhouse at last, we were so excited we ran for the little building immediately. I noticed a yellow-breasted meadowlark calling out his loud whistle of, "Spring-is-here! Spring-is-here!" from the electric wire above our heads, and said, "Look, Johnny," pointing up at the bird. I continued, "That's a good sign for us, Mama says Meadow Larks are good luck."

His face showed me that he didn't have time for such superstitions, and hissed, through closed lips, "Sissy!"

Even before we started cleaning out the sow's house, Johnny painted a sign on an old plank, "The Rangers' Club." He and Marcellus proudly nailed it over the door. Jimmy and I stood back and admired our new possession as they hammered in the last nail. Our dog, Bullet, our constant companion, yipped in agreement, running around and in between us. Bullet, a collie/spitz mix was a great dog and we were happy we had him. Grandpa Emanuel stuffed him into our car on one of our visits to his farm last summer.

"People are always droppin' dogs off out here in the country!" Grandpa laughed, pleading with us to take him, while at the same time, he was pushing him into the backseat between us kids. We had been begging Daddy for this dog all afternoon. With Bullet already in the car, and our arms already around him, he didn't have the heart to refuse Grandpa. This was especially true since Daddy had had a few beers at the reunion there that day.

"Now, you kids know what's gonna' happen when we get that dog home," Daddy admonished us as he drove along, "he'll chase cars and be killed like the rest of 'em." We had been through several dogs. Country dogs just couldn't get over their fascination with cars once they got closer to the city. There were few cars in the country. Luckily, that wasn't true of this dog. Bullet stuck close to the place and to us kids. Because Roy Rogers was our favorite cowboy, we named him after Roy's famous movie star dog, Bullet.

At first, our new home smelled like pig manure. Mama lent us her scrub brushes and plenty of "Pine-Sol" to clean out the fleas, ticks and dried manure. "I'll do anything I can to help you all with that clubhouse," she said as she happily handed over her supplies. "It's such a pleasure to see you kids working together instead of fighting." I was proud of us, too. *Even Roy Rogers would be proud of us,* I thought. We took Mama's cleaning supplies out to our clubhouse. While the humming birds buzzed in and out of the brilliant orange trumpet vine over by the pasture field fence, we scrubbed the clubhouse clean.

Daddy finished the sow's house in the nick of time before she birthed her litter, so he built it pretty rough. It was just upright studs holding walls around a plank floor with a tar-paper rolled roof on top. But, it sure looked like a palace to us. The floor space was about eight by eight and it was taller at the front than it was at the back. The back slanted down because the sow liked darkness for birthing. That would be the spot where we would sit for our future Rangers' Club meetings.

Next, we set about furnishing our clubhouse. Our goal was to spend nights out there. "It'll be like spending the night out on the range. Then we'll be real cowboys," we told each other. To make beds we nailed two by fours across a section of uprights on the walls at both ends of the tiny building. We laid planks over these two by fours to make beds. "Now we have a bunkhouse," we smiled, copying the sleeping quarters of the cowboys in the movies we loved. I riddled through Mama's "patchin' bag" and the Calfie's empty feed sacks to make blankets. I was pretty handy with Mama's treadle-powered sewing machine. It was fun to do some sewing that I wanted to do.

At the end of the second week, we sat huddled in a circle in the back of our new place, with a stub of a candle burning, and held our first Rangers' Club meeting. *At last we're official,* I thought. Each Ranger reported to the group about the discoveries they had made in their explorin' since the last meeting. This week, I reported on a new spring I found on Judge Jeffrey's property. It was near the cave Marcellus and Johnny found last summer, and not too far from the swimming hole across from the quarry. "Now, we can have clean water to drink while we're down at the woods," I offered excitedly.

Johnny's dark head shook from side to side. "That's not new, Deanna, I found that spring before, too. Mrs. Jeffrey, (the Judge had been dead twenty years, but this land was still called Judge Jeffery's Farm), puts bulls in that pasture with the spring in it. One chased me outta' there last week." I was disappointed that my great idea was such a flop, but, as president, I was careful not to let my feelings show.

Shortly after we moved here, Johnny and Marcellus found a swimming hole about a mile away on Hillcreek Road, but it wasn't as deep as the one Larney, our neighbor told us about in the woods. Larney was the youngest son of one of the older farmers around here. He visited us frequently to share a bottle of Fehr's beer that Daddy always brought home from work. Larney knew everything about Hikes Point, including the latest gossip. We kids stood around and listened – when Daddy would let us.

Then Marcellus spoke up, his blond head wagging from side to side. "I have some bad news," he said, "Deanna, there's a new subdivision going in where you and Jimmy found those horses last week. I heard Larney tellin' Daddy about it the other night when they were talkin' out by the barn."

"I hate these subdivisions, they are taking all our good places away," Johnny said, hanging his head. "We have to work faster to find those good places," I said hopefully. There was a moment of silence as we all looked down at the plank floor of our 'little palace.' To us the major benefit of living here was the open range, and it was fast disappearing.

"Those horses were pretty, I wanted to ride them so bad," Jimmy sighed, getting wrapped up in our dream and not remembering that he was only five years old.

"Me, too, Jimmy," I groaned in agreement.

"I heard Daddy tellin' Mama the subdivision was gonna' be called Houston Acres," Marcellus continued. "Next week they're gonna' start blasting for the basements." Then Johnny smiled, "At least we'll get some more blastin' wire." That was the thin multicolored wires that we had found around subdivisions before. It was used to set off the dynamite charges that blasted open the rock in order to build the basements. We used the wire to make bracelets and lanyards.

Johnny had to put in another two cents, "That's the trail that goes by the cave. We'd better be careful when we go down around there, now."

I interrupted, "If they're blasting, Daddy won't let us go near there. That means no more going to the cave." Tightening our lips to hold back the tears, we again, hung our heads in disappointment. The effects of outside limitations crunched into our innocent world.

Our mood slid back into excitement as we talked about the adventures that could happen for us in the coming week. "I have a good idea for a cut-through to get to the creek on Hillcreek Road faster," Marcellus suggested. "We can go down the Dusty Road behind our pasture field where those blackberry briars are and save a whole bunch a' time."

"Just so we keep our feet out of the crops," Johnny reminded all of us.

Now that we had the clubhouse clean and smelling better, we wanted more furniture than just our bunk beds. It should look more like a western place and not so much like a house that belonged to a hog. Most of our hiking for the next week was to comb through the neighborhood for any kind of lumber scraps we could use to build something. Marcellus and Jimmy found a couple of wooden orange crates up at the Point. They were in a garbage pile behind Bauer's Restaurant. There was no garbage pick-up in Hikes Point. Everybody burned their own garbage. The workman at Bauer's had already started the fire and was throwing stuff on it. The boys managed to rescue the crates just before the flames claimed them.

I helped Marcellus hold the larger crate straight while Johnny nailed it to the back clubhouse wall. "This'll make a good desk," Marcellus said. "I get to use it first." He put his favorite book, *Tom Sawyer*, on its shelf. Then I put in some of my comic books and papers. It looked just like the Wells Fargo desks in the Roy Rogers and Gene Autry picture shows we loved. We used the shorter crate for a stool by turning it up on its end, and setting it in front of the desk. I fashioned a quilt-patched pillow for the top and even Johnny said it looked pretty good. I couldn't wait to show off our masterpiece to my cousin Mary Jane when their family came to visit us on Sunday. They were always bragging about the clubhouses they showed off to us. Theirs were mostly built in the trees in the woods around their house. *Theirs look better than ours,* I thought, remembering the one high above the swimming hole across the street from their house.

Daddy would not be too happy with our next idea, so, of course, we didn't tell him. "We have to have a secret place to hide our strongbox (cigar box) in case enemies surround us and try to get it," Johnny exclaimed. It sounded like a real threat to us because we'd seen it in all the cowboy shows. So, he and Marcellus snuck into the tool shed and got Daddy's small handsaw. They used it to cut a trap door into the wooden planks of our clubhouse floor. Then Johnny lowered our cigar box, which was given to us by Uncle Mac, on a rope, down through the floor and into the dirt below.

All it contained were a few coins, marbles, and some Pepsi-Cola bottle caps that we collected from walking up and down Hunsinger Lane. The next time we went to Fontaine Ferry Park on Pepsi-Cola Day, we would use these caps to help pay for carnival rides. We made it a rule to never reach down into the trap-door (strong-hold), for the strong box because snakes lived in the dirt under a lot of farm buildings.

Every week we pulled the box up from the hole and added our treasures to it. We earned money by finding empty pop bottles along the road and taking them up to Jack Finn's Conoco Service Station for the three cent refund. Plus, we got a nickel a week apiece for an allowance. As president of the club, I used a scrap piece of paper to keep track of what each one of us put into the box. That paper was stored in our Well's Fargo Desk.

The boys put the planks back in place after the box was returned to its hole and Jimmy laid down a piece of a rug. He found it in a scrap pile in the Steidenburger's back field where he burned his trash. The rug made the floor look fine but I knew that wouldn't stop a hog, heavy with pigs, from falling through the planks and breaking a leg.

"Don't be a worry-wart, Deanna, we'll cross that bridge when we get to it," Johnny put me back in my place when I mentioned this concern during our last weekly club meeting. It was only almost August; we would surely know what to do with this problem by April when the sow was due to return here.

We were excited. "Now we can spend the night out in here!" Jimmy cried. Our dream of sleeping outside like the cowboys on the open range was finally coming true. Unfortunately, there was only room inside for two bunks. They were for Johnny and Marcellus, not me, even though I was the oldest, the president of the club, and helped make the bunks. I was not a boy, and this always presented a problem for me. This meant that Jimmy and I didn't get to spend the night out on the range. Jimmy hung his head and wished to be older, but I was beginning to accept the reality of my situation.

Johnny and Marcellus were Boy Scouts and spent several nights out there, having all kinds of adventures. Jimmy and I were jealous and hoppin' mad that we couldn't join them on their nighttime campouts. We pictured them sitting around a campfire playing the old harmonica Daddy got from a fellow at Fehr's Brewery, and listening to the howls of coyotes piercing through the night air, just like the cowboys did. Our daydreams increased our complaints as we searched for a solution.

Later that month, our problem seemed to be solved. Daddy bought Mama a new freezer to help us preserve the summer harvest. It was a big chest-type freezer and took up most of the back wall of the basement. I noticed that it came in a sturdy wood-braced box that was covered with cardboard. It was big enough to sleep both me and Jimmy in pallets on the floor. When we told Mama of our idea, she didn't think it was as good as we did and said, "You kids better not get ahead of yourselves. Ask Daddy first. He may have other plans for it because it *is* a big box."

We didn't have enough patience to wait for that. If he saw it already done, he would probably let us keep it. Instead of listening to Mama, we snatched on our idea for the extra bedroom. It took all four of us Rangers to drag the huge, awkward box up out of the basement and through the pasture field gate. While we had the long gate open, Bullet barked and stood guard for us. He wouldn't let the cow or any of the pigs out of the pasture. We struggled, getting it through the stands of purple iron weed over by Calfie's waterin' tub, and then we snuggled it right next to the clubhouse. It looked like a fine room addition to us. But still, we went to improving it. Using Mama's butcher knife, we cut a swinging "saloon-style" door, just like the ones we saw on a Lone Ranger movie. Then we cut a small window on the side so we could see the stars at night. Standing back, we admired our hard work.

Excitement got to us, and jumping up and down, we exclaimed, "Maybe, all of us can camp out here tonight!" But first we had to try out a cowboy adventure. We ran to the house for our cowboy gear: hats, holsters, cap pistols and kerchiefs. We were ready to play cowboys and outlaws right now. Johnny and Marcellus were the cowboys. Jimmy and I, with our kerchiefs pulled up over our noses, were part of "Black Bart's" outlaw gang. Bullet was loyal to first one side and then the other. We laid low in the daisies that grew behind the clubhouse and over by the walnut tree taking imaginary shots at each other with our noisy cap-pistols.

Pleased with ourselves, we continued our celebration. Yanking up the rope to strong box, we took out a few coins, changed into nicer clothes, and walked up to Jack Finn's Conoco, the only place around to buy treats. Jack's was working on Mr. Shellhamer's (Larney's father) car out in back by his smithy forge. "Get what you want and put the money on the counter," he yelled out from under the hood of Mr. Shellhamer's Oldsmobile. Jimmy got a Seven-Up candy bar, I got a Chocolate Turtle Bar. Johnny and Marcellus got soft drinks. The drinks were in a large chest-type cooler. The bottles hung from their throats between the long lengths of iron slats in the cooler. The boys pulled a Chock Cola and an Orange Crush down through the rows of slats until they reached the coin box on the end. There they released them with their nickels. The brown, rippled glass of the Orange Crush bottle made it look so refreshing as we walked home in the hot sun, that I wished I'd made that choice.

"Trade you a sip for a bite of my candy bar?" I offered to Marcellus, extending it to him.

"Heck no – I'm not sharing!" You shoulda' got one for yourself," he smirked as I bristled, knowing he was right.

When we got back home, Johnny and Marcellus put their empty pop bottles into a wooden box and lowered it into our clubhouse's strong-hold under the floor next to the cigar box. "Tomorrow we'll take these back to Jack Finns' for our three cent refund," Johnny said. *Darn*, I thought, jealously, *their treat even cost less than mine and*

Jimmy's, wishing again, that I had made the other choice. But, I had to admit, I did enjoy my Chocolate Turtle.

Then we changed clothes, and with Bullet romping along side us, we took off for the swimming hole, like we did everyday when our chores were done. Squeezing under the fence, near the cane reed break by Hunsinger Quarry, we ignored the "No Trespassing" sign, and marched down the trail edged with pungent creeping charley vine toward our swimming hole. It was in Judge Jeffery's woods, and over a mile down Hunsinger Lane from our place. First, we splashed the water with long sticks and threw rocks in to scare off the snakes. Then we jumped in and splashed each other plenty to cool off.

Looking up, Jimmy pointed, "There's a buzzard in the sky, Daddy says that buzzards mean bad luck. Somebody's gonna' get bit today," he shivered, still scared of the snakes that may have stayed in the water.

"No, Dummy, look again," Johnny said. "What yur' lookin' at is a good sign." Four faces looked into the sky, instead of seeing a buzzard, we saw a red-tailed hawk circling high above the trees. "Daddy said that seeing a hawk means there are no rats or snakes around because hawks eat 'em," Johnny went on, with a big smile to accompany his knowledge. He was so smart – we were proud of him.

****

When we returned home a couple of hours later, night time plans still bubbled from our lips. "Jimmy," I said, "we need to bring out our blankets and pillows and get things ready before I haf' to help Mama with supper." He giggled at the thought of our camping adventure and we all quickened our steps. Bolting though the pasture field gate, we were ready to get back to our preparations. Bullet made it through the gate first, barking furiously. Our good mood quickly changed as our clubhouse came into view.

"Oh, no!" we all screamed at the same time. We were not prepared for the horror of what we saw.

The cow and five of our six hogs were all standing around our room addition. They were eating it! We grabbed the longest sticks we could find, and Bullet nipped at their heels. Finally, we shooed them way. By then, they had eaten our fancy saloon style door, the top and most of the left side of our bedroom. In their feeding frenzy, they had yanked the huge box away from the clubhouse, and had it over near the hog waller, where they could get a better bite on it.

Our tears had not yet begun to start. When Daddy heard about the possibility of sick animals, we all got another visit from the switch. "I swear you kids ain't worth a bullet to shoot ya!" he boomed, his face stern and showing worry.

"But, Daddy..." we stammered, whimpering as we realized our dilemma.

"Don't give me your excuses! This is what you get for not askin' me about that box in the first place! I would a' told cha' that the animals would eat it." He shouted. He made all four of us sit up with him and the animals all night. We sadly listened to them bellow and grunt in pain as the cardboard went through their digestive tracks. We felt so bad for them, all of us cried, even Johnny and Marcellus who always bragged, "Nothing can make us cry!"

Needless to say, our clubhouse never did include a chance for all four of us to have our "home on the range," adventure. It seemed like many of our ideas came to a quick end, but sadly, this one was not over yet!

"Wait till Daddy finds that hole we sawed in the floor to hide our strong box!" I whispered to Johnny.

"Shh!" he gouged me in the ribs with his elbow.

Things change quickly, I pondered. *At our last meeting that problem seemed so far away.* But now, it was too late, I could feel it in my bones – we were going to get another visit from the switch, and probably never get to use our clubhouse again.

Chapter 9

Hogkillin' Days

The wind bit my nose and the frosty grass crunched beneath my shoes. I strained to see through feathery bits of snow swirling around me. It was 1952 and I was eleven. My brothers, Johnny, age ten, Marcellus, age nine, Jimmy six, and myself were helping Daddy feed the livestock.

"This is hogkillin' weather," Daddy announced as we threw cobs of corn to the pigs. "Yeah," his blue eyes danced at the thought of it. We knew Daddy loved this time of the year. "After Halloween," he continued, "when days get short and it stays good and cold, that's hogkillin' weather." I knew the weather had to be cold so the meat didn't spoil before Daddy could get it salted down and put in the smokehouse to cure.

Hogkilling was exciting for us kids, too, even though it demanded a lot of work from everybody. Daddy remembered it fondly from his days at Gethsemane and looked forward to hogkilling every year. There was a glimmer in his eye and quickness in his voice. Hogkilling made him most alive. So much work had to be done, and in such a small amount of time! He became the director of a great movie, barking orders and calling the shots. We ran around the farm doing the best we could to keep up with his demands, our faithful dog, Bullet constantly at our heels. The extra work called for extra help, so we had visitors. Our Uncle Bud and several of our neighbors would be coming by from time to time to help us get ready for the big weekend.

The work started several weeks before hogkilling day. Most of the outside tasks fell on Daddy and my brothers. First, they had to assemble the tools that were only used for hogkilling. They scouted them out from our many sheds and outbuildings. What we didn't have or couldn't find, we borrowed. It took a long time just to gather up all the equipment. Some of the things needed were a heavy, metal scalding trough, strong timbers to build a tall scaffold, huge iron cauldrons and tripods to hang over the fires, several five-gallon stoneware crocks to store the freshly rendered lard, hooks to hang the meat in the smokehouse, and sturdy chains for lifting and turning the hogs while the men worked on them.

Daddy sent the meat grinders and the lard press into the house for Mama and I to scrub out and oil for lard rendering and sausage making. After the tools were gathered, the work had just begun.

Many fires would be burning over hogkillin weekend, so piles of firewood had to be chopped and made ready by the boys. The wood came from the long lengths of barn lumber out by our pasture field fence beside the dusty, tractor-road that ran along Judge Jeffrey's property line. We called it the Dusty Road. The boys and I had helped Daddy stack that wood there after he tore down a dilapidated barn the first year we moved here. In the summer this pile was full of snakes, in the winter it was full of rats. The boys chopped wood everyday after school. It took them several weeks to get enough ready for the kill. Bullet sat by the barn and watched and waited, but the boys didn't have time to play with him.

Next, Daddy had my brothers scrub the manure and stale slops from the cement floor of the pigpen. They wore some of Mama's rubber gloves and their tall snow galoshes to protect themselves from muck. "I don't want to drag a fresh killed hog through that mess!" Daddy shouted to them as he gave instructions. Marcellus and Jimmy raked up the manure and shoveled loads of it into the wheelbarrow that Johnny kept pushing over and over again to the compost heap along the pasture field fence. The stinky manure became great fertilizer when Daddy did the spring planting. The smell was awful and the thick stench of it hung in the air for days. Pig farms are smelly, no doubt about it! Every farmer in Hikes Point did the same thing when it was time for their hogkilling, so nobody complained. This messy job was something that made me glad that I was a girl.

Highly important was the building of the sturdy scaffold. Different farmers in Hikes Point came by to help Daddy with it in the evenings after he got home from Fehr's Brewery. Farmer's were happy to help out because they knew they would need Daddy's help when they had their killings. Young Larney Shellhamer and Bud Singer were frequent helpers. The men only had a few hours to work before it got dark. The scaffold had to be strong and tall enough to hold all six 200 pound hogs at one time. It would be about seven feet high, because a stretched out adult hog needed a lot of room. After the men finished working for the night, they shared some bottles of Fehr's that Daddy brought home the brewery.

The extremely sharp hogkilling knives had to be re-sharpened for the butchering. Daddy's set of hogkilling knives was one of his most prized possessions. They were passed down to him from his father Demetrius, and had been in the family since pioneer days. Daddy was the only one allowed to touch them. Carefully sharpening them, he kept them like fine silver, wrapped in felt and tied with silken cords. "Ya' need a knife sharp enough to cut chur' fingers off, and I don't want 'em used for nothin' else." Daddy warned us when he caught us snooping in his tools to find a knife sharp enough to cut some of the cane reeds down by the quarry. We wanted to use the canes to make bows and arrows. Daddy's knives were locked up in his carpenter's chest out in the tool shed, where he hid his bottles of whiskey. We knew better than to mess around with anything in the tool shed, especially after we got caught a few times.

Then he cleaned the rifles. He didn't trust a pistol because your hand needed to be too steady. The hog had to be shot right between its eyes and one inch up in order to get in the center of the brain. A shotgun was easier, but the meat would be filled with buckshot – so that was out of the question. The bullet had to be found and dug out of the hog's flesh.

"This keeps the meat clean and puts the hog out of his misery real quick," Daddy explained to us kids, with a note of sympathy in his voice.

Still, Johnny asked, "Does the hog feel any pain?" Daddy could tell we felt sorry for the pigs. Sometimes we had already made pets of them. Daddy warned us that this was total foolishness for farm kids. But the little piglets, with their Necco-wafer noses were so cute when they were small that we couldn't resist them. Just as his had, our hearts gradually hardened as we got older.

To be able to take part in the shooting was a real rite of passage for my brothers. They had to prove their ability to Daddy by consistently hitting moving targets before he considered them ready. They practiced shooting their Daisy Red Ryder BB guns all year, killing birds and rabbits around the place and any rats they found in the barn. It hurt me to watch them. The day Marcellus killed a cardinal, I cried. He knew it upset me. As I picked up the red feathers from the ground, he said in his defense, "I'm sorry, Deanna. I meant to hit that sparrow next to him." It made me feel better that he didn't try to hit him on purpose. The birds were perched on the electric wire that stretched between our kitchen and the cowshed. Johnny and Marcellus were both able to win Daddy's approval the same year. Jimmy, being younger, was able to get his approval a few years later. They were between twelve and thirteen years old when they earned this privilege.

The Friday before the kill Daddy brought home several packages of fresh calf guts that he bought at the Haymarket. This meant that the work for Mama and me started the night before the men would arrive on Saturday morning to begin theirs.

"Josephine, boil these guts and get 'em ready for the sausage." Daddy's voice boomed as he entered the front door, coming home from work. He didn't need to give these orders to my mother. Having grown up on a farm herself, she had been through hogkillings every year of her life. But Daddy did like to give orders, especially during killin' time.

After the guts were boiled, Mama and I would need to cut their slimy twenty-five foot lengths into short eighteen-inch lengths, the size needed for sausage-casings. On Sunday these casings would be stuffed with the spicy meat. We cut the intestines down to size, then ran our fingers over them to make sure there were no holes. After that we tied a knot at one end of each one of them with the sturdy nylon cord that Daddy also bought at the Haymarket. Working with the guts took a lot of time, we would finish it tomorrow (Saturday), while the men worked outside with the hogs.

Saturday – the first day of the kill is finally here! This thought woke me up. The whole family was excited, whistling, singing and bumping into each other as we got the last of the preparations in order. It was early, Daddy stood in front of the kitchen window watching the flurries scatter through the brisk autumn air. As he finished his last cup of coffee, he told Mama, "I hope it don't snow too hard," It wasn't full daylight yet, but the men were coming in. They were gathering out in the pasture, not far from the pigpen, and circling the fires that were already blazing under the kettles. Daddy started these before he came in for breakfast. It took a long time to heat enough water to fill the large scalding trough.

From inside the house, we heard their deep voices laughing and shouting as they warmed their hands over the fires. Daddy and my eager brothers ran out to join them – Bullet running alongside. I stopped my job at the sink and stared through the dawn's light, watching them rub their hands together from the cold, and slapping each other on the back. Their voices were high with the anticipation of the day.

Uncle Bud and the main man in his garbage collection company, skinny Gus Ferris, (Daddy described him as, 'a long drink a' water), came to help us every time we had a kill. I knew Gus Ferris from the summer vacation I had at cousin's house a couple of years ago. I loved it when Uncle Bud brought his funny son, my cousin Bob, along. Bob was handsome and told jokes, and my energy always picked up when he was around. Neighboring farmers in this German farm community came by, too. Hank Kemper, Bud Singer, Larney, and Tom Dyer had arrived. And of course, our next door neighbor, Mr. Edsell. Older farmers came in for a while, like old Mr. Stiedenberger, Mr. Edinger and Larney's father, Mr. Shellhamer. They couldn't do the heavy work anymore, but they enjoyed the excitement and a "nip" or two of whiskey. "Have to do something to stay warm," they joked, pulling the bottles out of their mackinaws.

Daddy and my brothers, Johnny, Marcellus and Jimmy, went to the neighbor's killings too. Extra hands at a killin' were invaluable. My brothers were young, but they were well trained and efficient. More than just hard work, this was a social time for the farmers. In overhearing them from my work post in the house I could tell they loved it, and I wished I could be out there with them.

While the men were kept busy outside, Mama and I were kept busy inside the house with whatever they sent in for us to work on.

We were already busy preparing the calf guts for sausage casings, finishing the chore we started last night. When the boys brought in the organ meats, we would cut the gristles out of them and clean them so they could be added to the sausage mixture tomorrow. In the morning after church, we would begin to chop up the fat so it could be rendered into lard. Also, I would be checking on the baby, Mary Ann, one year old, while I did my work. When she got cranky, I would be moving her from the crib to the walker, and then to the Johnny-jump up swing in the doorway. I would give her bottles and change her diapers when she needed that done. This freed Mama up to do more important things. But our most significant work on both days was to fix a big noon meal for the hungry men. We did this while working on our other tasks.

Margaret Jane, age five, my closest sister in age, would be playing with Theresa, four, and Tony, three. Her job was to keep them out from under our feet and away from our flying butcher knives.

****

Good at judging hogs, Daddy made the choice of which piglets would fatten up best for our table, back in the spring when the old sow gave us a litter of about twelve of them. His experienced wisdom as a farmer was all he needed for this decision. The other piglets he fattened up and sold to the Bourbon Stock Yards located down by the Haymarket, close to where he worked at Fehr's Brewery. Now, we had six hefty 200 pounds hogs to be killed on this hogkillin' day. Johnny and Marcellus already had them corralled in the pigpen. This was done before breakfast too, while Daddy milked Calfie and got the fires going.

At last, it was time for the kill to start. Daddy took the lead and readied to shoot the first hog. Shouldering his rifle, he took careful aim, then felt the jolt as his arm absorbed the gun's kickback. Immediately, a black and white hampshire boar fell to its knees. You would think the animals would scatter, screaming in fear, but hogs are fascinating creatures. Instead, they lined the front of the pigpen with their hooves up on the wooden rails, looking at the men in a frozen gaze. Always hungry, they seemed to be thinking, "You must be here to feed me." They didn't notice or care about their brothers getting shot. Our dog, Bullet was smart enough to stay back out of the way, and sat over by the corncrib.

As soon as a hog went down, the men immediately sprung into action. Gus Ferris and Uncle Bud grabbed the Hampshire's legs and turned it over on the pen's cement floor. This was the same floor my brothers had cleaned earlier in the week. Using the longest of the hogkillin' knives, Gus slit the hog's throat. As it went through death throes, the men watched it kick and bleed. That's when the older farmers came into the pen and collected the blood from each of the hogs as they went down. The men used the blood to make blood sausage. "Oooo-weee, a real delicacy," Mr. Edinger exclaimed, handing a mason-jar of warm blood to Mr. Steidenberger, who nodded his head in agreement.

Gus Ferris, was an interesting fellow in his own right. He loved the fresh blood and always drank a cup of it. "Once you taste fresh blood you always want it," he said, "it warms you up and makes you strong." Banging his fist on his chest, he slurped some down with great gusto. Then he bragged of his younger days when he worked at one of the slaughterhouses in Butchertown. A true hobo of the Depression Era, Gus spent many years jumping trains, and crossed the country several times. Learning to travel light, he boasted about how little a person really needs to get by in this world. So little, in fact that he used his pocketknife for almost everything, even eating. "Forks and spoons is a waste of space," he told me one time while juggling some peas on the knife's sharp blade. I was afraid he would slice his tongue. My eyes had widened, as I watched him roll the peas into his mouth without losing a one.

Back on the kill floor of the pigpen, Uncle Bud yelled to his son, "Bob, you grab that back leg," motioning with his hand. "Go over there and help your Uncle Bud and Bob drag that hog," Daddy shouted to Johnny and Marcellus, who were alert and waiting for their next assignment. Each took a leg and the four of them pulled the hog from the floor of the pigpen out to the scalding trough about thirty feet away. It was important to remove the hog immediately, "Ain't no need to fill 'im with an accidental stray shot," Daddy told the men who already knew what he meant. When the hog got to the scalding trough, Bud Singer, Tom Dyer, and Hank Kemper took over for my brothers and cousin Bob. They rolled the hampshire onto long chains and prepared to lift him.

"Ready, on the count of three, let's dunk 'im," Uncle Bud said as the other men joined him in lifting the hog into the steaming water of the scalding trough. Grabbing the chains the four men rolled him back and forth in the hot water.

"They gotta' keep rolling him," Johnny told Marcellus and Bob, trying to show Daddy and the men that he knew exactly what to do. Gus and the three of them worked with the heavy chains, wiggling him over and over in the scalding water. The water temperature had to be exact, almost boiling. Too cold and the follicle would not release the hair, also, if it was too hot the hair would set in and not be removable, either.

"Grab that end of the chain – time to take 'im out," Daddy beckoned to Bud Singer and Tom Dyer. It took all four grown men, one on each end of the chains, to pull the water-soaked hog from the trough. Only the experience of the farmers involved told them when it was time to remove the hog to the scraping table. Mr. Edsell and Hank dragged over the next hog; Larney and Daddy helped them to lift him into the trough.

Once the first hog was out, all the available men descended on him with the rounded scraping bells (dome-shaped metal tools with wooden handles) and worked furiously to scrape the hair from his hide. "Hurry, it's gonna' freeze up," Larney yelled grabbing another swig of whiskey to encourage his mood. There was only a small window of time before the hog's body temperature cooled down, then the hair would not release. While they were scraping, Mr. Kemper, Hank, Mr. Edsell, and Daddy pulled the next hog from the scalding trough.

After the scraping, the hog looked like a big bald cloud. Daddy pushed sharp poles called "gambling rods" through the hog's Achilles tendons. Then Gus, Uncle Bud and Larney used other chains to hoist him up and attach him to the scaffold where he would hang and drain most of his blood.

"This _____ of a _____ is heavy!" Larney yelled out. That was another feature of hogkillin – the liberal sprinkling of curse words.

"That's a good reason why I don't want you outside, Deanna," Daddy had told me when I complained of having to stay in the house and cut up stuff with Mama. "The language from a bunch of men is too loose for a young girl to hear." I knew this excuse was not completely true because Daddy used words worse than these around us on a daily basis. I liked to watch the men laugh and joke when they had a drink or two in them. the sad truth for me was that I was more valuable in the house.

As the killing continued, each man got a turn to shoot. When my brothers got old enough, they got their shot, too. Never did any of them ever miss his mark. If he did he would be humiliated and not get a turn here next year, or at any of the other pig shoots in the neighborhood.

Before long, all six of the hogs were hanging from the scaffold. The men started gutting them. They removed the head first and set it aside. Mama and I would work it into souse (a meat-grain product), on Monday. When the entrails came out, several colored men were on hand to take the guts. Daddy let them have the kidneys, too, if they wanted them.

"I don't like the way the kidneys make my sausage taste," he told Uncle Bud.

"I never use 'em either," Uncle Bud agreed, shaking his head.

These colored men hung around the Haymarket or worked for Uncle Bud's garbage collection company. They always had an ear open for a hog killing during the cold weather, and were able to find one somewhere in the county every weekend. Most of Jefferson County was farm country.

"My wife's been after me to get some more fresh chitlins," one of them laughed to Daddy, pushing back his sleeve so he could dip his hand into the pile, and fill his canvas bag with the slippery guts.

Jimmy brought the organ meats into the house for Mama and me to prepare them for being ground into the sausage. Still working on the sausage casings, I gladly stopped my job of cutting the wiggly calf guts, to open the kitchen door for him. When I saw the excitement on Jimmy's windburned face, I again wanted to be outside. Staying inside with the chopping, cooking and the babies didn't seem nearly as exciting to me as being outside with the laughter of the men. He lifted my spirits slightly when he said, "You're lucky to be in this nice warm house, Deanna. It's cold out there." Hank Williams crooned

Your Cheatin' Heart, on the little brown Motorola on top of our Westinghouse refrigerator, as I took the bloody meats from his chilly hands. With a "Harrumph" from my throat, I let him know I didn't completely agree with him. Jimmy didn't care, and took a minute to run to the dining room and stand in front of the potbelly stove, where he removed his gloves and rubbed his red-chapped hands together.

I set the organ meats aside. *Later,* I thought. Besides the sausage casings, my most important task was helping Mama fix noon time dinner meal. The men would be coming in the house for it, starved, in a little while. Soon after Jimmy delivered the organ meats, Marcellus came in with the tenderloins. These were considered the tastiest and tenderest part of the hog. He told Mama, "Daddy said to tell you to fix these for dinner," Mama took Daddy's orders in stride. She knew these tenderloins were the most coveted part of the meal. They were cut from the muscles that ran alongside the hogs' spines. Even from six hogs – there wasn't much of this precious meat. She divided the amount in half. Knowing that the men loved the tenderloins, she wanted to save some of it for those men who would come back to help us again tomorrow. Soaking the fresh meat in salt water, she put it in the refrigerator for later.

This was the most incredible meal we fixed all year, and we gladly did it for the workers. They got a feast, and they well deserved it. Earlier in the morning, we had baked several apple pies from our fall crop of winesaps. There were also sweet potatoes, green beans and corn from some of the canning we did last summer, cornbread dressing, mashed potatoes and, of course, tenderloin gravy. *Umm! It all smells so good,* I thought, my tummy rumbling in excitement.

As I fried up the juicy meat, the temptation to nibble on some of it was too much. It smelled delicious when I turned it over in the bubbling grease. I wanted to taste it, but I knew there was just enough for the men. Unable to stop myself, I sneaked a corner from a piece as I lifted it from the skillet. Mama caught me and smacked my hand. "Deanna, those men are out there in the cold killing our hogs. These tenderloins are for them. If there's any left after they have their fill, then you can have some," she said sharply. After my eleven years of going through hogkillin', I knew there wouldn't be any left.

Embarrassed, I didn't try again because I knew she was right. Looking out of the kitchen window while working at the stove, I noticed the snow thickening. The men huddled around the warm carcasses, working quickly with skillful, deft fingers. Johnny, Marcellus, Jimmy, and Bob ran from place to place, fetching tools for them and stoking the fires. I had to admit that I was really glad my work, though unsavory, was at least in the house, where we could listen to country music and be warm.

****

"Josephine, you sure are a good cook," Uncle Bud said to Mama, his older sister, as he took another helping of mashed potatoes and gravy. Mama beamed him a smile, and Daddy shot a proud glance at his energetic wife. She and I weaved around the men refilling bowls, platters, and milk pitchers. My brothers and cousin Bob sat at the big table, too. I was proud that they were being treated like the men because they deserved it, too. Daddy, Uncle Bud, Gus, Hank, Mr. Singer, Mr. Dyer and Larney ate hearty. The kitchen filled with the sound of their deep voices, lip-smacking, and laughter. It was good to hear them relax. We women-folk knew hogkilling was hard work.

Mama and I ate later with the little kids. Naturally, the tenderloin was gone. I wondered if Mama, who was in her thirties at the time, had ever even tasted it. Gobbling our food down quickly, we spent a good deal of time doing up the dishes. After that, we returned to our assignment with the sausage casings and the organ meats.

Before they had to leave for the day, the men were doing their best to crack all the ribs and quarter all the carcasses. They worked at makeshift tables put together with long planks on top of Daddy's sawhorses. The cold sped up their work but made their fingers stiff. The hogkillin' knives were so sharp, they had to be careful in their use of whiskey to keep warm, and help them tolerate the heavy work. But they had enough alcohol that we heard their laughter come all the way into the house while we did our work (without the benefit of whiskey). "I think they're keeping warm enough," Mama laughed. "It feels good to hear 'em laugh," she smiled, cutting the gristles out of one the hog-livers.

"I wish I could be out there laughing, too" I said under my breath. Mama caught me and said, "Deanna, this is what it's like to be a girl and you're gonna' haf' ta stop fightin' it." Her comment didn't help me much, as my face twisted into a grimace – still jealous of my brothers. I knew they were working hard, too, but they got to be more a part of the things of the world, and I was always stuck in the house. But, I realized that Mama was stuck, too. My lips wrinkled as I thought, *house is another name for prison when it comes to bein' a girl.*

Daddy fixed a salt brine for the meat. He put sage and pepper into his recipe with the water and the rock salt. As the hams, shoulders, backbones, and bacons appeared, he rubbed the salty mixture into them and packed them into the brine recipe for the night. Larney's strong hands helped him push the salty mixture into the crevices of the different cuts. Tomorrow (Sunday), all the meat would be removed from these barrels and hung in the smoke house where Daddy would cure it with hickory smoke. But first the meat had to sit overnight in the salt mixture. It could still spoil without this important step even though the weather was cold. The salt drew the rest of the blood out of the meat.

What a waste that would be, I thought, *after raisin' all those hogs from spring piglets, to lose the meat, now.* The afternoon sped by quickly. Soon it was milking time and the men left to take care of their own animals. After supper, Daddy and my bothers went back out to finish putting the fresh cuts into the salt brine. This step had to be done on Saturday.

Mama and I had to finish our Saturday work in the house. The casings and the organ meats would be needed tomorrow. We weren't done with our work until these tasks were finished. In the morning we would be busy cutting up fat, lots of it, into one-inch cubes for rendering. Working continually, all of us fell into bed, exhausted, but finished, around nine o'clock that night.

****

Sunday morning we got up earlier than usual. We had a lot of work to get done before the men returned. We drove into all the way into Louisville, and went to the five-thirty Mass at St. Francis of Assisi on Bardstown Road, because St. Bartholomew's only had a seven and a nine o'clock Mass. We never missed Mass no matter how much work had to be done.

140

Sadly, not all the men were able to return to help us on Sunday. They had their own farm work to tend to and some of them went to work at other kills. We hurried home from Mass to find Uncle Bud, Bob, and Gus waiting for breakfast. Mr. Edsell and Larney would come over later, after church. The breakfast on the day after the kill was an important meal. Mama had mixed the hogs' brains into our scrambled eggs along with our morning biscuits.

As we sat down for breakfast, Gus declared, "I love 'em hog brains. Tha's what got me ta' come back and hep' out today!" He flipped open his pocketknife, showed a toothless smile, and juggled the fried eggs and brains on its sharp blade. Then he poured some coffee into his saucer and slurped the hot liquid down with the eggs, saying, "As fine a delicacy as ya'd find in any restaurant!" Daddy smiled in agreement. We kids, including cousin Bob, turned up our noses, "Yuck!"

I'd never been to a restaurant, but I knew none of the girls at St. Bartholomew's ever talked about ordering this so-called delicacy at any of the restaurants they'd ever been to. To us kids they were disgusting. We struggled through the salty, scrambled brains while the men teased us about the funny looks on our faces as we choked them down. The brains had to be eaten today because they didn't keep. We knew it was a sin to waste the good food God gave us. Even though we hated the salty brains, we could understand that God, like Daddy, didn't like waste.

After breakfast, the men were back out working with the hog-meat again. Johnny and Marcellus already had fires going. At least it wasn't snowing, this day was very cold but sunny. The men removed the fatty hides from the meat and trimmed up all the side cuts. They took the trimmings into the barn for Daddy and Mr. Edsell to prepare for the sausage mixture. Jimmy and Marcellus brought armload after armload of the pigs' fatty hides into the kitchen. Mama and I started with our work of cutting them into one-inch cubes. Six hogs provided a lot of fat. So much that Johnny and Bob were cubing some of the hides up outside, too. Sighing at the mountain of pearly fat, I tried to speed up my progress, thinking I could get outside faster. "Cut that in half, Deanna, it'll never render up fast enough," Mama said eyeing one of my pieces. That put an end to my plan of escape, and I sighed again, accepting the reality of my gender.

Even though we worked fast, the sharp hog killing knives had me cutting carefully. With dinner to fix as well, Mama was afraid the men would be calling for the fat cubes way before we had a chance to get them done. The refrigerator was filled with about 100 sausage casings and the organ meats we got ready before we went to bed the night before. Both of these things were swimming in salt water. After dinner the men would need these for the sausage-making. We shifted from one job to the next, cutting, chopping, cooking, peeling, and frying. "Hurry up, Deanna, we have to have these done on time." Mama urged. I was already working as fast as I could.

Again, we made another fabulous meal for the helpers. Today the men would finish off the rest of the tenderloin. I drained off the salt water it soaked in, rinsed it, breaded it, and fried it. Mama made banana pudding, and I made banana croquettes to go along with the same kind of food we served yesterday. Again, the men relaxed, enjoyed the meal and took some time to warm up in the cozy house.

After dinner, Jimmy was sent inside to do the dishes, so I could get back to work on finishing the hides. Noticing the time, Mama started acting just like Daddy – shouting out orders like an army sergeant. She was nervous that we might not have the fat cubes ready before the men wanted them. If that happened, the men would waste valuable time waiting on us, and she couldn't bear the guilt of that. "Keep those kids in the other room," she said sharply to Margaret Jane. With all this commotion going on, Theresa and Tony were chasing back and forth and whining for our attention. "Deanna, go fix Mary Ann, who was crying, another bottle, and change her diaper," she continued, her voice getting higher. Grateful for the break from the jiggley fat, I wiped my greasy hands on my dirty apron and raced off to scoop up the baby up from her walker. I changed her diaper in the babybed as I settled her down with her bottle. She sucked on it fiercely, her blonde curls mashed against the blankets, as I worked.

When the fires licked the bottoms of the kettles, Daddy yelled to Marcellus and Johnny. "You boys go inta' the house and get that fat they been cuttin' up in there," the boys jumped at the opportunity to enter the warm house for any reason at all.

Once the cubes of fat hit the hot kettle, they melted quickly. Uncle Bud and Gus tended the kettles and stirred the bubbling grease. While this was going on, Daddy, Bob, Johnny, and Larney cut the rest of the hogs' scrap trimmings into three inch pieces. This made them easier to grind when it came time for doing the sausage making. After the fat cubes rendered, Uncle Bud took the *renderins*, to the lard press and squeezed out all the grease. What was left was called *cracklins*. Cracklins' were the pigs' skin with all the grease removed. Both the men and we kids considered them delicious, and looked forward to this treat all year. The salt in the hides made them taste like potato chips, and that's the way we ate them – like potato chips. The men and my brothers nibbled on the hot cracklins' all afternoon to help them keep warm. Marcellus brought some in the house for Mama, me and the little kids to enjoy.

Gus and Mr. Edsell poured most of the scalding grease into the heavy stoneware crocks. As it cooled, the hot fat hardened into lard. We would use it to cook with for the rest of the year. It was time to make the soap. Last night, Daddy had gathered up some ashes from the fires of the weekend. He knew exactly which ashes to choose. He added water into the ashes he had in one of Calfie's old milk buckets. Now, he threw the dissolved ashes into some of the rendered lard in the kettle along with some lye. When this mixture cooled, the men poured it out in a thick layer on a countertop in the tool shed. In a few says, this amber colored mixture would harden, and Daddy would cut it into bars of lye soap. This was our major source of soap. We used it for everything, laundry, dishes, and even bathing. Harsh and caustic, it made our skin rough and our hair stink, and of course, we didn't like it.

"Don't complain. You're lucky to have soap." Daddy would answer us, never having much sympathy for our opinions. The only time we used *city soap* was when we visited Aunt Bertha or Aunt Ida down near Shawnee Park. All my country cousins used lye soap like us, and they didn't like it either.

The men cleaned out the pig bladders and used a piece of cane reed to blow them up into tough balls about the size of dodge balls.

The bladder's thick hide made them sturdy enough for the kids to play with for several days. Mama and I heard the men laughing as we worked in the kitchen. They were taking a break from their work to test the strength of the bladders by popping them back and forth like playground balls. Hearing the laughter of the men, Mama called over to me, "It's time for the kids to go outside and play." I stopped my work and helped Margaret Jane get coats, hats and gloves on Theresa and Tony. *Darn-it, the little kids get to go out and I'm still stuck in here!* I thought, my jealousy heating up again.

Daddy wasn't too happy to see them, fearing they would get underfoot. "Margaret Jane, you better keep 'ose kids back outta' the way," he shouted to her as he saw Theresa and Tony running toward the pasture field gate. The afternoon was disappearing and that aggravated his mood. He knew his helpers would be leaving soon. Lovable Mr. Edsell, who always had time for children, gave the kids the bladders that hadn't been popped yet. He chuckled as he watched them chase each other, carrying the bladders, off to the orchard and play dodge-ball with them.

The men pulled the large pieces of meat from the brine and brought them into the smokehouse where they hung them from the rafters on strong hooks. Daddy fixed a special fire in there earlier in the day. He made it of oak and hickory woodchips and contained it in a metal five-gallon drum. The smoke smelled delicious as it began to cure the meat. Filling the little smokehouse, some of it could be seen escaping through the open eaves by the edges of the roof. While they worked, the men poured water on this fire every so often to keep it from flaming up and burning down the shed. For the next four nights, Daddy would have to get up during the night to continue this procedure.

It took four to five days to completely cure the meat. Mama tended the bucket of fire during the day, until the boys got home from school and took over the task. All the neighbors on Hunsinger Lane knew what Daddy was doing, but many strangers driving down the road pulled up into our gravel drive and shouted, "Hey, Mister, your shed's on fire!"

By now, it was getting late on Sunday, and the sausage making was still not done. Daddy got increasingly nervous about the time. "Jimmy, go inta' the house and tell yur' Mother to give ya' Grandma's cookbook," he shouted over the noise. "And, get the organ meats and the casings, too, while yur' at it." To me, Daddy's sausage was so good, I thought he should enter it in the Kentucky State Fair. Grandma's cookbook was written in German, and the sausage recipe was the only one he could read. It called for some interesting spices. Those I can remember were whole mustard seeds, sage, caraway, and thyme, which we grew in the herb garden by our driveway.

When Jimmy got to the kitchen door to make his requests, I was ready! My inside chores with Mama were done. It was so exciting to finally get outside. I was dressed warmly for the cold, with a wool scarf tied under my chin and wool gloves on my hands. Grabbing the large pan of prepared casings, I took them out with me along with the cookbook. Jimmy carried the pan of organ meats. Bullet greeted me as I got down to the bottom of the steps, and bounced along by my side. It felt so good to be with him and outside at last.

Daddy ground the side trimmings and the organ meats together. Watching him twist the handle on the grinder, the ground sausage meat looked like some creature escaping from the machine. Then he and Larney used their bare hands to squeeze the chunky rock salt and spices through the corse meat they as they mixed it together in Mama's large metal washtub. Daddy checked the taste of his mixture by pinching off a bit of the raw meat and rolling it over in his mouth. If it didn't meet with his satisfaction, he added more of whatever he thought it needed, usually more rock salt, Daddy loved salt. When he considered the sausage ready to stuff, he pulled each empty casing, one at a time, over the end of the long metal tube that was connected to the lard press. He pushed the lever down, and the sausage meat oozed into the intestine. I watched each calf-gut casing blow up like a long, skinny, red balloon.

Marcellus and I took turns tying tight knots to the back ends of each casing with a nylon cord as it came off the press. Then Larney tied the two ends together, so the eighteen-inch sausage took on the shape of a big loop. We strung the loops on a broom handle that rested between the backs of two kitchen chairs we had taken outside for this purpose.

Inside the smokehouse, the air was thick with the hickory smell and cloudy smoke. Johnny and Bob sat high up in the rafters. They scrambled from one rafter to the next like circus monkeys. "Shove 'em sausages up 'ere," Bob yelled down to me as I came into the Smokehouse with my arms full of sausage loops. In the smoky haze, I couldn't see anything, it sounded like a ghost talking from the clouds. I struggled to find him. Marcellus, Jimmy and I ran back and forth to the smokehouse with armloads of the stuffed sausages. While we kids carried the sausages into the smokehouse, Uncle Bud, Mr.Edsell, and Gus were still hanging the heavy pieces – the hams, bacons, shoulders and ribs on the study hooks so they could cure. We weaved around them in the haze.

As I walked back and forth from the sausage press to the smokehouse with Jimmy and Marcellus, I thought about the next day, Monday, when Mama and I would finish the work of hogkilling. On this day, we would work up the hogs' heads and their feet. By the time I got home from school, Mama would have the gelatin made from boiling the hogs' feet. It would be congealed in a pan. My job would be to pick the small bits of meat from the hogs' heads. This meat was called mincemeat. Mama would mix the mincemeat with oats and some of the spices in Grandma's cookbook. Then, she would put the whole mixture into the dark brown gelatin that she boiled up from the pigs' feet. Farmers called this mixture souse. We poured the souse into loaf pans that I took to the smokehouse. There it would be cured along with the rest of the meat. The souse would harden into a kind of lunchmeat that we kids hated worse than we hated the hog brains. I shivered when I thought of the most disgusting words Mama ever said, "Deanna, go out to the smokehouse and get the souse. Slice off a piece for each of us, and fry it for supper tonight." *Thank God, that stuff takes a while to cure*, I thought. Then I smiled, realizing that the delicious sausage would be ready much sooner.

****

The sound of cars crunching down the driveway, and loud good-byes brought me out of my daydream. The excitement of hogkilling was winding down. All the men were gone now, but Larney. He and Daddy sat out by the barn enjoying a last bottle of Fehr's for the day, and chatted about the weekend. Hearing their muffled voices as the boys put the fires out, I leaned against the pasture field gate and absorbed some of the feelings of the hectic weekend. Scratching Bullet's head, I looked over the fields beyond our fences. In the clear cold weather, I could see past Judge Jeffrey's farmland that surrounded our property, and on out to the blue knobs of Fairdale, about thirty miles away to the south of us. The only building around was a place we kids called the "Old Brick." It was a decaying Civil War mansion, in the field behind our pasture. Too dangerous for us to play in, it was hidden behind trees and covered over with columbine vines.

Everything looked peaceful under the sunset's pink glow. The old sow was the only hog out grazing in the pasture now. I wondered if she missed her children. In the spring she would give us another litter. I felt kind of sorry for her. Spreading my elbows out on the top rung of the gate, I leaned over and pressed my chin on top my gloves, mellowing as the excitement came to a close. Then I remembered Mama sighing as she told me, "Deanna, that's what it's like ta' be a sow, that's her lot in life – ta' have babies and let 'em go. She don't know nothin' different." I sighed again, thinking how my life was similar in some strange way to the sow's – first hope, then disappointment. *Being a girl will always be my life, and I'll never be able to change it or outgrow it. Darn...*

Chapter 10

Risen From the Dead

It was January of 1953. I was eleven years old and wouldn't be twelve until February. On a particular Saturday night during this month, one of the most frightening events of my childhood took place. Strangely, it concerned the indoor bathroom that Daddy had installed the summer before.

But first, I'd like to describe a little background about our lives in Hikes Point before we got this room that we had begged for for so long. We had been living a pioneer life in our drafty and inconvenient farmhouse for over four years before our indoor bathroom finally arrived. Life here was never easy. For a long time, we were on well water, used an outhouse, and had very little electricity. There was one ceiling socket in each of our major rooms. Still, Daddy was convinced this was a good place to raise a family. The farms here were beautiful and fertile. The neighbors were friendly and hardworking. But this house! – it screamed at us! Over a hundred years old, it was first used as a tenant house (we believed), for the decaying, old, brick plantation house seen in the distance from our pasture field, that we called the 'Old Brick.'

With our help and his skill, Daddy slowly fixed up the place one room at a time. He did some incredible things in order to give us a more settled life here. He worked the most difficult tasks with the help of Uncle Bud, or our talented neighbor, Mr. Edsell, but most of his daily help came from us kids. We worked tirelessly, desperate for the improvements. With most of the work falling on Daddy, we followed his directions, and did some amazing things. We helped him dig a basement out of the old root cellar, add three rooms to the back of the house, and build out three sleeping rooms under the eaves in our large attic. We also helped to repair the pasture field fence so our animals wouldn't escape, rebuilt a pigpen, and planted the fruit trees in the orchard. As things got easier we started to appreciate life here, but we still thought that living in Lexington, Indiana was the good life. There we were close to school, friends, and, most of all close to stores.

Whenever Daddy overheard us complain about our unfortunate move to this desolate area (according to us), he put us right to work. "You kids stop griping. If ya' ever want life to be better, ya' have to work for it. Now, hold up this board so I can get it nailed," the chores fell easily from his mouth. Sometimes he called on us to sit on the end of planks so he could saw them in half. Using the long handsaw that we watched him rub with linseed oil every night, he worked next to our bodies. It was slow, time-consuming work. I watched the muscle in his arm bulge while he moved the saw tediously up and down through the wood, sweat seeping from the corners of his brown hair. Because of him, we knew the difference between an eight-penny and a ten-penny nail. When he said, "Go to the tool shed and bring me a bucket full of those eight-penny nails," he got mad if you brought back the wrong size. Daddy only showed us something once and he expected it to take.

My brothers, Johnny age ten, Marcellus nine, and even Jimmy at age six, did most of the house and farm projects with him. Daddy only called me away from my chores with Mama when a lot of hands were needed. I enjoyed getting a chance to help with this exciting work. Watching wooden boards grow into walls and cabinets was much more interesting than doing dishes, sweeping floors, and changing diapers. When I helped Daddy, I felt that I had done something really important, like I did when Mama and I made dresses grow out of empty flour or feed sacks. Working on the improvements we made to our place allowed us kids feel an independence many kids didn't get to feel. We knew we were as necessary as adults and capable of doing anything we put our mind to.

It took a long time and lots of hard work by the whole family before our house became barely livable. Finally, last summer, Daddy added the room we'd begged for for so long – the indoor bathroom. "I have to do the most important jobs first," he explained to us without sympathy, "you can go to the toilet in the outhouse." Both he and

Mama had grown up with an outhouse and they really didn't consider a bathroom necessary – only convenient. Early in June he hired our neighbor Bud Singer to dig a huge cistern in back of the orchard. This was the first step toward getting our bathroom.

"We'll need a lot more water if we're gonna' get indoor plumbing." Daddy told us, as we watched the bulldozer grind deeper and deeper into the ground.

Mr. Singer joked to us from the seat of his dozer after he finished digging the twelve-foot by eighteen-foot hole. "When it's cemented on top you kids'll have a great place to play basketball." We didn't really care about that, but we held our breath when we thought about getting a bathroom. After the cistern was finished, Mr. Singer helped Daddy to put in a septic tank on the other side of the house. We all helped in digging the lateral lines for the drainage. Daddy stretched binder's twine on little pegs to measure out where he wanted the lines to go.

Buying the supplies for these household projects was expensive, it didn't matter that we did most of the labor ourselves. Daddy believed in only purchasing what he could pay for in cash. He even bought our house and car in cash. "My parents were strapped with debt at Gethsemane the whole time I was growin' up," he told us whenever we *tried* to beg him for anything that cost money. "It controlled our lives and I'm not gonna' have it!" He tightened his lips and walked away.

Daddy finally got enough cash together to buy the toilet, tub, and sink for this new luxury. Mr. Edsell came over and helped him hook up the plumbing and the electricity. Daddy's first words to us were, "Now don't you kids go hog-wild, and be flushing that toilet just to watch the water go down. Remember, we're still on well water, and there hasn't been a lot of rain this summer." We were so grateful for an indoor bathroom; we'd do anything he said. Seeing no reason to remove it, Daddy kept the outhouse in the orchard behind our cowshed. We used it when we worked outside, or if we were too impatient to wait in the line for the indoor bathroom. That line did seem to move awfully slow. It formed every morning and evening and several times during the day. Located next to the kitchen, the bathroom was the most popular room in the house.

Finally feeling that our life here was almost normal, I daydreamed about inviting some of my girl friends over to visit, once school started in the fall. So many things embarrassed me about our life here on this farm, particularly since most of the kids at our suburban school did not live on a farm. Some examples of the things I fretted over were: the constant flies that came in from the barn that was located close to the house, the bare bulbs that stung our eyes from the ceiling fixtures, the hand-crank pump at the kitchen sink, the caustic lye soap that burned our skin, the slop bucket that we kept in the kitchen corner to feed the pigs, and my smaller brothers and sisters constantly running around with smelly, dirty diapers. But, the part of our lives that I really didn't want anybody to know about was that we used an outhouse. I couldn't ask my friends over and have them use an outhouse! Imagine the teasing that would cause. I doubted that these suburban kids ever in their life had had to use an outhouse. Daddy said that the way we lived was our business and that our lives were as good as anybody else's. "Stop worryin' about what other people do!" he said when I complained about our embarrassing life.

****

Unimagined by me, this bathroom got me into a lot of trouble on this particular Saturday night in January. Several circumstances jarred us out of our usual routine. Mama was exhausted and went to bed early. We would be having company tomorrow, and she and I had worked all day getting the house and food ready for them. After Sunday Mass, Uncle Bud, Aunt Lena, and their nine kids would be spending the day with us. I was tired, too. Daddy, who always ate his supper later than the rest of the family, had usually eaten by now, but he was late in getting home tonight.

A neighboring farmer, Mr. Edinger, had finally decided to sell his land and needed some help in getting ready for his farm auction. Mrs. Edinger died the year before and he was ready for an easier life in town. Daddy joined several other neighbors and helped him lift and sort over fifty years worth of equipment and belongings. After the men finished the job, Mr. Edinger bought them all a beer at Bauer's. This made Daddy late in milking Calfie. Looking through the evening twilight out of the kitchen window, I saw his light burning in the cow shed, next to the barn. Through the drafty window, I heard Calfie

152

lowing in her stall, waiting as Daddy gathered up the milking stool and pushed the cold metal bucket under her full udder.

All the kids, except Johnny, who was already finished, were waiting in the bathroom line before going to bed. I'd been standing in line for at least ten minutes, crossing and re-crossing my legs to ease the discomfort in my bladder. *Heck, I'll just go out to the orchard and use the outhouse,* I pondered, impatience getting the best of me. Looking out the kitchen window again caused me to reconsider, as I watched the snowflakes thicken under the light over the barn door. *No, darn-it, it's January, and, besides, I'm next.*

Finally, Jimmy finished his turn and I jumped over the threshold. Before using the toilet, my reflection in the mirror over the sink caught my eye. Sighing, I started experimenting with different hairstyles, as young girls tend to do. In a few weeks I would be almost a teenager and I wanted to look like the girls at St. Bartholomew's. I pulled it up, then back, checking the mirror for the results. The only other mirror in our house was over my parents' dresser, but this one was so much nicer because Daddy had Mr. Edsell put in a light fixture above the sink.

****

Suddenly, a hand grabbed my wrist and flung me back out into the hall. Furious – I screamed. I hadn't even used the toilet! Marcellus decided his needs were more important than mine. This was it! Years of my parents' preferential treatment of the boys reddened my face. The heat of anger rose in my body. Because I was a girl, Mama's message to me about any argument had always been, "Deanna, it's the girl's job to be the peacemaker and besides, you're the oldest. You have ta' show the others how to behave," she'd say. Then, even worse, her instructions were, "If you don't argue back, the boys'll just go away. Don't let 'em get your goat!" I never found Mama's philosophy to work, but I did it out of respect for her wishes.

However, tonight neither one of my parents was close by. Temptation got the best of me, and I gave in to my anger. Venom throbbed in my muscles, giving me the strength to yank Marcellus right back out of the bathroom. Assisted by some unknown super power, I pushed him all the way down the hall, past our long kitchen table and the slop bucket in the corner.

My confidence soared! Without thinking, I shocked myself, letting my new boldness carry me away. Kicking open the basement door at the other end of the kitchen, I shoved him down the basement steps. I was so angry I didn't notice what I had done.

The other kids in the line were dumbfounded and stared at me with their mouths open when I returned to the line. Ignoring their complaints to, "Hurry up," I went back to my rightful place in the bathroom, and thought, *This is my turn and I'm gonna' take my time!* Steadying my pounding heart, I pressed my hands against the cool porcelain of the sink.

"Good enough for him," I grumbled. Still too angry to consider the consequences of what may have happened to Marcellus. *He's so mean he deserves to be layin' on the concrete floor in a pool of blood.* I pulled my shoulders up straight and re-assured myself that whatever I had done was justified, recalling the bible story about Jesus throwing the money-changers out of the temple. *I showed him! I'm not some seventy- pound weakling. Maybe now those two boys will leave me alone.*

Poor Marcellus, this night I got him back for all the things that both he and Johnny had *ever* done to me. "Oh well, it'll take a while before he can get up here and get me back," I mumbled to my face in the mirror, unconcerned. After using the toilet, I looked back into the mirror and returned to primping my hair. My blond friend Betty Lou always looked pretty, and even though my hair was brown and bushy, I parted it down the side like hers.

"Hurry up, Deanna. Come onnnn!" calls from the line outside the tiny room came in through the door, but I didn't pay any attention. "Yes, it sure feels good to take up for myself!" I spoke again to the face in the mirror. Humming, I used bobby pins to pile my unruly hair on top of my head. I admired the new me, even ignoring my freckles.

Suddenly, however, strange, new thoughts started coming up. Thoughts that didn't feel so good – thoughts concerning the consequences of what might have happened to Marcellus. *Where is he? He should be up here by now,* I thought, getting worried. *God's gonna' punish me for being so mean.* Guilt crept in and I started doubting my former conviction. *What have I done? What if I killed him?* My new sense of power turned to panic, and my heart began to pound again. The blue eyes in the mirror widened in terror. *What if I'm a juvenile delinquent?* Always a shy person, I never considered that I would ever be in a situation like this. Startled, I felt trapped. I had been reading about juvenile delinquents in the *Louisville Times.* They were *always* caught and they *always* went to jail. I panicked, my heart pounding harder. *I'll go to jail; I'll go to Hell at the very least! This is what I get for disobeying Mama and not letting Marcellus have his way in the first place.* Ignoring the smiles of relief from my younger brothers and sisters when I finally left the bathroom, I moved in a hurry.

No longer smug with self-satisfaction, I ran to Mama's room, scared to death. *God listens to her, and she needs me to help her run the household. She'll pray for me.* Mama had just gotten the youngest, Mary Ann, off to sleep in the baby bed – she looked very peaceful lying there in her bed, saying the rosary. I knelt down beside the bed and looked directly into her face.

"Oh, Mama," I sobbed. "I've just killed Marcellus! You have to pray for me and save me from Hell." Tears splashed on my hands as they pressed into the mattress alongside her body.

"I declare! You've done no such thing," she said, "Now, shush, you'll wake the baby." She shook her head like she knew a secret I didn't know.

My fear turned back to anger again. *Darn-it,* I bristled, *she never listens to me. Here I am desperate, gonna' burn in Hell for eternity, and she's not even hearing what I have to say.* Then Mama continued, "Settle down, Deanna, here comes Marcellus, now."

Turning around, I saw his silhouette in the last of the evening's pink glow coming in the west window. He shocked me, jumping out of my parent's closet, his face was frozen into an angry mask. I was relived to see him alive, until he came after me with both fists in the air. It seems he managed to catch himself on a shelf Daddy had just finished building at the top of the stair's second level. I didn't know about this shelf, but considering the possibilities of this night, I was sure glad it was there. Marcellus had grabbed the shelf and sprang back up the steps. While I returned to the bathroom, he snuck into Mama's room, only too delighted to tattle on me.

Now I was in for it – screaming, I pulled my bare knees up from my parent's cold linoleum floor and ran outside into the snowy yard. Marcellus followed close behind me. His feet slipped in the snow as he chased me through the front yard. The empty arms of our winter maple trees reached up into the twilight and prayed for my safety. Running from one tree to another, and slipping in the snow, myself, he easily caught me. We fought, the flakes falling all around us, without the benefit of our winter coats. Anger's heat warmed our bodies. Daddy finally came out of the cowshed and pulled us apart.

"Hey, you stupid kids, stop fighting in the front yard," he demanded. "What will the neighbors think!?" Neighbors were the last thing on our minds. Both Marcellus and I were black and blue, but he never pulled me out of the bathroom again. Mama's idea about how to handle arguments turned out to be false, as I suspected it was. However, I still had to do it to follow her wishes – I was still, and would always be a girl. *Would my life ever get any better?* I wondered.

Chapter 11

Pepsi Cola Days at Fontaine Ferry Park

The big day had finally arrived – like waiting for Christmas, it took a whole year! We'd been saving every penny of our tiny allowance, and had combed Hunsinger Lane, Hikes, and Taylorsville Road for pop bottles to return for their three cent refund, and also for Pepsi-Cola bottle caps. Our pockets jingled!

This Sunday would be Pepsi-Cola Day at Fontaine Ferry Park. (Louisvillians pronounced the name of this park as Fountain Ferry Park.) On Pepsi-Cola Day bottle caps could be used to help pay for carnival rides in the park. I was twelve years old and Jimmy was seven. Excited for weeks, Jimmy and I talked as we went about the farm doing our chores. "We'll go to the 'Hilarity Hall' this time. Johnny says your money goes further in there," I told him. My other brothers, Johnny, age eleven, and Marcellus, age ten, had lots of money because they mowed Aunt Ida's grass every week and caddied at Big Spring Golf Course. Aunt Ida (one of Grandma Anna's sisters), was one of Daddy's elderly aunts who lived in the West End along Broadway near Shawnee Park. The boys would be doing more expensive things than Jimmy and me, but we didn't care because everything was fun at Fontaine Ferry.

Fontaine Ferry was Louisville's most popular amusement park, having big city rides like roller coasters, Ferris wheels, and merry-go-rounds. Fun contests for prizes went on in the park all day long. And, most important to me was Fontaine Ferry's pony ride. The park had real ponies, provided by Aubrey's Dude Ranch. Aubrey's horse stables were located near Shawnee Park, which was close to the amusement park. That's what I really wanted to do, feel the wind in my hair, as I became a genuine cowboy. *I'm gonna' be like Roy Rogers and Trigger*, I daydreamed. Roy and his spunky wife,

Dale Evans, were my heroes. Much of my anticipation for this day revolved around my dream of feeling the power and freedom of being a cowboy.

Nothing moved fast enough! After Mass, Mama and I rushed through packing the picnic basket with the fried chicken and potato salad we fixed yesterday. Daddy kept things in financial perspective when he said, "No sense in buying food when we can bring it. We're not going to Fontaine Ferry for food anyway – we're going to enjoy the park," he continued, standing over the picnic basket as he spoke. "Josephine, be sure you and Deanna pack enough for the whole day!"

This is what Daddy said about every place we went. Johnny and Marcellus helped him pack our cumbersome army cooler with ice tea, water, and milk for the baby. Due to the polio scare of the '50's, it wasn't safe to drink out of public water fountains.

We wore our best Sunday clothes. "I don't want my kids to look like field hands." Mama reminded us. "And hold yur' shoulders back," she continued. The boys wore their Sunday trousers and white button-up shirts. Daddy did not believe in blue jeans or tee shirts, and his rules were never questioned. All of us girls, Margaret Jane age six, Theresa age five, Mary Ann, age two, and I wore dresses because it was the curse of being a girl in the early 1950's. I was a tomboy and couldn't stand dresses. *I don't wanna' ride a pony in a stupid dress!* I complained to myself.

Reading my mind, Mama said, "You may as well get that notion out of your head, Deanna. I declare, no daughter of mine is gonna' ride a pony and have the wind blow her dress up, and let everybody see her bloomers." 'Bloomers' was Mama's old fashioned word for panties. I didn't usually plan on being disobedient to Mama, but I knew I was going to ride my pony, I didn't care what she said, I'd just have to find the right moment. Mama looked pretty in her flowered smock and the navy skirt that concealed her ninth baby. She also wore summer pumps and a navy hat, other curses of being female. Her dark hair shone in the sun and I was sure she would be one of the most beautiful women in the park.

Daddy looked handsome in his summer-weight linen trousers and straw hat. He liked to wear white long-sleeved shirts with the sleeves rolled to three-quarter length. He chose a blue and yellow checkered tie. Like most farmers, he was tall and muscular. *Daddy's so handsome,* I thought, even though his brown hair was starting to thin. He was sometimes stern, but I was still proud that he was my father.

My mind flashed back to the days when Grandma was alive, *she looked so pretty when we went to Fontaine Ferry.* I remembered her in her Sears and Roebuck turquoise dress, proudly topped off with the white shell necklace Uncle Mac brought her from his days in the Pacific during World War II.

By nine o'clock, not too long after we finished breakfast, (having gone to early Mass), we took off for the long ride from Hikes Point to the West End. Fontaine Ferry was at the foot of Market Street, by the junction of Northwestern and Southwestern Parkway, and right next to Shawnee Park. Being eager to get there made the trip seem to take forever. Daddy couldn't stand noise in the car so we kids settled into watching the countryside turn into the city. We passed restaurants and stores and beautiful homes. Everything seemed to get bigger and we got more excited, as we got closer to the West End.

"Are we almost to Aunt Bertha's, yet?" Jimmy asked, knowing that she and Uncle Victor lived near Shawnee Park. "And Aunt Ida's?" he went on. Finally, we heard Daddy's announcement. Now, we knew we were around the corner from Fontaine Ferry. We couldn't help it, the excitement made the noise rise up in the car again.

"There's the Seven Gables Restaurant." He shouted over our racket. "I deliver Fehr's Beer there," he bragged, loving to talk about his work outside the farm. This restaurant was one of Louisville's finest eateries. According to Daddy, this place was named after a famous house in Salem, Massachusetts. I had no idea about this important house, but he made it sound like such a famous place that I always counted the gables to make sure they were not cheating on that name.

Immediately, the white twin columns came into view, and flashes of bright flags waved in the breeze over the colossal park entrance. The reverence in our car was almost church-like – eyes widened and mouths opened. Each one of us had visions of how to spend the day. Fontaine Ferry's front yard was filled with bicycles chained to benches and trees. Driving past the entrance, Daddy took us to the back fence of the last parking lot.

"J.H.," Mama said speaking to Daddy, "I declare, why do you have to park so far away?" Unconcerned, he said flatly, "You'll be glad we're not coming back to a hot car." He brought our '34 Chevy to a stop under a tree in the fence line. Everybody grabbed something to carry and we made the long haul back up to the front gate.

Our noses pinched at the strong smell of the pine mulch covering the entry area as we waited for our turn to get into the park. Other smells like cotton candy, hot dogs, and Caramel corn, came from inside the gate, luring us in and increasing our impatience.

The twin columns were only the front part of this immense building that was called the Entry Hall. The enormous ceiling was rounded, and open latticework arch supports were repeated several times every few feet down the length of the huge hall roof. Besides being the entrance, this building also contained many fun booths and games of chance. The ceiling arches had yellow light bulbs placed every few inches. Almost all the attractions at the park also had these rows of lights. They were lit in the evening to cut down on the mosquitoes that came up from the Ohio River on the northern end of the park. When the lights went on, the whole park look like a fairyland.

While we stood in the crowd, waiting to get inside, I noticed the Cracker Jack boxes stacked several rows high behind the entry gate, on the back counter. The red, white, and blue box with the little boy in the sailor suit fascinated me. "Toy in one end and nut in the other" was the motto of Cracker Jack. Uncle Mac always brought us some when he came to visit. The Caramel corn was tasty, but I'd eaten it before and decided to save my precious coins for more exciting ventures inside the park.

Daddy presented a bottle cap for each of us kids, and ten cents apiece for he and Mama to get inside the turnstile gate. We kids were all under twelve, (actually I was twelve, but even the honesty of my mother suggested I pass for eleven today). She made Daddy tell the lie to the attendant. Now, all of us kids got in free.

Slowly, we made our way past the many attractions of the Entry Hall. Carnival "hucksters" tapped their skinny reed canes on the cement floor and begged the crowd to spend money at their booths. "Come on up Sir, try your luck on our wheel of fortune – win a nice prize for your pretty wife." *Boy! Are they wasting time talking to my father,* I thought. Daddy did like the shooting gallery, but that was not in this area. What he wanted now, was to relax with a cool beer. I could see that look on his face.

Large numbered wheels like the wheels that St. Bartholomew's used for their summer picnics were everywhere. People put money down on different numbers and hoped to win a prize. But here, the prizes were not homemade cakes and pies like at church, they were much more exotic! Some of them were fancy glass dishes, painted dogs made of plaster of Paris, or Fontaine Ferry hats with red pom poms. One booth had poor, unfortunate canaries with saucers on top of their tiny cages. We begged Daddy to throw a nickel on them, knowing what a good shot he was. "Please, win us a bird!" We begged.

"Move-on you kids, don't you know they have those saucers waxed? No nickel will ever stick to 'em." Another booth had strange "rag mop" looking dolls that appeared easy to knock down for a Cupie Doll prize. I reached into my pocket for a nickel. "Don't waste your money on those Deanna, most of them have poles running up the middle – they won't go down," Daddy warned me. Then he reminded us, "I've told you kids until I'm blue in the face about how tricky they are down here." *Daddy's makin' that up – Fontaine Ferry wouldn't cheat us like that,* I thought, defending the park in all my innocence.

Then Daddy stopped all of us and looked directly into our eyes, and he mumbled in a low tone, "I'm tellin' you kids, again. There's all kinds of tricks they use in this park to get your money away from you." Then he said, even more seriously, "And be careful of pickpockets – they're everywhere! Now move on," he shouted. "We need to find a picnic table before they're all gone."

The left side of the entry hall housed an attraction called the Penny Arcade. Everything in that attraction cost exactly one cent. Sneaking a peek inside as we passed, I thought the many, small, hand-cranked moving-picture machines looked interesting. Jimmy caught my eye – *we'll be back here later in the day,* I could feel it, and my whole body tingled. Finally, we emerged from the long Entry Hall, and off we went to the picnic area by Kiddieland, which was the area of children's rides.

"I want to ride that," Theresa said about the little train going around Kiddieland. At least three of the other kids yelled, "Me too!" But Margaret Jane had her eye on the little boat ride.

"Well, I'll swan' – will you kids move on!" Daddy was exasperated.

"What baby stuff!" Marcellus and Johnny snickered. Because Aunt Ida's house was close by, they visited the park frequently after they finished cutting her grass. "We'll show you kids what's fun," they bragged, nodding at each other.

"We're not doing anything until we eat," Daddy reminded us, again. Carrying our load, we kept on walking, passing the "Test Your Strength" stand, and the "Guess Your Age or Weight," stand.

"How can they ever tell how much you weigh?" I made the mistake of asking Johnny.

"Deanna, if you had a brain, you'd run backwards!" he quipped back at me, shaking his dark head. "They're smarter than you'll ever be."

Boy, if we weren't in public, I'd let that smart-alec have it with both fists, my face reddened and snarled, but I did my best to control my temper. I knew better than embarrass my parents in public. Daddy might get fed up with us and march us back to the car. He'd done such things before.

I settled back into my appreciation of the park itself, enjoying the mature trees that made it nice and shady and the pea gravel that covered the ground and kept down the dust. I liked the buildings that housed the booths. They had the look of the Victorian Era and were all wooden and painted white with the same color of forest-green painted on the trim. The twin columns at the entrance were painted the same way. Daddy liked history, "This park was built in 1904," he announced as we walked along – but our minds were elsewhere.

Before finding the picnic area, we passed the "Mirror Maze." This attraction was 100 standing mirrors, turned in all directions, like a forest of mirrors. "Don't any of you kids go in there," Daddy warned. "You'll get lost and throw away your whole afternoon. His warning wasn't wasted on me. I moved fast past it. Johnny and Marcellus had done it many times.

"No, it's a cinch," Johnny mumbled to me. I ignored his boasting.

When we got to the picnic area, a balloon-blowing contest for the kids was being held. "Let's see who can blow up their balloon the fastest and win a prize!" the barker yelled to the crowd. The picnic area was cool and shady, and the tall maple trees were whitewashed half-way up their trunks, making it look very pleasant. Contests would go on in this area continually throughout the day. Daddy's plan was to station the family here for the whole day. He didn't like the rides and wanted to relax under the trees. The summer heat was already pressing on his mood.

"Johnny, hightail-it up there and grab that table by the beer booth. I want to see who delivers beer here," he shouted. But I knew what he really wanted – a nice cool bottle of Fehr's. He also liked to talk to bartenders and swap World War II stories with other beer patrons. Even though he didn't fight in the war because he was a full-time farmer, Daddy loved hearing about their European adventures. War talk also gave him a chance to brag about the medal his brother, Uncle Mac, won from his time fighting in the Pacific. "Beating the Japanese was important, too," he'd boast.

As we spread our noon meal, we watched an egg-rolling contest. This one was for adults only. Contestants knelt down on the ground and rolled eggs with their noses! Even women in dresses participated. All the women in the park wore dresses. Most of them had on smocks like Mama. I kept hearing on the radio that this was the postwar "baby boom" era.

We laughed so loud that eating was hard. I didn't care to eat chicken, anyway, but yearned for one of the tasty charcoal-smelling hot dogs from the little man in the white uniform standing across from us. "Hot dogs. Get your grilled hotdogs here," he shouted. I swallowed, knowing better than to torment myself with Daddy's food policies.

Finally, we were off to the rides. My parents stayed at the table. Spreading a picnic blanket, they were ready to relax. Mama liked watching the contests, and Daddy wanted a nap. A three-legged race was starting up just as we left. I took Margaret Jane and Theresa with me, Johnny and Marcellus took Jimmy and Tony. Mary Ann was only two, and stayed back for her nap with Mama.

The first thing I did was to take the girls to the bathroom. Even the Ladies Room was fancy. It was painted white with a long screened porch and tile floor. "Don't walk so fast Deanna," Margaret Jane screamed. Her blonde pigtails swung to the side as her head spun around. "We might get lost!" Theresa cried, holding her bigger sister's hand, her light brown hair blowing in the breeze. This huge crowd had the girls as scared as I was when Mama and Grandma first took me down here to the park, over six years ago.

I remembered to do for the girls as they did for me and said, "You two see this Ladies Room? If you get lost just ask somebody to show you how to get back to the Ladies Restroom. I will come here to find you." Now they felt better, and so did I, knowing that if they got lost, they would know what to do. The girls would both be together because that's the way they did everything. Now, I didn't have to worry so much about losing them.

First, I took the girls to the Novelty Stand and the Fish Pond. I wanted some new trinkets for my Roy Rogers T Bar V Ranch set, and thought this was just the place to get them since Hikes Point had no stores. I found some plastic figurines that could be used for Roy's cowhands and a tiny set of chickens for the barnyard. If I didn't get this stuff first, I knew I would spend all my money on the rides.

We only went for the rides that cost a nickel and a Pepsi-Cola bottle cap. Daddy gave me a little money to spend on the girls. For myself I used my allowance. Margaret Jane and Theresa got a big kick out of the boat ride in the Kiddy Area. We watched people throw coins for the duck pond with little yellow duckie's swimming around in watery circle. I joined them on the little train ride, myself, even though I felt silly there as a big twelve year old.

Mama wanted to join us for the ferris wheel and the merry-go-round. A "watermelon eating contest" for kids was going on in the picnic area when we went back to get her. Loving watermelon, I wanted to be in the contest. Mama put an end to that notion when she warned me, "Deanna, if you get that dress of yours messy, you'll have to spend the rest of the day back here in the picnic area with the kids." *I can eat watermelon at home,* I thought, and changed my mind instantly.

First, we went to the merry-go-round. Made in Germany, it was beautiful. Victorian murals of pastoral scenes were painted on the sides of the motor casing. Carved oval mirrors and laughing faces surrounded its top level above the murals. Lively, mechanical calliope music poured out from inside the machine. The circus melodies played constantly, putting the toe-tapping crowd in a happy mood. I noticed my own feet moving, too. *The people at Fontaine Ferry sure know how to make people feel good!* I told myself again, *they're not full of tricks like Daddy says.*

The convincingly carved and painted animals looked almost real to me. They all had saddles on them with a tall brass pole for the rider to hold on to. There were wooden horses, and wild animals like giraffes, jaguars, lions, and zebras standing majestically on the merry-go-round's huge wheel. "I love the music on this ride, Deanna, it's my favorite," Mama said as we helped the girls onto their animals. I chose a zebra, and she selected a nice safe chariot-styled bench that she shared with another lady who was expecting. They chatted during the whole ride.

Walking past the scooter cars to get over to the Ferris wheel, we saw Johnny and Marcellus inside. Driving separate cars, they bumped each other around like it was something they'd always wanted to do. Long metal connecting rods snapped electricity from the ceiling as they bumped and charged along. Jimmy and Tony were watching them from the fence. That didn't look like any fun to me. *The ponies are more my style,* I smiled smugly to myself.

After the merry-go-round, we had to go through the picnic area again to get to the ferris wheel. Weary, Mama decided to sit down and rest awhile. Of course, another contest was going on. Laughing ourselves silly, we watched the lady's "nail driving" contest. The ladies banged their hands, shook their fingers, and sucked on them. Most of them missed the nails completely. Then, I couldn't believe what I heard Mama say to me. "I bet you could drive a nail faster than that, Deanna." Her comment delighted me. In our farm family strength and accuracy were considered very important; and usually only attributed only to the boys. I sat up straight and pulled my shoulders back.

We stayed for the men's wheelbarrow race. The man in front had to walk on his hands while the man in the back held his ankles, wheelbarrow style. People loved to get into these contests because the park gave "Fontaine Ferry Medals," and the Pepsi-Cola sponsor gave the winner a wooden, twenty-four count case of Pepsi's. Cheers burst forth as contestants took their places. Those Pepsi's would taste awfully good for our picnic, but we couldn't interest Daddy in getting into the fun, when the barker begged the crowd for more volunteers. *His beers may have something to do with that,* I snickered to myself.

Picking ourselves up again from the picnic blanket, we took off for the ferris wheel. When the ride lifted us to the top of the ferris wheel we could see all over the West End, past the river and into New Albany, Indiana. Mama held Theresa on her lap and I held MaryAnn. Margaret Jane sat between us. Mary Ann squealed with glee and clapped her hands. The wind blew through her blonde curls as we sailed down the other side.

"This ride tickles my stomach!" Theresa giggled. Even though Mama was expecting a baby, the ride was gentle and didn't bother her. This was probably because she loved it so much. Besides, her baby wasn't due for quite a while, yet.

When we walked past the Caterpillar, she laughed, rubbing her stomach, "Now, I sure wouldn't wanna' be riding that!" On the Caterpillar, the kids squealed in delightful dizziness as it ripped around in circle after circle. We stood and watched a striped yellow, orange, and green canopy go up and over the riders. It looked very much like a huge version of the caterpillars I had to pick off our cabbage crop. Under the canopy, the girls screamed even louder as their beaus tried to steal a kiss from them.

Finally, we got to the part of the park I was seeking – Frontier Land. This was the location of Aubrey's Dude Ranch and Pony Rides. Frontier Land was the section of the park that was dedicated to all the little "buckerettes and buckaroos" who loved cowboys. In other words, every kid in the park! Frontier Land was surrounded by stockade fencing. On top the left side of the entrance was a huge painted cutout of a cowboy on a horse. Smiling, he threw a lasso at a running Indian on the right side of the entrance. At the back of the lot

I saw my dream ride – the Aubrey Dude Ranch Pony rides. I begged Mama, to the point of embarrassment, to let me ride the ponies. "I promise, I'll sit on my dress. I'll make sure it doesn't fly up." I pleaded, pointing to other girls who were successfully accomplishing this very thing. Mama didn't have the iron will of Daddy, and she finally gave in. Ready for a place to sit down, she found a wooden bench under a shady oak. The girls joined her while I tried my hand at my long awaited fantasy.

Now, I get to be a real cowboy, I told myself, tingling, as I thought of Roy and Dale again. When riding my bike down Hunsinger hill to the rock quarry, I pretended I was on a pony. But today I would get to feel real horseflesh beneath me. It was important for me to wait for Aubrey's fastest pony. He was very popular and I had to wait a long time for him. Plus, he cost a full dime – Aubrey stables had no use for Pepsi bottle caps. *Darn!*

While waiting my turn, I foolishly did a little bragging to Mama. I laughed at how silly all those sissy, city kids looked bouncing up and down on his quick little back. "That will never happen to me," I boasted, "I'm strong enough to hold him in." Now that my turn was finally here, I eagerly mounted the little chestnut pony, noticing his neck was covered in sweat. He had been working hard for Mr. Aubrey. While I was adjusting my dress and enjoying the smell of the leather saddle, all of a sudden he took off, yanking me off balance. Already, losing control of my mount, the same thing happened to me that had happened to the city kids. I bounced up and down on his back like the dasher in our butter churn, as he sped swiftly around the track. My long awaited ride lasted less than two minutes.

Getting down from the saddle, Mama said, "I hope you learned your lesson about making fun of other people." Dazed and embarrassed, I focused my eyes on the ground. Luckily, my little sisters were quickly distracted by a contest going on in Frontier land and didn't say anything about it.

The funny looking potato race was getting ready to start. Contestants held spoons in their mouths with potatoes on them. They could only look down because, if they turned their heads to either side, the potatoes would fall off and they would be kicked out of the contest. They looked so silly, we laughed until our sides ached.

Watching the contests were almost as much fun as going on a ride, and they were free. *Fountain Ferry sure knows how to make people feel good*, I smiled again.

Leaving Frontier Land, we heard music coming from the outdoor dance floor of Gypsy Village. This dance floor was for adults only. A polka was playing. We kids sat down on the grass while Mama found a shady spot on a crowded bench. Everyone watched the dancers. Mama's feet tapped to the music. I could tell she would rather be dancing than traipsing around the park with us kids. The musicians stopped for a break and the dancers stampeded the park. They could ride anything for free just by showing their Gypsy Village handstamp.

"Whew! I think I've had enough fun for awhile," Mama said, standing up and taking Mary Ann's hand. She did look tired. They went back to join Daddy at the picnic table. I didn't have much money left from the seventy-five cents I had saved. I looked around for something else to do that was free. The girls and I went inside the skating rink and stood behind the rail. Tall, standing fans blew loudly, their thick breeze making it cool in there. We watched the skaters and listened to the lady play the rollicking organ music that guided them into circles and dances on the slick wooden floor. Lulled into the beat of the music, we found ourselves swaying from side to side. I could make my bike go pretty fast, but these skaters whizzed by me so quickly that it was scary. I saw two of my friends from St. Bartholomew's, Betty Lou Lendin and Ann Watson, racing around the rink. Betty Lou's knee was already skinned. They waved at me as I stood outside the rail with Margaret Jane and Theresa.

When we turned back toward the picnic area, we watched young boys trying to impress their girlfriends at the "Test Your Strength" stand, and took a few minutes to watch how this worked. A pillar stood up about thirty feet high into the air. The participant slammed a sledgehammer down on the bottom of the pallet as hard as he could. A puck slid up the pillar to announce his strength to the audience. The scale went from 100 to 1000 points. If you hit 100 the announcement was "weak and wimpy," 400 was "not so hot," 700 was "macho." If you hit 1,000, the announcement said, "You're the champ!" *Mama said I was pretty strong*, I thought, my vanity starting to catch my attention. *I'll hit 700 at the very least.* But fingering my coins, I knew the Penny Arcade and the Hilarity Hall would be more fun. Besides, I had learned a little humility from what happened at the pony ride.

"Look at that!" Margaret Jane and Theresa exclaimed together, pointing at the cascading waterfalls of the swimming pool. "Take us over to see the pool," they begged, yanking my hand. Fontaine Ferry had the most beautiful swimming pool in the city. Swimmers went up tall ladders and slid down water slides. Diving off the diving board, they looked like swans. They were surely cooler than I felt in my sweaty dress.

You didn't need to bring a swimming suit with you to swim because all the pools rented suits. Most people didn't own such a luxury. Women bathers were required to wear swimming caps, they could be rented, too. Fontaine Ferry wanted to keep ladies' hair out of the pool's water filter. Looking at the different kinds of suits and caps was fun. Some caps had colorful pieces of rubber in the shape of flower petals. "Mama would look pretty in one of those suits with a little skirt," Margaret Jane said.

If her stomach was ever flat, I chuckled to myself.

Even if I had the money, I didn't want to waste time swimming and be stuck in one place. There was way too much to see and do at Fontaine Ferry Park. Besides, we swam plenty in the creek back home.

"Enough of this," I said. "Let's move on." I noticed that the hot sun was starting to get to the girls tender skin

They begged to ride the little airplanes hanging on long chains that went around in a circle. The sign said, "Lindy Planes" after Charles Lindbergh. I told them, "He was the first person to fly across the ocean." They didn't care much about that, and they ran for them as soon as the attendant let them in. When the little planes landed on the ground, the long chains that held them to the machine went slack, allowing new riders to enter.

I just had enough money left from the fifty cents that Daddy had given me for the girls, to pay for this ride. That is, along with the bottle caps, of course. Listening to their laughter, I watched the Tilt-A-Whirl ride located near by. My head swayed from side to side as I watched it go halfway forward and then halfway back all the while it traveled up and down hills and around in a circle. The riders screamed with such delight that I could feel it in my bones.

Seized by the fear that a pickpocket had gotten into my loot without my knowledge, I checked my coins and bottle caps again, pushing my hand deep into the pocket of my dress. Daddy said they were so fast and clever that you never felt them till the damage was done. With my money safe, I noted that there was enough left for the plans Jimmy and I had made before we got here today.

We girls continued to walk along the pathways, past lemonade, ice cream, and cotton candy vendors. Margaret Jane and Theresa begged for treats. "We're not at Fontaine Ferry to eat – we're here to have fun." I reminded them about what Daddy told us before we left the house. "If you girls are hungry, I'll take you back to the picnic table, where you can get something to eat." I didn't need to say any more.

Years ago I learned to talk myself out of the tasty-smelling treats that filled the park. I was still, however, always intrigued by the beautiful pink or turquoise fluffs of the cotton candy clouds – having never tasted one. I used to beg Mama for this pretty treat, but she always said, "That cotton candy might look pretty, Deanna, but it gets caught in your throat, and it will choke you to death!" Now, I just knew I would rather save my money for the rides. Quickly, I pushed the girls past the enticing smells coming from the concession stand.

"Let's go see the 'Comet,' they begged. This ride was famous as the world's largest wooden roller coaster. We had to walk almost all the way down to the river for it. The Comet was painted white with red trim, not white with green trim like the rest of the attractions. A huge octopus – it covered several acres!

When we got there, I pushed the girls into a shady spot because I was concerned about the sunburn that was developing on their faces and arms. We saw Johnny and Marcellus getting into the front seat. This was one of those rides that required the full price. *The boys have plenty of money,* I reminded myself. Jimmy held Tony's hand along the fence in front, waiting for them to get finished. I prayed they wouldn't get killed. There was no way I wanted to ride such a machine! Margaret Jane screamed at them but she was unable to get over the noise of the crowd, "Don't do it! You-all are gonna' be scared to death!"

Under my breath, I jealously mumbled, "Good enough for ya, and I hope ya' are!"

When they finished with the Comet, the boys joined us in walking down the avenue of trees. Suddenly, we were surprised and delighted by raucous laughter. Johnny and Marcellus knew what it was, but the rest of us started running.

"Hey you kids, stop that running – there's no running allowed in here," one of the many security guards stationed around the park shouted at us. Embarrassed, I knew this was a time when Mama would not be proud of me.

Red-faced, I apologized to the man in uniform, not wanting him to think that we didn't know how to behave in public. The walkway opened up and there it was – the Hilarity Hall. The loud laughter was coming from Hilarity Sam and Hilarity Sue standing on either side of the entrance to the enormous hall. A crowd stood with us. Everyone was enchanted by Hilarity Sam and Sue. The huge hobo figures, with their painted clown faces, laughed and rocked back and forth, as they welcomed everyone into the Hall. Margaret Jane, Theresa and Jimmy pointed at them and laughed, while Tony rocked back and forth with the figures. Many of the rides in the Hilarity Hall were really too dangerous for the younger kids. Mama wanted us to bring them back to the picnic table when we were ready for this attraction. Besides, they were tired and ready for a nap.

Free of the little ones at last, Jimmy and I ran back to the Entry Hall where we saw the Penny Arcade when we first arrived this morning. Putting in our pennies, we laughed at the antics of the Keystone Cops and Charlie Chaplin, and thrilled to the cowboy adventures of Tom Mix and Tex Ritter on the one-minute movie machines. These old movies struck me as out-of-date, but I enjoyed them just the same.

There were several human-size dummies made up to look like gypsies in large glassed-in cages. Across the top of these cages were requests like, "Let me tell your fortune" or "Show me your handwriting." Teenage boys and girls holding hands seemed to really like these booths. Smiling at each other, they pushed their nickels into the slots and hoped for predictions of their secure future together. There were strange signs of the zodiac drawn all over the cages. At that time, I was fearful that they were of the devil, and pushed Jimmy as we quickly ran past them.

The rest of our day was for the Hilarity Hall. It was gigantic with a thousand things to do, all covered by the entrance fee of twenty-five cents, just like Johnny and Marcellus had told us. First, we ran for the bucking broncos. These were mechanical iron ponies that gave you a fast ride back and forth. *I don't have to worry about my dress flyin' up on these,* I thought, recalling Mama's fears.

We saw Johnny and Marcellus going up the steps for the Alpine slides. There were two slides, the "Angel" slide and the "Devil" slide. They were both several stories high. Jimmy and I started out with the Angel slide. We must have gone up 200 dusty steps get to the top of the slide. Before we got on the steps an attendant handed us a scratchy burlap bag that had been sprinkled with dance powder. When we reached the pinnacle, we sat on the bag and folded it over our bodies from the lap down. Not only did this bag hold my dress in, it kept my bare legs from sticking to the wood. The dance powder on the bag made me fly down the slide. We loved the Angel slide and took several turns on it.

Finally, we decided to go for the Devil slide. It was much more popular and the kids screamed even louder as they went down this steeper slide. There were even more dusty steps to climb in order to get up to the top of the Devil slide. When we reached its top, and looked down, we were scared to death. Where was the bottom? All you could see was a big bump standing out at the top of the slide.

Looking at each other, our eyes wide with fear, no doubt about it , our courage was gone, neither of us wanted to go down that slide. The crowd behind us didn't care and shouted, "Hurry-up, slowpokes! Are you going to take all day – we want a turn, too!" Jimmy and I took our bags, turned around and slithered past all the others waiting in line on the narrow stairs. "Chicken! Chicken!" they taunted us as we passed them on the way back down. We were crest fallen scaredy cats, but we didn't care.

We knew there was plenty of other fun stuff to do when we got down to the bottom, and immediately went over to the Sugar Bowl. A large, round depression in the floor, the bowl's sides were covered in wooden slats. Only about fifteen people were allowed in it at a time. The attendant had everyone sit in the middle before he started up the ride. The centrifugal force of the spinning bowl sucked us from the center area and soon flattened us out on its large sides. Always scared of my dress flying up, this time I didn't have to worry. The powerful centrifugal force had it flattened on my skin, like a peeling on an orange!

After we collected our brains back from the powerful spinning, we walked across moving floor slats called the Turkey Trot. The slats jogged back and forth making it hard to stand up, especially in our dizziness. Even though there were rails to help out, people laughed as they stumbled along. These slats had to be crossed in order to get to the next attraction. Bumping into each other and also into total strangers, Jimmy and I finally made it to the Dinner Plate. To ride the Dinner plate, the crowd gathered in the middle of the large wooden disk. Some people linked arms with each other. The attendant made the girls sit cross-legged to fit more people into the eager crowd on the plate. Nervously, I pulled my dress under me as tight as I could.

When the wheel started spinning, it was impossible to hang on. Everyone was flung off to the floor. Strangers bumped into each other, laughing from the delirium. As careful as I had tried to be with my dress, when I stood up, hidden air jets in the floor made it fly up to my waist. All the girls, and even the women, screamed as theirs did the same thing. Men and boys pointed at us and bent over laughing at what they saw! Unbeknownst to us ladies, men hid behind cracks in the wall and when enough women stood over the jets, they turned them on. I was sure glad Mama was back at the picnic table.

Next, we found the Barrel, a large wooden cylinder about twenty feet long and six feet high, was the next attraction. As it rolled over and over, the challenge was to walk from one end to the other, trying to stay only on the flat part at the bottom. Mostly, people soon fell and just sat on the bottom as it spun over and over them. Jimmy and I joined the crowd sitting on the bottom. Some men and teenage boys stood spread-eagle with hands and feet clinging to the barrel's sides as it spun them over and over. We heard the squeals of laughter from their wives and girlfriends. When the barrel stopped rolling, we watched several people from the crowd run in and grab for the coins that had fallen from the pockets of these riders, before they were able to get their senses back. We finished our time in the Hilarity Hall by going down the Bumpy Slide. This was a series of about ten large, carpeted rollers placed in descending order going down a gradual incline. Our bottoms got sore, but it was a piece of cake compared to those other slides.

Johnny and Marcellus had long disappeared from us – to take in some more expensive stuff. After we tired of the hall, Jimmy and I decided to pool our last bit of money and share a cotton candy cloud. Eager to try its fluffiness at last, I said, "We'll take a pink one." The vendor took a long white paper cone that he ran around and around the large spinning aluminum tub, collecting feathery bits of pink cotton. Finally, a fluffy sugar cloud formed. All twelve years of my desire to taste the pretty treat came to my mouth at once. In my first attempt to eat it, I bit off too much, and it got caught in my throat. Just like Mama had always said it would.

Oh no! I panicked. *I'm chokin' to death!* It went down my windpipe, I couldn't breathe. A mother in the line behind us heard me gagging and banged me vigorously several times on my back before I coughed it up. After thanking her, I was disgusted with the cotton candy. Still red-in-the face from choking, I gave the rest of my share to Jimmy. He didn't seem to have a problem with it and was delighted.

Later in the day, we all gathered back at the picnic table for a supper snack. The little ones were tired but nobody was willing to leave the park. We knew Fontaine Ferry stayed open after dark and hoped our parents wanted to stay as much as we did. They had shared a pleasant day in the picnic area, relaxing. Daddy felt especially good after having a few cold beers in the hot August heat. *I like to watch Mama and Daddy have fun,* I thought, as they smiled into each other's faces, *they always work so hard.*

When the mosquito lights turned on, the yellow glow made the park look enchanted. We lounged around watching informal dancers gather on the bricks in front of the beer garden to the music of an accordion player. "J. H?" Mama cajoled Daddy, "Ask me to dance."

"No," he teased rubbing her belly, "You're expecting." Then he took her hand, leading her to join the other dancers.

We kids lay back on the picnic blanket under the stars and the glow of the mosquito lights as our parents glided across the brick dance floor. Their laughter made us mellow. I admired their movements and thought that it must be fun to dance.

Sadly, Daddy told us it was time to start back to the car. Picking up our belongings, we filled the bushel basket. Of course, there wasn't a scrap of food left. Johnny and Marcellus poured out the bits of ice and water left in the army cooler. Jimmy and Margaret Jane carried the bushel basket that we had used as our picnic hamper. Mary Ann slept on my shoulder and Daddy had the sleeping Tony on his. Johnny and Marcellus struggled along with the empty, but still heavy army cooler. Theresa held Mama's hand.

As we made our way back to the car, Daddy found his favorite booth, the shooting gallery, located next to the Skeet Ball Booth. Being a rabbit hunter, he was a crack shot and always won several prizes at this attraction. We watched him take aim at the rows of tiny metal deer, turkey, and duck silhouettes. They were attached to a slowly moving rotary chain that the attendant sped up as soon as he saw that Daddy was a good shot. It cost a dime for three shots, and no matter how fast the attendant set the chain, Daddy never missed. He won Mama some glass beads, a Fontaine Ferry plate, and a stuffed poodle for the future baby. His day was now complete. Our faces beamed as a crowd gathered around to watch his skill. The sharp shooting cowboys of the Wild West were nothing compared to *my* Daddy.

Continuing toward the parking lot, we watched the sunset gather over the river as dancing diamonds of light sprinkled the water. Passing the Old Mill Stream, we watched lovers get into the heavy wooden boats in order to go into its dark and mysterious moat. This attraction was also called the Tunnel of Love and was filled with intrigue. And, I later found out, mischief, as well!

The mischief was from teenage boys, called "Hoods." They caused the boats to pile up in the water by holding on to the supporting posts of the moat's roof from the boat in which they were floating. In the dark, the other floating boats collected together, instead of flowing downstream. These pile ups certainly put a damper on the romantic plans of most of the riders. On this night I heard angry shouting as we walked past the Old Mill Stream, and wondered why such a peaceful ride could make people upset.

Exhaustion made us walk slower, but it did not make us want to leave the park. We walked as slowly as we could. Daddy was mesmerized, remembering his childhood, when he, Uncle Mac, Grandpa Demetrius and Grandma rode the train to town from Gethsemane to Louisville. They spent the weekend with Aunt Bertha and Uncle Victor or Aunt Ida and Uncle Gus just to take a trip to Fontaine Ferry. Grandpa Demetrius had to get a neighbor to take care of the farm animals, like Daddy did tonight.

Satisfied with his winnings, Daddy allowed us to linger. Where he usually said, "Hurry-up you kids, ya' all er' slower n' Christmas!" He was quiet and he meandered, too. Luckily, Mr. Edsell was milking Calfie, so we really had no need to hurry. We enjoyed our last look at Fontaine Ferry for this year. Lightening bugs popped on and off, but we were too tired to chase them.

Suddenly we were surprised by the most unique attraction of all. Away from everything else, and under a huge sycamore tree, we heard the delightful sounds of a large self-standing German organ. It was powered by gasoline. Carrying our picnic stuff, we waddled toward it in our exhaustion. Surrounded by darkness, it seemed mysterious and we wanted to hear it better.

I'd seen this organ before, and hoped we would find it before we left this year. Being on wheels, the park moved it from place to place. I loved this organ, and remembered how much Grandma and her sisters, Aunt Ida and Aunt Bertha loved it, too. They swayed their rotund bodies to its haunting music, right in front of their unwilling husbands, Uncle Gus and Uncle Victor.

It was beautiful and about the size of a small car. The sides were cream colored and painted with woodland scenes, ornate carvings decorated the top. It was obvious to me that the same company that made it, had made the merry-go-round. Their style looked so similar. It never stopped playing, and unlike a Jukebox, you didn't have to put any money in. Daddy was intrigued with it, too.

"That's well-made," he said, walking over to touch it. We knew how much Daddy appreciated things that were well-made and took this as a sign that we could stay longer in the park – knowing he would want to check it out. Daddy liked to build things, if he could figure out how to build one of these; we would be the envy of Hikes Point. "I know this came from Germany," he said, crediting the German part of his heritage. "In fact, I bet this came from Alsace Lorraine," he continued. Feeling Daddy's contentment, we sat down and laid our burdens on the grass. As the organ played my parent's favorite waltz, *Over the waves,* we watched them dance again, this time under the moonlight.

It was a perfect ending to a perfect day!

Two views of O'Daniel Gethsemane farmhouse 1918-1946.
Now Thomas Merton Retreat Center called Bethany Spring

1904-Wedding of Anna
Hegenauer to Demetrius
(Dee) O'Daniel

1964-Wedding of Deanna O'Daniel
to Kenneth Costelle

1939-Wedding of Josephine
Boone to John H. O'Daniel

Dee O'Daniel, (hands on hips) at Gethsemani Abbey helping with
Voting Day-1928

1920's Backyard at Gethsemane home: From left: Dee, Aunt Ida
Brakemeier, Aunt Rose, Grandma Anna, Uncle Gus Brakemeier

JH O'Daniel, Mama, Deanna age 3 months at Gethsamane,Ky.-1941

Grandma Anna headed to the spring for water-1940s

1945 Gethsamane, Ky. Back left: Marcellus, Daddy, Uncle Victor Packwood, Mary Jane Packwood, Aunt Bertha Packwood, her favorite dog, Deanna holding doll.

1940s Aunt Gen and Uncle Mac

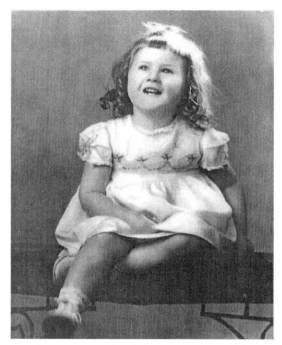

Deanna O'Daniel age three-1944

Johnny and Marcellus ages 3 and 2 -1945

Mama's birthplace and childhood home in Howardstown,Ky.

Howardstown Store, formerly Howard's Mill

1930's-Sam and Sudie Howard and their 10 children. Grandma
Lucy is woman on left. Uncle Virgil is man behind Sudie(woman
with necklace), Uncle Linn is young man between Sam and Sudie.

Josephine Boone (Mama) and her
sisters-1930s. Left: Saloma, Josephine,
Mary Cora, Aurelia

Emanuel Boone,
1907 – Mama's
father

Josephine's brothers-1930s left: Cyril, Irvin,
Edward, Garland, Leon. Bud in service at the time.

Riding Old Jack back to the barn. Left:Johnny, Deanna, Marcellus

1946-Goldsmith Lane, left: Marcellus,
Johnny, Jimmy in stroller, Deanna

Deanna, Age 6 First Grade-1947

Goldsmith Lane, Deanna holding Theresa, Margaret Jane standing

1950-Wedding of Aurelia Boone to Earl Cecil

Uncle Ed and Aunt Lila-1954

1954-Emanuel and nine of his ten children. Back row left: Garland,
Bud, Irvin, Emanuel, Saloma, Aurelia, Josephine, Mary Cora.
Front left: Cyril, Ed (seated) Leon took picture

1968-Mama and her siblings after Emanuel's funeral. Front left:
Mary Cora, Aurelia, Ed(seated), Josephine, Saloma. Back left:
Garland, Bud, Cyril, Leon Irvin

1950s-Daddy, Tony, Margaret Jane, Theresa

1953-Tony's First Communion, Left: Mary Ann, Theresa, Tony,
Margaret Jane, Jimmy

Billy and Pat, 1964 just before
the move to Alta Aveune

Phillip, age 9, holding
Snowball-1964

1964-Alta Avenue, Phillip pulling
wagon, Pat, dog, Billy

Our Hikes Point House on Hunsinger Lane 1949-64

Our home on Alta Avenue-1964-2001

O'Daniel Siblings 1974. Left front: Bill, Pat, Mary Anne, John. Middle left: Theresa, Margaret Jane, Deanna. Back left: Phillip, Tony, Marcellus(Morris) Jim

Chapter 12

First Time in Charge

Summertime fun was over, we were back in school. It was fall of 1953 and I was twelve years old. Mama would be having her ninth baby soon. All of us were eager for that, but I was nervous about her leaving. This would be my first time to be in charge of the household while she was in the hospital.

****

A clear, crisp autumn day found me slamming my schoolbooks down on the dining room table as I came in from St. Bartholomew's where I was in the seventh grade. Hearing humming coming from the kitchen, I found Mama on her hands and knees scrubbing the red and gray squares of our linoleum floor. *She oughten' be doin' that,* I thought. Mama had been more sickly than usual during these last few weeks of 'waiting.'

"I feel so energetic!" She smiled up at me, her blue eyes sparkling. "I got a lot 'a work done today!" Accomplishments always excited Mama and she went on, "Now, you know this baby's due in three weeks, and I don't wanna' to leave you with all the work. You'll have enough ta' do just keepin' those boys in line!" She laughed, as she beared down on her scrub brush again, her belly swishing from side to side.

Daddy usually got Mama's cousin from Howardstown, named Dorothy Mae, to take care of us when she went to the hospital to deliver one of her babies. But now Dorothy Mae was married with kids of her own. Mama warned me this was coming up when she told me last spring, "Deanna, at twelve years old, you're old enough to take care of things while I'm gone for a few days. My mother had all her kids at home so I was in charge much younger than you are at twelve."

Fearfully, I had been watching Mama's stomach grow since she told me about this plan. Every time I thought about being in charge while she was at St. Anthony's Hospital, I shuttered. However, on this day, it seemed that three weeks was long time away. *I got plenty a' time to learn how to do what I don't know,* I considered. *Tomorrow, I'll watch how Mama starts everything.* I always knew what to do once things got started because we did the same tasks every day.

Right now though, I just wanted to be free of my afternoon chores so I could get back to reading my latest novel, *Little Women,* by Louisa May Alcott. Spunky Jo March showed me the way I wanted to be. This book was so popular in my seventh grade class, I had to wait three weeks for it.

Running to the basement, I grabbed a clean bushel basket from the pile stacked in the corner and went to the orchard to collect the dry clothes. Our dog, Bullet, left his favorite spot behind the water pump and bounced along beside me. *Mama's been feeling good today,* I chuckled, *she must a' washed everything in the house.* The balmy October breeze dried the cottons to that "crisp linen" smell that I loved so much. Unsnapping the clothespins, I threw the clothes in the basket as I took them off the line.

My little sisters, Margaret Jane and Theresa, ages six and five, followed along. Mama had sent them out to give me a hand. Grabbing the ones they could reach, they giggled and chased each other, their light brown hair blowing in the breeze, as we worked. After folding and sorting the clothes, we then put them away in everybody's chest of drawers. Finishing the task quickly, I stole a few minutes and got back to my novel. Snuggling deep into the cushions of our fuzzy upholstered chair in our dining/family room, I gratefully jumped back into the lives of Jo and her sisters in the March family, before Mama called on me to help her fix supper.

****

The next morning I got a scary surprise when I heard Daddy's voice boom up the stairwell. "Deanna, come on and get up outta' that bed, and get on down here – you gotta' get the biscuits going." His urgency replaced Mama's usual calmness, he continued, "And, get those other kids up outta' their beds while you're at it."

At 5:30, my usual time to get up, it was hard to roll out of the warm cozy bed I shared with Theresa, and into the unheated upstairs bedroom. I knew the others would grumble, too, when I shook them. *Oh-oh, what's going on?* I wondered. *Where's Mama?* Usually, she didn't have me call for the little ones until after I had the biscuits in the oven.

The autumn frost made our rooms under the eaves nippy. Shivering, I removed my nightgown. Daddy's frugal policy on the heat was that he refused to turn on our oil furnace until November unless there was a snowstorm. Sadly, we no longer had the toasty potbelly stove in the dining room that we used to dress in front of, anymore. Putting on my navy blue school uniform, I shook Theresa and Margaret Jane. Johnny and Marcellus had heard Daddy and were already climbing into their bib overalls. They roused Jimmy and Tony.

"I'm taking your Mother into the hospital today." Daddy told me as I descended the stairs. "The baby's early." His face was strained and his voice seemed nervous. Going into the kitchen, I half-heartedly started breakfast, feeling pretty scared with this new development. Slicing a piece of jowl bacon for each of us, I then filled the syrup container with "Bob White" molasses. Starting the biscuits, I sifted the flour and cut in the lard for the six-dozen biscuits we had every morning. *Oh heck,* I wondered...how *much baking powder goes inta' these biscuits?* I could ask Mama, she was in the other room, but that would show her my ignorance, and I couldn't do that – how could trust me while she was gone? *I can't remember anything!* I panicked, but I tried not to be anxious as I waited for the rest of the family to appear.

Margaret Jane and Theresa stumbled down the steps, already dressed for school. Still sleepy, they set the breakfast dishes on the red and yellow flowered oilcloth that topped our fourteen-foot-long kitchen table. Johnny and Marcellus, anxious to get out of their work clothes were already out feeding the pigs and filling up the water tub for the cow. Jimmy was in the hen house doing the morning care for the chickens.

Daddy milked Calfie while I made his coffee. I didn't know how to make coffee so I copied what I saw Mama do everyday. During the week she just added another scoop of grounds to those in the pot and put in some more water. Always thrifty, Daddy thought the grounds could get more than one day's use. On Sunday she poured out the whole mess and started the new week with a fresh pot. The kitchen soon filled with the comforting coffee aroma. The perk of our aluminum coffeepot chirped beside me as I finished frying up the bacon.

My mind started to wander again, *Could I ever be as brave as Mama?* Me, who cried over the thorn that poked its way through my bare foot down by the creek last summer. I even had to be carried home by Johnny and Marcellus – that was humiliating.

"You've got to be a lot tougher than this to be a woman, Deanna," Mama said to me that day, rubbing the stomach that contained this, her ninth child. Now, she was bent over in pain and dressed for the hospital. Her familiar leather suitcase was packed and leaning against the front door.

Popping the last pan of the biscuits into the oven, I again hoped I had made the batter right. While they baked, I helped Mama get Mary Ann, the baby, age two, and Tony, age four, dressed and ready to go to Mrs. Edsell's. The Edsells were our wonderful next-door neighbors who helped us out many times. Today, Mrs. Edsell would keep the young ones while I was at school.

The house began to have that welcoming, "Good Morning," smell of fresh baked bread, as the biscuits browned. Glancing into the oven, they looked good, and I started to feel comfortable again. "Stop daydreaming, Deanna. Better get those biscuits out before they burn," Mama said, pulling my brain back into the room. She stumbled around, gathering clothes as she finished packing the black baby satchel for the little ones. It went to Mrs. Edsell's along with the kids. Mary Ann was still in diapers and took the bottle to go to sleep for her nap. Mama tried to muffle her moans, but I heard them. She wasn't one to direct attention to herself, but I could tell she was in pain.

Doubting my abilities, I asked, "How am I gonna' do all this stuff that you do Mama?" Hoping I could loosen my fears.

Smiling at me from her chair, she reassured me saying, "You know how ta' do everythin' I taught ya'. You' been doin' it all your life. Don't worry, I'll be praying for ya.' Now, you be sure to make those boys mind ya.' Daddy's going to whip the tar out of 'em if they don't. But, <u>you</u> gotta' be the one to let him know!"

My face twisted. *Boy, Mama don't know half of it.* Since I was ten years old I'd kept the kids on many occasions. Tattling on the boys seemed simple enough, but when I tattled they got me back. They slugged me in the stomach where the bruises didn't show, and they called me a tattletale. I didn't like that, either, because it made me feel like I couldn't handle my duties as the oldest girl.

Mama continued, "Now, don't cha' forget to pick up Mary Ann and Tony from Mrs. Edsell's on yur' way home from the bus this afternoon." The Edsell's farm was the closest one to us. Mrs. Edsell had no children and welcomed any opportunity to watch the little ones. All the rest of us eight kids were in school. I was in the seventh grade, Johnny the sixth, Marcellus the fifth, Jimmy the third, Margaret Jane the second and Theresa the first.

Daddy grabbed a quick cup of coffee while he changed from his farm clothes. He looked handsome, appearing in his Fehr's Brewery navy twill uniform – he carried his authority well. He stood tall, his wavy, but thinning brown hair caught a glint of the morning sunshine that was coming in through the side window. Looking at all of us sitting around the breakfast table, he said briskly, "Alright you kids, now Deanna here is in charge while your Mother's in the hospital. You better do what she tells you to. If I hear of a one of you that doesn't, he'll wish he did what he was supposed ta' do when I get home!" He looked straight at Johnny and Marcellus when he made that last remark. They looked at each other.

My parents left and took Mary Ann and Tony with them. Panic set in immediately, I felt totally isolated. But, needing to show a strong front, I wasn't going to let the other kids know how scared I was. Instantly, the boys started making fun of my biscuits.

"These biscuits are as hard as rocks," complained Johnny, totally ignoring Daddy's warning to behave. Shaking his dark head for emphasis, he threw several on the floor.

"You expect us to eat stuff like eat this?!" Marcellus chimed in, and said, "I'm gonna' get some of the white bread," as he moved toward the cabinet. Jimmy glanced at me with a look of sympathy, but this was not enough to sway the attention of Johnny and Marcellus. They thought they could do whatever they pleased when I was in charge.

"Oh brother," I sighed as a familiar feeling of defeat crossed my mind.

An immediate fight broke out. The white bread was for school sandwiches, which still had to be made. There wasn't enough white bread for both breakfast and lunches for six school children. With as much strength as I could muster, I reminded them of Daddy's comments about my new authority. Disgruntled, they settled back into their biscuits. I didn't have time to eat, so I didn't really know if the biscuits were bad or not. But, I believed them, and told myself that tomorrow I would cut more lard into the batter. Now, we were busy getting ready for school and still had to walk the quarter mile down Hunsinger Lane to the bus stop. Being the only kids that lived this far away from Buechel, our bus driver turned the bus around and drove on back to St. Bartholomew's if he didn't see us standing up at Bauer's.

I was suddenly distracted from this daydream by another fight. This one was over whose turn it was in the line for the bathroom.

"Johnny's lying, I got into line before he did and he jumped in front of me." Marcellus screamed, his blond head moving from side to side and his fist in the air. Johnny faced him, his body rigid and squared off.

"Go ahead, move me, just try it!" He dared. Their anger frightened me and my shoulders jumped up around my ears. Totally guessing at what to do, I settled this quarrel by putting Jimmy in front of both of them.

"Now, you've both lost your turn and if you keep arguing," I threatened, "I'll put the girls in front of you, too!"

Quaking in my boots, I was afraid they would both attack me at once, but they backed off. Ruling these boys was not easy. They did what Mama said because they loved her, but they hated me. I was less than a year older than Johnny and smaller than both of them. Besides, I was in their words, "Just a dumb girl." *It's a curse to be the oldest!* I complained to myself.

My day at school was distracting. I couldn't concentrate on anything but the situation at home. Jumping off the school bus that afternoon, I headed to Mrs. Edsell's for the little ones. They were having such a good time with her, they weren't particularly glad to see me.

"You don't have to rush off, Deanna," Mrs. Edsell said. "Sit down and visit a spell," she continued, motioning to a chair in her living room. I decided to agree with her.

"I've been praying for your mother today," she told me. "You know she's a real strong woman, I'm sure she'll be okay." These were the words I needed to hear. Mrs. Edsell was a very calm person. I didn't want to leave, but I was getting nervous about all the things that had to be done at home, so I made an excuse to go.

"They sure are sweet children." She said, giving each of them a lollipop for the trip home. She gave me one, too. "Now Deanna, you be sure and call me if you need anything," she continued. I loved Mrs. Edsell. She always remembered to say the nice things that Mama didn't even have time to think about. Letting Mary Ann and Tony run down the back steps of her yellow brick bungalow, I juggled my schoolbooks and the baby satchel. She also gave me eight pieces of hard candy to share with the rest of the kids after supper. I hid them in my pocket.

"You bring those little ones back up here in the morning on your way up to the bus stop," she called after us as we trudged through the large cornfield that separated our two houses. The dried autumn stalks crunched beneath our feet as we stumbled along. Mary Ann and Tony enjoyed their orange lollipops as we struggled through the field. Bullet ran out to greet us from our backyard, enjoying chasing at the blackbirds that swooped down for leftover corn laying in the field from last week's harvest.

Being in charge meant I had to make sure the boys did their chores of caring for the animals and doing anything special that Daddy might have told them to do before he left for work in the morning. These were orders like bringing in any ready vegetables from the garden, or putting the hogs into separate pens, or moving the cow to a different part of the pasture. Today he wanted them to pull up some turnips and gather some kale. He also told the boys that he wanted them to work less at the golf course this week, so they could be around the house to help me more. *Is this a good idea?*

I doubted it, but I knew Daddy's heart was in the right place, and I appreciated that.

Because I was the only one in the house with the little ones and fixing supper, they had to do my afternoon chores of feeding and watering the chickens, and cleaning up their messy coop. Not used to this unpleasant task, they naturally they balked about it. *Who do I think I am, expectin' these boys to do what I tell 'em?* My face twisted as I laughed at myself.

The hens pecked at their hands when they collected the eggs from under them. I heard the boys' squeals from the hen house and I snickered because by <u>now</u> I knew how to approach the hens, and they didn't peck me anymore. *I'm not so dumb afterall,* I thought, wishing I could convince the boys of that.

That morning, I had been nervous about preparing the biscuits by myself, but tonight, I was really doubtful about getting supper. I knew the boys would complain, no matter <u>what</u> I fixed. I wanted to impress them about deserving to be in charge, after all, I had been helping Mama all of my life. Feeling like I deserved a little credit, I didn't realize that this was <u>not</u> the place to find it! Watching Calfie, our Guernsey cow, lazily chew the pasture grass as I worked at the kitchen sink, I tried to remember what I knew how to cook without any help. The Pet Milk commercial on the radio that said, "Our milk comes only from contented cows," crossed my mind and I started to envy Calfie. I grumbled, "Wish I was a cow... Why do I have to be the oldest, and a girl?" I sighed loudly about my double stroke of bad luck.

Coming back from my daydream, I recalled what Mama said to me before she left this morning, and told myself that I should know how to fix anything that Mama did. However, it was not until this moment that it occurred to me that she never really showed me how to do anything from the start. I just did what she told me to do. *I'm only good at following directions,* I realized – this thought scared me to death! I knew how to open the jars of the food we canned over the summer. But, what if it was spoiled!? *I know there can be some kind a' germ in canned food that makes you go blind and get paralyzed,* my hand quivered. *How can I tell if it's bad or not?* Mama always knew automatically, although I never saw her throw anything out.

Examining my memory from last summer, I hoped that I had scrubbed out and scalded those mason jars well enough when we did the caning. Mama and I put up at least 500 quarts of tomatoes, beans, corn, beets, pickles and sauerkraut. The basement was full of food for the winter. But the truth was that I hated that scrubbing job and rushed through it, envying my brothers who were finished with their chores and already down in the woods swimming in the cool creek. Mama had promised me, "Deanna, when you're finished sterilizing those jars, you can go join the boys." Naturally, that was all I was thinking about. Now, I was worried that I may have been too careless.

"I will have to pray about that." I mumbled to myself, guilty for my summer sins. *What'll happen if I poison the whole family?* Then I hit on an idea. *Jimmy can help me figure this out.* He was a sensitive child and much smarter than his seven years. We would both smell the food and taste it. I would hear what he had to say about it. Always honest, Jimmy didn't try to scare me to death like Johnny and Marcellus.

While the boys were out doing their chores that afternoon, Daddy called me on the phone. Something in his voice told me that things were not right. "Tell Johnny to milk Calfie tonight," he said, wearily. "I'm gonna' stay here at the hospital with your mother. Put my supper on the hotplate (a special steam plate we used to keep Daddy's food from drying out), for me to eat when I get home." I gulped when I realized I was going to have to be in charge during another meal. I had hoped he would be here to help me manage the boys.

Trying not to think about that, I went back to fixing supper, slicing off a piece of pork shoulder for each of us and two for Daddy. As the meat crackled in the heavy, iron skillet, I opened up a canning jar of green beans and one of sauerkraut and put some potatoes on to boil. *This is enough for supper,* I thought, sneezing as the pungent kraut stung my nose. The kitchen started smelling like sauerkraut as I cooked it with some bacon grease we had stored in a can that we kept on the stove. Calling Margaret Jane and Theresa in to set the table, I calmed down as they sang and tossed dishes across the table to each other as they did their work. *Now, they have the right idea,* I thought. The girls got along well and respected me; it was fun to have them around. Pouring each kid a glass of milk, they set it by their plate. Soon, we were ready to eat. Leaning out the kitchen door, I rang the dinnerbell. The boys marched in from the barn and smelled like they had brought the barn into the house with them.

Their criticism came quickly enough. "Deanna, do you expect us to eat this slop? I wouldn't give this to the hogs!" Johnny and Marcellus both complained as they entered the back door. They hadn't even tasted anything! Acting nonchalant, I ignored their remarks, but they cut me deeply.

Taking the bucket of Cafie's warm milk from their hands, I strained out all the flies and pieces of straw with a strip of cheesecloth. Then, I poured the milk into the heavy stoneware crock, and put it in the refrigerator to "mend." By morning it would be okay to drink. Somehow, we thought that the coldness of the refrigerator killed all the germs. Luckily, none of us ever caught anything from dirty milk.

"Did you take care of the chickens for me" I asked Johnny, trying to re-establish my power.

"Go and look for yourself," he smirked at me. I had to again remind him of my authority. He bristled, but settled. "I'm gonna' tell Daddy how mean you are!" He threatened. Johnny always had to get in the last word. But I didn't care, I was used to that and ignored him.

The kids sat in their usual assigned places at the table. I lead the grace. The meal seemed quite content, now that the complaints were out of the way. At the end of the meal I passed out the candy from Mrs. Edsell and everyone fell into their after supper chores. Jimmy scraped the dishes, wiped the oilcloth clean, and swept the floor. Margaret Jane washed the dishes and Theresa dried them.

We put all the dinner scraps, plus the dishwater itself, into the slop bucket in the corner of the kitchen. Daddy said the hogs liked the dishwater because we did our dishes with lye soap and that helped to fatten them up. Never mind what it did to our hands! Then Johnny and Marcellus took the stinky bucket out to the pigpen for the hogs to enjoy. By the end of the day it was heavy. I silently admired how strong they were. I was always embarrassed that our family even had a slop bucket. My job was to fix Daddy's supper on the hotplate and to repackage the leftovers for the refrigerator. Glancing at my brothers and sisters, I was proud of them all for doing their evening chores without a fuss – this almost made me feel a mother myself.

It was time for homework. Johnny, Marcellus, and Jimmy worked together and so did Theresa and Margaret Jane. I did my own and was around to keep order and answer any questions. Sometimes Johnny had a better answer for their questions than I did and that was fine. For an hour the dining room table buzzed with homework talk.

Mary Ann, feeling lonely for Mama, sidled up to me. "I want my mama." She whimpered. Taking her to her babybed in my parent's bedroom, I changed her diaper. The baby powder smelled sweet as I sprinkled some on her tiny bottom. Bringing her back into the dining room with me, I put her on my lap and stroked her hair while finishing up my arithmetic lesson. Tony loved Jimmy and sat on the floor leaning his little brown head up against Jimmy's chair. He held his raggedy teddy bear, the same one he took to Mrs. Edsell's. It went everywhere with him.

After finishing my homework, I got the little kids ready for bed, sitting both of them up on the kitchen counter and using the kitchen sink to wash off their faces and hands. The others listened to "Abbott and Costello "on our little brown Motorola and started taking their turns for the bathroom. The routine went much better that night than it did that morning. They were all tired and there were no fights. Having the radio on made it seem like there were other adults in the house.

"Mama is at the hospital bringing you a new little brother or sister to play with," I explained to Mary Ann and Tony as I brushed through their curls. "And tomorrow, you get to go to Mrs. Edsell's again."

"Yay," they said at the same time. "She's nice to us and gives us candy! We love Mrs. Edsell."

"I love her, too." I said, continuing to brush their hair. They didn't take baths tonight because it was not Saturday. We were on well water and only took full baths on Saturdays.

I stayed up till nine o'clock waiting for Daddy. Sure my new sibling was born by now, I was curious to see what sex it was. Mama always said, "I don't care if the baby is a boy or a girl, so long as it's healthy." But I cared, I was sick of bossy boys, and wanted it to be another sweet little girl.

****

By the time Daddy came home it was raining hard. He was in a somber mood. I never had much luck in talking to him and was embarrassed to approach him now, but my curiosity made me persevere. We had always communicated our needs by way of Mama. I noticed he did not have his usual proud smile at the birth of a new child. His eyes looked down, his tone was heavy. "Get my supper heated up," he said without looking at me. His tone scared me, *something's not right*??? I pondered.

It took all my shy courage, but I managed to push out the words, as he sat down. "Daddy, was it a girl or a boy? How much did it weigh?" Going through all Mamas' pregnancies with her, I almost felt the pains – somehow they nearly seemed like my pregnancies.

Daddy's face was drawn. It was obvious that he was tired. He stared across the room and didn't answer me. Then he changed the subject. "Did you tell Johnny to milk that cow like I told you to?"

By now I was getting scared and stammered, "But, but..., what about Mama? What about the baby?"

His voice fell on me like lead, "It was a girl, weighin' nine pounds – born dead this morning," he sighed and let his eyes drop down to the table.

My heart jumped into my mouth and tears of fear automatically came to my eyes.

"Is Mama okay?" even though my voice shook, I didn't want Daddy to see my tears as I reached over to fill his coffee cup.

What I saw next really shocked me. Daddy's head sunk to rest on his folded arms that lay on the table. Looking at the bald spot at the back of his wavy brown hair, my fears choked me. I had never seen this before, *he's not gonna' tell me*. This thought scared me even more because I knew that Mama had lost her own mother in the delivery of her tenth child. *Daddy can't face it*, I panicked.

"D-D-Did Mama die, too?" I stuttered, afraid of the answer.

"We almost lost your Mother, too," Daddy said, slowly raising his head, clearing his throat, but keeping his eyes lowered. "Gangrene had already set into the baby. Dr. Duncan had to pull it out. He told me the baby died two weeks ago – the cord wrapped around her neck. It's a miracle your Mother's alive at all – she'll be in the hospital longer this time. She's real weak." Then, as if he realized he was telling all these intimate facts to a child, he pulled his coffee cup up to his lips and changed the subject.

"I'll be late tomorrow night, too. Tell Johnny to milk the cow again, and iron me another uniform when you get home from school tomorrow. Now go to bed." By now his head was again resting on his folded arms on the table.

With this terrible news, I knew sleep was impossible. My former excitement turned to worried tears as I climbed into bed next to Theresa. We both got out of bed and knelt in prayer for Mama. I didn't tell her anything except that we needed to pray. Tense, we both got back under the covers and waited for the patter of the rainfall on the tin roof above our heads to distract us into slumber.

****

All too soon it was 5:30 in the morning and Daddy called up the stairwell. I went down to fix the biscuits. It felt good that it was Friday. The rest of the kids stirred into their morning routines. When everyone was settled around the breakfast table, Daddy told all of us the bad news. There was a hush over our usual lively breakfast chatter.

"I think we should say the rosary for Mama tonight." Jimmy mumbled through his tears. Nobody spoke, the sad news about Mama and the baby, dampened our usual Friday mood. Everyone was more cooperative today. The difference between their actions today after Daddy left, than yesterday amazed me. Johnny and Marcellus even helped me fix the kids' school lunches.

After school, when I came to gather the little kids from Mrs. Edsell's, she told me how sorry she was that Mama had lost the baby. Daddy called her earlier in the day on the telephone. She gifted me again with the eight pieces of hard candy. I hid them in my pocket and we trudged through the cornfield, the blackbirds jumping into flight before us as we walked along.

After finishing an after-school snack of some biscuits that were left on the cabinet from breakfast, I went down to the basement to take care of Daddy's uniform. Getting a clean unironed uniform shirt, I sprinkled it down with water, then rolled it up tight to let the moisture seep through. Turning the iron up to its highest temperature, I still had to press down with all my might because the thick drill cloth was difficult to iron. The light blue shirt had "Fehr's Brewery" embroidered in red threads on an appliqué over the chest pocket. After it was ironed, I hung it up and admired it, particularly the creases in the sleeves and the pleats on the yoke in the back.

The trousers were another matter. Daddy always wanted to look sharp, so they had to be cleaned and pressed. He wanted them to show a nice crease. Made of wool and gabardine, they couldn't go into the washer. Aunt Lena showed Mama how to use gasoline to clean them. So, I followed Aunt Lena's plan and took a small amount of gasoline out of the one-gallon can Daddy kept in the basement just for this purpose. I poured it into a saucer. I loved the greasy smell of the gasoline and enjoyed using it. Nobody else was allowed to touch it. Getting to work with such dangerous materials made me feel like an adult. Using an old rag, I rubbed the gasoline into the black marks that were caused by the heavy beer cases Daddy lifted all day. Watching these marks magically disappear fascinated me. Mama called this, "Poor man's excuse" for dry cleaning. When the job was finished, I carefully poured the rest of the gasoline back into the container and closed it tight.

Mama told me once, "If you're not careful with that gasoline, Deanna, it will make an invisible trail and go to the pilot light on the hot water heater. That will catch fire and the whole house will blow up." I had just enough information in my head to scare me to death! Ironing Daddy's uniforms like this every week had never bothered me before. *Why do I doubt myself over such regular stuff?* Hoping I had put the top back on the gasoline container tight enough, I checked it again and prayed that the house wouldn't burn down while we were sleeping during the night – and kill all of us.

Before I had time to turn around, it was time to fix supper again. *Mama must feel like this everyday,* I thought. Tonight was our usual Friday menu. Meat wasn't allowed for Catholics on Fridays. I made salmon croquets from the same recipe that I used every week. A can of salmon drained, mixed with an egg and salt and pepper, then fried in a cornmeal batter. The kids loved them, but mostly what they loved was Friday night.

Margaret Jane ran down to the basement and got me a jar of tomatoes, and Theresa brought up some potatoes. I sliced and fried the potatoes, then added some chopped onion to the tomatoes that I served cold. They were always a favorite. Their cheerful red brightened the table and lifted my spirits. The meal was finished with no comments about the food. Anticipation of Mrs. Edsell's candy treat made it go faster. Feeling her support was a big help to me.

There was no homework hour tonight. On Friday nights we always listened to the "Friday Night Barn Dance" on the radio. Mama loved the fiddle music. When the square dance-calling started, it felt like Mama was in the room with us. I could almost hear her say like she did every week, "That old time music reminds me of Uncle Charlie. He was the best fiddler in Howardstown. Everybody gathered on his and Aunt Margaret's porch to pick and sing." Then I would watch her smile with that happy memory from Howardstown.

While we listened to the radio, we played our usual game of cards that Daddy called, "Three-card Rummy." We looked forward to Friday nights all week.

But this night our hearts were heavy. After Friday Night Barn Dance, we gathered around my parent's bed and knelt down. Whenever Mama was scared, she prayed the rosary. Tonight, we prayed the rosary for her. Using the "Sorrowful Mysteries," I lead the first decade (a series of ten beads representing the Hail Mary prayer, each decade had a separate title for contemplation), "Jesus' agony in the garden..." I started. All the others said their decade when it was their turn. There were no elbows in the ribs, as in our regular nightly rosary times. Our young fingers slid over the beads. I'm sure God felt our sincerity. We finished our evening prayers by saying the short prayer called the "Glory Be," and begged God to bring Mama home safely. The girls started crying about Mama. "God knows how important she is to us," I told them, keeping my lip from quivering, "He'll bring her home safe. Now, you all go on to bed." I hoped they couldn't tell that I was worried, too. We were too sad to stay up any longer and everybody headed for bed – but me.

I waited up for Daddy again. The other kids had turned in around Eight-thirty. It was after nine o'clock before he came in. I was tired, but too stirred-up to sleep.

Daddy came into the kitchen from the back door, his shoulders slumped and his face looked worn out. "I'm not hungry," he said, pushing away the warmed meal I set before him. "Your mother and I named the baby Josephine Ann, after her," he said. "I got a little white coffin today," he continued, pulling his chair in toward the table as I poured him some coffee. "And I got five cemetery plots at St. Edward's Cemetery in J-town (Jeffersontown), just in case." His voice was heavy and trailed off.

In case? In case of what? I was afraid to ask. *Do I really want to know?* Feeling a little closer to him tonight, I pressed for the information I needed.

"How is Mama?" I asked, trying not to start crying.

Daddy looked at me like I was being way too nosy for a kid, but said. "She's weak, but Dr. Duncan says she'll make it. Now, heat this coffee up some more," he continued, pushing his cup away, "this ain't good an' hot like I like it." Looking at Daddy, I thought he looked tired, and that his nerves were worn out, so I sat on my curiosity, guessing at the information I didn't get.

"You get my uniform ready?" He continued, casting a look in my direction. "This situation made me miss a lotta' work this week and I'll have to work tomorrow. Those taverns want their beer. If I don't get them Fehr's, they'll switch to Fall City or Sterling (Louisville's other local breweries). That means I'll lose customers, and I can't afford that with these hospital bills comin' in!" Pushing the chair back on its hind legs, he pulled a pack of Lucky Strikes cigarettes from his chest pocket and struck a match against the side of his shoe. The plume of smoke curled into the air, floating up to the bare bulb above the table. His head bowed as he stared blankly into his coffee cup. *It's hard bein' an adult*, I thought.

Daddy rambled on, easing some of his tension while he drank his coffee and finished his cigarette. We had really never fully talked before. During his supper was when he talked to Mama, I was usually in the dining room doing my homework with the rest of the kids. But now, I was listening to the events of his day, like Mama would be doing. It felt good to be treated like a confidant. Daddy didn't say anything like, "You're doing a good job, or, thanks for helping out." But his tone told me he was satisfied enough.

"Tomorrow's Saturday," he continued. "The boys'll be going ta' caddy at Big Spring. Make them get up early enough to milk the cow before they leave." In listening to Daddy, I thought, *this is like the list of chores he leaves with Mama every day.* He was showing me the respect of a grown-up and that made me feel important.

****

My sense of strength continued into the next morning because of the conversation I had with Daddy the night before. *This is the support Mama promised me,* I thought, letting this realization throb through out my body. Now, I was ready for any grief Johnny and Marcellus might cause. I sprang out of bed quickly on Daddy's morning call and bounced down the steps to fix the biscuits. Putting on the coffee, I started frying some eggs and bacon for Daddy. He was in a hurry today and left before the rest of the family got up. Because it was Saturday, I didn't have to wake up the little kids till seven o'clock. I just had to get Daddy off to work and the boys out to take care of the animals.

The boys grumbled when I called them, of course, at having to take orders from me, but with my new found power, I bristled, and shouted from the bottom of the steps, "You lazy boys. Daddy said you better get out of bed now, if you know what's good for ya." I realized they had no idea that Daddy had already left the house. The power in my voice surprised me and it sure felt good. Up they sprang! Delighted, I chuckled as I heard them scramble around on the floor above my head. By now, I felt really good about my biscuit making skills and hummed as I put them into the hot oven, that had also warmed up the kitchen on this chilly morning.

Their aroma filled the house, and I called up the steps for the girls to come on down and bring Tony with them. The biscuits continued to bake while Margaret Jane dressed Tony. Theresa started setting the table. Mary Ann had already climbed out of her babybed and stood before me. I took her back there to change her diaper. Being Saturday, the little ones would stay here with me instead of going to Mrs. Edsell's. They were disappointed and so was I, having grown used to the daily pep talks that lifted my spirits.

Margaret Jane and Theresa laughed as they tossed the dishes back and forth to each other, showing their playful Saturday mood. They poured the milk after I removed the heavy crock from the refrigerator. Calfie gave us about a gallon of milk every day, and we always drank all of it and wished for more. Before the girls could fill the glasses, I carefully skimmed the cream that had formed overnight from the top of the milk. Pouring it into the quart jar with the rest of the cream that had been saved during the week, I recalled that Saturday was churning day. I would turn this quart of cream into next week's butter. The task was easier now that we had a Sunbeam Mixer. Instead of the hours we used to spend complaining and beating the cream with the hand-crank churn, the mixer made the butter solid in minutes.

When the biscuits were good, the boys always ate eight to ten apiece. They came in from their chores and surprised me. Today, they really seemed to like my biscuits, and actually scrambled for them, each grabbing almost armloads of them. *I finally got the mixture right,* I thought, *or maybe my bossy manner this morning made `em stop complaining.* Allowing myself to be in good spirits, I enjoyed a bit of self-congratulation.

Later, however, in cleaning up the kitchen, I found out why the boys were so anxious for my biscuits. Through the back window over the sink I heard laughter and screaming coming from the orchard. This area was right in back of the house and we also used it for our play yard. Glancing through the window to check out this racket while I did the dishes, I was disgusted at what I saw. The boys were hiding behind the fruit trees and throwing my biscuits at each other, using them like rocks in a rock fight.

Oh! My high spirits fell to defeat immediately. Humiliated, I quit my work in the kitchen, went to the basement and found Bullet asleep behind the water pump. Waking him, I pulled him close to me and sobbed into his dusty fur. *Bein' a mother is hard.* Bullet licked my hand as I hugged him. Then, magic thoughts of re-empowerment came to me. "I can tell Daddy the boys wasted food," I told Bullet's smiling face. Any kind of waste, especially of food, was a cardinal sin in Daddy's eyes. They would really get it now. He'd also be upset they took time to play around and hadn't left for Big Spring Golf

Course, earlier. Saturday was a good day to make double money by caddying two rounds.

My mind wandered to the other things I needed to get done today and I allowed Bullet to return to his slumber. The baby was almost out of diapers and everybody would be out of socks and underwear by Monday. *I gotta get in a wash today*, I thought, *the clothes 'll be dry in no time!* Looking out the door, I watched the morning clouds quickly lift up into white puffs in the periwinkle sky on this sunny October day.

Margaret Jane and Theresa giggled and chased as they ran around the house gathering all the dirty clothes they could find. I enjoyed the way they made a game out of their chores. *Why don't the rest of the kids get along as good as these two*, I thought. Today was really hard for Mary Ann and Tony. They not only missed Mama, they also missed Mrs. Edsell and all the extra attention they had gotten used to at her house. Whining, they took turns clinging to the girls, and then to me. Mary Ann hugged her dolly and Tony hung on to his raggedy teddy bear. They were lonely, we just did not understand, and kept pushing them away from us.

"You kids go play and get out of the way," we snarled at them, jealous that they got to do what we wished we could.

Taking the clothes to the basement the girls and I separated them into piles of whites, good-colored, old-colored, and darks. I filled up our ringer washing machine with hot water and added detergent to the chips of lye soap I put in there earlier to soften. I let the machine agitate for a long time to allow the clothes to release their dirt – putting in the whites for the first batch. Then I turned on the wringer at the top of the tub and carefully placed each article one by one between its motorized rollers. Again, Mama's words crossed my mind, "Be careful that you only place a corner into that wringer Deanna, or you'll get your hand caught and your whole arm will be mashed as the rollers keep pullin' on it." For emphasis, she added, "This is what happened to my cousin, Agnes." I remembered Mama's cautions, but I smiled because this was something I knew how to do well.

However, I didn't have the same skill with making starch. Three times I tried to make the starch for Daddy's and my brother's shirt collars. Mama always dipped them into the wet starch before we hung them out to dry. Mixing the flour and water and heating it on the stove like Mama did, I was disappointed that my starch was a flop each time. Finally, I gave up and called Aunt Lena and asked her how to do it. Mama had told me to call her if I had any problems. Aunt Lena did things the way Mama did them. Mrs. Edsell used a ready-made box mix for her starch. Daddy would never allow us to use anything that we had to buy.

My shyness prevented me from calling Aunt Lena about my many questions. I was scared to talk to adults, even my favorite aunt. She greeted me with a smile in her voice. Pleased that I needed her help, she gave me her suggestions, "You need to whip it with the beater and get the lumps out before you heat it. And make sure you add more water to it as it cooks. Don't let it get too thick. That's been your problem, Deanna." She laughed again. Aunt Lena could always find something to laugh about. I wished Mama was as sure about everything as Aunt Lena was.

"You call me again if you need anything else," she said cheerfully, before I hung up. I had to admit to myself that it wasn't only my shyness that prevented me from phoning her sooner, there was another side to this story. The truth was that I wanted to appear more capable than her two daughters, Lucy and Mary Jane. They were the closest grandchildren to me in age. Giving in and making a call about so many of the things that confused me would show Aunt Lena that I didn't know how to do everything like I wanted her to think I did. It was hard for me to admit my vanity. I also feared it would look like Mama hadn't trained me well in the matters that all young girls have to know how to do expertly, in order to become successful women.

Calling in Margaret Jane and Theresa from play, I had them help me hang the wash. Using the clotheslines in the orchard for the best clothes, I hung them from tip to tail with the wooden clothespins we kept in a small feed sack hanging on the clothesline with a coat hanger sewn into it. The girls took the rest of them over to the orchard fence. This fence separated the orchard from the pasture field. They laid blue jeans and dark clothes on the top of the fence, and hung the socks and washrags on its rungs. Bullet ran from one of us to the next, entertaining us as we worked.

Theresa fell and skinned her knee on the gravel driveway as she and Margaret Jane held the wire handles on either side of a bushel basket of wet clothes. Wanting to get their chore out of the way as fast as they could, they were running toward the orchard when it happened. Sniffling, she brought her bloody knee into the house for me to take care of. I washed out the cut and applied rubbing alcohol to it. Mama and I had always put the stingy liquid on all the flesh wounds in our household.

"Ow!" she screamed, pulling her knee away. "That burns!" she said, tears rolling down her face. I told her the same thing that Mama had always told me, "Don't look a gift horse in the mouth. Be glad it hurts, that means it's working." Theresa didn't seem comforted, bending over her knee and blowing on it over and over again.

****

Slowly, the days toiled on. Discontented, but steadily enough, we fell into our routines each day. Of course, we were all scared for Mama and prayed the rosary every night. At last it was Sunday, again. Struggling to be on time for the early Mass at seven o'clock, I got Mary Ann and Tony ready while the other kids dressed themselves in their Sunday best. Turning the girls around, I tied the bows on the backs of the dresses that I freshly ironed for them the day before. Theresa carried the black baby satchel packed with an extra set of clothes and a bottle. Jimmy checked the younger ones over for tied shoes and Margaret Jane helped me check for closed buttons before we left the house. *We are a good-lookin' family*, I thought as we stuffed ourselves into our new 1951 Chevrolet two-door sedan. Uncle Bud had a car with four doors and I couldn't understand why Daddy didn't think of getting us one like that, but guessed that it probably had something to do with the price. Calming down, I held Mary Ann on my lap in the coveted front seat, as Daddy pulled the car out on to Hunsinger Lane.

We kids loved Sundays, especially me because I didn't have to fix biscuits. After church we were eager for the delicious cinnamon toast we had only on Sundays. Just remembering the smell of the cinnamon was making my mouth water. Going to communion at Mass meant we couldn't eat beforehand, not even have a drink of water. Sundays were a treat day for us with white bread for breakfast, in order to save a little time.

As Daddy drove us back from St. Bartholomew's, he yanked us from the daydreams about our yummy cinnamon toast, by making a surprising announcement, "I'm bringing Mama home today," he said "I'll get her after we eat dinner."

"Yay!" We screamed and clapped our hands. The energy in the car changed completely. The somber mood of Mass was now one of laughter and anticipation.

This dinner was the happiest meal I fixed since Mama left. Daddy was completely helpless in the kitchen and could not even boil water. "You take care of that, Deanna," he said to me about any food preparation. "That's woman's work, and you better learn how to do it while you're young, if you ever wanna' get a husband."

He did kill me a fresh chicken, however. This was something I usually did for our Sunday noon meal. Since I was busy with the cooking, he not only killed it, he scalded it, plucked off the feathers, and cut it into pieces. I gratefully took his chicken, rolled it in breading mixture of flour and milk, and then placed it in the bubbling grease of the skillet. It crackled and started browning nicely. Smiling again, I felt good about frying chicken.

The boys brought in fresh greens. This time it was their turn to search for the kale slugs because Daddy was there to make them. Jimmy measured out flour and milk and I cracked the eggs, and finished the batter for our Sunday cake. Margaret Jane greased and floured the pan. Theresa set the table. The kitchen hummed like a well-oiled machine. The aroma of the chocolate cake soon filled the kitchen as it baked. We were so excited about Mama coming home that nobody complained about the meal, even though several kale slugs wound up on our plates. As always, the cake and the chicken were good. Neither food nor mischief was on our minds, Mama was coming home today!

****

Anxious to see her, we ran to the screen door on the front porch when we heard the car grind to a stop on the crunchy gravel drive. Bullet waited, sitting alert next to the front porch door. Daddy lifted Mama from the front seat of the car. She had on her pretty baby blue silk gown and satin robe. She wore these nice things whenever she went to the hospital to deliver a baby. Johnny and Marcellus opened the doors for them, and we all started crowding around, wanting to see her.

"You kids get back out of the way," Daddy called out as he carried Mama in his arms. *She looks like a feather,* I thought. He laid her gently on the bed. She was pale and her face looked way too white against her dark hair. She was as weak as a kitten. Her frailness worried me. My stomach clinching in fear, I ran to the refrigerator and brought her some milk to drink. Mama made us drink milk when we felt weak.

"Deanna," she said, "that was the hardest birth I ever had. That delivery was even harder than when you were born, and you weighed over ten pounds and were the first one. Getting that dead baby out was like pushing out a nine-pound rock. Little Josephine Ann wasn't able to help me at all. I didn't realize how much the other babies helped me when they came out into the world. Dr. Duncan tried to pull her out but the gangrene had made her skin so soft, it just kept falling off. He cut me pretty bad and had to use forcipes to get all of her out." Mama's lips quivered, as she remembered the pain. "I lost a lot of blood," she mumbled, weakly.

Kneeling down beside Mama, I wanted to get as close to her as possible. Maybe some of my strength would rub off on her. I had always been Mama's confidant and listened to all her trials. She was very brave and never complained through any of her hardships. Seeing her like this scared me. I fell to the floor, my body heaved with sobs. *What if Mama dies?* I panicked, trying not to remember her own mother's young death in the delivery of her last child, my Aunt Saloma. Letting go of some of the tensions that had accumulated during the last ten days, the crying wouldn't stop.

"Cut that out, Deanna, and get up," Mama's voice was weak but stern. "God is helping me through this. He didn't give me all these kids to leave them without a mother." *How can she read my fears?* "You can stop worrying. We have to have faith, that's all," she continued. "And trust God's will, He always takes care of everything, you know that." I wished I had Mama's powerful faith. But, the thought of being in charge of the family for good was too much for me to bear. The certainty of Mama's faith lifted my spirits. I had seen God help her through many difficult struggles.

Relieved, I went back to my chores, knowing my biggest help to Mama was to do what needed to be done, without her having to think about it. The sets of pretty baby clothes went back into the bag and up to the attic for the next time. *For the "next time?"* I wondered, *can Mama have another child?* I waited until she went to sleep before I did that task, fearing that if she saw the tiny clothes they would make her cry. As it turned out, Mama did have three more, next times. To my dismay, *they were all boys*! Our family ended up with seven boys and four surviving girls.

Mary Ann, remembering the little sister I had promised her, cried for her new playmate. Margaret Jane entertained her by putting a new dress on her dolly. Mary Ann grabbed it and ran out to play under her favorite tree in the orchard. Tony joined her with his little raggedy teddy bear. Tomorrow, they would go to Mrs. Edsell's again. Reminding them about this cheered them up.

I wanted to stay home from school the next day and hear all the stories of Mama's stay in the hospital, but she insisted that I go. She always stayed in a dormitory room with several other ladies, and came home with some interesting tales about how the rest of the world lives. I felt too important for seventh grade lessons. The girls in my class would be talking about boys and the shopping of the weekend. They would harass me because I wasn't much fun to be around – I had bigger things to think about than boys and shopping.

I worried about Mama. Mrs. Edsell had promised to look in on her during the day. A prayer for Mama's safety drummed in the back of my head. "Oh God, don't let her start bleeding again." When I had come down to fix the biscuits that morning I found her lying in a pool of blood. Daddy was already out doing the milking. I cleaned up the mess and put new sheets on the bed. Mama was helpless and unable to help me. That scared me even more. Wobbly, she sat crying on a chair and waited for me to finish.

But mostly, my thoughts were about how good it felt to have Mama home again. She was there to answer all my questions, instead of me guessing and making mistakes all the time. Just Mama's presence would keep the boys off my back! They wanted do what she told them to. Now, she was the one to tell Daddy if they were bad and I didn't have to! No more stomach punches for me!

****

It took several weeks before Mama got completely well. Daddy finally gave in and called Aunt Aurelia to come over and help us. "I don't want to put you all out," I overheard him say when he talked to her on the phone. Daddy was a proud man and hated to admit he needed anything – particularly help.

Aunt Aurelia was happy he called her. She was only three when their mother died, and she saw Mama as her own mother. Uncle Earl moved himself, her and their little boy, Ricky, into one of our upstairs bedrooms. They stayed with us several weeks, until Mama was on her feet again. I was so happy to have them here. Uncle Earl worked at Reynolds Aluminum. I looked at my handsome uncle and smiled. He was tall, slim, and muscular with a full head of blond hair. *Yeah, I'm sure glad Aunt Aurelia married him.* I thought, recalling the weekend a few years ago when she told me the good news about their wedding plans.

When he came back home from Reynolds in the evenings, Earl helped Daddy around the farm.

"It sure feels good to work the land again," he told Daddy, "City living is pretty boring." Daddy was grateful for the help from our country relatives who knew what needed to be done on a farm, and did it without any instructions.

Aunt Aurelia and Uncle Earl were young and lots of fun. The boys couldn't wait to do what they asked. She was a great cook and we all played card games together in the evenings after homework. Uncle Earl enjoyed a Fehr's beer with Daddy after they finished the farm work. Sometimes our neighbor, Larney, came by to join them. I heard them laughing out by the barn as Aunt Aurelia and I got the kids ready for bed.

Life was a lot easier for all of us with Aunt Aurelia and Uncle Earl there. Mary Ann and Tony got the new playmate for a few weeks in the form of Cousin Ricky, who was just a few weeks younger than Mary Ann at age two. They all played on the floor together. Daddy changed his stubborn rule about the heat and turned on the furnace, even without a snowstorm. But he still didn't fool Aunt Aurelia and

Uncle Earl because Daddy had a reputation in the family about being tight-fisted with money.

We were having such a good time that it lifted Mama's spirits, and she was eager to join in. Soon, she was able to sit up at the table with us. Mama's illness was scary and uncertain, but turned out to be an important time in our family's history. I learned a significant lesson about faith. When Mama said, "Deanna, God will take care of everything. All you have to do is trust." I knew it was true because I had seen it happen!

Chapter 13

Eighth Grade Summer Days

Summer again, this was always my favorite time of the year — no school, no homework. *What'll this un' be like?* I wondered, planning ahead. Having graduated from the eighth grade at Our Lady of Lourdes Parish School, I was now fourteen, full of myself and wanting to enjoy my last free summer. Surely, next year I would have a job in town, or somewhere. My thoughts about life had changed a lot this year.

Our family had been transferred to Our Lady of Lourdes while our new parish, St. Barnabas, on Hikes Lane was being built. The change in schools was thrilling to me. Lourdes had a different attitude than St. Bartholomew's. Also a suburban parish, it was located in St. Matthews rather than in Buechel. Wealthier than my old school, the people at Lourdes didn't seem to think or talk about money. The girls were outgoing and friendly. I thrived in this new atmosphere where I was no longer teased for being a hick and out of step.

Whether they realized it or not, these girls did many things to help me change my feelings about myself. They saw me as a unique individual and accepted me for that. Because of my fast running ability, I was immediately put on the girl's softball team, and they showed me they were grateful to have me there. Lourdes had other teams, like tennis and field hockey, in which girls could participate. However, my need to come home immediately after school and help Mama with chores, limited me to just one activity.

Also, the girls at Lourdes enjoyed my essays and told me I was a good writer. They complimented me on my clothes, too. The eighth graders at Lourdes had the privilege of not having to wear uniforms. Finally, I gave up the need to be a tomboy, and gladly wore the nice clothes that my cousins Pat and Alice, and Uncle Mac and Aunt Gen had given me. I actually felt pretty and began to care about being a girl.

Mama was delighted with the change in my outlook. She had been baffled as to how to help me when I came home from school crying last year, and was now glad to see me come home from school with enthusiasm. However, despite the positive changes, I still considered myself mostly shy and backward. Being tall, skinny and having pimples didn't help. I was five foot and five inches and weighed only eighty-four pounds.

Daddy tried to offer me his wisdom by talking about reputation. It didn't really fit, but he considered it his most important message as a parent. "Deanna, you're the complaininest' girl I ever laid eyes on. Don't you know the most valuable possession a person can have is a good reputation – and that's what I gave ya' – y'r good name. Make sure ya' don't ever lose it," he said. Then he went on, "It don't matter how skinny ya' are, you'll gain weight in due time. It's yur' name that follows you wherever you go, forever. It's the only thing that gets you through in this world."

My parents wanted to be helpful, but I could tell that neither of them had any idea what it was like to be a country teen trying to fit into the ways of the city. Of course, I was nice to everyone, I was too shy not to be.

Being a teenager was confusing. I didn't want to have battles with Mama. But now that I had experienced some good friendships, conflicts begin to develop between us. My desires started to clash with Mama's needs. I wanted to spend a lot of my summer joining in on some of the activities of my new girlfriends from Lourdes. They would be swimming, going to movies and dancing at the teen clubs. Doing my chores at home seemed pretty stale, now. I especially found it hard when I noticed that Johnny and Marcellus got more privileges outside the farm.

However, the truth was that being the oldest girl gave me no choice about helping Mama. I didn't have the money to do the things that my friends liked to do, and Mama had to have my help. Running this family took a lot of work and I would feel too guilty to leave her alone. Besides, she was expecting again.

After complaining to her and fighting with myself, I realized that even though I wanted to be with my friends, I felt unsure about how to enter their world, anyway. Daddy bought us a TV last fall, and I noticed that I had nothing in common with the teens I saw there. They were from the city and acted stylish and smart. On "Father Knows Best," for example, the teenage daughter, Betty, seemed privileged over her brother Bud, and was called "Princess," by her father. This was the opposite of the way our family worked. I didn't know how to be a princess. My lessons on the farm taught me that feminine stuff was sissy and silly, either of which was about the worst thing any country girl could be called. Farm chores and taking care of babies were all I felt comfortable with, and felt inadequate to do anything else.

Disgruntled, and unable to do anything about it, I comforted myself by knowing I would follow my girlfriends to Assumption High School in the fall. Ignoring my predicament, I decided to enjoy what I could of the summer. The beauty of the farm inspired me, even though I quarreled with its constant chores. Complaining didn't solve anything, so, I threw myself into helping Mama and enjoying our time together. We did laugh a lot and cut-up while we worked. Daddy and the boys considered what she and I did the "women's work" of the farm: food processing, taking care of the little ones, mending, and "washin' and ironin'," of the family wardrobe. To them that meant necessary but inferior work. To me, the part of all this that I hated the worst, was that most of these tasks took place in the basement. The jobs were unending – and gave me no time to worry about what my friends were doing.

However, other dilemmas going on in my world were confusing to me as well.

Hikes Point was changing from a peaceful farm community to a crowded suburb. Strangers were everywhere. This upset me, even though this meant that some new opportunities were opening up. We had lived here since 1949 and I held deep affection for the splendor of the meadows, pastures, woods and fields. Quickly, many of these beautiful things were disappearing. Farms surrendered to subdivisions and shopping centers. Old farmer friends of ours died, and their children, not willing to work so hard, saw more profit in just selling the land. The county accelerated this process by taxing the land on its future financial potential, rather than on the money that the farm could produce.

"This is not fair," I complained of the policy to Daddy one night. He shook his head in agreement and said, "You can't fight city hall. America's gonna' be sorry for lettin' go a' all these farms," he lamented more than once. This "progress" had angered Daddy, too. This was one time we both saw things the same way. Witnessing the majesty of the open countryside dissolve into common bricks and asphalt was troubling to me, somehow making me feel disposable, too. Catching on to Daddy's fears and regret made my heart weep at the changes we both resented, but couldn't stop. I felt like the countryside was being stolen from me.

I remembered the day during the spring when I came home from school and couldn't stop crying. Loud screaming and crunching noises assaulted our ears as our school bus pulled up in front of Bauer's. *Some kinda' monster's loose in Hikes Point,* I feared, as I descended the bus steps. Johnny saw it first and pointed it out for the rest of us. A bulldozer was tearing down Al Rohleder's large Victorian house that had been nestled behind the tall hickory trees of his front yard.

The giant trees were already on the ground, humbled by the screaming chainsaws slicing away at their mighty limbs. Mr. Rohleder's son had sold the farm and the land was becoming a shopping center. Seeing the porch columns chewed like toothpicks in the dozer's mighty jaws started the tears that just wouldn't stop.

Mama didn't share mine and Daddy's feelings about the farms, "Well, I declare! Stop that cryin' over spilt milk," she admonished me when I got home, "cryin' won't change things" *True!* I thought, nothing I could do would stop this thing called progress and this reality saddened me even more.

However, the extra population sometimes meant good things. For example, Father George, our parish priest at Lourdes, made a surprising announcement at Mass on the first Sunday in June: "There will be free swimming lessons for the kids of St. Matthews, Buechel, Hikes Point, J-town and Fern Creek," he told the parishioners. "They will start July 12th, on Tuesdays and Thursdays, and will go on for six weeks at Light House Lake Quarry on Gardiner Lane." This was about five miles from Hikes Point. Free swimming lessons! I couldn't believe it. I was so excited I couldn't wait till Mass was over.

The new subdivisions that brought more kids into the East End turned out to be the reason the Red Cross was giving us the free lessons. *I guess I should be happier about all these new people,* as I realized that, now, I wouldn't have to ask Daddy for money to get out of the house, anymore. My requests never worked anyway, he was an expert at holding on to his cash. My pleading only produced a frown, a lecture and a subsequent denial of funds. Now, I could get out into the world without his help. Begging Mama to talk Daddy into leaving the car home for us, two days a week was my first task. This was quite a sacrifice for him, and he balked at having to give up the car. But, he knew it was good for his children to learn how to swim. And, with the free lessons, he didn't even have to pay for it, so, reluctantly; he gave in and walked up to catch the Blue Motor Coach on Tuesdays and Thursdays.

Johnny and Marcellus wouldn't be taking part in the lessons. After they finished their morning chores, they would be speeding off to caddy at Big Spring Country Club, as usual. Making money at caddying was more important to them than swimming. Besides, Big Spring had special times set up for the caddies to use the club pool. Johnny sneered at our lessons, saying, "Light House Lake is not so special, that old joint is full of rough-necks and dope-dealers." I thought he was just mad because he couldn't join us, but Daddy said something about this, too. But, then Daddy added that their reputation for dope stopped back in the `30's when the police ran the gamblers out. "See how hard it is to get yur' good name back, once you lost it," he reminded me.

"You wouldn't catch me swimming in that dump!" Marcellus piped up, wanting to agree with Johnny. I recalled hearing stories from the girls at Lourdes, who were joking about dead bodies being lost among the quarry's rocky ledges since the `20's when this was a popular swim club. The girls made cracks about this being a "tacky-place" before school let out for the summer when they talked of swimming at the country clubs where their families belonged, like the Louisville Country Club, River Valley, and Big Spring.

I wouldn't think about these tales. Light House Lake was old, I knew that, but any swimming pool looked good to me. When it was time for the lessons to start, it turned out that none of us had to worry about getting caught in the rocky ledges, because the lessons were held in Light House Lake's new above ground pool and not in the famous lake. Unfortunately for me, I found out that at fourteen, I was too old for the lessons, and Mary Ann was too young, at four. They were only for kids from six to twelve. But I went to the pool anyway. Mama needed me to help her with the other kids, and I was always ready to find a chance to get away from my chores in the basement.

The instructor felt sorry for me because I didn't know how to swim *at my age*, so he allowed me to splash around at the other end of the pool. Desperate to learn in case one of my friends at Lourdes asked me to a swim party, I practiced the instructions he gave to the class. By the end of the summer I still couldn't swim, but felt more comfortable in how to handle water over my head.

****

This particular day, a typical summer day, was Tuesday and a swimming lesson day. All of us kids were eager to be finished with our morning chores so we could go swimming at one o'clock. The lessons also came at a good time in our life because Daddy wouldn't let us swim in the creek anymore. The constant blasting for new subdivisions in the woods made it too dangerous. *Yuk!* I had outgrown the desire to swim in creeks with crawdads and snakes, anyway. Also, watching the woods disappear into housing made me too sad to be near there.

To be on time for the lessons, we raced from one task to the next. A lot had to be done before we left the house at 12:30. Our first chore was to go out to the garden before the summer heat got too bad. Gathering the vegetables was the most important work of the day. We were out there by the time the sun first came up around 5:30 or six o'clock in the morning. Dew was heavy on the grass and fog hovered over the ground. Walking past the blue morning-glory blooms by the chicken house, our bare feet were wet before we reached the fields. 'Picking' was done everyday of the week but Sunday. It was a sin to work on Sunday, or we'd be out there on Sunday, too. Instead of hating this chore, it would have been nice for me to be grateful for the bounty nature had provided for us.

Golden Writer spider webs greeted us as we went down the garden rows. Attached to the tangles of milkweed vines and vegetables, the delicate orbs hung one after the other as we crouched along the ground to pick. About the size of dinner plates, they sparkled with droplets of dew – looking like diamond platters. The spider's body was striking in patterns of yellow and black. Large spiders, about the size of a fifty-cent piece, they looked frightening as they raised their front legs at us in anger, attempting to protect their artwork. Unconcerned, we pushed them aside with our sticks.

Mama said, "Golden Writers are not poisonous, they just look scary. They'll be back tomorrow." They always were, and tomorrow, their webs would be even more beautiful than today. The spiders never gave up, no matter how many times we tore down their houses.

Uncle Mac told me once when he and Aunt Gen had visited us in the summer time, "Look at nature, Deanna, to see how life should be lived." Uncle Mac was so wise. *The spiders are tellin' me ta' stop bein' a cry-baby,* I thought. Smiling, I remembered sitting on his lap when he shared his philosophy with me.

On this day, we gathered peas, beans, tomatoes, some beets, and a few early cucumbers. Also, the sweet corn had started coming on. Before we pulled the rosin-ears from the stalks, we pushed aside the pearly green husks and checked the kernels for tenderness with our fingernails. The ready ones popped forth a gush of sweet liquid. Daddy loved sweet corn but only planted two rows of it, just enough for us to eat before it got tough. It was a funny crop because it could get tough overnight. When that happened, we allowed it to dry and then stored it in the corncrib with the rest of the corn that we threw to the hogs. *Heck no, we're not given' them our best corn,* I thought. Daddy planted three acres of yellow corn for their pallet. The family ate on that too, using it for corn-on-the-cob, slathering it with our home-churned butter. We also cut it from the cob and fried it in the skillet, seasoning it with bacon grease and slices of green pepper. Yellow corn was tough and not as tasty.

Mama, Johnny, Marcellus, Jimmy, Margaret Jane, Theresa, and I bent over the crops for about two hours, our backs aching. Mama was on her knees, her belly bulging with my brother Phillip, the fifth boy, who would be born in a few weeks. This birth meant that I would be back in charge of the family again while she was in the hospital delivering the baby. Now that I was older, being in charge wasn't as frightening as it used to be.

I was concerned for Mama. Seeing her work so hard made me want to work faster so she could go and sit down. Since she lost her last baby, little Josephine Ann, I took her health seriously. This was her eleventh baby. She lost a baby before I was born and she lost her ninth one – little Josephine Ann. As she aged, her pregnancies were harder on her. By the time we finished with the pickin' the sun was scorching, tanning my brother's summer skin, but it was burning Mama's and mine. This chore was never put off until after breakfast.

The little kids, Tony age six and Mary Ann age four, gathered the eggs while we worked in the garden. Daddy said they were too young to know what to pick, and too little not to stomp on the vegetable vines. This would kill the plants. Gathering the eggs was important work, too. Daddy let the chickens roam in the summer so they didn't use their nests in the hen house. "Chickens need to roam to stay healthy and make their eggs sweet," he told us. This was also the time of the year when the rooster fertilized the hens. This meant that several of the eggs had bloody splotches in them. To us they looked disgusting.

Noticing the frowns on our faces one Sunday morning, Daddy said, "Those bloody eggs have the strength of two eggs, which means they make ya' twice as strong." His story had us fighting over them because all farm kids want to be strong. I wished these disgusting eggs would make me as strong as the boys. But, I knew more than just physical strength was needed to be a teenager. "How do I get to have self-confidence?" I asked Mama, "That's what I need to be a teenager." Confidence was gushing out of the girls at Lourdes.

With their summer freedom, the hens laid more than just their eggs all over the yard. We had to watch where we stepped because having stinky chicken poop squish between our toes was a nasty surprise! The eggs might be anywhere, under bushes, behind drains, in the front yard, side yard, or the orchard. It took Mary Ann and Tony quite a while to find all of them. This was like a daily Easter Egg Hunt. But, being kids, they soon got bored of the job and started chasing each other in and out of the evergreens that grew behind the hen house. Sometimes they even stepped on the very eggs they were sent out to find.

"Don't they know we want to go swimming today?" I said to Mama, shaking my brown hair and looking up from my row of tomatoes.

She had noticed them chasing, too, and nudged my arm, "Deanna, go over there and make those kids get back to work, we can't let the hot sun ruin the eggs." I gladly left the pungent tomato vines with all the Golden Writers staring at me. Giving commands in Mama's name was something I loved to do as the oldest. It gave me a great feeling of power, even though my siblings didn't seem too moved by it.

After the vegetable gathering, and grabbing some of the Daddy's leftover biscuits, Johnny and Marcellus left quickly on their bikes for Big Spring. It was about six miles away on Dutchman's Lane. They wanted to be there by eight o'clock to catch the early golfers. I envied their exciting day of meeting rich people and making money. It would be nice to join my friends from Lourdes who belonged to this club. They would be swimming at the country club's Olympic-size pool and playing tennis.

But, again I reminded myself that I didn't know how to do any of these things. My shyness reared up and doubts filled my mind. *I wouldn't know how to dress, an' I'd most likely act stupid. Wha'd I talk about all day?* I would probably drown and that would be embarrassing. This over dramatizing was a frequent method that I used to keep me from being too jealous about the things I didn't get to do.

****

Falling back into the rhythm of the farm, I enjoyed watching the flashes of quick little Goldfinches dash above my head as they headed for the thistles that grew along the fencerow by the side-garden. The kids and I pulled the several baskets of the freshly picked vegetables over to the outdoor pump, in our Radio Flyer Wagon, and the wobbly wheelbarrow. The pump was just outside the kitchen door by Mama's bed of bright "Four-O'clock" flowers that only bloomed in the afternoon after four o'clock. Right now, the colorful blooms were folded up tight, looking like tiny closed umbrellas.

Jimmy jumped up and down with the swing of the pump's long handle. He, Margaret Jane, and Theresa scrubbed the mud off the vegetables before they took them to the basement to be canned. I helped them too, before Mama called me in to finish getting breakfast together for the rest of the family. I had made the biscuits earlier before Daddy went to work.

This summer of 1955 was another summer of drought, the pumping would take more effort as the summer got dryer and the water table got lower. It was important to use our outdoor water whenever we could, in order to conserve our house water supply in the big cistern in the orchard. Everybody talked about rain. Uncle Bud and Aunt Lena complained about the dry weather, too. Even Uncle Victor and Aunt Bertha who lived in the city, and didn't care about it as much as farmers did, complained about the drought, too. A cooling rain was the daydream of everybody I knew. During these hot days, I just wanted to lie down under a tree and let the drops fall on me.

I brought several unripened tomatoes with me when I entered the kitchen after leaving the outside pump. They were in the rolled up bottom of my dress – I had used it like a basket. Putting them on the sash of our sunniest kitchen window to deepen their color, I then started frying the eggs and bacon. After choking down my biscuits, the rest of my day, like my past summers, would be spent in the basement, canning with Mama and butchering chickens. Recalling the anger of the Golden Writer spiders when we tore up their handiwork, I swallowed hard, realizing that they may be just spiders, but I felt the same way about my situation. As the oldest, I was stuck. I had to help harvest the crops and can them for winter because Mama obviously couldn't do it by herself. The other kids did their part, too, but I was Mama's right arm, and she totally depended on me. I had no choice for anything else. Like the spiders, my choices were changed by others' needs.

"Aunt Aurelia is doing this same thing out in Howardstown," Mama tried to console me, noticing the unpleasant look on my face. She and Uncle Earl hated city life so much they moved back to the country to help out Grandpa Emanuel on the Boone Brothers Farm.

"Har-ump," I sighed. Mama's comments didn't soothe me much as I stumbled down the inside basement steps, *going back to my prison.*

At least it was cool down there. My bare feet welcomed the sweat coming up from the cement floor. If I stood at the back of the table while I worked, I could look up the outside basement steps and see a sliver of summer sunny sky. I pretended I was outside, but sighed, knowing that Mama was in this prison, too, and just as stuck as I was.

When Mama looked at the cucumbers she said, "These don't amount to a hill o' beans, Deanna, fix 'em for salad tonight."

Agreeing, I said, "I guess we'll start canning them next week," wanting to feel I had some say in the work we had to do.

She grunted in agreement and started putting the ears of corn by the cool back wall to keep them from getting tough. "We'll have corn-on-the-cob for supper tonight, too," she went on, rubbing her belly.

After peeling and slicing the cucumbers I put them in a mixture of vinegar and sugar to steep for tonight's supper. Thinking that my mother's life as an adult was almost the same as it had been in her childhood, I promised myself that there would be a better future for me. Looking over, my heart sank when I saw that the front of the basement was filled with the vegetables that Jimmy and the girls had washed up at the pump outside. Pickin' was good this morning – there were several baskets of work to do here.

****

Being a skinny nine year old, Jimmy had a busy day in front of him, too. It took him several trips to carry enough water and feed for the cow and the pigs and chickens. Later, the salad garden by the dusty tractor road next to Judge Jeffery's property had to be hoed of weeds. Tomorrow, I would help him pull the Johnson grass, a stubborn weed growing out by the peas and beans. Then we had to 'sucker' the corn in the big garden on the other side of the house. Suckering meant snapping off the weedy parts of the cornstalk that took strength away from the developing rosin-ears. It was a while before I learned to recognize the difference between a sucker and a real blade of the corn plant.

Like our parents, we also prayed for rain. If the crops got too dry, Jimmy and I had to carry buckets of water to them. Some of these chores belonged to Johnny and Marcellus, but since they started caddying, they decided that we should do most of their work. Daddy, happy that the boys were making money, let this go on until Jimmy and I pitched a fit. Then he made them pay us a dollar a week to do their share. In 1955, a dollar was a lot of money. Anyway, that's what I told myself to keep from getting too angry about the extra work. But, the truth for me was that I enjoyed doing their chores because at least they got me out of my prison in the darkness of the basement for a while.

Using the short-handled pump at the basement sink, I filled the deepest pan we had. Almost every task needed boiled water. Our cistern ran dry last week, so again, I reminded myself to be conserving of its precious contents. Daddy paid ten dollars for a load of 10,000 gallons. A truck delivered it from some place in J-Town (Jeffersontown). *Where does that company get the water to sell to us,* I wondered, knowing that J-Town was not on city water. Ten thousand gallons sounded like a lot to me, but for a family of ten and our farm animals and the crops, I knew it wasn't.

"Don't waste that water!" was Daddy's constant refrain. I understood, and joined him in his lament.

Feeling like a copy-cat, I called out, "Don't waste that water," when speaking to the others.

With the strength in my young arms I lifted and struggled the heavy pan from the sink over to the coal oil stove. The burner had to be lit with a match. To get to the matches, I reached up into the joists of the kitchen floor above my head and retrieved the old coffee canister we kept tucked into the basement ceiling. Daddy insisted that matches be stored in a metal container because he feared the field mice would find them and start a fire by chewing on them. This made sense to me because our house was full of field mice. Pulling a long kitchen match out of the canister, I struck it with a snap of my wrist, by rubbing it against the brick wall of the basement. It was called a "strike-anywhere," match.

Since the water took a while to boil, I decided that this would be a good time to run out to the orchard and start on my job of killing chickens. Twelve to fifteen had to be done every morning. The chickens were fryers size now, which meant they were the perfect size for good eating. Fryers get tough fast, and I had to work my way through the 400 baby chicks Daddy gave Mama for Mother's Day a few weeks ago when they were cute and fluffy. It had been my job to raise them in the multi-layered chicken brooder in the hen house. Smiling, I was delighted with a chance to get out of the basement.

Running toward the chicken house, I heard Tony screaming when I reached the orchard. After the little ones finished eating their breakfast, he and Mary Ann had returned to their job of searching for the eggs, but were not really working very hard at it. The fresh grapes coming on in the arbor tempted Tony to climb up to the vines and help himself. A yellow jacket that had the same idea stung him.

"Good thing it wasn't Margaret Jane," I told him unsympathetically, as I turned up his pants leg. We were all scared of her getting stung. Being allergic, last year a sting caused her head to swell up like a pumpkin! Quickly, I searched the weeds for some broad-leafed Plantain. Daddy showed me how to do this a long time ago when I was stung by a nasty wasp. Rolling the long leaf over and over between my palms until it was juicy, I applied it to the sting.

"Darn-it, hold still, this will make it feel better," I said, as Tony continued to squirm and wiggle in my grasp. The redness soon left, and when the pain settled down, he climbed right back up the vine to nibble at the sweet purple grapes, again. "If you get another sting," I grumbled, suddenly jealous that he got to be outside all day, "I'm not gonna' feel sorry for ya'!" From the ground, Mary Ann looked at me with a guilty face and stopped drawing pictures in the dirt with her stick. Jumping up quickly, she stretched on tiptoes to tug at Tony's pants leg. "Tony, Mama wants us ta' get the eggs," she reminded him. "Come on!"

Suddenly, remembering my reason for coming to the orchard in the first place, I started running for the chickens. Managing to turn my job into a game, I tried to make it go faster. *Yay! Hurry up, Deanna,* I cheered myself onward, *only five more to go.* Chasing another squawking, red-feathered pullet around the peach trees, I snatched her under the leafy rhubarb bushes. Grabbing her by the feet, I looped them into one of the nooses that I kept tied on the clothesline. Finally, I had the twelve chickens needed for the day.

With a sharp butcher knife, and without emotion, I briskly began to remove their heads. They hung, I cut, they squawked, I cut, they thrashed and drained, I went for the next one, having no concern about how the poor chickens might feel. Caring about that would take time, and time was something I didn't have. It was really getting hot outside, I bristled, as the sun beat down on my shoulders.

By the time I finished with the last chicken, the first one had drained its blood, and was ready to drop in the basket, then the next and the next and the next. I gathered up the chickens' heads and threw them over the orchard fence and into the pasture field where the hogs grunted and waited. Then, removing the dirty apron that kept the blood off my cotton work dress, I returned it to its nail by the door of the hen house.

When I brought the chickens in from the clothesline, the water was boiling nicely in the kettle, and the basement was filled with the sharp smell of the first batch of tomatoes Mama had bubbling on the other burner. She put down her paring knife, and together we plunged, scalded and plucked the red feathers from the chickens. Mama then scrubbed out the pan and refilled it with water. This time it would be used to sterilize jars for the canning.

She called upstairs for Margaret Jane and Theresa. They came down the inside basement steps from doing the breakfast dishes and cleaning up the kitchen.

"You girls need to go and find us some quart jars," Mama said. "We're gonna' need five for the peas, then we'll need another twenty for the beans, six for the beets, and twenty-five for the tomatoes. "Now, go find 'em, then go back and finish your work upstairs." Mama's skill at judging the piles of vegetables amazed me.

As the girls scampered off to the laundry room, which was the room behind us, they started singing, "Oh, the sun shines bright..." from *My Old Kentucky Home*, which was one of our favorite songs. Mama and I joined them in their singing, as they pulled jars from the shelves that lined the walls in there. Singing played an important part in our work. It calmed us down and helped us ignore the boredom of our mind-numbing chores. When a song ended, one of us chimed in with another one. Singing made the time go faster, at least until Mama's soap opera, "Stella Dallas", came on the radio. While we sang, Mama and I continued to remove the innards and cut the slippery chickens into recognizable parts of breasts, legs, wings and thighs.

Wrapping each chicken in layers of waxed paper, I readied them for the freezer. Mama went back to her work with the tomatoes. She was cutting out the tent caterpillars that had hatched in them before we squished them through the hand crank grinder to become tomato juice. I waited until the girls finished finding the jars and stacking them on the table before I opened the freezer. After they went back upstairs to sweep the floors, I reached up into the basement rafters for the secret hiding place of the freezer key. Mama only trusted me with its location, and I enjoyed being her confidant. I had to admit, there were a few privileges to being the oldest.

Daddy insisted that the freezer stayed locked. After Fehr's went out of business the year before, he had returned to his old job at Sealtest Dairy. The workers there were given several tubs of surplus ice cream from time to time.

He told Mama and me, "I know those kids'll keep sneakin' inta' that ice cream, and that lets all the cold air outta' the freezer. The chickens in there are gonna' spoil!" Continuing to speak, he then frowned, "Worse, it makes the 'lectricity bill go up." All of us knew that any kind of waste made Daddy mad. Keeping Daddy happy was always a goal of the whole family.

Mama and I passed the time talking about the secrets of life while we worked. She liked to tell stories about her life before she married Daddy and about my aunts and uncles when they were just little kids in Howardstown. Her being the oldest in her family meant that she knew of all their adventures. These stories made me feel close to them, even though most of them lived far away. She repeated many of her tales, but I didn't mind. "Did I tell you about the time Uncle Bud got caught selling Moonshine?" she asked as I bent down into the freezer, stacking the wrapped chicken packages in neat rows. I laughed as I remembered the details of Uncle Bud's antics of the 1920's.

I started on the jars, and in no time, Margaret Jane and Theresa were down in the basement again, having finished their upstairs chores. Using jar mops and sudsy water, they helped me scrub the jars out for sterilization. After I put them on to boil, we gathered our chairs, and sat around in a circle, hulling peas and snapping beans. We laughed at the "Art Linkletter Show," on the little brown Motorola radio that we kept in the basement during the summertime, while we waited for Mama's favorite show, "Stella Dallas."

When most of the job was done, she reminded Margaret Jane and Theresa, "Now you girls go on outside and get the rest of the eggs from Tony and Mary Ann. Help 'em clean 'em off at the pump. Then pull some carrots and radishes from the salad garden, and get the table set for dinner. We wanna' get out of here on time," she continued. The girls giggled and chased each other up the outside basement steps to the yard, happy to get out of that prison, again. I envied them, and took this opportunity to run up the inside basement steps myself, to check the time on the clock above the kitchen stove. Mama didn't want the kids to get cramps in the Pool, so dinner had to be ready by eleven o'clock.

"It's already 10:15, we'll never get to Light House Lake!" I whined down the steps to Mama.

"We'll burn that bridge when we get to it. Now, get down here and help me and stop bein' so desperate," she answered my complaints.

Blanching the peas in boiling water, we then filled the sterilized jars. Mama put ten jars at a time in our large pressure cooker. I filled the smaller cooker with six at a time. All the burners on our coal oil stove were busy. We watched for the steam in the pressure-cooker to go up to ten pounds of pressure, while we continued to work up the tomatoes.

Before going upstairs to fix dinner, I gave the clabbered milk in the cotton-gauze sack hanging over the laundry tub another twist. It was becoming cottage cheese. This cement tub was in the back room next to the ringer washing machine. The yellow whey poured out of the cheesecloth bag as I collected it in a bowl. I went upstairs to put the meal on, and poured the whey into the five-gallon slop bucket for the hogs. Everything edible or drinkable went into the slop bucket. On the farm we wasted nothing.

It's disgustin' that my family's gotta' have that nasty slop bucket, I thought, cursing the existence of the large, greasy, crusty container.

None of my friends at Our Lady of Lourdes had even heard of such a smelly thing! But none of them had hogs either, or lived on well water.

I let my mind wander to the time was mortified when Claudia Gilbert, Shirley Singer, and Tim Quimby dropped in to visit me. They had walked down Hunsinger Lane from the new Hikes Point Bowling Alley that was now up at the corner of Hunsinger and Hikes Lanes and across from Bauer's Restaurant. It was delightful to see them, but I feared what they might find at my house. Immediately, I ushered them past my embarrassing, whiney and dirty little brothers and sisters, and took my friends into the living room where the other kids were not allowed. After we four took a few turns playing *Chopsticks* and Hoagy Carmichael's *Heart and Soul* on the piano, my friends suddenly left. Despite the closed door, the sounds of screaming, yelling and crying came in through the living room walls. I could see in their faces that they didn't know how to cope with the chaos going on at my house. Uncomfortable for me, they quickly made an excuse to leave, and return to the safety of the bowling alley.

"I guess they'll never come back," I sobbed to Mama. "Why can't we live like normal people?" She shook her head and rolled her eyes up to the ceiling, "Well, I declare, what 'm I gonna' do with you?" she sighed, not having an answer.

Going to my room that night, I spent the rest of the evening working on my embroidery designs. I poured my discontent into practicing the new stitches that Aunt Bertha had taught me the week before. The pretty colors of the spring garden design on the large doily that I was embroidering for my Hope-Chest, lifted my spirits and gave me something to dream about. I went to bed feeling a little better than I had when my friends left me, earlier in the evening.

****

But on this particular morning, I finally entered the kitchen and brought my mind back to getting dinner together, so we could get to the pool on time. Mama stayed in the basement to finish canning the tomato juice – *we're a pretty good team*, I thought. I opened up a jar of last summer's sauerkraut, and served it cold with some of the cottage cheese that was made two days before. Then I sliced off some pork shoulder to fry. The smoke-cured meat was stored in the metal drawer of our Hoosier Cabinet. All my relatives called this type of cabinet a baking cabinet. It held a twenty-five pound sack of flour that was inserted above a sifter, and had shelves to hold all our sugar, baking soda, and spices. There was also an enamel counter-top that pulled in and out. Mama and I used its cool surface for rolling out dough for biscuits and piecrusts.

The hickory-smoke smell of the cured meat I was preparing, made me hungry. As I sliced it, I brushed the maggots from the shoulder's salt encrusted rind with my butcher knife. They were deposited there by the flies that flew in from the barn because our kitchen screen door was constantly being swung open and shut. The flies buzzed around me and were aggravating me as I sliced on the pork shoulder. They landed on my arms and in my hair. Frustrated, I shooed them away, but they continued to lay new eggs on the rind as I worked. *Darn-it!*

"Don't worry about any germs from those maggots," Deanna, Mama told me years ago, "The heat from the skillet kills 'em all." I cut seven slices, one for each of us. Margaret Jane and Theresa scrubbed up the carrots and radishes they brought in from the salad garden. I sliced some tomatoes after frying up the pork.

We were so eager to go swimming that the dishes were done in no time, and the kids got ready just as fast. Because of the polio scare nobody drank out of public water fountains, so I filled two large water bottles to take along with us. The pictures we saw of children in iron lungs on TV scared us all.

Mama sat behind the wheel of our 1951 Chevy two-door sedan and the kids climbed in. Getting into the car last, I made sure all the kids had their towels and a change of clothes. Right now, we were all wearing our swimsuits. Excited to go the city, we started singing again because Daddy didn't believe in spending money on a car radio. Cautiously, Mama carefully pulled the car out of the driveway onto Hunsinger Lane. There was more traffic here now than in the old days, and it had been asphalted for several years by now. We rolled down the windows, wanting to feel the breeze in our hair as Mama drove along. It felt very suburban to be going off to swimming lessons.

We didn't lock the door of the house, because nobody ever locked doors in Hikes Point.

"Who'd want Aunt Bertha's hand-me-down furniture from the '37 flood?" Mama joked. Besides, our trusty dog, Bullet, would protect us from any intruders that may happen on the place. Bullet was a good watchdog. When he wasn't trotting around the farm with us kids, he slept in the cool corner of the basement not far from the water pump. This pump was used to bring the water into the house from the orchard cistern. Bullet was my best companion, and followed me everywhere I went. Any unfamiliar sound on the property pulled him away from his cozy corner, and "he barked up a storm."

****

The relaxing break at Light House Lake was soon over. To keep from coming home smelling like Clorox, we washed off at the stand-up showers at the pool, before we went into the bath house to change. The songs, *Dance with Me Henry,* and *Rock Around the Clock"* from the jukebox, were rumbling around in my head as Mama drove along. While the kids were swimming, I had watched the skilled moves of the dancers on Light House Lake's patio. Sighing, *I'll never learn all the stuff you need to know to be a teenager,* I despaired, fearing that jitterbugging' would just make me fall all over the guy's feet. But, I was still jealous and yearned for the fun the other teens were having at the pool.

Nothing special was going on on this day, so, we came straight home. Sometimes in the *Louisville Times* we found out about the Grand Opening of a new shopping center. Earlier in the summer, we enjoyed one at the opening of the Gardiner Lane Shopping Center. We signed up for door prizes at Taylor Drugstore and got free cookies at the Woolworth's Five & Dime. To get anything free was exciting to us. New shopping centers were opening all over the East End. We thought Grand Openings were great events and were always on the look out for them. Slowly, I realized these opportunities were some of the good aspects about becoming more suburban.

Hearing our car crunch the driveway, Bullet ran up the basement steps to greet us as usual. He followed me back down into the cellar to put the outer rings on our canning of the morning. I also checked the jar lids and make sure the canning had been successful. If the lid was stuck tight against the jar when it cooled down it was good. If it popped up, it was a dud that may cause food poisoning, and had to be thrown out. That never happened, our pressure cooker always did a dependable job.

Putting away the canning of the morning, I counted sixty quarts of beans and seventy of tomatoes that we already had on the shelves. The beets had just started coming on. Even with this drought, we were right on schedule. Before the summer ended we would get our usual 100 to 125 of each of them, plus at least sixty-five of pickles, fifty of sauerkraut and thirty Chowchow, a green-tomato relish, and several of beets. We also had fruit: apples, peaches, pears and several of grape juice and jelly. By winter, the basement shelves would be filled with about 500 jars of our summer food to eat. I was proud of our hard work. It took the effort of the whole family to keep us fed. All of us, even Mama, went out in the fields to help with the spring planting. Daddy and the boys worked hard, too, doing most of the outdoor work that was needed for our food supply. Without their work in the fields and with the animals, except for the chickens that I raised, Mama and I wouldn't be canning and butchering.

Daddy made good sour-kraut. Before leaving the basement I checked on the balloon that he put on the lid of the large, stoneware crock of cabbage he sliced up a few days ago. As it fermented, the cabbage turned into sour kraut. The fermenting process caused gases to push the balloon erect. Checking the balloon let me see how many days before the kraut would ready to can. Daddy also liked to ferment elderberry wine that he made out of the sweet smelling bushes that grew at the end of our cornfield, and dandelion wine out of the pesky yellow blooms that he made us collect for him in the spring.

****

We were always famished after swimming. Thanks to Daddy, we got to have a snack on this day. The day before, he traded a farmer out by Sealtest Dairy, a tub of surplus ice cream for a watermelon. Watermelons were so delicious, we begged Daddy to grow some for us. He said they took up too much room in the garden, and they couldn't be canned for winter use, so, "They're not worth the effort," he replied. Jimmy grabbed the melon, we had it cooling against the back wall in the basement, near where we had the ears of corn. While

Mama was down for her afternoon nap, I sliced off a big piece for each of us and put the rest in the refrigerator for Daddy and the boys. The sliced watermelon made the milk and butter taste funny, but that was part of summertime.

Jimmy spread a blanket under the maple trees in the front yard. Each kid took their melon slice and I grabbed the saltshaker. We laughed as we gobbled the tasty melon – the juice running down our faces and arms.

"Deanna, Tony said that a watermelon will grow in my stomach because I swallowed a seed. Is he lying to me?" Mary Ann asked nervously.

Laughing, I remembered Johnny teasing me in just the same way a few years ago. I looked over at Tony who was snickering behind his hand and enjoying a good laugh as well as his watermelon. "But, but, I heard it on TV…" he stammered giving me a serious look.

Reassuring them that it was still false, no matter where they heard it, I wiggled around for a comfortable position in my dress and stretched my legs in the itchy grass. It was great just being outside. Acting my age was far from my mind as I proved that I was just as much of a kid as the rest of them. We ended our treat with our usual seed spitting fight between the boys and the girls. Soon we were so drenched in stickiness, that the flies were driving us crazy. We washed the watermelon juice off our skin, in the bucket of water that Jimmy had waiting for us by the hand pump. Then he took it to the cow's watering tub.

Before long it was time to fix supper. While the little kids watched "Howdy Doody" and "Clarabell the Clown," on the TV in the family/ dining room, Jimmy and I were back out at the pump again. This time it was for removing the husks and corn silks from the rosin-ears. We threw the scraps over the pasture field fence to the grunting hogs, with their ever-ready stomachs, while we talked about how our life would change one day. Our supper would also include fresh sliced tomatoes, the vinegar-sugar cucumbers I fixed that morning, cottage cheese, fried country ham with red eye gravy, and a mess of beans flavored with the ham grease.

****

At this time, I wasn't thinking of supper though. I had my mind on more important things than that. Watching the clock, I was thinking of teen-age things. Daddy liked the evening paper, the *Louisville Times*. It was delivered right before he came home from work around five o'clock in the afternoon. Sneaking over to the mirror in my parent's bedroom, I combed my hair and straightened the fresh dress I put on after our watermelon fight.

My heart beat a little faster as I thought of handsome young Paul Steidenberger. He was home for the summer from University of Kentucky to plant and care for his elderly father's farm. Their potato farm was across Hunsinger Lane from us. I couldn't help having a teenage crush on him. When it was time to collect the evening paper from our paper box, I hoped young Paul would get a glimpse of me from his tractor as I walked across Hunsinger Lane to the to get it. Everyday that I could, I waited behind the screens on our front porch, watching for his tractor to get closer to the road before I came out to get the paper. One time he was close enough to the road to actually say "Hi" to me. The memory made my stomach tingle as I thought, *that's been my biggest thrill of my summer,* and I hoped it would happen again. But, today my dream was not to be. Paul was plowing a field behind the pasture on the other side of his house.

Disappointed, I comforted myself by reaching up into the basement rafters for the freezer key when I went down to get the beans for supper. My favorite Sealtest Ice Cream flavor was called, Cherry Nugget. Filled with crunchy chopped almonds and cherries, it was cool and sweet, and distracted my temper.

Soon, I heard Johnny and Marcellus shouting at each other as their bikes bit into the gravel of the driveway. Full of themselves, they were bragging about who made the most money caddying today. *Time to get supper,* I sighed, and ran up the inside basement steps to join Mama in the kitchen.

After the meal, Margaret Jane and Theresa did the dishes. It felt good that they took over some of the chores I used to do. When the girls came outside Jimmy and Tony challenged them to play 'chicken,' by running down our long driveway and sliding on the gravel in their bare feet. Johnny, Marcellus and I used to dare each other to do that when we were younger. Now, the boys were in the bathroom primping and getting ready to go to the Sky-Way Drive-in with some of the older caddies who were able to drive. I wished I could go with them, but they sure didn't want me, a sister, along. They were interested in flirting with the girls. For me, being a teenager was hard. I didn't want to play with the little kids, I didn't have any money to go out with my friends, and I knew that having them over here was impossible. As the oldest girl in this family I felt so left out.

Playing on the old water heater that Daddy threw out years ago, I killed some time and watched the evening go by. We kids called the old heater, "the barrel" and made a game out of it by challenging each other to roll on it, going back and forth across the side yard, like a lumberjack rolls on a large log. We went from the corn crib to the pasture field fence. My long toes clinched the cool metal as I rolled it over to the maple tree near the cow's water tub, my head ducking under its lowest limb. I knew I was too big for this activity, especially when the younger kids begged me to get off and give them a turn. They must have noticed my mood because they decided to play Fox and Geese, instead. *That use ta' be fun, too,* I complained, *nothin's fun anymore.* My mind rumbled on, feeling sorry for myself.

Did Mama feel like this when she was a teenager? I wondered, shrugging my shoulders and watching Daddy take Calfie into the barn for the evening milking. He checked over the crops and the work we did every night. He also checked the animals to make sure they were healthy. If any were weak or sick, he weaned them from the pack at once. Animals are very cannibalistic, and quickly killed the weaker members.

After finishing his outside work, Daddy ate his supper alone when the kitchen was quiet. He steered clear of our hectic supper times. Mama always put his meal on the steamed hotplate that she kept warm for him in the oven. Then he and Mama sat together at the table, filling in the holes of their day.

It was a lazy summer evening and I continued barreling back and forth from the corncrib to the cow's watering tub by the fence. As I liked to do in the evenings, I watched the sun go down and bring new color into my world. The sunglow changed the broken windows in the 'Old Brick,' the dilapidated Civil War mansion behind our pasture field, to gold with its reflection. The blue hills of Fairdale, way off in the distance, framed out the picture. My mind wandered as I let the sky inspire me as it gradually turned from gold to pink and purple, and then to mauve.

Life is passing me by, I thought. *Farm chores are all I know how to do, and the farms are disappearing. What am I going to do when I grow up? How will I live?* City ways, as much as they intrigued me, also scared me. I felt as worthless as the suckers Jimmy and I nonchalantly cast aside from the corn stalks.

"Is this what it's like to be a teenager?" I had wailed to Mama the night before.

"Deanna," she told me then, "you're a girl and you're gonna' feel different than those boys. Girls have the blues, sort of like the baby blues I have after each one of my babies is born. There's no explainin' it. Now boys, 'phsaw,' nothing bothers them!" she said, pursing her lips and squaring her shoulders, obviously, being aggravated by that thought, too.

Bullet trotted over to be with me, smiling and wagging his shaggy tail. I jumped off the barrel, and welcomed him into my arms. Whimpering into his sandy brown fur, I pulled him in close. His buoyant spirit always cheered me up, and with the reality of Mama's words soaking in, I allowed my sadness to slide into better feelings.

"Maybe I'll have a good-looking man like Paul Steidenberger in my life when I grow up," I told Bullet. "Next year I'll be in high school and have a job, and things will change then." Bullet's tail wagged in agreement. We chased down through the pasture field, avoiding all of Calfie's squishy cowpies, going beyond the stinky hog 'waller' and on to the sinkhole down by the back fence.

Collapsing into the clover between the stands of delicate Queen Anne's lace, I rolled over on my stomach and leaned up on my elbows. Bullet beside me, I watched the lightening bugs come up out of the thorny jimson weeds and pasture grasses. This spot, by the sinkhole, was woodsy and it felt like I was somewhere else. On a flat rock at the edge of the trees, Jimmy burned our weekly trash. On the Fourth of July, this was the place where we had our wiener roasts and bonfires. Lying there together, Bullet and I just enjoyed the coolness of the summer evening settle in. Soon, stars twinkled in the sky through the leafy ash trees that grew by the sinkhole's edge, and the lightening bugs blinked on and off around us. The beauty of the evening calmed my raging teenage mind, and I let myself be settled by it.

Too soon it all ended. "Deanna, come on back to the house, I need you," I heard Mama's voice over the noise of the screaming locusts and Katy-dids and Kady-didn'ts. "I never get much time away from my obligations," I complained to Bullet. I never thought much about whether I was loved or not. I knew I was valuable. "Oh well," I said to Bullet's smiling face, "school will start soon." Then I realized that school and homework were my way out of here.

My Orange Blossom Cookie Canister

Sweat drips from our
brows, Jimmy and I
work the cornfields
in the hot afternoon sun.

Hoeing out Johnson weeds,
plucking off sucker shoots,
collecting the rosin-ears.
August heat moves us slowly.

Each coping silently,
sliding into private worlds
of daydreams that arise
to release our burdens.

Mentally, I return again
and again to a hiding place.
A darkened bedroom corner
under a pink taffeta skirt that
hides a wobbly table.

Secreted on the shelf behind
my sketches and writing tablet.
I recall a favorite treasure
and imagine my sunburned face
welcoming the touch
of its cool metal surface.

An empty canister, decorated
in shades of turquoise with
sumptuous clouds of
orange sugar cookies
painted on its lid.

Gingerly opening it, I
allow the orangey fragrance to
escape. Surrounding my face, and
filling my lungs, it
waters my mouth
with desire for the cookies' taste.

The canister holds only
this aroma and my imaginings
of what life must be like
for those wealthy enough
to own such frivolity.

"For your crayons," I recall Aunt
Bertha saying
when she gifted me
this empty vessel – the tinkling
voices of Pat and Alice, her
granddaughters, filling the air.

My mind sees their sophisticated
neighborhood by Shawnee Park –
where ladies have afternoon tea
on white linen tablecloths, and serve
cookies such as these –
lighter than air, more fragrant than
lavender.

This daydream allows me
to forget the sun's blaze
and the thirst in my throat, as
I ponder a place where
ladies don't work cornfields, kill
chickens or water cows.

I picture ceiling fans and potted palms,
breezy rooms with cool tile floors.
My scorched body relaxes back
into my chore as I move

among the corn stalks,
eager to be done,
so I can again delight
in the fragrance
of my canister –
and dream of future days.

Chapter 14

Flashlight Dance

My feet tapped to the music of, *Wake Up, Little Suzie*, by the Everly Brothers. I wanted to dance, and hoped some cute guy would ask me. I thought I looked pretty in my blue 'Ivy League' shirtwaist dress with the three crinolines stuffed under it. The crinolines, which were fluffy lace petticoats, kept me from looking so skinny. I had just had my brown hair cut in a cute little 'bob,' that all the girls at Assumption High School were wearing this year. *Why aren't the boys asking me to dance*, I wondered?

My friend Betty Lou came over, shook her long blond curls and said,

"These boys are just not in a dancing mood tonight, they're all scardy-cats. You and I should dance together. That way they'll know we want to dance, and break in on us."

Grabbing my hand, we ran for the terrazzo dance floor of St. Steven Martyr's school cafeteria. It was Friday night in late August of 1958, and very hot. I was seventeen and ready to go into my senior year of high school. Betty Lou and I were attending what teens called a 'mixer.' Mixers were how the five Catholic girl high schools and the three Catholic boy's high schools got the opposite sexes together. These dances were held on Friday and Sunday nights every weekend by the Teen Clubs of the local parishes. St. Steven's called their club "Mar-teen." Betty Lou and I went to at least one mixer every week. Not only did we get to meet boys, we met people from all over Louisville. It was especially fun to meet teens from the West and the South Ends of town. I was amazed at how different people could be, who were from the same city. It was almost like traveling to another town.

Last week, "Aga-teen," from St. Agnes had a 'sock-hop' in their gymnasium. No shoes were allowed. Everybody danced in their bobby sox. Sock-hops were always fun, though sometimes a bit smelly. *What is it about stinky feet that makes guys want to dance? I pondered.*

After *Wake up Little Suzi*" the rollicking beat of, *Good Molly Miss Molly*, by Little Richard, pounded in our ears and excited our feet – we decided to take in another dance.

She yanked my arm toward her in a jitterbug twirl; my skirt flew up, exposing the frilliness of my puffy crinolines. *Now, I really look like a good dancer*, I thought, *the guys'll be flocking over here ta' ask me for a dance.* But, I commented to Betty Lou, "What's wrong with these guys? They're usually more willing than this." We finished the dance, breathless, with sweat rolling down our necks, and no dance offers.

Although the parishes housed these mixers, it seemed like the Nuns still played a big role in the way they were run. There was dress code: You must wear nylon hose or bobby socks, no bare legs, you must have sleeves in your dresses, no bare arms, and definitely no low-cut tops. You were not allowed in the door if you looked inappropriate. There was also a dance code: No 'Alligator' or 'Dirty Dog Dances,' and no holding your partner too close. Committing any of these infractions got you kicked right out of the event.

The mixers cost twenty-five cents, and they usually served punch. Standing around the punch bowl was a great way to meet people. It was just like Uncle Mac told me about the water cooler at Swift and Company, where he worked in Detroit. After our unsuccessful dance, Betty Lou and I headed to the punch table for a cool glass of punch. The breeze from the tall floor fan standing by the table blew through our hair, and dried our sweaty necks. Mary Lou and Claudia, both wearing ponytails, joined us. These girls went to Presentation High School.

"What Duds!" they lamented, contorting their pretty faces. "I guess they're too hot to dance," said Claudia, backing up to the fan and shaking her ponytail into its breeze.

"The only one who wants to dance is that creep you brought, Deanna."

Embarrassed, I looked over at the wall, and said, "Oh well, I had to get here didn't I?

"Me too." Betty Lou spoke up. "He brought both of us."

I guess I actually had a date tonight – of sorts. Joe Speed, he was a graduate of Trinity High School. When he called me at the last minute, I asked him to give Betty Lou a ride, too. Her boyfriend, Larry, had to work tonight, at the local burger joint called the "Ranch House." He would come to the mixer later and take her home.

"If Joe didn't bring us," Betty Lou explained, "we'd have to take that long bus ride from Hikes Point to Audubon Park to get here," she continued, "Mama couldn't get the car tonight." Her mother usually took us to the mixers that were far away. With all my younger brothers and sisters at home, my mother could never leave the house. Besides, she was afraid to drive at night. Betty Lou and I took the bus to the mixers that were close by. The one time that we took the bus out here to Mar-Teen, the ride required several transfers and took almost two hours.

Betty Lou had gone to St. Bartholomew's with me a long time ago, but at that time, she lived in another part of town. I was delighted when, three years ago, her parents decided to move to the subdivision on the other side of McMahan Shopping Center at Hikes Point. Betty Lou's father had grown up in Gethsemane, like mine. We always helped each other out with rides when we could.

Joe and I had gone out a few times, but we were not really dating. I thought he was obnoxious, constantly talking about himself, and always had a roving eye. Even more embarrassing, he kept his keys on a long chain that he kept twirling back and forth on his index finger. Joe didn't like to go to mixers alone, but once we arrived, he spent his time flirting, and dancing with other girls.

That made me happy because I really was at Mar-Teen to meet somebody else, somebody that I could be proud of dating. I was glad that Joe was willing to take Betty Lou and me all the way out here to Audubon Park. Glancing up, I found him twirling his keys with a group of girls from Mercy High School, near the table that held the box of records. The disk jockey for the night was Father Brown, St. Steven's assistant pastor.

"Father, do you have *Blueberry Hill*, by Fats Domino, or *Shake, Rattle and Roll*? by Bill Haley." Joe and his friends pestered him with requests, as Father Brown searched through his record box for the next selection.

Oh brother, I sighed, recalling the earlier conversation that I had just had with my girlfriends. Now that I knew how all my friends felt about him, I was embarrassed. Like my parents, I judged myself by how the people who were connected to me acted.

As the evening grew darker, a spotlight shined on the rotating "Disco" Ball, revolving from the ceiling, scattering stars around the cafeteria. Now, this place really looked like a dance hall, and felt almost as good as when Assumption held a dance at the Crystal Ballroom of the Brown Hotel, downtown, at Fourth and Broadway.

Joe looked as hot and bored as the rest of the guys here. I watched him crunch his cigarette into one of the ashtrays on a window ledge. He turned around and started coming in my direction. "Come on Cutie, let's cut a rug," he chirped, wrapping his clammy hand around mine. *Oh, Brother,* I moaned again, *why does he always say such ridiculous things?* Blushing at his corny words, my mind continued, *Joe, if you only knew how little the girls like you're brazen attitude, you'd tone it down a little.*

I lead the way onto the dance floor. A slow piece by the Platters called, *My Prayer,* was playing. Grabbing my waist, he turned me around like a sack of potatoes, and pushed his sweaty palm into the back of my blue shirtwaist dress, smudging his greasy 'Brill-Cream' hair dressing against my cheek as he brought our heads together. At least I was dancing, I thought, as I looked over at my girlfriends. They were still dancing with each other in order to keep from being dreaded wallflowers.

The heat of the evening had most of the dancers cooling off by the open windows that unfortunately emitted very little cool air. Hardly a breeze stirred. Even though there were plenty of ashtrays inside, many smokers chose to smoke outside in the parking lot. Most of the boys smoked. Some snuck into their car to drink something. If they were caught with any alcohol on the premises, the priest would throw them out. Their name would be put on a blacklist and they would be banned from all the Teen Clubs across the city. They were very careful, at least until it got darker.

When *My Prayer,* ended, Joe disappeared again. Suddenly, the parish priest, Father Jones, came into the room wearing his long black cassock. Priests generally wore cassocks when they were not saying

Mass. *He gotta' be hotter than me*, I thought, mopping my neck with a piece of toilet paper I had swiped from the bathroom. The heat didn't seem to bother Father Jones.

He announced, "Okay Folks, things are too dead out there on the dance floor, tonight. So, we're going to have a little ice breaker."

"What we need is an ice pick," Betty Lou whispered to me, as our circle of girlfriends chuckled.

"All right, you Guys and Gals," Father said, as he stood in the middle of the floor, walking around in a wide arc and holding a flashlight, "It's not too late to have some fun, here – Mar-Teen never gives up!"

Joe came back over and grabbed my hand. If there was anything weird going to happen, he wanted everybody to know that he started out with a partner.

Then Father gave directions, "I want all the girls on the left wall, and you guys go to the right wall. He motioned with his flashlight. With as much obedience as we had shown in elementary school, we moved forward and waited for the next suggestion.

"Now, Father Brown, who is the disk jockey," Father Jones chuckled and did a courtesy toward Fr. Brown, "is going to put on a record for us. I'm going to go from one side of the room to the other. I'll shine my light on first a girl," then he cracked a little joke, "You remember the rules boys, 'Ladies First!' Then I'll shine it on a boy," he continued. "You two to are to dance with each other as partners."

I watched Father Brown, the DJ, who was also wearing a cassock, use a piece of gauze to wipe off a record and put it on the turntable. His choice was "Volarie," a popular Italian song about the constancy of "tomorrow." Father Jones came down the line, as he said he would, going from one side of the room to the other, shining his flashlight first on a girl, and then a boy. Everybody tingled as the room filled with suspense. Soon all of us were dancing. My partner was a tiny freshman from "Boys Haven" nicknamed, "Bird," who went to Flaget High School. I had danced with Bird before, not a bad dancer, but a freshman! He was way too young for me.

When the music stopped, Father Jones refused to let us off the dance floor.

"That's a nice start," he said, "but I think we need another one for good measure. This time we are going to do the Schottische. Start with the partner you now have." He told Father Brown to put on special song for this. "We'll be dancing the Schottische to 'Patricia'," he said, with a lilt to his voice.

The rollicking organ music of "Patricia," filled the room. The schottische was a Swiss American folkdance, and a real icebreaker. The dancers moved in circles and did all sorts of movements with other couples. It was like square dancing, and we switched partners many times. Dancing with some cute guys and some ugly guys, some good dancers and some bad ones, I chewed my gum and tried to act nonchalant.

One of the last guys that I danced with was a tall, dark-haired, senior from St. Xavier (St. X), High School, named Johnny. Like me, he seemed a little preoccupied, we had to move fast through the movements of the Schottische, but while we were partners, we did find a few things to say. He seemed at least interested. When the music stopped I expected him to go back to his date. Instead, Johnny left the crowd standing near him and came over in my direction.

I was delighted when he asked, "Would you like to get some punch?" I looked around quickly because I wanted to check on what Joe was up to. I found him, a cigarette dangling from his lips, a plume of smoke rising into the air. He was flirting with a girl I knew slightly from Holy Rosary High. I was relieved.

"Sure," I smiled shyly, and followed Johnny to the crowded punch table. We stood in front of the fan and cooled off. Its rattle drowned out the tinkle of the glass dipper, as Johnny fumbled with the punch cups.

Holding the tiny handles of our glass cups, we found a couple of vacant folding chairs, near an open window. Gratefully, my body welcomed the cool metal seat. The locusts and crickets outside the window were almost as loud as the song, *Tenderly,* by Nat King Cole that was playing for the dancers. The icebreaker had worked! The dance floor was now filled with chatter and laughter, replacing the former skepticism.

"Everybody is dancing now," we both said at the same time, a bit nervously, trying to find something to say. Chuckling, both of us took a gulp of the cherry Kool-Aid and smiled at each other.

Johnny said he lived in the West End. *Oh good,* I smiled. *Now, I got a lot to talk about,* I thought, thankfully. Since Daddy's elderly Aunts lived down there, I had been there many times and knew most of the landmarks.

Opening our stalled conversation again I said, "My Aunt Ida lives near you on West Broadway. Do you know a Mrs. Brakemeir at 3517?" A smile spread across Johnny's face and it lit up immediately. He answered, "You mean the Mrs. Brakemeir that lost her husband, Gus, not too long ago? Sure I do, I deliver papers to her." Then we talked about his paper job, about his getting up at four o'clock in the morning, carrying two heavy bags, one on each shoulder, the agony of taking them up and down steps, especially of the apartment buildings, etc.

I was impressed, and felt like little kid because I had no job. "I wish I had a job," I volunteered, "but I'm the oldest of ten kids and Mama is pregnant. She needs me to stay home and help her with the work."

After explaining some of my chores to him, he shook his head and said with a chuckle, "That sounds a lot harder work than delivering papers." Exhaling, I felt reassured that he didn't look down on me because I wasn't part of the world.

Lucky for me, the next dance was a "Sadie Hawkins Dance." That meant it was a "Ladies Choice Dance." Naturally, I chose Johnny. "Do you like to jitterbug?" I asked as sounds of, *Johnny Be Good,* by Chuck Berry bounced up at us from the terrazzo floor.

I couldn't believe my good luck, a cute boy, a nice boy, a St. X Senior. St. Xavier was considered Louisville's finest boy's high school. Finding our place on the crowded dance floor, we jitterbugged, twirling, swinging each other in and out, and ducking under each other's arms as we moved to Chuck Berry's lively beat. The heat made our sweaty hands slip from each other's grasp more than once.

After the jitterbug, we stayed on the floor to slow dance to Pat Boone's, *Love Letters in the Sand.* He held me comfortably, taking my hand in his and placing both our hands on his shoulder. He didn't push his other hand up my back, instead, he let it encircle my waist. As I moved in close to him, I noticed the smell of his, Aqua Velva, aftershave lotion. *Oooo, he's so sophisticated,* I thought, beaming him a big smile. As we danced, we lost our inhibitions and chatted like we had known each other forever.

I found out Johnny volunteered for the Red Cross, and helped deliver blood to the hospitals. He was in St. X's Marching Band, and played saxophone. *If I date him,* I thought, planning ahead, *I'll get to wear his letter sweater, and go to all the games. I need to move things along, here.*

Finally, I got the courage, and asked, "Do you drive?" hinting for a ride home. "Yeah, I drove tonight," he said. "I have my father's '52 Plymouth." Before we were able to finish the thought, the DJ, Father Brown interrupted us on his microphone, saying he needed to take a break. The music stopped. Distracted, Johnny and I both used this opportunity to dash to the restroom.

When I got to the Ladies Restroom, I found Betty Lou in there.

"Deanna, what are you doing? Don't you remember you came here with Joe and me? He's mad as hell, and told me to see if you had your head screwed on right!" she exclaimed, as she looked in the mirror and rearranged her blond curls.

I was so excited, I just couldn't help blurting, "Oh Betty, his name is Johnny and I think he's going to ask to take me home. You can just tell Joe to go jump in the lake! If John doesn't ask me, I'll take the bus home."

Betty Lou turned me around, our blue eyes met as she stared me straight in the face, "Oh no, you won't Deanna, if he doesn't ask to take you home, I'll get Larry to give us both a ride."

Smiling, I said, "I knew I could count on you, Betty, thanks."

Johnny waited for me outside the bathroom door. He looked cute in his Ivy League Indian madras shirt and dark slacks. I was so glad to see him. It seemed we had been separated for years. Father Brown returned and started the music up again. Johnny led me right back the dance floor to do another jitterbug. Elvis was belting out the sounds of, *You Ain't Nothin' but a Houndog.* Afterward, when we returned to our chairs, he asked, a bit breathless after the dance, "Do you have a ride home, did you come with anybody? "Oh yeah" I admitted, my heart pounding, I came with my girlfriend Betty Lou."

Then Johnny added, "But I thought I saw you dancing several times with some tall guy earlier."

"Oh him, he brought Betty Lou and me." I didn't offer any more information. "Well in that case, can I drive you home? Where do you live?" he asked.

"I live in the East End," was all that I offered. If I told him I lived all the way out in Hikes Point (about 15 miles away) he might refuse, and if he didn't know how to get to my house, I might not see him again.

Our conversation was interrupted once more, this time by the dance's ending song, *Goodnight, Sweetheart*. This was how all the mixers ended. We took this opportunity to hold each other one more time before the evening was over.

On the way to my house, I was glad that Johnny didn't take a shortcut through the park. Seeing all the parked cars clogging the roadways with other kids necking inside them, would have embarrassed both of us. Johnny must have felt the same way. As we drove along, he said, "I like driving in the East End, but you really live out in the country. Then he laughed, "I hope I can remember how to get home from here." He walked me to the door of our screened porch, and shook my hand.

"Can I call you?" He asked. I melted as he spoke, but tried to act nonchalant. "I'm sure it will be okay with my parents." I replied, my heart pounding, again. His hazel eyes twinkled as he said goodnight and walked back to his car in our driveway.

With school starting in two weeks, the next week Johnny asked me to a St. X Football Game. He did remember how to get to my house and came in to meet my parents. He looked sharp in his green St. X Band Uniform; the school's colors were green and yellow. I could see that my parents were more impressed with Johnny than any of my other dates.

I was so proud of him. If he noticed the slop bucket in the corner, or my curious siblings peeking around the corner from the dining room, he didn't let on.

I felt important sitting up in the stands while the band cheered on the football players. The yelling and cheering from the crowd told me when it was an exciting game. I never did care much for football, and had no idea what they were doing down there on the field. I just cheered when the crowd around us did, and kept my eye on Johnny.

I especially like it when the band went down to march and do their formations during half time. It was thrilling for me to know that one of the band members was *my* date.

After the game, he told me, "When school starts next week, I'll buy you a yellow mum with a green "X" on it for the games. All the band members get them for their dates." Delighted, I gave him a big smile. "That would be lovely," I said.

Three weeks later, he gave me his green St. X letter sweater, with the bright yellow felt "X" appliquéd in the center of the green yarn. A few weeks after that, when the senior rings came in, we traded rings. My Assumption ring arrived the same week as his St. X ring did. He wore mine on his little finger. I liked to watch it catch a glint of the fluorescent lights at the stadium when he played the saxophone.

I wore his, like all the other girls wore their boyfriend's rings, on a long chain around my neck. This was called 'going steady.' I was so happy to be going steady with Johnny.

Holding my breath every week, I waited for him to call and set up our weekend plans. We saw each other on either Friday or Saturday nights. Sometimes both, if there was a dance happening at either his school or mine. We went to all of the St. X and Assumption dances, including each other's proms where we stayed out, going to parties, for the whole night. I felt good showing him off to my girlfriends.

****

In looking back on my life, I now feel that my relationship with Johnny was a major turning point in my decisions about my future. He encouraged me to go to college, and later, to get out and live in a place of my own.

Chapter 15

Snails, Snails, and More Snails...

This story begins in the fall of 1958. I was seventeen years old, a senior at Assumption High School, and I was going steady with my boyfriend, Johnny. Assumption was wonderful experience for me, and did so much to change the way I felt about myself. Though still battling shyness, the closeness of the girls in this small, but fast growing school, helped me develop courage. Our principal told us over the PA (public announce system), continually, "Girls, be proud that you are an Assumption Girl!" I was proud, and grateful to Daddy for paying my tuition.

Eager to move out into the world, I still hung back because Mama needed my help at home, at least that's what I told myself. This was only partially true; I was really very scared about venturing away from home. There was always plenty to do around the farm. My little brother Phillip was only three, Billy turned one in June and Mama was pregnant with my last brother, Patrick, who was due in February. The two brothers right under me, John age 16 and Marcellus (changed his name to Morris) age 15, were already "out into the mainstream," of life. I was proud of them because they were both handsome and popular – many of my girlfriends wanted to meet them. The girls at Assumption teased me by saying, "Deanna's the O'Daniel boys' sister," like I didn't have an identity for myself. Although, I didn't think it was very funny because I really didn't feel like I had my own identity.

John and Morris also had money from their after school jobs at "Winn Dixie and Woolworth's. These jobs gave them nice clothes and even cars, (though they were jalopies, they at least drove). Also, my brothers knew important people from their old days of caddying at Big Spring Country Club. These people kept up with my brothers and were influential guides as they shaped their teenage years.

Happy for Johnny and Morris, and liking the way they were budding into such successful young men, I could hardly remember the way we used to fight and scrap as kids. Their good fortune made me even more eager to move out into my own life. I obligated to Mama, but helping her around the farm and with the babies made me feel even more left out of everything that mattered to a teenage girl. I had been engaged in this fight with myself since my eighth grade summer when I was just sure that I would have a real job by now. My girlfriends at Assumption showed me a larger picture of the world, too. When we walked to the "Gardiner Lane Shopping Center" after school, they had money for the clothes and make-up I yearned to have. "You can do it, Deanna," my friend Juanita Maynard told me, "you can get a job like I have. They always need help at Our Lady of Peace Hospital. She worked at the hospital's kitchen after school. But, I wanted to meet new people, and hoped for a more social job. Doing kitchen work was too much like home.

During the summer I earned some money babysitting in the subdivisions around Hikes Point, but that was only enough for my bus fare and an occasional movie at the Bard Theater with another Assumption High School friend, Marcella Cameron. I wanted a real job that would get me away from the attitude of the farm, and with a set wage that I could depend on.

Finally, Daddy affirmed my feelings when he said, "Deanna, it's time for you to get out of the nest. Margaret Jane and Theresa are ready take over your work here for your mother." This delighted me, now I wouldn't have to feel guilty for deserting Mama with all her chores.

My cousin Mary Jane had a real job. She was having a ball and meeting lots of cute guys by working at the Bard Theater on Bardstown Road. Seeing her there on one of the Sunday's that I came in with my friend, Marcella, made me thrilled but jealous. *Why didn't I think of this?* I thought, as my anger at myself made my stomach burn. Delighted to see me, Mary Jane proudly showed me her duties in running the popcorn machine at the concession stand. Then she pointed out the best part of working at the Bard – her boyfriend,

Frank. Frank was an usher and a good-looking Trinity High Senior who also worked Sundays with her.

I was impressed that she dated an usher, in their snappy red uniform coats and matching caps. I knew that theirs was an important job. Carrying flashlights, they assisted latecomers to their seats in the darkness of the movie. After the start of the feature, they stood behind the four foot counter at the back of the Bard. This counter separated the audience from the coat hooks on the rear wall by the restrooms – where mischief sometimes occurred.

From this vantage point, the ushers managed the crowd. If they heard talkers during the show, they shined their flashlights in their faces, as a warning to be quiet. After a second chance, the talkers were removed from the theater. The Bard was a popular theater, and had two or three ushers for each double feature.

I wanted a job like Mary Jane's. Interacting with the public would get me into the mainstream and take away my shyness. The babysitting jobs I had showed me that most people were nice, and even interesting. Using all the courage I could muster, I made myself get going. Mama prayed to St. Jude, the saint of impossible causes for me. She lit the candles at our parish church, St. Barnabas, and made a special Novena. "St. Jude will help you find a good, safe job," she assured me. I smiled at Mama's faith.

Taking the bus, I visited the local theaters: the Bard, the Uptown and the Vogue. Unfortunately, they had all the help they needed. "You should have applied last summer," they said, shaking their heads. Some of them needed ushers, but girls weren't allowed to do that.

I asked my girlfriends at Assumption if they heard about any job openings. Linda Boyd told me the bakery where she worked near downtown needed another counter girl. She and her friend Judy Hubbach, another girlfriend from school, both worked there. Frances Woods, (another senior) dropped them off on her way to work. "She'll take you along, too." Linda told me. Excited, I called Mama from the principal's office, and rode in to work with them that very afternoon.

The bakery was named, Fannimen's, it was located in a one-story modern brick building, mixed in with many taller surrounding older buildings. Upon entering the sunny showroom, I noticed light filling it from the tall plate glass windows that spanned across the front of the store. Mesmerized, I tried to take in the whole scene before the manager called for me. Linda and Judy began to fill me in about the place as I looked around.

The floor, done in striking diamond patterns of black and white linoleum tiles caught my attention right away and gave the bakery a dramatic appearance. Yet, other parts of the show room gave it a cozy feeling. Along two sides of the showroom, glass cases sparkled. The pastries attractively displayed on lace paper doilies looked delicious, and begged me to make a purchase. A wide marble counter at the bakery's back wall held a large old-fashioned cash register – shiny brass and traced over with fancy filigree.

"Ding, Ding!" I heard a loud bell ring out announcing a sale as numbered placards popped up to show the sale's amount in the little glass window at the register's top. Behind the marble counter I saw more shelves. They were going up the wall so high that the clerks had to use a stool to reach them. "These shelves hold the more expensive bakery goods," Judy said, noticing the flow of my eyes. "They have all types of Danish pastries, cinnamon swirls, Kuchens, streusels, and jellyrolls."

Near the bread slicing machine were the many kinds of fresh baked bread that Fannimen's carried. Linda told me about the breads that I was looking over. "We have pumpernickel, salt rising, wheat, sourdough, and a Jewish braided bread called Challah. We call that one "egg bread" because the clerks can't pronounce its Hebrew name correctly," she whispered, chuckling.

A tall stack of flat white cardboard box forms rose up from the floor in the corner, by the can on the wall that held a ball of string that was used to tie them shut. The clerks called this container, the 'string minder.' "We fold these boxes for purchases that are too large to fit into small white paper sacks," Linda continued. On the other side of the swinging door that separated the showroom from the bakery itself, was a refrigerator case. I looked at the fussy, fancy items inside, like the custard pies, éclairs, petit fours and Neapolitans.

"This case is for the really expensive stuff. We don't want it to spoil," Judy took over and Linda moved toward swivel door at the back of the showroom. As I listened, my eyes bulged and my stomach stirred. *Oh boy, I'm wanna' taste all of these goodies.* I thought, and wondered if they tasted as good as they looked.

Fannimen's was a very busy bakery. Several clerks (all female) moved quickly behind the counter, waiting on the hungry crowd. Others washed and shined the fronts of the glass cabinets from the constant fingerprints made by eager customers. My head pivoted from one side of the store to the other. While we talked, I noticed fresh bakery items were continually being brought in and arranged handsomely on the glass shelves.

All of the ladies wore hairnets, and white dresses, with decorative aprons. In their chest pockets, like the waitresses at the lunch counters downtown, they displayed a colorful flowered handkerchief. "One of the policies about serving food is that you have to wear a hairnet," Judy frowned, "I don't like them; they make my hair go flat."

When three of the ladies saw us come in the front door, they walked through the swinging door to the back area, undoing their aprons as they went. They were ready to punch out. The shift was changing. These ladies had been working since 6:30 this morning, when the store opened. An older woman, the showroom floor manager named Mildred, started later, at nine o'clock, and stayed on till closing at 6:30 in the evening.

Suddenly, we heard a gruff voice, "You got girl for me." It was the voice of the manager, Mr. Baughmeyer, (out of earshot, he was known as Mr. B), calling to us from the bakery area behind the swinging door.

His blunt voice, manner and broken English made me tremble. "Sent her back," he bellowed. I pushed through the swivel door into the back room with my friend Judy, and could see why he didn't come out into the store. An older man of about 60, he was heavyset, unshaven, totally dusted with flour, and looked like a bizarre snowman.

His tight fitting tee shirt stretched over a bulging baker's belly that was covered by a long muslin apron, reaching almost to his feet. Wiry gray chest hairs protruded from the v-neck of this dirty shirt. Several food and coffee stains were smeared throughout the filthy apron. His disheveled shock of oily gray hair tumbled down into the bushy salt and pepper eyebrows above his beady gray eyes. Whiskers poked through the flour on his face.

263

"How many brothers and sisters you got?" This was the only thing he asked me, and I thought it was rather odd. When I told him I was the oldest of ten, with Mama expecting another child in February, he asked me about work availability. Nodding his head, he hired me, with no further questioning. *If I had known it was this easy to get a job,* I thought, *I wouldn't have waited so long.*

My first job! My mind spinned. Linda and Judy showed me how to punch the time clock, so that my wages could be determined. It was located in a tiny dusty alcove by women's bathroom, which was located in the backroom. Everything in the bakery preparation area was dusty with old looking flour that had obviously been sitting there for years. Inside the bathroom they showed me the women's lockers.

"You can share space with me." Linda said, as she pushed her maroon Assumption uniform jumper to the side. "You need to go to Robert Hall's Clothes, at Bardstown Rd. and Stevens Ave., or some dime store on Fourth Street and buy yourself a white nurse's dress. Today, Mrs. B will let you just wear a baker's apron over your uniform, but she doesn't like it for us not to have white dresses."

"You have to wash the apron and bring it back to let her see it before she'll let you go to work the next time you come in," Judy added. "Cleanliness is next to Godliness," Linda chanted in a teasing way, rolling her eyes up to the ceiling. The three of us laughed.

I piled my purse and school sweater into Linda's locker. "Here, you better take this," she offered me an extra hairnet that she kept on hand. "Even though this is your first day, you still have to wear a hairnet, everybody does, whether they're on the showroom floor or in the back – it's the law," Linda explained. However, I noticed that Mr. B didn't wear one. *What if one of his greasy hairs falls into the dough?* I wondered as my face twisted.

I loved bakery goods, but except for an occasional doughnut, I knew nothing about them. When Grandma was alive, she was always baking. She made fruit stollens, jellyrolls, and kuchens. She died so long ago, I hardly remembered what these items looked like, now. Daddy never bought food he considered unhealthy or unnecessary, which included bakery goods. I was embarrassed, when I had to ask what several items were. But, I had to let it go and thought, *if the other clerks think I'm from the sticks, I'll just have to give myself away, and not care.* I was eager to do a good job.

Luckily, Mildred, the floor manager, took the phone orders. I knew I would have gotten them all wrong. When we were really busy, Mr. B yelled from the backroom, "Make dos' people on 'da' phone vait! "A bird in 'da' hand is verth two in 'da' bush." I was impressed with his ability to hear through the wall, and felt that he must have had life pretty hard during the Depression in the 1930's.

Making change was even scarier than giving people the wrong piece of bakery goods. Most single items were a nickel, but the fancy ones like the chocolate éclairs were a dime, the Neapolitans were fifteen cents. It was easy enough to keep the figures in my head unless I started worrying about looking stupid, then I lost concentration.

Items of sixty-five or seventy-five cents like the streusels and the kuchens threw me off completely. Showing everybody that I was no whiz in arithmetic, I added them up on a piece of paper. The other girls were human calculators. *I'll be that good soon,* I assured myself. I loved my job. Helping people in the busy showroom was fun. I also enjoyed watching the day go down as we worked, and the sun set through the west windows before darkness came around 5:30 in the evening.

The customers smiled as they came up to the glass counter to order what they wanted. "When people come to buy treats," Linda explained, "they're always in a good mood." Even when I felt like I bungled, they were patient and helpful. *I'm glad the world's not as scary as Daddy talks about,* I thought.

Frances let me ride along with Linda and Judy to get to the bakery on the four afternoons a week that we worked. Our hours were from three o'clock to closing, and we were paid fifty cents an hour. After work, I walked to the corner and caught the bus home. John, the friendly bus driver was still driving the Blue Motor Coach Bus. The city bus now came to Hikes Point, but John worked hard to keep the business of us school kids. He sold us discounted bus tokens that he picked up for us himself, at the car barn whenever we needed them. We just gave him the two dollars, which bought a whole month's supply of rides, so I rode the Blue Motor when I could.

I usually got back to the farm around 7:00 O'clock at night. Being tired, I had a quick supper and started my homework, wanting to make sure I graduated in May. Life was much easier for me at home since I had a job. Now, I was considered an adult – Mama had supper ready for me, and Margaret Jane and Theresa helped her to prepare the meal and do the dishes. My turn for home chores was finally over. Since I was making money, I was as important in Daddy's eyes as the boys were, and this new respect felt good.

Because of the bakery goods, even the boys treated me differently. All the kids, including Johnny and Morris, listened for my foot steps coming down our gravel driveway in the dark. They all ran out to meet me because I carried a grocery bag of, day-old bakery goods. The first night I carried these home on the bus, I noticed the delicious smell of a cinnamon swirl roll coming up from the bag. We girls were not permitted to eat any of the stock at work. *I've always wanted to try one of these,* and thought about grabbing into the bag and eating it right there. I deliberated however, fearing all of Mama's warnings about such a practice, "Eating in public is common," I recalled her saying, emphatically. But, I felt the moistness of extra saliva accumulating in my mouth, and Mama wasn't here. On the crowded bus I helped myself to its sweetness, and allowed each bite of the sensuous cinnamon treat to melt on my tongue. Stretching my legs and relaxing into the sway of the packed bus, I thought *life is good.* The murmur of passenger's conversations fell on my ears as they hung on the long overhead pole above my head, I knew they were enjoying the scent of my grocery bag of goodies, too.

Every day before I left the bakery, Mr. B said, "You eat, you have big family. Dey' not good for my customers. Nobody ever say ve sell stale bakery goods." Mr. B stuffed the large sack to the top. Carrying this along with my schoolbooks was quite a balancing act. Puzzled by the way he singled me out, I feared that the other clerks didn't like it. *Maybe they're just tired of stale bakery goods,* I hoped. My family loved any bakery goods they could get, day old or not, and so did I.

On Saturdays, I caught the bus at 7:30 in the morning and worked from eight o'clock in the morning, till closing at 6:30 in the evening. I didn't even think about being tired when I got home, because my anticipation had been building all day. I would be going out with my boyfriend, Johnny after work! Having Johnny as my boyfriend also helped me build the confidence I needed to face the outside world.

Proudly, I wore his ring around my neck on the gold chain I bought at Woolworth's Five and Dime in the Gardiner Lane Shopping Center. We had been going steady for a few weeks now. This meant that we dated nobody else. To me, he was just about the most handsome boy in the city and I felt very lucky.

****

Things changed at Fannimen's when a Sacred Heart girl named Laura suddenly quit. Another girl quit soon after that. Then Judy quit for a job closer to her house. Linda, being Judy's best friend and next door neighbor, followed her to her new job. Now, instead of being counter girls, they sold clothes at "Simmons's Department Store," near Douglas Loop. "We don't have to get a ride anymore, or take the bus home in the dark," they explained, looking relieved, when I expressed my disappointment at their leaving Fannimen's. They may have had a good reason for leaving, but I felt an undercurrent, like there was something else going on. Too many girls were leaving in a huff. Most left just like Laura, with no warning or reason.

I had heard some whispered gossip about Mr. B chasing girls through the back room, grabbing them and trying to kiss them. *That's gotta' be a silly rumor,* I thought, considering his repulsiveness. Frankly, I couldn't imagine him moving fast enough on those short, fat legs, to catch a teenage girl. I looked so innocent, when the other girls saw me coming, they quieted their rumors, and I had decided not to worry about it.

Daddy insisted that I not work at the bakery on hogkillin' weekend. My hands would be needed at home at that busy time. I flinched when I told Mr. B, knowing he would yell at me, and of course, he did. "Mine Got, girl, you think I get off vhen I vant? You got job here!" But he did let me off when I got Norma, one of the counter girls from Mercy High School, to take my place. She usually only worked weekdays, and did me quite a favor.

Mr. B and his wife were Europeans who had escaped the horrors of World War II by coming to America. They ran the bakery, but were not the owners. For all their gruffness, we had to give them credit. They were great bakers, and because of their skill, ours was the only fancy, "European Style" bakery in town. Mr. B made all the doughs and Mrs. B was in charge of decorating. They obviously loved what they did, and worked almost around the clock. Mr. B came in before dawn around 4:30 to fry the fresh doughnuts for the morning crowd. The bakery opened early – 6:30, and we were told that there were usually people waiting at the door.

Totally dedicated to her work, Mrs. B made many types of icing for her cakes on the big old cast iron stove in her area – like the boiled caramel, penuche, and one-minute sugar frosting. She was proud of the work she did. I loved to watch her build roses from flakes of butter cream, then lift them with a spatula to insert them on the tops of her pretty cakes. Her wedding cakes were an artistic masterpiece. She used non-parells that looked like either little silver balls or pearls, and built up her icing to make the cake look like a fairy castle.

Our bakery carried treats you would find in Vienna, Berlin or Paris. Besides the usual bakery items already mentioned, we also had macaroons, marzipan, cream horns, cakes and pies of all flavors and doughnuts of all types. We carried prune and apricot kolatchen and poppy seed items that the Jewish people loved for their celebrations, too. Jewish people from all over the city came to us to buy the specialty items that were dear to them. Even though the Baughmeyers were sometimes gruff, I was proud to work in their bakery.

****

After working for a few weeks, one Saturday, Mr. B's assistant baker called in sick. In a snarly mood, Mr. B growled in the door of the showroom for me to come in the back and take the baker's place. I didn't want to go back there and moved reluctantly. This was just like being stuck in the basement with Mama while the boys were out seeing the world. I was sure my red face didn't conceal my anger. Obviously, Mr. B didn't notice or care. When I got to the dimly lit backroom, he said, "You not silly like utter girls, you have serious head on you shoulders. You oldest girl, you hard verker, I vatch you." He situated me across from him on the huge wooden baker's table – about eight feet wide by twelve foot long.

"First, ve make snails," he snapped, in a hurry to get me started. *Snails! How repulsive, snails in a bakery?* Unbeknownst to me, I had been selling them for weeks. "Snails" was baker's talk for Danish pastry. Mr. B walked over to the tall rack of metal trays that he kept by the outside brick wall. This wall kept the dough cool. He pulled a

268

long tray and took it to the table, where he cut off an inch of length from the eighteen inch wide slab of dough. Tapping it on the table to loosen the elasticity of the fibers, he held one end down with his left hand while rolling and twisting the length of dough with his right hand towards his large belly. Then he curled it into a rounded, flat snail shape, and fastened the open end underneath the dough.

"Dhare, now you have snail" he said, popping it onto a heavy metal baking pan. "Vhen you get 'da pan full, I show how do eggvash, now get busy." The room was cold, but I was boiling inside – *this job is awful!* I thought, disgusted. Saturday had always been my favorite day to work. But today, I wouldn't get to take pleasure in the customers that came in to buy their goodies for Sunday breakfast, or to have fun with the other clerks as we walked over each other in the rush to satisfy the hungry crowd. Anger rose inside as I realized that indeed, I would be stuck in the backroom all day. I swallowed hard, it stung too much to think about it.

Working across from me, Mr. B leaned his rotund belly against the table's edge. It wiggled back and forth following either his arm movements with the rolling pin, or his mighty hands as he kneaded and punched doughs of various types. I continued to work on the snails. A full pan contained ninety-six snails. When I finished, he took a grimy paint brush out of an even grimier looking coffee can and washed all the snails with thinned raw eggs. *Yuk!* I tried not to show my displeasure.

"Dis' eggvash makes 'dem brown nice, vhen dey bake, don't you miss any, or I haf to vaste it." After the eggwash, we put on the fruit with streusel topping, or nuts or poppy seeds. I made 600 snails before lunch. Unfortunately, I was too good at this job. Mr. B soon fired the other baker, because I was cheaper at fifty cents an hour. Now, I was only allowed in the showroom when one of the other clerks was sick. My usual place was the backroom. Growing up a lot, I realized I wasn't getting paid to have fun, I was getting paid to work at whatever I was told to do. My job was very different than my cousin Mary Jane's at the Bard where she got to enjoy the public and look pretty all the time. Jealousy and anger, jealousy and anger – *I can't afford to think like this*, I realized as I felt my face turning red again.

I worked twenty-three hours a week, and earned about $9.00, after taxes. That was pretty typical pay for an after school job. Being in the back was hard to take, especially when Norma, the clerk that had helped me out on hog-killing weekend, asked, "How can you stand working across from Mr. B? He's so disgusting." Not keeping my disappointment a secret, I shook my head and rolled my eyes. I told Norma how much I missed the camaraderie of the other girls, and that I wanted to get to know the new girls Mr. B had hired, other than just saying hello in passing. Her lips tightened, not knowing what to say.

Like the old days in the basement at home, I was trapped. *But what can I do? I don't want to get fired.* If I complained, Mr. B, very prone to outbursts, might fire me. Then Daddy would think I was a failure, and my brothers would make fun of me. Ignoring my disappointment, I tried to remember the benefits I got from the family because of having this job.

Daddy, however, was pleased with my promotion, "Now, you're now an experienced baker. You're well on your way into a good career, Deanna, you can get another job as a baker anywhere in the city if this one runs out," he said, smiling. He always tried to secure my future. But, thanks to my days of helping Mama in the basement, I knew there was no way I would work in back rooms for the rest of my life. When I complained of how bad life was in the back of the bakery, Daddy had no sympathy, "Do you expect life t' be a bed of roses, Deanna? You better not look a gift horse in the mouth, just be glad you got a job!" he bellowed, shaking his now balding head, and again calling me the complainest girl he ever saw.

Besides myself and Mr. B, there were two teenage stock boys back there, and also, Mrs. B. She stood over on the other side of the vast dimly lit cavern, decorating her cakes, unseen by us. The stock boys were brothers, named Barney and David, from St. X High School, like my boyfriend Johnny. To make matters worse than just the gloomy surroundings, there were brutal rules for the back room. We joked that Mr. B didn't leave Hitler in Europe, he brought him to Louisville!

The boy's jobs were to lift and tote the fifty to 100 pound flour and sugar sacks, and to run the huge mixers for the many kinds of doughs Mr. B worked up. No talking was allowed from any of us. Mr. B was afraid that we might spend a minute laughing, and that would be a waste of wages. "Time is money," he yelled. "Now get busy." These were his constant refrains. Waste was a word that made Daddy cringe, and all of us kids at home shiver. I understood waste.

When Mr. B went to the bathroom, the boys and I shared a few laughs and lots of complaints. Mrs. B seemed deaf to us. We felt she tattled on us later, but we were never really sure what kind of injuries she sustained before they escaped from Europe during the war. Maybe she was really deaf.

"Shh," one of us would whisper, "Simon Legree's coming back," when the Men's Bathroom door slammed. We immediately shut up upon his return. I wondered if he washed his hands in there before coming back to work with the dough. Mr. B was the only one allowed to talk in the back room, and he drove us crazy rambling on and on, mumbling in his broken accent. Over his protruding belly, in the greasy tee shirt and filthy apron that he propped on the side of the table across from me, he shared his philosophies. "You know how be smart in business," he suggested, "You vatch da hardest verker," he said, pointing to me, "and da laziest verker," he continued, looking over at Barney. "Dey da vuns dat gives da best ideas." I shook my head in agreement, trying to figure out how this applied to my life.

Pondering his words, *I guess this means that if I could be lazy like Barney, I would still be in the showroom having fun – Harrumph!* I grizzled. Since the table was eight foot wide, I could pretend not to hear him, like everyone else did. Usually, his voice was just a low background noise of complaining. Sometimes he called out instructions to Mrs. B, sometimes he yelled out at the boys. To him, nobody ever did anything good enough or fast enough.

But, I have to say, he never yelled at me. I was so shy, he probably thought his yelling might make me cry. That would be a loss of wages, and he could never take a chance on that. Maybe he could tell that I wanted to do a good job, even though I hated being back there.

Mrs. B spoke in a loud chirpy voice, which convinced us teenagers of her deafness. Everytime she came into the backroom, even if it was just from taking fresh bakery goods into the showroom, she squealed, "I'm baaaaaaack!" at the top of her lungs. *Why does she do that! It's so annoying.* I complained to myself. It was difficult at first, understanding the broken English of either one of them. Both of them used the "d" sound for the "th" sound, and "w" for the "v" sound. "Put'dis in the Wegtable pan," I finally figured out, meant to put the flaky dough in a certain part of the refrigerator. I had nothing against the way they spoke, and after I got used to it, found it rather interesting. In those days, Louisville had very few foreigners. We considered them unique and welcomed them here.

****

One Saturday when returning from lunch at "Nancy's Shine and Dine,'" a combination greasy spoon, and shoeshine grill across the street, I heard a scream. Walking into the backroom, Mary Beth Macan, a pretty, Presentation High School counter girl ran past me, "No you don't!" she shouted, "Stay back, don't you touch me!" Her face was red and her eyes were wild. I couldn't believe what I saw. Mr. B was chasing her around the baker's table. I'd been working here for weeks by now, and this was the first time I was really sure this was going on. When he saw me, he let her push him away.

"Ve get back to verk," he announced to the air. But instead, Mary Beth ran to the Ladies bathroom, grabbed her jacket and purse out of the locker and quit right then.

Happily for me, I got to spend the rest of the afternoon working in the showroom. But, I missed Mary Beth and her easy laughter. *So the gossip is right,* I thought, *and I have to work in the back with him all the time.* I caught Linda at school the next week and begged her to fill me in. It was time for me to let go of my innocence.

"Oh yeah!" Linda explained, "that's why Mrs. B yells, 'I'm baaaaaaack!' when she returns to the backroom, she doesn't want to catch him and embarrass herself. You're too valuable, Deanna, you are doing the job of a baker. Counter girls are easy to replace, but bakers are not. He won't bother you," she assured me. I sighed, feeling relieved.

I knew the counter girls hated coming to the back area. They stood at the door and yelled to the boys or me to bring them whatever supplies or pastries they needed. I thought it was because they didn't know where anything was located. If Mildred was working, she usually went in the back to get the requested items. Mr. B never bothered her either, she was valuable, too.

****

The weather was changing. Crispy autumn air stirred colorful leaf swirls past our windows. I walked through the showroom slowly, savoring its mood, certainly not eager to punch my time into the clock, or to get to my place by the baker's table. Thanksgiving grew near and Mildred took orders for baking customer's turkeys and hams in our huge ovens. Cutouts of pumpkins, pilgrims, turkeys and corn shocks hung through out the showroom, giving it a comfy holiday look. Anticipation of the days coming up warmed me from the inside, out.

Fannimen's made special treats for every season. For fall we used lots of cinnamon, cloves and nutmeg. I filled Mr. B's pie shells with pumpkin and sweet potato fillings. Mrs. B cut fresh apples for special order pies. We rolled all the stale cookies together and made "Mountain Spice Cookies." They were only available for Thanksgiving and everybody considered them quite a treat, not knowing what they really were. Mrs. B decorated turkey shaped sugar cookies with colorful feathers. I iced her cakes in caramel icing, and she decorated their tops with turkey outlines.

Whenever I took something to the showroom, I enjoyed its hum of activity. Customers chatted as they waited their turn, which was decided by a numbered card they drew from a hook when they entered the store. Music played in the background from the little white Zenith radio atop the refrigerator case.

Mildred was in charge of selecting the station. She liked the station for light listening called, "WINN." Their motto was, "WINN, the station of the Men with Music, instead of the Boys with Noise." This later reference was to slam Louisville's newest radio station, WAKY, which was loud and catered to the teenage crowd. Adult Louisvillian's were disgusted by WAKY, and considered it insulting to the intelligence of our city. Fearing it would lead to the degradation of our youth, they called it "downright tacky."

As we continued to get closer to the holidays, the sales girls were so busy they rushed back and forth like robots. "Ding! Ding!" The cash register rang continually. Taking bakery goods from the

273

shelves with the wax paper leaflets they pulled from a ceramic dispenser on the glass counter top, the clerks popped them into white paper bags. Folding bakery boxes for the larger items, they pulled off string and tied them up. The low gurgle of the bread slicer rumbled in the background constantly, adding to the noise of the cash register and the customers' conversations. The lively showroom was a total contrast from the bleak monotony of the backroom. I jumped at any opportunity to get in there and enjoy its throb of excitement.

****

Coming in to work on the Monday after Thanksgiving, I found the showroom completely enchanting. This day was our first snowfall of the winter. Snowflakes flurried in front of the windows as I came inside. Colored lights glowed from the Christmas tree Mrs. B had decorated with the help of the morning crew. Excitement and a Christmas feeling stirred in the air. Shiny ornaments hung on ribbons from the fluorescent lights high above on the ceiling. A snowy, cotton draped manger scene stared down from the top of the refrigerator case that held little Zenith radio. Snow gathering outside on the sidewalk set the scene. *Walking through the Winter Wonder Land*, played softly as I reluctantly strolled through the showroom to the backroom. My eyes widened and I felt like I was indeed walking through a winter wonderland. Mildred, our floor manager, was already busy on the phone taking Christmas orders.

"Yes, Mrs. Hammond," I heard her say, "we will be happy to bake your two hams and a turkey," I overheard her say as she pulled a pencil from behind her ear and took notes. The holidays came closer, and the crowd in the showroom got thicker. I always took as much time working my way through it as I felt I could get by with. Just being there always lifted my spirits. I needed that because we were very busy in the gloomy backroom.

Many extra treats were made just for the Christmas Season. I was amazed at Mr. B's ability. The metal clips on the special order clothes line started filling up right after Thanksgiving. His fruitcakes were especially popular. I saw fifty of them in metal springform pans when I entered the back area. They were on a makeshift table near Mrs. B's area. Everyday, she laced them with a bit of whiskey. As

274

Christmas grew near, you could almost get drunk just by walking around back there.

Mrs. B had her own specialty, too. Mildred took orders for Mrs. B's beloved decorated Gingerbread Houses. Some of the Christmas treats were familiar to me because we had them in our house when Grandma was alive. In addition to Fannimen's usual goodies, we sold special German Christmas cookies, Springerles, peffernusse, and a molasses cookie called Lebkuchen. Grandma baked these for us, too, and the smell of them reminded me of her. Remembering Grandma always brought a smile to my lips.

Mrs. B showed me how to decorate the hair of the gingerbread men with her tube of white icing, and to use small raisins for the mouth and eyes. *Thank God! A break from the snails!* I thought, delighted. Her personality was as cold as the weather. She followed Mr. B's orders of no-talking with great care. But then I remembered that perhaps she didn't hear well. At least she was more pleasant to look at than her sloppy husband.

She wore white dresses and decorative aprons under her protective baker's apron. Mrs. B removed this dirty, work apron when she brought her freshly decorated items into the showroom, where she placed them attractively into the glass cases. Her colorful handkerchief was always in her chest pocket or the corner of her hairnet. She had bushy gray hair and was a pretty woman except for her thick "coke bottle" glasses. I was impressed with her expensive jewelry, usually a necklace with matching earrings.

****

Christmas passed, winter grew colder, and snowdrifts were everywhere. It was February. "When you birthday?" Mr. B surprised me. I didn't know how to answer him, so I pretended to be too busy to hear him. He didn't quit, and asked over again and again. When no one was in earshot, he said in a loud whisper, "I get you present." I still pretended not to hear. With his reputation, the last thing I wanted was a gift from him. The news would spread to each of our teenage workers — and them being from most of the different Catholic high schools in town, this news would soon be all over Louisville. "Did you hear, Mr. B gave Deanna a birthday present, wonder what's going on there??" In the wild imagination of my teenage mind, I could just see my boyfriend Johnny finding out and dumping me, on the grounds that I was involved with a married man albeit, the disgusting Mr. B!!

Mr. B must have looked at my job application because on the Saturday closest to Feb. 10, he pushed a small white box with "Stewart's" written in gold lettering on its top, across the baker's table to me. Stewart's was Louisville's finest Department Store. Before he presented his surprise, he had sent Mrs. B to the grocery to get some more red dye for the Red-Velvet Valentine cakes. I was naturally curious, and I could tell from his wife's neck that he had good taste for expensive jewelry. I didn't know how to handle being put on the spot like this. Ignoring the box, I pretended not to notice it, though my curiosity tingled.

"Take it, it for you," he repeated and started to get loud. This was another thing I didn't want, him getting loud, embarrassing me in front of Barney and David. Hesitantly, I wiped my greasy hands on my apron and opened the box. It was a lovely white gold necklace with matching earrings. Embarrassed, I stammered, "Thank you," and slipped the box unceremoniously into my apron pocket. I don't know if his feelings were hurt that I didn't act more pleased, but I didn't care. Removing myself from this embarrassing situation, I walked over to the sanctuary of Mrs. B's marble topped cabinet. There, I went to work icing the red heart shaped Valentine's Day cakes. When Mrs. B returned she used white baker's icing to write messages of love on these individually ordered cakes.

I didn't want anything to bother me tonight, this Saturday evening was a special night for Johnny and me. We were going to a school dance for St. Xavier in one of the beautiful ballrooms in the Henry Clay Hotel in downtown Louisville. It was a St. Valentine's Day Dance. Nothing would bother me today, my excitement mounted as quitting time neared.

Mama helped me button the many tiny cloth buttons on the red taffeta dress I bought at Bon Tons' for the occasion. "You need some jewelry with this dress, Deanna." She said, taking time from her chores to help me get ready. *Mr. B's white gold necklace gift would really pick up this dress,* I thought.

But, if I wear it, Mama will ask questions, my face will turn beet red. She'll think I did something illicit. Then I realized that I'd probably never wear it. "Can I borrow the rhinestones Aunt Gen gave you for Christmas last year?" I asked, knowing that Johnny would bring me a corsage for the dress, too. I took the little white box from Mr. B upstairs to my bedroom and hid it in the drawers of the tall, walnut dresser in my Lincoln Bedroom suite. There it stayed.

****

On Ash Wednesday, all us teens that worked at the bakery came into the store with ashen crosses on our foreheads. Our Catholic Schools had had Mass that day. It was Lent, and for the next six weeks Mr. B and I were busy making Hot Cross buns. I enjoyed icing these by dipping my bare hand into the baker's white icing that Mrs. B provided. I traced a vertical, then a horizontal line up and down each row of the "cinnamony" buns. Hot Cross buns were delicious and very popular. Churches from all over town ordered them. We could hardly keep enough of them in stock, and made thousands.

The weather began to warm as spring came on. Orders for the baking of Easter hams and turkeys were coming in. Mrs. B and I were busy making Bunny Cakes when I wasn't working on the snails. These creative projects were fun to do, and gave me another break from the snails. To make these we took a regular white cake layer, cut it in half, iced it back together in a semi circle, then re-iced it all over in butter cream, white icing and sprinkled it with coconut. A smaller size cake was cut and iced the same way for the rabbit's head and tail. White cardboard ears were inserted, and jellybeans were used for the eyes.

We iced lamb cakes in shredded coconut, too, from the "Pascal Lamb" molds that I carefully greased before baking. "If you miss spot, ve must vaste dem." Mr. B warned me again. We set both types of cakes on beds of green Easter grass. *My, they're beautiful,* I thought, taking a minute to admire my work. *Maybe Daddy was right, I should be a baker.* Mrs. B decorated cookies shaped like Easter eggs, and baby chicks. I went back to the never-ending snails, immediately extinguishing my baker possibility desires.

With the coming of spring, life opened up for me. I got a wonderful surprise at school. Because of my good grades at Assumption, I had been accepted for a teaching scholarship at Nazareth College, located next to Presentation High School on Fourth Street. Thrilled to get to go to school downtown, I was already making plans to sneak off between classes and shop in the many department stores down there. Fourth Street was still Louisville's major shopping area.

However, there was one stipulation before Nazareth would okay my scholarship. I was missing an Algebra Two Class. Math was never easy for me. I had put off this class and forgotten it. My boyfriend, Johnny promised he would help me through it. He was accepted at U of L's Speed Scientific School and loved math. I was grateful for his offer of help, but this class almost made me dread summer. *I am stupid at math, what if I fail it?* Then my fears bubbled up like carbonated water, afraid that I'd lose my scholarship because I'd be showing the Nuns I couldn't keep the 'B' average it required.

The Algebra Class would take place at Holy Rosary High School on South Side Drive. Holy Rosary was a long bus ride across town. I would have to transfer three times to get all the way from Hikes Point to the south end. Worse, I needed to be there by eight o'clock in the morning. It would take me more than an hour travel time each way. But, I was raring to go – being a teacher was the job I had always wanted. I had some anxiety, *am I going to be able to do all this and still work twenty-three hours a week at the bakery?* In fact, with school getting out, Mr. B was already talking of having me work more hours during the summer. I was his chief assistant baker.

Needless to say, doing a good job for Mr. B was less important now that I was more certain of my future, and less convinced that I had to keep up a good reputation as a baker, like Daddy had said. Inadvertently, I began taking liberties in the back room, and took more chances with my talking back there. After all, remembering what my friend Linda had told me about being a baker should give me some privileges, I reasoned. What I really wanted was to quit this job and get started on my future. I had some emergency money put away and enough saved to pay for my summer classes at Holy Rosary. Still, Daddy wouldn't let me quit. He was as fond of the "A bird in the hand is worth two in the bush," philosophy as Mr. B. "You never quit a job until you get a new one," he told me, emphatically.

The warmer weather made the doughs difficult to manage. They were gummy and stuck to my hands and to the rolling pin. I had to sprinkle everything with so much flour to cut their stickiness that I sneezed continually. The beautiful days outside increased the boredom of my imprisonment in the dimly lit cavern. This didn't feel like a job anymore, but more like my days of captivity in the basement back home. Also, the workroom was hot, big ovens roared at us, and the heat seared our skin.

The only ventilation came from the back door. That wisp of air was not enough to cool this large room. Enjoying the small strip of sunlight was my only connection to the real world beyond this dungeon. Little kids played in a yard close by, running, laughing, and jumping. I reminisced about my little brothers and sisters playing in the meadows of our farm. Feeling stuck in my situation, I thought of myself as stuck as the dough was glued to my rolling pin.

****

One hot day when David and I were working, we started talking, even boldly cutting up in the backroom. We laughed so hard, we didn't hear Mr. B slam the Men's Bathroom door. Returning to the table, Mr. B was furious at these, "goings on." In a fit of temper, he scoffed, "You boy, you fired! Punch out!" to David, and pointed at the time clock. His face reddened and his beady eyes widened as he did so. I felt guilty for David losing his job. He would have never talked carelessly if I hadn't been part of it. I made an attempt to stand up for him. This really surprised me in myself, and pleased me with the changes that the thought of going to college had made in my personality.

"I was laughing, too." I admitted to Mr. B.

But, to me he only said, "You better watch you self, Missy, or you lose you job, too."

Surprisingly, I continued with my newfound bravado, "If you fire him, I'm leaving, too," I threatened. This put Mr. B on the spot, his mouth falling open, giving a perplexed look to his flour-dusted, whiskered face. Could the mouse be speaking up? I was so naïve that I thought my being a baker would actually make him hire David back. But Mr. B knew stock boys were easy to replace, and he hesitated, staring at my face.

"Owwn, mine Got!" he snarled, red-faced and shaking his chubby, doughy hands in the air, at a loss for words. Now *he* was stuck!

This was my chance to get out, my chance to get my summer and my life back. I quit, not caring about Mr. B's reaction. I was sick of working across from him and sick of his no-talking rule. I didn't care if Daddy did get mad. There were new shopping centers opening up in Hikes Point and I would find another job to help me with my college expenses.

No more dark rooms for me and no more snails. I was going to college! A new sense of freedom glowed through the flour on my face. Yanking off my grimy apron, I threw it on the floor, and punched out of the bakery business, forever.

Chapter 16:

Supper at Aunt Ida's

"Aunt Ida, Aunt Ida," I called for the third time, continuing to knock on her door. *Why won't she answer?* I wondered impatiently. *I hope she remembered that my boyfriend Johnny and I are coming over here for supper tonight.* I thought, pondering why she wasn't coming to the door. *Old folks get forgetful.* Starting to doubt my own memory, I tried to reassure myself that I wasn't wrong to be on her porch. It felt odd standing out there all alone. I paced from one end of the long porch on her tiny bungalow to the other. Truly, with all the unfortunate news about this neighborhood, lately, I didn't feel safe. Aunt Ida lived down in the West End by Shawnee Park.

It was a balmy springtime Sunday afternoon in 1959. As a senior at Assumption High School, this was the first time I had ever gone to the West End by myself. As recently as a couple of years before now, this lovely area of town was considered one of Louisville's finest neighborhoods. Presently, it was the sight of civil unrest, and going through a lot of upheaval. The *Louisville Times* and WHAS television station called the situation, "White Flight." Houses were being sold rapidly and people were moving out 'in droves.' According to the news media, there was a lot of crime going on all through the West End, and all around Shawnee Park.

This area was about a forty-five minute bus drive from Hikes Point. "Don't walk around by yourself down there, Deanna. It's not safe," Dad had told me before I left the house. Then he expressed sadness that his gentle, elderly aunt, who had lived there all her life, should have to spend her last years widowed, with the neighborhood turning against her.

I thought about my boyfriend, Johnny. Like most of the rest of the homes around, his family also had their house up for sale. They lived close to Aunt Ida and he was her paperboy. The week before, when he came by her place to collect his fees for the delivery of the *Louisville Times and the Courier Journal,* Aunt Ida and Johnny had set up plans for us to have supper together tonight.

Johnny told me of this when he called on Thursday night to talk about our weekend plans. "Your aunt, Mrs. Brakemeir, has invited us to come to her house for dinner on Sunday evening. "She wants us at her house by five o'clock, Deanna." He continued, "I told her that after we helped her get the dishes done, we would take her to hear the Shawnee High School band concert in the bandstand in Shawnee Park, and maybe we could drive by the lily pond, beforehand, if we have time," Johnny continued our conversation. I was thrilled, remembering all the times we kids wandered around that park, in our many visits to Aunt Ida and Aunt Bertha's houses. We loved the lily pond, covered over with beautiful lotus blooms.

"She would really like that, "I had answered. "I know she doesn't get out much since Uncle Gus died, she loves Shawnee Park and any kind of music," I told him, agreeing with his good idea.

"Johnny is so thoughtful," I told Mama after I hung up the phone.

"Yes, your Aunt Ida has been pretty lonely since Uncle Gus died last winter," Mama said, shaking her head and grimacing. "They were married over fifty years."

Aunt Ida liked Johnny and was delighted that he was dating me. She wanted to do something special for us. She and Uncle Gus didn't have any children and she took an interest in the children in my family and those of her neighborhood. I was overjoyed. She always did nice things for my brothers, Johnny and Marcellus (who now called himself, Morris), when they cut her grass a few years ago.

"Now, it's my turn," I told Mama, gleefully, rubbing my palms together. I knew Aunt Ida was a great cook.

"We'll probably have roast beef," I mentioned to Johnny later, when we talked again on the phone, trying to impress him that not all the cooks in my family fried everything like Mama and I did. She wasn't a country cook like we were. My mind was on a pot roast with gravy, potatoes, carrots, and onions. From looking over the magazines, this was my idea about how city people ate.

Mama added a suggestion about our plans, "Aunt Ida is getting pretty old, Deanna," she said, "sometimes she gets tired easily, you better get there early and help her with the meal."

****

"Oh, Aunt Ida… please answer… Darn it!" I mumbled, eager for everything to be perfect by the time my beau arrived.

Johnny was also taking the bus on this day. His father needed the 1952 Plymouth they shared. Johnny had used the bus to get to the ball field where he played his sax in the marching band for the "St. X Tigers," football game. The Tigers hardly ever played a game on Sunday, but this was the only time they were able to face "Francis Bacon," a high school from Cincinnati, Ohio.

I usually went with Johnny to the games and enjoyed watching the band do their maneuvers on the field during half time. However, on this particular Sunday, I had to work at the bakery until two o'clock, so we traveled separately.

Increasingly, I grew anxious about my Aunt. *Something's happened… this is not like Aunt Ida. She's always so happy to have company,* my mind started to spin. I walked over in an effort to peek in the front porch window. A dark green blind was pulled and I couldn't see anything. My wrinkled face stared back at me, along with the reflection of the maple limbs, showing tiny, fresh new leaves, and dancing in the spring breeze, from her front yard.

I don't like the feel of this, I thought. *I know Aunt Ida loves a sunny house.* I remembered the shelf of beautiful blue African Violets blooms near the window in her living room. *This shade should be up by this time of day,* I deliberated, pursing my lips.

Suddenly, I was surprised by a man's voice calling over from the house next door. Their porches were so close together I could have jumped across to it. "Do you know this woman?" the voice boomed at me.

Startled, my face blushed and I stepped back. From what Daddy had said about the West End lately, I expected to be jumped by some stranger. But, noticing his smile and the small woman by his side I felt I was safe. However, I felt instantly guilty for being on Aunt Ida's front porch.

He thinks I'm an intruder, trying to break in, I thought. Looking down at my high heeled shoes and sheath skirt, I wondered how he could think that. But then I recalled the recent problems of the neighborhood. Embarrassed, I managed to blurt out, "Yes, she's my Aunt."

Almost before I could finish my sentence, the man and his wife were on the porch with me. He was the minister at the Lutheran Church on the corner. As kind neighbors, he and his wife looked out for Aunt Ida.

My embarrassment eased and the redness left my cheeks as he explained, "We're the Spencer's, we've been watching the house for the last two days." Then the woman spoke up, "And we haven't seen your aunt. Mrs. Brakemeir hasn't been out to get her mail or to pick up her paper. We've been concerned about her."

Now, I was humiliated that I had only been thinking about myself. I was so eager for Aunt Ida to come to the door, so that I could get things ready and impress my boyfriend. I hadn't noticed the papers accumulated on the porch floor, or the mail crammed into her letterbox. But, knowing these nice neighbors looked out for her relieved me as to her safety.

Mr. Spencer really startled me when he suddenly said, "We're afraid she may be in there dead." I gasped at the thought, and couldn't imagine such a thing. Then a cloud fell over my face. My memory flashed back to 1947 when Aunt Ida's older sister, my Grandmother, died unexpectedly of a stroke. The memory made tears smart at my eyes.

Then the couple both took turns banging loudly on the door, shouting her name and trying to peek in the window. "Mrs. B... Mrs. B," they called, increasing their volume. Nothing! The three of us stared at each other, perplexed.

"My boyfriend Johnny will be here in a few minutes, he'll know what to do," I said, trying to ease the tension that was building up. Then I explained why I was there on Aunt Ida's front porch in the first place.

"What a nice boy!" they exclaimed. "He's our paperboy, too, you're a lucky girl to have him for your boyfriend."

Blushing again, I said, "I feel the same way."

Then Mr. Spencer spoke up, "We don't need to wait for Johnny. I'm calling the fire department right now." I was still in a daze about *anything* being wrong with Aunt Ida.

Within five minutes, firemen arrived in their black helmets and slickers. The chief approached the couple and asked, "So, how long has it been since you've seen her? When the Spencers' answered, he shook his head and continued, "Well, I think you are probably right, we see this sort of thing happen with these old folks, everyday."

The chief took a small ax and broke a glass pane in the front door, then reached his hand inside and unlocked it. Thinking about the crimes going on in the area, I was scared to see that a house could be gotten into so easily.

Following the three of them, I entered the dark living room. Tears sprang to my eyes when I saw Aunt Ida's small crumpled figure sitting in her easy chair by the fireplace. On her lap she clutched a little bowl of pin curlers with her right hand. Half her dark hair was curled. With her left hand she clutched her heart. Her head was slumped over. On the coffee table was the familiar cut-glass candy dish filled with chocolates, just like I always remembered. To the left of Aunt Ida's chair, sunlight streamed into the room, through the door of her bedroom. Coming from an upper-level stained glass window, it slanted through the glistening bottles and jars of her *Helena Rubenstein* perfumes and cosmetics that sat in front of the mirror on her bedroom dresser. I remembered the time she had showed me how to use them, particularly the squeeze-top atomizer sprayer. "Not too much," she had said, laughing, "or you'll smell like a gypsy." She had crinkled up her nose at that thought. I didn't know what a gypsy was, and told myself that I'd ask Mama about it when we got in the car to go home.

"I should call my parents and tell them," I said gathering myself together and walking toward the phone in the hallway by the stairway landing.

"Oh no, Miss, you can't touch anything in here," the fireman said. He walked in front of me with his arms extended, "especially not the phone. "We have to send an Investigation Unit in to check things over in case of foul play."

285

Fingerprints didn't come to my mind, I knew Daddy would want to know about the death of his Aunt. My tears began again.

"I was afraid this might have happened when we didn't see her in the yard," Mrs. Spencer said. "Mrs. Brakemeir was such a nice lady," tears were in her eyes as well. Looking into my face, she said, "I'm sure sorry," and she put her arm around my shoulder, as we all gathered on the porch again.

The couple helped the fire chief fill out the report. Then the chief secured the house with a sturdy chain and a large bolt. "There's a lot of crime on Broadway right now," he said, affirming what my father had told me earlier. Then, looking at me, he asked, "How are you going to get home, Miss? Do you need a ride?"

About that time, Johnny bounded up the porch steps, obviously bewildered at all these goings on. Mr. Spencer looked at him and explained the situation. "You know, Mrs. Brakemeir was pretty old," he said, when he noticed the surprise on Johnny's face. At the same time Mr. Spencer glanced in my direction with a sympathetic look, trying to comfort me, as well. *What a kind man*, I thought.

Johnny wound his arms around me, and whispered in my ear, "I'm sorry, Deanna," as I cried onto his shoulder. With Johnny's support, this astonishing situation was easier to bear.

The fire chief spoke up again, "I'll send the police over here this evening to check things out and take care of the body. Can somebody be here for them?" he asked.

I didn't want to do it, and stammered, "Uh, uh…..

Mr. Spencer came to the rescue and said, "the wife and I will be home all evening, come knock on my door." He pointed to the house on the left. Then he said to us, "You kids go ahead and have your date this evening." Both Johnny and I sighed with relief and thanked him.

Abruptly, everything was over as fast as it started. The Spencers went back to their house next door. The firemen returned to the firehouse. Johnny and I were left standing on the porch by ourselves, confused. Our plans inalterably changed, we were both pretty shaken up.

Taking my hand, we walked two blocks away to his house. His mother, Mrs. Ulrich, fed us a lovely dinner and spoke sympathetically about, "Mrs. Brakemeir." She knew her as someone who had lived in the neighborhood even longer than she, herself, and her family had. We waited for Johnny's father to return with the car, and lost our mood for the concert at the bandstand in Shawnee Park. We stayed home to play Canasta with Johnny's mother and his little brother, Paul. I decided not to call Daddy. I would tell him when I got home, being afraid the tears would start up again.

"Good Bye, Aunt Ida," I said, as Johnny and I drove past her house on our long trip back down Broadway to Hikes Point. The little bungalow was dark and looked lonely, the same way I felt. Now, only one of Grandma Anna's sisters was left, Aunt Bertha, the baby of the family. Her brothers had died long ago. *The end of an era*, I thought.

Chapter 17:

"Roll Me up Some More Vanilla"

September of 1959 found me as a freshman at Nazareth Girls College, (presently, Spalding University) on Fourth Street. College was great, finally, I felt like an adult. Carrying thirty-two hours in my first semester, it was hard to keep the "B" average my scholarship required. Study, study, study...that's all I did! The priest who was paying for my education wanted me well-prepared in order to start teaching in his school with just two short years of college training.

The priests who donated these scholarships, called the 'Father Pitt Scholarships' had a lot of help in making us girls serious students, from the Nuns who ran Nazareth College. "Girls," Sister Walter Ann, the head of the Education Department, told us, "you need to spend at least three hours studying for each hour you spend in class." I did a quick calculation in my notebook and swallowed hard – *that's ninety-six hours,* and started to panic.

But, even with all this studying to do, I still needed to find a job. The expenses of summer school and my books, fees and bus fares, had dissolved my savings from the bakery job. I was tired of the lecture I got when I borrowed anything from Dad, "You've got to learn to stand on your own two feet, Deanna. You can't depend on me forever," he admonished, whenever I stuck out my hand. *I wish I lived close enough so I could walk to school,* I thought.

****

Lucky for me, my best friend Betty Lou did me a big favor. She married her childhood sweetheart, Larry, and they moved to Texas. I knew I would miss her, but before she left, she suggested to Mr. Harding that I be the one to take her place as one of the soda jerks behind the lunch counter in his drugstore. He trusted Betty Lou's word enough to hire me over the phone.

I would be in training for the first few nights. My hours were from five o'clock to closing, four nights a week, plus weekend time as needed. I had a lot of energy and enough determination that made me sure I could handle the job, along with my schoolwork.

****

In walking to work on that first Saturday evening, I noticed how much life was changing at Hikes Point. Coming up to The Point from our farm on Hunsinger Lane, I crossed in front of a Blue Motor Coach bus on Hikes Lane, then continued walking, going over the long front porch of Bauer's Restaurant. Now, I was on Taylorville Road because Bauer's sat right *on* the point where Hikes Lane and Taylorville Road crossed over each other. Bauer's was Hikes Point's most famous local landmark, built around the 1880s'.

The buses on Taylorville Road were city busses – their colors were green and yellow. They were becoming more plentiful each day as our farm area became increasingly urban. The blue busses on Hikes Lane served the county. When I was younger, Hikes Point had only the county busses of the Blue Motor Coach.

I passed what used to be Hal Rohleder's Farm and The Edinger Farm, both of which were now shopping centers and subdivisions. My lips pursed as I recalled how pretty both of those farms were, and I tried not to think about that. Looking west on Taylorsville Road, I noted that the lovely, white columned plantation home was still visible behind the leafy trees in its long front yard. Last year the owner had sold the east side of this property to a new church. Sadly, the church and its asphalt parking lot covered all of the former meadow. My heart really sank when I remembered the chestnut horses that romped and grazed there.

Crossing Taylorsville Road and cutting through "McMahan Plaza Shopping Center, I entered the, "Triangle Center Medical Plaza," across Browns Lane. Harding's Drugstore was located at the end of this medical center and a couple of doctor's offices were next door. A good-sized parking lot separated the drugstore from a small Tastee-Freeze ice-cream vendor that was located diagonally across from it.

A long line of people stretched through this parking lot from the Tastee-Freeze to Harding's front door. I sighed, and walked in front of them – I didn't want to be late for work. Somebody in the line admonished me saying, "The line forms at the rear, Miss." Surprisingly, I found out that I was still suffering from shyness because my face instantly blushed.

I mumbled, "But, but, I work here." Noticing that I had on a hairnet, the man stepped back and let me pass. I couldn't imagine what was going on. *I didn't know Harding's was this popular!* I thought. However, when I got inside Harding's' I found out why the people outside were so worried about me jumping ahead in the line.

There was a banana split sale going on! *My goodness,* I mused, when I saw the crowd inside, *people must be driving in here all the way from Jeffersontown (J-town), and Buechel.* Every seat was taken; I walked past the kids twirling each other around on the stools while they waited their turn, with their parents standing behind them, also waiting their turns for a "split."

The store was bright and pleasant, lit up from the sunny south wall that was made up of large plate-glass windows. The soda fountain, on the right, was the first thing you saw when you entered. About twenty pink leatherette swiveling stools stood in front of a beige Formica counter.

Two thoughts immediately struck me: *It'll be exciting working here,* and at the same time, *Can I handle all this?* Squeezing past the aromatic, roasted-nut machine at the back end of the fountain, I went behind the Formica counter and into the fountain.

Mr. Harding, a small, slender man with a balding head, and dressed in a white pharmacist coat, greeted me. The size of the crowd had caused him to leave his station behind the pharmacist's area and help out at the soda fountain. His face lit up with a smile as I came in. Obviously, he was relieved to see me.

"Here," he said, "take over with this banana split sale." He tapped the ice cream dipper against the side of the metal rinse dish, and let the water splash over it. Then he handed it to me, clearly anxious to get back to his pills.

The thick smell of the banana peels hung in the air. The sale was a good deal for banana split lovers. At nineteen cents, the price was reduced from our usual twenty-five cents. This really undercut the Tastee-Freeze price of thirty-five cents! *No wonder the long line,* I shook my head.

"Ball up me up some more vanilla, Girlie," my partner for the night, Rose, called out to me, bringing me back to the situation at hand. Sweat rolled out of the edges of the hairnet covering her short red hair. She was an older woman, maybe in her forties. I later found out that she had teenagers and that her husband had lost his job the year before.

Rose turned out to be cheerful enough, and we had as much fun as we could, considering the constant demands of the banana splits. I proceeded to dip vanilla, chocolate and strawberry from the two-gallon cardboard ice cream tubs in the freezer behind the counter.

This went on for the full six hours I worked that night; dip, roll the ice cream, rinse the dipper, dip, roll the ice cream, rinse some more. Mr. Harding was proud of the ice cream he served – it was the best: "Sealtest." From Daddy's workdays there, I was familiar with the goodness of Sealtest and remembered it jingle on the radio, "Get the best, get the best, get *Seeealtest!*" Its rich thickness was why it was so hard to dip.

We served well over 100 splits that night. Finally, at ten o'clock, Mr. Harding locked the door. Saturday was our only late night – during the week the store closed at nine.

"You're a good worker," Mr. Harding called over from the pharmacist's counter, as Rose and I washed up the dirty soda glasses. Thank God the splits were served on plastic walk-away "banana boats." He continued, "Be back tomorrow after church. We open at one on Sunday."

I left the store, dazed, exhausted and with a blister on my thumb. I was more than ready to see this evening end. With Harding's fluorescent lights behind me, I entered the night ahead. The moon was up and I could see the neat rows of Mr. Stiedenberger's potato plants as I crossed the road on the south side of Harding's. This road was Taylorsville Road. With lightening bugs flitting all around me, popping off and on like fireworks, I stepped onto a part of his dusty fields that edged this major highway. Mr. Stiedenberger's farm stretched from Taylorville Road to Hunsinger Lane, and in front of our house.

I knocked about a half mile off my trip home by cutting through his farm and old Mrs. Kindle's yard, which was next-door to his property. My siblings and I always saved a little time by coming home from the Point this way. *On the way back home, your shoes don't have to stay clean,* I smiled smugly, to myself. He never minded us doing this unless we stepped on the crop. If that happened, Daddy was called. It made my father furious that any of his kids would embarrass him in front of his neighbors, and he never spared his razor strap.

I reached Mrs. Kindle's house and thought about her situation. She was an old lady in her eighties, and had been bedridden since her stroke a few years before. I visited her from time to time. Always happy to have visitors, she passed out pieces of hard candy when she had them.

Tonight, it was late and I didn't want to disturb anyone, as I tried to go quietly through the weeds at the back of Mrs. Kindle's lot. However, I was so tired, I wasn't as careful as I needed to be. Slipping on some of the walnuts that had already fallen from the tree that arched over her screened-in porch, I fell with a thud, ripping the green hulls off the nuts and releasing their pungent aroma. The old woman's daughter, Margie, who was in her forties, lived with her husband, Bobby, in the house next door. Their last name was McKindle. I always thought it was odd that Margie's married name only took her from Kindle to McKindle.

Margie's head popped out from the back door of her house and she yelled,

"Who's there?' When I picked my limp body up from the ground and called out, she laughed, "Deanna, why are you out so late tonight?"

After I explained, Margie assured me, "I'm gonna' get me one a' them splits, too," Bobby and me 're goin' up 'ere after church tomorrow, an' we'll let 'chu be the one to wait on us." She laughed again as her screen door banged shut behind her. Apparently, the news of the banana split sale had reached everybody.

On the farm, we were simple people. Now that Daddy wasn't delivering Sealtest Ice Cream anymore, we only had home-churned ice cream. It took hours to make. We tossed the churn from one of us to the next to share the chore of cranking the handle. It took quite awhile, before the dry ice made the cream hard enough to serve.

"Homemade ice cream ruins you for anything else," Daddy said. But we knew the truth behind his statement. He considered ice cream one of those unnecessary foods, and he didn't want to spend money buying it.

Mama put strawberries, peaches or bananas into Calfie's fresh cream and I thought it was quite a treat on a hot Sunday afternoon. We never thought about doing anything else with it, but enjoying a saucer of it. At Harding's soda fountain, I found out people ate ice cream in all kinds of interesting ways. Not only in cones or dishes, but in sodas, splits, sundaes, milkshakes, malteds, and floats. Each treat was served in its own special dish – I was eager to try them all. You can tell I didn't get off the farm much. When we visited our country relatives, they served the same kind of homemade ice cream we did.

There were many other things I needed to learn in order to work at the soda fountain. I was afraid that if I got it wrong, the food would be wasted and that Mr. Harding would fire me. In my imagination, I felt his eyes piercing through my back when he looked up from his mortar and pestle, behind his stand at the pharmacist's counter. This stand was located across the aisle from the soda fountain. However, I was confident that no matter what, he wouldn't fire me until the banana split sale was over.

****

The next day, Sunday, was even busier with the banana splits. Because of the "Blue Laws" the only stores that were allowed open were the drug stores. Even then, nothing could be sold in the store, despite all the products we had, but prescriptions from the pharmacy, and treats from the ice cream fountain. My partner was Donna, a girl I knew from Assumption. She wore her dark hair in large curls, which she had to poke up and mash under her hairnet. I was sure that broke her heart. Being, 'all girl', she liked to wear lots of make-up, and smacked her gum when she spoke. All her sentences started with, "Oh Honey." Donna was a junior and only worked two days a week. Her being here for over a year, made me feel she was far superior to me, even though I was older and in college.

In between serving up the banana splits, Donna, smacking her gum, rattled off all the ins and outs of working at the soda fountain. A lot of it was proceeded by, "Oh Honey, Mr. Harding likes us to do it this way," or, "*Oh Honey*, Mr. Harding *doesn't* like it when such and such happens." I had heard Rose using those phrases the night before, too. Giving anything away or wasting anything were big items on his "no-no" list. I could understand this because I had dealt with Daddy, who thought the same way.

Donna showed me how to make the batches of fountain soft drinks from the large bottles of pure syrup, in the most economical way. This was the way Mr. Harding liked them made. There were Cokes, Dr. Pepper, root beer, and 7-Up drinks served from the shiny, chrome levers on the fountain. All these drinks were all mixed with measured amounts of carbonated water.

When we ran out of Coke syrup, Donna took me to the back room and showed me the shelves where the items for the soda fountain were stored. She took me to the freezer where we kept the extra tubs of ice cream, as well as extra Sealtest half gallons of the many ice cream flavors we carried. People bought these, as Donna called it, "off the shelf." The half gallons were displayed in the store in a glass refrigerated cabinet near the pharmacy counter.

She told me how to make all the ice cream treats, and how to hand pack the fountain ice cream, "Oh Honey, this is for those people who are too cranky to buy it off the shelf," she sighed, rolling her eyes. "They think the soda fountain ice cream is richer in flavor." I couldn't imagine people refusing any kind of ice cream.

My head swam from all the information. "If I can keep my "B" average in college, I can surely remember all this stuff," I told Donna. We talked and laughed about Assumption High School and its silly uniforms of maroon jumpers and saddle-oxford shoes, while we made the banana splits. I missed Assumption, but not those crazy uniforms. "And what about those gym suits with the maroon cotton skirts?" Donna laughed, and I joined in.

Time wore on toward evening and I didn't get to make many of the new treats Donna had explained to me. Most people didn't want anything but the nineteen-cent banana splits, and I couldn't blame them. My blister throbbed beneath my band aid, as I dipped out the balls of vanilla, chocolate and strawberry, ladled on the pineapple, strawberry and chocolate syrup, squirted on the whipped cream and smacked a cherry on top, over and over again.

The line of banana split fans was unending and stretched from our front door through the Tastee-Freeze parking lot, until Mr. Harding locked the door, despite the groans from the crowd. On Sundays we closed at six pm. My hands were relieved – I had added three more blisters.

Donna and I still had to wash up the pile of dirty dishes before we left for the evening. "Oh Honey, don't forget." She reminded me of an earlier conversation, "Mr. Harding is having a sale on Revlon make-up next week!" She winked as we put the dishes back on the shelves.

Again, on my way home, I cut through Mrs. Kindle's property, this time avoiding the area with the black walnut tree. The McKindle's were sitting in their porch swing next door reading the Sunday paper.

"Sorry, we didn't make it up there for our splits," Margie said, speaking loud enough to be heard over the noise of the seventeen-year locusts screaming at us from the bushes behind their swing. "We'll do it the next time, Mama felt real bad today and we couldn't leave her."

Margie didn't fool me for a minute, everybody knew that Bobby was too much of a tightwad to splurge even nineteen cents on what he called foolishness (to me, he was too much like Daddy). I glanced over at him. He was smiling back at me, holding the paper and staring up over the top of his reading glasses. I recalled the rainy day when he and Margie offered me a ride home. They were coming home from shopping in the Highlands, when they happened to see me walking up Taylorville Road from Bowman Field because I had missed the last bus to Hikes Point. I was sure glad to see them pull their Nash Rambler over to the side of the road for me. When we got to their house Bobby pulled the car right into their garage and said, "Well, we're home," of himself and Margie. I had to walk the rest of the way down the road to my house in the rain.

"Oh, yeah," Dad had said to me as I struggled in soaking wet, "that Bobby is tight as the wax on the floor." I had to smile at his remark and thought; *it takes one to know one.*

The next morning I caught the city bus in front of Bauer's at seven o'clock, for my eight o'clock classes at Nazareth. I was in school until five o'clock everyday. When my afternoon bus reached Hikes Point, I returned to Harding's instead of going home. I would be working until closing tonight and for the rest of the week, at nine o'clock.

The banana split sale was over. *Thank God!* I felt relieved.

Rose smiled as I entered the fountain. This was my last night in training, and she was my partner again. With the break from banana splits, she helped me get a better handle on learning the skills of the soda fountain.

"Are you ready to learn some more stuff?" she teased. There was a new contraption called an infrared oven on the shelf under the plate glass windows. It was a kind of microwave. "The infrared rays are lower than the light spectrum," Rose explained, "they are captured by this little oven, and it cooks lickety split." I watched the red glow inside the glass door. Then she added, sucking in her breath, "Don't ever let your hand get caught in it!"

The sandwiches for the infrared oven were wrapped in special paper that distributed the heat evenly through the food and kept it from burning. The infrared menu contained barbeque, hotdogs, chili dogs, hamburgers and chili soup. Except for the chili dogs, none of it was very tasty. But that didn't really matter because we cornered the market – there were no other lunch counters around. The infrared was popular because everybody was fascinated by this latest invention. Mr. Harding was always on the top of the curve.

"I'll take a Cherry-Coke, please, Miss," requested a tall man in a seersucker suit. I was surprised to find out there were different kinds of Coke drinks, and looked at Rose. She showed me how to add a squirt of the cherry syrup into the cup before I added the fountain drink. Customers also liked Chocolate Cokes and Vanilla Cokes.

Some people asked for phosphates. *What a word*, I thought, *it sounds so old fashioned.* "Just put in a teaspoon of lemon, cherry or strawberry syrup, whatever they ask for, and then add the carbonated water," Rose told me. The syrups smelled fruity and delicious. The bubbles of the carbonated water tickled my nose. The first time I lowered its lever, the strong pressure surprised me. A powerful stream shot the glass right out of my hand and shattered it on the tile floor.

I knew this was one of the things that Mr. Harding didn't like, as the sound of broken glass caused him to yank his head up from his mortar and pestle behind the pharmacist's counter.

"Now, I've done it!" I whispered to Rose.

The truth was however, that Mr. Harding was really much more of an understanding man than I had thought. Everybody loved him. I just imagined my own father's impatience with anything being wasted or broken.

Rose showed me how to make coffee in the twenty-four cup percolator, and how to keep the hot fudge syrup cooker from drying out. "It's very expensive," she explained of the hot fudge. "People have to pay an extra fifteen cents to have hot fudge put on their sundae." Rose also used the phrases of the lists of what Mr. Harding liked and what he didn't like. "He really doesn't like for the pot of hot fudge to burn." She said, "Be sure to keep an eye on it." I watched her stir in a bit of water to it as I washed and dried the tall glasses for ice cream sodas and root beer floats.

It was an easy night and we were able to keep up with most of the dishes as we dirtied them. And, we had time to chat. Rose shared with me the concerns about her teenagers. She was happy they were switched from Fern Creek High School, which was several miles away out in the county, to Seneca High on Goldsmith Lane. Due to the growth in our area, Hikes Point had finally gotten its own high school. But, Rose explained that her oldest girl was a cheerleader and hated to leave Fern Creek High, which had one of the best football teams in the public schools.

Taking money for the purchases made me nervous. I tried to add everything in my head. But, like at my bakery job, when there were several items, I got lost in my figures, and had to add it up on paper. Many parents brought in large families, and adding their purchases was confusing. Using a notepad made me feel stupid because Rose did everything in *her* head. I also feared counting the change back correctly. When we returned change, we counted it back to the customer, out loud. That was good because it helped me keep the money straight. Since we were not so busy with the banana splits, I got to take in more of the money, and I did fine, just like I did at the bakery. The customers smiled and were very patient with me, as the new girl. Their pleasant attitude helped change my nervousness into confidence.

After work, I again cut across Mrs. Kindle's yard on the way home. When Margie came out, I wished I had been able to sneak her a banana split, or a quart of hand-packed vanilla. Between taking care of her mother and Bobby, she didn't seem to get out much.

"Mama's been feeling better today; she sure would like to see you, Deanna. Do you have time for a short visit tonight?" she asked. It was late and I really didn't as I faced several hours of homework. But, I knew that cutting through her yard saved me a lot of time in the long run, and besides, I liked Mrs. Kindle.

"Sure, I love to see her," I found myself saying.

In addition to being bedridden, the stroke kept Mrs. Kindle saying the same things over and over again. I remembered Grandma when I saw Mrs. Kindle lying there in the bed. I swallowed, as I thought how scary it must be to grow old. I recalled Mrs. Kindle's laughter a few years ago, when I used to help her peel apples on her front porch and watch the traffic go by. I enjoyed being around old people, they were always so grateful.

Mama had told me one day when we visited her together, "If you visit the old and the sick now while you're young, you'll get plenty of visitors when you get that way." We were returning from shopping downtown, and our arms were filled with school clothes we had just bought on Fourth Street. This visit was important to Mama, so we stopped in to see her, even though we were both tired.

Nothing seemed worse than being old and lonely. I never knew what to say to her, but I guess that didn't matter because Mrs. Kindle's face always lit up when she saw me. Her tiny body was surrounded by sprays of gray hair that also framed her smiling face. Holding out her thin arms, she welcomed me when I entered the room. I leaned down over her bed and gave her a hug. My heart melted, *she's so sweet,* I thought. I was glad that I took the time for the visit, because she died later in the month. Her death surprised me as much as Grandma's had, several years before. I never guessed about her dying, either.

Finally it came, my first night to work alone. I was nervous, fearful I wouldn't know how to make anything. People asked for many of the things my teachers Donna and Rose had shown me how to do in our crash courses. I fixed what I remembered how to do, for what I didn't, I just asked the customers to show me. They all knew the recipes, or acted like they did.

Mr. Harding smiled at me several times from his perch behind the pharmacy counter, which was an open wall behind the cash register. I could tell he liked the way I interacted with the customers. Of course, from his post, he couldn't hear that I was asking them to show me how to do my job. Surely that would be on the "things Mr. Harding doesn't like" list.

I was grateful that Mr. Harding let me study when there were no customers at the fountain, unless there were a lot of customers in the store. At first, I went over to the drug and sundry side of the store whenever I could get a break from the fountain. I wanted to get used to the job there, so I could help handle it when the crowd was thick. When customers paid for their purchases, we had to handwrite the list of what they bought in duplicate, on a metal rollup box, including each product description and cost. At the top we had to write the words, "drug" or "sundry." We yanked off one copy for the customer's receipt and rolled the other one into the box for the store's records. I found that if there were a lot of customers to take care of, nervousness made me sometimes misspell words. I was too distracted to notice it, but the customers never missed it

"And, you think you're going to be a teacher next year!" they teased. All the customers seemed to know my ambitions.

Credit cards had another metal box. Here, we slid a roller over the raised name and numbers on the plastic credit card, and filled out the purchase receipt in the same way as any other purchases. *This is a stupid system... I'm surprised anybody ever buys anything!* I complained to myself, looking at the long line in front of me and writing as fast as I could.

Harding's was a busy drugstore. Besides myself, and the other fountain girls, there were three drug clerks and two delivery boys. Then, of course, there was Mr. Harding and the other pharmacist, his son, known as "Young Mr. Harding," who was also balding. The Hardings were well-respected, soft-spoken men. Not only did they know their jobs well as pharmacists, they also dispensed valuable medical information. In those days druggists were allowed to do this.

One day, a lady in a print house dress, with her hair styled up in a popular "bee-hive" hairdo, told me her story. "Mr. Harding saved me from having to take my Emily to the doctor, and drive all the way to J-Town," she said. "My husband would a' had ta' take the bus to work, and he'd a' had a fit! Mr. Harding told me to treat that boil on my daughter's leg with bacon fat. It didn't cost me a nickel," she boasted. "I jes' strapped a slab a' jowl bacon ta' the bak a' her leg fore she went ta' bed and put a sock ore' it, she laughed.

Here today for another matter, the lady and I chatted while I served up fountain cokes for her three little kids, who spun round and round on the stools. Mr. Harding was smart enough to pass out free-Coke coupons for pharmacy customers to enjoy while their prescriptions were being filled.

The Hardings went the extra mile for their customers. They even came to the store after hours if a family was having an emergency. Harding's had the loyalty of most of the customers in Hikes Point. The other drug stores in the area couldn't compete with us. They were just chain stores.

The three pharmacy clerks were women. There was Iris, Nancy and a pear- shaped blonde named Polly. Polly was the most fun. She wore her hair in a Rosemary Clooney hairstyle and had a personality like the "Millie" character on "The Dick van Dyke Show –," being full of funny wise-cracks.

Both Nancy and Polly were, as we Louisvillians used to call it back then, "from the north." So were a good many of the customers at Harding's. Their husbands had been moved to Louisville by General Electric, at Appliance Park, in the 1950s. These families came mostly from Erie, Pennsylvania.

Daddy complained that the northerners were unfriendly and looked down on us Louisvillians as backward, but I didn't find that to be true. It was fun getting to know them and listening to the way they talked and teased. These people didn't talk about babies and crops all the time like my relatives.

I enjoyed hearing how they got used to their new life here in the south. They made it sound like an adventure. There were lots of comments about our use of "you-all," instead of "youse guys." They also chided us about the slow way we talked. One of their constant refrains was about money. "Things are so much cheaper down here in the south. My money goes so much further," they commented, smiling from ear to ear. We people who lived here, thought Louisville was so sophisticated, but to the Northerners, we were just a sleepy southern town.

The pharmacy clerks laughed about the jokes they heard on the "Jack Parr Show." I had never watched it, but was sure I'd like the sophisticated humor. Jack Parr came on late, at eleven o'clock, and Daddy wanted the TV off at nine. It was always off when I got home. Between my studies, my work and dating my steady, Johnny, I had no time for TV, anyway.

These clerks were nice and talked to me like an adult. They wanted to know how I liked Nazareth College, and, like some of the customers, asked me if I thought I would really be ready to teach a class of elementary students with just two years of college. Some of them had gone through a full four years of college, and frankly, they doubted that I would be.

Being a good mother was the most important job of women in those days. Even with their college degrees, these women didn't work outside the home until after their children were in school. Nancy and Polly also wanted to know how I was getting along with my boyfriend, and joked about their available sons if Johnny and I should break up. This was conversation Mama didn't have time for. Iris was older than Nancy and Polly; her sons were married, with families of their own.

They teased me about being "as small as a minute" (I weighed ninety-six pounds). They remembered when they were my size, and wished they were again. I had never felt good about my skinniness before. It had always been seen as a negative "hillbilly" trait. In grade school, my classmates sneered the ugly nickname, "bones" at all us skinny kids. These ladies changed my attitude about my weight. Delighted with their compliments, I stopped drinking the raw egg milkshakes that gagged me every morning. Mama guaranteed they would fatten me up, but they never seemed to.

Sometimes young boys came into Harding's to buy Kotex for their sisters. They blushed so much, you could light a match on their cheeks. The first time they asked me for them, my face was as red as theirs. Polly took over for me and finished the sale while I scurried off to the ladies room in the back of the store and put cold water on my face. When men wanted to purchase "rubbers," (condoms) they didn't have the nerve to go to any of us women. They asked to see Mr. Harding, himself. He kept them under the shelf behind the pharmacist's counter.

Working at Harding's was like going to a party every day. I relaxed with the routines and learned a lot from talking to the customers. These were the suburban people who were filling up the cornfields with subdivisions. I had always resented the loss of the beautiful farmland, and I still didn't like it. But now that I saw how nice these people were, it was easier for me to handle these unwanted changes.

A distant cousin of mine, on Daddy's side of the family, named Gene Gwinn came to the soda fountain frequently. He was a Bellermine student, and liked to have a cup of coffee on his way home from school everyday. He lived in Hike's Point's most expensive subdivision, "St. Regis Park."

Gene's family had lived in the West End by some of my father's other relatives. Due to the dangerous racial tensions presently happening in the West End, many residents were now moving to Hikes Point. This situation started in the late'50's, and it was really accelerating at this point. I enjoyed talking to Gene because he was from the city and I thought he was very suave. He dated a fellow Assumption graduate of mine, Barbara Harvey. I was thrilled when they married after he got his accounting degree.

The hardest thing for me to learn how to do at Harding's was to handle the kids from suburbia. They were different from country kids. They dressed well and were abrupt at times. Sometimes they sassed their parents, sometimes they sassed me. I wasn't used to children acting this way. The local children always addressed me with "Yes, Ma'am, or No, Ma'am." Many times the new kids came in without their parents. They liked to sit in the magazine corner near the plate-glass windows at the front of the store and read the comic books. They constantly came over to the soda fountain and asked for drinks of water. Mr. Harding said, "Only give them one, then tell them they have to pay for the cup if they want a second one," so I had to keep track. Our cups were made of cone shaped paper that fit into little plastic-handled pedestals.

By the backside of the fountain there was a wooden telephone booth. These kids continually checked its lever for stray change. A phone call only cost a nickel and many patrons forgot to take their change from a dime. The kids used this money to buy ice cream cones. It was only five cents a dip.

Many colorful people patronized our store. A skinny, short reporter for the *Courier Journal/Louisville Times*, named Mr. Garrison, came in every day just after I arrived at five o'clock. In his business suit, silk tie and fedora, he looked very elegant. He ordered the same thing each day, "Honey, get me a glass of carbonated water, I like the way it settles my stomach,"he explained to me. (This was before the women's rights movement made it wrong to call waitresses and store clerks "honey" or "dear"). My busy schedule and my nervousness about keeping up my grades had my stomach acting up, too, and I thought I might give it a try. The carbonated water worked, but probably what worked was the power of suggestion. I was learning about bits and pieces of information like that from my "Introduction to Psychology" Class at Nazareth.

Some of the boys from Wickham's Service Station across the street came in and flirted with me and any of the other girls that worked at Harding's. One, named Bill, was really cute and reminded me of the movie actor Tab Hunter. One day I fixed him some chili in the infrared oven.

His teasing had me so rattled that I put it in a waxed, cold-drink cup to go. I even had to charge him the three cents extra for a "to go" item. In those days, all eating places charged extra for food packaged to-go. It was cheaper to wash the set of dishes that the restaurant had on hand than to keep re-purchasing paper and plastic items.

The next day Bill came in and told me that the paraffin in the wax made him sick at his stomach. Embarrassed that I had done such a foolish thing, I snuck him another chili for free. Working nervously, I hoped Mr. Harding didn't catch me as I poured the spicy soup into the proper container, while the overpowering smell of chili powder hung in the air. I wasn't sure if he would be more upset about my giving away free food, or flirting with the customers. Both of these activities were on the "things Mr. Harding doesn't like list."

One of our deliverymen was a funny black man named Franklin. In between deliveries, he laughed and cut up with all of us. He liked to impersonate lines from famous actors. Around Valentines Day, Schraft Candies had a special heart-shaped candy box with the ad line, "I'm Shrafty-dafty about you!" Franklin thought the line was cute and went around chanting it to all us girls. We laughed until our sides ached. Doing this was bold for a black man to do in the 1950s/early sixties.

The other deliveryman was a Bellarmine student named Albert, who was tall, dark and handsome. Although I would never give up Johnny, Albert was a secret heartthrob of mine, and of all the other girls. He wanted to be an attorney.

****

Mr. Harding, a very good businessman, could see the wave of the future. Sadly, drugstores were getting too busy to have soda fountains. He closed ours in May of 1961, and switched me to the other side of the store. This meant a raise in salary, from fifty-five cents an hour to 60 cents.

Rose got on as a counter-girl at McCrory's Dimestore on Fourth Street, where she earned more than she did at Harding's. Donna, loving fashions and make-up as she did, was delighted with her new job at Ben Snyder's Department Store downtown on Jefferson Street.

My cousin Gene caught my attention one day when he said, "In six months, there will be a minimum-wage law in effect. Regular people will have to get paid at least a dollar an hour."

My mouth fell open, "A dollar, just for waiting on customers," I said, remembering the really hard work I used to do on the farm with no pay.

I never got my raise to $1.00 an hour because I only worked at the fountain for the rest of the summer. I started teaching in the fall of 1961. The job at Harding's Drugstore was one of the most enjoyable part-time jobs I ever had. It was certainly a complete contrast to the gloomy interior in the back of the bakery where I rolled snails during my senior year at Assumption High School.

Chapter 18

Teaching is Enchanting

Shivering, I woke up excited, but scared. It was September 6th, 1961, the first day of the new school year – and the day I was to begin the thirty-year career that put me on the other side of the teacher's desk. At twenty years old, I was younger than most beginning teachers, and that made me nervous.

Time to get dressed. I looked into the mirror, and remembered the "no-no" list of inappropriate clothing for lay teachers that Sister Walter Ann at Nazareth College recited to us almost daily when I was a student there the two years before. "Lay teacher" was the title the Nuns gave to the non-religious men and women who were helping with the teaching load in the Catholic Schools at that time. Due to the crunch of the immense "Baby-Boom" population, as well as, the decrease in the number of Nuns available for the classrooms, the parishes had no choice but to accept lay teachers in the schools.

A memory of Sister Walter Ann reminded me of the attire that the parish priests required."Girls," her voice droned in my ear, "you may not show your bare-arms, no revealing tight skirts, and dresses or blouses must be buttoned to the neck. No! You may not show your collarbones. *Absolutely* no cleavage, Girls, not even toe cleavage. Wear hose and sensible shoes, no bobby-sox." *I'll be safe in the navy linen dress with the pleated skirt that I ironed last night,* I smiled at my reflection. *I'll look professional and definitely older.* Jealously, I thought, *all the Nuns have to do is jump into their black and white habits.* I saw my face twist in the mirror. My envy dissolved as I realized that I was glad I didn't have to wear that, and gave my outfit a quick approval.

Like a strong parent, Sister Walter Ann was back in my head again, "Girls, you should be so grateful for choosing Nazareth

College, because we are the toughest girl's school in the south. In your two year program here, you will be as competent as anyone the public schools can graduate in a four years! Be proud you are a Nazareth student."

Yes! I thought, *I am proud of being a Nazareth student.*

I was what Nazareth referred to as a "Father Pitt Girl." When I earned my scholarship, I was delighted. "What a deal, free college!" I exclaimed two years before, to my high school boyfriend, Johnny. I knew I was well trained, but I was also exhausted. In the past two years, I had accomplished 109 college hours, and only 136 hours were needed to graduate with a full Elementary Education Degree. In order for Nazareth to present me with an 'Emergency Teaching Certificate,' I had to agree to finish the rest of my degree on my own within five years.

This 'make 'em or break' em' scholarship, was designed to see if you had the self-discipline to teach in the Catholic Schools. In short, to see if you were able to make sacrifices like the Nuns. Completing this program showed the parish priests that you were willing to put in the long hours it took to be a teacher. My pay would be low, at $50.00 a week, but it was a fortune compared to the sixty cents an hour I made at the drugstore where I worked while I attended Nazareth.

Competence was only one component of being a good teacher. *What if those kids don't like me?* As I finished polishing my navy pumps to complete my outfit, my mind began to spin again. I remembered the smart-mouthed youngsters I dealt with at Harding's Drugstore. *If my students put me down, I'll look stupid, then competence won't mean a thing...* spin, spin, spin... *No, no*! I made a quick prayer to St. Jude, *help me – this day is too valuable!* Forcing a smile, I left my sister Theresa sleeping in the bed we still shared, and ran down the steps to get Mama to pray for me, too.

At Nazareth, the identity of our sponsoring Parish was kept secret until the last month of school in the spring. The priests were afraid we might not like the location of the school that paid for our tuition, and quit the program. It was true that some of the schools were in dangerous areas. My pastor turned out to be Father Frank Maloney of Holy Name Parish, in the South End. I would be teaching one of the Fourth Grades there.

Oh, good, I thought of Iroquois Park located close by, and felt relieved. However, Dad gave me his opinion as he shook his head doubtfully, and said, "That's down by the racetrack, Deanna. There's all kind 'a crime 'round Churchhill Downs." I had ignored his warnings that day— I had to. I wanted with all my might, to be a good teacher and I wasn't going to let his fears get in my way!

****

Father Frank, as he was lovingly called, was a kindly old gentleman in his '80's. He left the running of the parish in the able hands of his two assistant priests, Father Bob and Father Ed, and put his waning years into what he believed was his most important calling, the running of the school. This mission, to Father Frank was the continuation of the Catholic Faith.

"A good Catholic education is where a young Catholic mind is trained. It is where the faith is continued and strengthened." His unsteady voice wavered as he spoke to us three new lay teachers at our introductory meeting during the summer before. We were to be Holy Name's first lay teachers. Wearing his long black cassock, Father Frank welcomed us into the formal drawing room of the priest's rectory.

"I hope you young girls know the seriousness of your job here at Holy Name," he said, his voice continuing to quake. "You are not only teaching academic lessons, your most important job is to grow the Catholic Faith. Surely, God himself has called you here." He lifted both his eyes and an unsteady forefinger heavenward. His sincerity touched my heart. But, cynically, I thought, *he's been talking to Sister Walter Ann, he sounds just like her.* I had listened to these same words at least ten times a week for the past two years at Nazareth.

Then he presented us three young ladies with keys to the school building saying, "I'm sure you new teachers need to come here often this summer in order to get your classrooms ready for the arrival of the students in September." It was obvious to me he didn't think we could ever do as well as a Nun in teaching the principles of the Faith, or anything else. I swallowed. *Can I really do the job of a Nun? Who do I think I am, anyway?*

My mind returned to the present and I grabbed a couple of biscuits to chew while I was on my way to school. I was too nervous to sit down at the table. It was only six o'clock in the morning, and I felt late already. Living all the way out in Hikes Point, I was several miles from Holy Name. Getting to the South End of town took three bus transfers: Hikes Point to Eastern Parkway, Eastern Parkway to Fourth Street and Winkler, Fourth and Winkler for the last mile to Fourth and Heywood Avenue.

Dad saved me some aggravation by dropping me off at Eastern Parkway and Bardstown Road on his way up to his new job at Wideman's Brewery, near Broadway.

He didn't make me feel any better when he said, "I hope ya' know what chur' gettin' inta', Deanna." I nibbled at my biscuits as we drove along. "Ya' better watch out for those worthless "Ne'r do-wells" that hang out around racetracks. And make sure ya' keep an eye out after yur' purse. If ya' let those kids get the upperhand, they'll run ya' around like a circus clown." *Dad thinks I'm still a child.* Knowing to take his warnings with a grain of salt, I forced the corners of my mouth to move upward.

****

Though anxious, I was also excited to get started. The night before, I had talked to my new boyfriend, Bill, who was also a teacher from the Father Pitt Plan. He got his education from the the boys college, Bellermine, and had been teaching seventh grade at Holy Infant Parish for three years. *Bill's so dreamy. Tall, slim and with lots of dark hair, he looks like that English actor, Laurence Harvey,* I let my mind take off on another trip. He was the brother of a good college friend of mine, Louise. Bill was able to calm my fears by giving me some pointers on how to handle difficult students. *Boy,* I thought, *I hope my students are never as bad as his,* but that was before I knew how badly middle school kids behaved. My former St. X High School steady, Johnny, and I had decided to stop dating, but we were still good friends and talked frequently. *Johnny might be smart,* I thought, *but, he can't help me with classroom advice like Bill can.*

Dad sped on after I jumped out of our turquoise Chevy station wagon. I soon boarded the Eastern Parkway bus across Bardstown

Road from the Whitecastle Hamburger Shop. The ride along the Parkway was lovely and I relaxed again. Passing Parkway Field, where Louisville's baseball team, the "Louisville Colonels," played their games, the bus stopped, at "University of Louisville's Speed Scientific School, next-door. College student's scrambled off the bus to get to their early classes.

This is where my old boyfriend, Johnny, was now completing his chemistry degree. *He's still in school.* I thought, *and I'm out on my own... A teacher, wow*! I let myself feel a little pride in my accomplishment. *Teachers <u>are</u> important people,* I lifted my head a little higher.

Soon the bus screeched to a halt at Winkler Avenue. Finally, I was in the neighborhood of Holy Name. Now, I felt more in control of my schedule. *It's after seven o'clock...Darn-it!...I'll be late for Mass at 7:30.* I panicked. Bounding down the steps, and being too uneasy to wait for another bus, I decided to walk the last mile. A group of youngsters familiar to me from my summer classroom work circled around as I walked along. These children had helped me count books and arrange desks.

"Good Morning, Miss O'Daniel," a youngster named David Nold, smiled as he came up beside me. A blond towhead I'd not seen before was behind him, "Is it true you are going to be the new Fourth Grade teacher?" he asked. When I answered, his face beamed, "Good, I get to be in your class." He was Ronald Clark. His next question was, "Can I carry your books, Ma'am?" *A young gentleman,* I thought, and smiled.

As we walked along, other students joined us. The rest of the kids wanted to carry something, too. I separated my books and papers, and despite Dad's warning, even my purse among the members of the group. But, I kept the bouquet of flowers I had picked the night before, wrapped in wet newspaper. *I'm going to like these children,* I thought, again getting excited about being a teacher.

We walked under the tall sycamores and maples of Fourth Street. The neighborhood was up and getting out into the day, people filled the sidewalks. Some were headed to the bus stop, some grabbed doughnuts at Bader's Bakery, or milk at Elmore's Corner Grocery. Wagner's Drugstore, a block down at Fourth and Central was open, and the spiraling candy-striped tube next door showed the barbershop was ready for the morning crowd. The area around Holy Name was only about a mile from U of L, and students weighed down with books were walking back toward that direction.

The children and I continued walking on past Leo's Variety Store, Thornby's Hardware, and several Victorian frame houses. Across the corner from our school was Cecil's Bar and Grill, where the sidewalk showed some evidence of last night's Labor Day reveling.

When we reached the location of the school building, I wanted to run across the street right there, in my haste to be on time. But, I knew it would be a bad example for the children, to have them cross with me in the middle of the block, though they probably did it all the time without me being present. So, I guided them to the corner of Fourth and Heywood Avenue and we crossed with the light.

As we hurried through the playground to the school, I noted that Holy Name's cornerstone, located below the gingerbread adorned front porch, showed the date of 1902 chiseled into the limestone. The school faced Fourth Street, while the church was across the large playground and faced Third Street. Since we were almost late, the children and I ran across the playground toward the back door of the school – I needed to drop off my materials in my classroom.

"Unlock the door," I called ahead to David, who was carrying my keys as we reached the school building. A little girl named Penny held the door for me, and all of us charged up the back steps, our noise thundering throughout the empty building. The children beat me to the room, and held the door open as I sailed through. They deposited my purse, books, papers, and my school satchel on my desk, while I put my bouquet into a vase that Ronald had filled with water from the fountain in the hall. I knew kids were not allowed in the building before school, but at that point, I didn't care. I felt a little bit like a disorganized pied piper, sort of like Maria in the *Sound of Music,* a popular movie that Bill and I had seen at the Rialto Theater during the winter before.

Tomorrow I'll catch an earlier bus, it's not good to wait for Dad's ride, I lamented, checking the clock above my side blackboard, and noting I was already two minutes late for Mass. We ran to the bottom of the steps, relocked the outside school door and chased through the rest of the playground to the church. None of the classroom doors were locked.

Entering the church's vestibule, except for our intense breathing, we became immediately quiet. The principal, Sister Phillip Martha, dressed in her long black habit with the starched-pleated bonnet of the Sisters of Charity, raised an eyebrow. *Late – on my first day!* I felt terrible. Sister gave me a 'clicker,' which was to be used to signal the students at the end of Mass, and pointed me to the location of my class. Our place was in the middle of the church and right in front of the brilliant blue and red stained glass Blessed Mother window. I felt good knowing that Mother Mary would be shining on me every morning before the school day began. Most of my students were already waiting for me in the pews. I knelt behind them and noticed that they kept turning their heads to sneak a peek at their new lay-teacher.

The September morning sunshine poured through the virgin's kindly face and landed on my shoulder. I felt her say, "Don't worry Deanna, I am at your side." Eagerly, I surveyed my class of thirty-five Fourth Graders. They knelt up straight because the Nuns had trained them, and the Sisters frowned on slouching. I had eighteen girls and seventeen boys. Their mothers had sent them off in freshly ironed clothes. *Such beautiful children,* I thought, as I surveyed the curly topped heads of the girls and the stiff flattops of the boys. Today, on the first day of school, the students didn't have to wear their navy and white uniforms.

They're so young. Then, getting distracted, I prayed, *Mother Mary, help me to set the class straight, like Bill told to me last night.* I didn't know if I would be able to do that, but what I didn't realize yet, was how delighted these children were to have their first lay teacher, instead of a Nun. Their parents were disappointed; most of them felt that a lay teacher could never teach as well as a Nun. As for the children, I would have had to be as mean as a witch and have a hairy wart on my nose for them not to like me.

****

Holy Name was an old church, showing the Victorian elegance of the turn of the century. Gold leafed murals depicting the life of Christ were interrupted repeatedly by large stained glass windows. These windows were unusual, showing teenagers in the attire of 1902. The boys wore dark suits and the girls were in long dresses. Each window featured these young people receiving one of the Seven Sacraments. Glancing over the eighth grade classes across the aisle from my students, I saw the other huge rounded Blessed Mother window. It flanked mine on the north side of the church's nave. Stained glass colors danced all over the students and the floor.

Large Celtic knots carved into the tall marble corners behind the altar showed me that this church was built by Irish immigrants. *Those people must have sacrificed many pleasures back then from their meager immigrant earnings, in order to build this beautiful church,* I thought. I realized the importance of what Father Frank said about carrying on the Catholic Faith to their children. Then I affirmed without a doubt, "God will help me do a good job for them, too," knowing that they deserved it.

Suddenly, the church was alive with the sound of the clickers. My daydream burst and I realized Mass was over. Butterflies gathered again in my stomach. My teaching day had officially started. Now, it was time to lead my class over to the school. Looking down at my clicker, I found it was nothing but a child's toy, red with black polka dots, and shaped like a ladybug. Standing up, I depressed it and my class began to file out of the pews and onto the pink and yellow squares of the terrazzo floor in the aisle. When they were all out, I joined them and depressed the clicker again. The class went down in unison with me on one knee, when the clicker popped on its way up, we all came up too, completing the genuflection. When we left the church each child made the sign of the cross on his or her forehead with holy water from the font beside the door. I did the same.

The whole student body, led by the eighth grade, filed two by two through the narrow opening in the yellow-brick Blessed Mother wall. This seven-foot wall separated the church from the rectory and protected our playground from view of the Third Street traffic. Its name came from the life-size statue in the center of the wall celebrating the feast of Our Lady of Fatima.

My students kept a straight line and chatted quietly. *"Sister Robert Imelda did a wonderful job with them in the third grade,* I smiled, affirming *they're nothing like those smart-alec kids at the drugstore.*

Marching across the playground from the church to the school, I realized that we would be doing this every morning for the rest of the year. Suddenly getting impatient, I became eager to get to my students over to my bright and sunny classroom. I was so proud of the way I had it prepared for them.

The school was old fashioned and, in those days, so was the equipment. The student's wooden desks looked like they had also arrived in 1902, the same year as the building. They were the ink-welled type that my parents talked about using out in Nelson County. Heavy and awkward, the Men's Club had long ago bolted them to long wooden slats to keep them from falling over. David Nold and another boy named John Berry helped me scoot them into place the week before school was to start.

I wanted my room to be special. I liked the sweet potato vine that the principal, had in a jar atop the filing cabinet in her tiny office, so I brought in one of those we had growing on top of our refrigerator at home. My classroom ceilings were at least twelve feet tall. I put up several bulletin boards to bring in the colors I wanted. The one I liked best was in the alcove between the door and the cloakroom. It simply said, "Welcome to the Fourth Grade." Sister Robert Imelda gave me a packet of my student's third grade pictures to hang up for the display.

As I put up the bulletin board that day last summer, one of the office clerks, Mrs. Williams, who also came to school to prepare for the new year, happened by my classroom. Happy to meet me, she cheerfully told me all about my class. Because of her comments, I felt I already knew my students. She gave me a brief synopsis on each child as I hung their picture on the blue burlap background that I had just purchased at Leo's Variety Shop on the way in that day.

"That Doreen Briggs, her mother had to get married, and Doreen seems to be going down that same path. The saddest thing is that she seems to be taking little Betty Brown along with her! Betty is such an impressionable child," the clerk lamented, shaking her curly red head. As I put up the picture of the stringy haired blonde with the coke-bottle glasses, I felt sorry for Betty. It was easy to see that in a small school like this one, there were no secrets. I appreciated Mrs. Williams' desire to help me understand my class, but I was also torn. I felt like she was treating me as a confidant, and I liked that. But, I knew from my teacher training that I shouldn't be listening to gossip about my students. I was too shy to know what to do about this interaction. I certainly didn't want to lecture an adult because I knew I would need all the help I could get this year, being a new teacher.

As I pondered my dilemma, Sister Walter Ann's words came to my mind, "Never color another's attitude about a child before they get them, or you will cause labeling. On the other hand, don't let another person color your attitude about the children, either. Labeling curbs a child's ability to perform, because you will subconsciously treat them differently." I hoped I wouldn't let this be true for me since I had already listened to the gossip. I was sure the clerk, Mrs. Williams, was just trying to welcome me to the school and only wanted the best for me. So, that was the thought I went along with.

Getting my classroom ready during the summer had helped me get to know the Sisters, too. I met all of them and had conversations with each one before the school year began. I noticed that even after all their years of experience, the Nuns took their jobs seriously, as well, and put as much effort into readying their rooms as we new teachers did. I found them to be very generous, as they frequently came by my room offering materials. It was evident that they wanted me to succeed.

I shook things up a bit when I put my desk in the back of the room, instead of the front. At Nazareth, Sister Walter Ann suggested that we try new methods, and I wanted to show the Sisters at Holy Name that I had been paying attention during my training. They seemed pleased with my plans. "My, you new teachers, you come up with such innovative ideas, Sister John Margaret said, "But how can you keep order if they can't see your face?"

"Oh," I said. "Sister Walter Ann's advice at Nazareth was to walk around the room to keep your students on their toes. She said it doesn't matter where you put your desk because you don't use it during the day." After my remark about never sitting down, I hoped I didn't make Sister John Margaret feel as though I thought she was a slacker. I knew that she wasn't, and realized that all the Nuns worked very hard. Again, I was at a loss for the right words to help me smooth things over. *Why don't I watch what I'm saying,* I admonished myself.

Outside my windows, which were on the second floor, was the roof of the priest's garage. It was attached to the school on one side and the convent on the other. Tall trees poked up on the other side of the convent's tile roof. I was surprised to find out that the garage was handy for other reasons, too. There were rumors that students (usually, only boys were guilty of this), who were kept after school for talking in class, sometimes jumped out of the large classroom windows onto the garage roof, and slid down the drainpipe and escaped to freedom.

If the teacher of this room, or the one next door (which also shared the garage roof), returned from the office and found this to be true, she immediately called the parents and informed them of their child's disobedience. Training a child to be self-controlled was the most important partnership of both the teacher and the parents, and was considered to be the most vital part of character development. A disobedient child was guaranteed to be punished at home. To the Nuns and the Catholic parents, behavior was the most important component of education. "We must first show them what discipline is, so they will learn the ability to discipline themselves," our principal, Sister Phillip Martha said. This made sense to me.

****

Finally, my students were in the room and seated. After months of anxiety, I was at last ready to begin my first day of teaching. Rehearsing many times about what I wanted to be the first words to my class, I was able to keep them as planned. "Good morning, boys and girls, I am your new teacher, Miss O'Daniel." I wrote my name on the blackboard as I spoke. When I called their names, each student answered, "Present, Miss O'Daniel," in a clear voice with good diction. As the students had entered my classroom, they sat themselves automatically in alphabetic order. They had used this format for three years, and cheered when I told them that as soon as I learned their names, I would move them every other month.

All the teachers, even the Nuns were required to turn in their lesson plan books for Sister Phillip Martha's perusal a week in advance. If she found anything that she felt could be removed or strengthened, she suggested it. Nazareth had done a good job with my training – my lessons were always well prepared.

As the Catholic School rules required, I started the day with the Catechism lesson.

Sister Phillip Martha had insisted at that first faculty meeting, the week before school started. "The teaching of the Faith is the reason the parents send their children to a Catholic School, that is why it must be the first class." My students were good in their religious knowledge. It was delightful to hear them open up to me, a stranger, and to each other. The children told of things going on in their families and of beliefs they had about life. Their innocence was refreshing and our interesting discussions made the day fly by.

Teaching was more fun than I imagined. Bill had told me that it was enchanting. "You feel like a magician when the class is well behaved and involved in the lesson," he had said to me the night before on the phone. As the oldest child in my family of eleven siblings, I had spent my life asking children to do things, and mostly getting refusals and smart remarks. But these students were delighted to do as I asked and couldn't wait to show me how much they remembered over the summer. They loved writing in their tablets and running to the blackboard to demonstrate their competence to the other students. I was grateful for their good training and felt sure that this would be a great year.

Sitting up straight on the wooden seats of their desks, the children smiled enthusiastically, happy to be back in school. Every answer they gave me included the phrase, "Yes, Miss O'Daniel or "No, Miss O'Daniel." If they had a Nun for a teacher, it would have been, "Yes, Sister" or "No, Sister," which actually came out, "Yes, Stir' and No Stir'." This was required etiquette in all the Catholic Schools. It had been required from me, too, the whole time I attended Catholic School, even at Nazareth College.

When the students wanted to answer a question, they raised their right hand for permission. My heart thrilled to see the hands flying up for every question I asked. When I chose a child to give an answer, that child slid across the desk's wooden seat and got out and stood beside it. Their answer was given in a full sentence. This behavior was also expected for all the Catholic Schools, and I had done it in grade school myself, though we didn't need to stand for answering in high school or college.

However, I feared this wonderful behavior was only a honeymoon period, and began to look for all the problems Bill and Dad warned me about. Happily, I didn't find them. I didn't know about this, but because neither the Nuns nor Father Frank really trusted us new teachers yet, they gave us only the best students.

Thrilled with my class, and like a racehorse from the "Downs," I galloped them through the schedule, leading them into spelling, math, English, and three reading groups, all by noon. To make the students feel at ease, I kept the same names Sister Robert Imelda used last year, the "Redbirds, the Bluebirds and the Blackbirds." When David Nold and John Berry helped me put the reading books on the shelves in my bookcases during the summer, I was surprised to find out that we would be using the same reading texts I had used in the Fourth grade at St. Bartholomew in 1951 – ten years before this! Even more surprising, these books were printed in 1933. *Schoolbooks must really be expensive,* I thought.

The students read with good expression. Holy Name taught reading using the phonics method, and it obviously worked. The top group, the Redbirds read at a strong fifth grade level. The Bluebirds were a good fourth grade level. But sadly, the Blackbirds were behind, reading at second grade to weak third grade level. Luckily, there were only three in that group. I had one new student, a boy named Teddy Beckman. Being a very shy, almost non-reader, I put him in the Blackbird group.

After hearing Teddy read, I was struck by the difficult task in front of me. The other students in the group gave him sympathetic, but impatient looks. Teddy was embarrassed. *I hope they're not making poor Teddy feel worse than he already does,* I thought, recalling the trouble I had learning to read in the first grade. My heart went out to him. Unfortunately, too, he was also big for his age, and felt awkward because he had already been held back once.

In those days we knew nothing about learning disabilities, now we call his problem "Dyslexia." Sister Phillip Martha informed me when first she brought him to my room, and pulled me out into the hall, "He's rather slow, he came over from the public school. You need to show his mother what we can do for him here at Holy Name." *That's easy for her to say,* I thought, *with her thirty years of teaching experience.* I was glad Sister talked to me outside the door, but I saw Teddy's downcast eyes when I came back into the room. *This has happened to him before,* I reflected, my lips tightening.

The day ended before I was ready. Both my class and I were surprised when the final bell rang. Because of the September heat, we had no lunches and only half-day classes for the first two weeks of school. Holy Name had a definite dismissal procedure. The students were not allowed to run wildly out of the building when it was time to leave. All the classes were required to stay in line as the whole school filed down the front porch steps, two by two, and on to the Fourth Street sidewalk.

Each teacher led her class along Fourth Street to the corner of Fourth and Heywood. This was the same corner where I had crossed to get to church this morning with my little helpers. The students were dismissed from here, even if they lived in the other direction, and had to turn around and walk back. If a teacher held any students after school as punishment for talking in class, tutoring, or to help her clean the classroom, these students also walked with the class down to this corner, and then turned around and went back to the school building with their teacher.

The public school, Heywood Elementary, located one block away on Heywood Avenue dismissed at the same time. Sister Phillip Martha wanted Holy Name students to behave in an orderly fashion as they left for the day. Any pushing, chasing or shoving they did, was done after they left this corner. They did plenty of it once they blended with their friends from Heywood.

Some of my students followed me back to the room, as they would do everyday for the rest of the school year. "Going home is boring," David Nold told me. Parents thought it was a privilege to get to help the teacher. "My Mama said it was all right to stay after and help you, Miss O'Daniel, if it's okay with you," several students told me, as we walked down to Heywood Avenue. "Can I stay today?" "Can I stay?" a number of them asked me. I was thrilled that they wanted to return to school.

For the most part the mothers didn't work and were usually not in a rush to do anything special. They were just glad their child was not out getting into mischief somewhere. The kids had always been welcome to stay behind and help the Nuns. I was now seen as an extension of the Nuns. At that time, Holy Name didn't maintain a full- time cleaning crew, so the children's help was important to me.

Most of these children were the ones who helped me to get my classroom together during the summer. Some of them were, David Nold, a curly headed blond with sleepy brown eyes. John Berry, a small boy with a flat top and round blue eyes. Sally Major, a brown-haired beauty with "Shirley Temple" ringlets, and sometimes Penny Smith, looking like a little Dutch girl, with her blond bangs and pigtails. Sally's mother ran a 'Rooming/Boarding house across the street from the church. Ronald Clark, who had spent the summer in the country, (it turned out to be Howardstown, and he turned out to be a distant cousin of mine, but I didn't find this out till years later), also came in to join them from time to time.

If there was a need like a doctor's appointment, etc, the mother called Sister Phillip Martha's Office, and had me send the student home. My helpers were called 'walkers,' because they lived in the neighborhood. Most of the students at Holy Name were walkers. The only ones who didn't walk were the wealthier ones who lived in the big homes on Southern Parkway. Sometimes their mothers picked them up, but usually they took the city bus. Families had one car and the father took it to work unless there was a special reason not to.

My helpers were serious about cleaning the classroom and begged for their favorite chores. "Can I dust the erasers? Let me wash the blackboards. Can I sweep the floor? I'll empty the trash cans." We didn't have overhead projectors or dry erase boards, so the blackboards, which covered three of the walls in my classroom, were in constant use. I enjoyed teaching most of my classes in drills, and found myself going through almost a whole box of chalk every week. The students loved going to the board, so I called them up several times a day. It was used for penmanship, diagramming sentences, having spelling contests and math races. This made my classes active, plus we saved paper. The majority of the parents had several children to raise and appreciated that.

But, getting back to that first day. After the classroom cleaning was done, some of the students walked with me down to Fourth and Winkler for my bus ride home. Disregarding Sister Walter Ann's warning to us Father Pitt Girls of, "Don't become friends with any of the students, or they won't see you as the authority figure," I smiled to the children as I took back the supplies they had carried for me, before I boarded the bus. Also recalling her cardinal rule for new teachers, "Remember girls, don't smile until after Thanksgiving," I laughed to myself. My students waved good-bye calling out, "Good-bye, Miss O'Daniel," as I looked out the bus window. *I can't help it, I smiled back at them and waved good-bye, these young people are just too sweet.*

Riding the bus home was a great time to take the class's school papers out of my satchel and grade them. Even on that first day, I was amazed at their good spelling and sentence structure. *Wait till I tell Mama about my good group,* I thought. She probably prayed to St. Jude most of the day for my success.

****

The Catholic Schools saw no need to hire special teachers for art and music. We taught our own, whether we were good at it or not. The Catholic System used the, Arsis/thesis method of teaching music. "Put the music in their bodies, so they can *live* the music," was the idea of the program. The children raised their arms and made swirling movements to the rhythm of the song. The music books had these swirls drawn over the song lyrics and notation, and we simply followed them. *Thank goodness,* because I knew nothing about reading music. The students were well-trained last year and led me along. I found out that they loved to sing. Whenever I wanted to perk things up a bit during a slow day, I just asked, "Okay, Boys and Girls, what would you like to sing?" Some of the songs they loved best were sung in rounds like, *Row, Row, Row Your Boat,* or *Deep in the Distant Forest, I Hear the Cuckoo, Cuckoo Sing.*

I had feared at first that they wouldn't like my country ways, happily, I was wrong. These city kids loved to hear my stories about the farm and what things were like when I was their age. They were thrilled by anything I brought in for them to examine, such as beans to shell or hard corn that we used on the farm to feed the hogs. My class and I threw it out the window to feed the squirrels that ran across the roof of the priest's garage there. Then we laughed at the fights it caused as the squirrels stole from each other.

When I brought in my record player, the students were overjoyed. It only held one record at a time, but that was plenty. Uncle Mac had given it to me for Christmas when I was in the eighth grade. I played classical music for the children when they wrote stories and Nursery Rhymes for Sing-along during art class on Fridays. In their innocence, they didn't consider themselves too big to enjoy the nursery rhymes. Before any holidays, the students took turns bringing in their favorite records. The Sisters thought this was very inventive and praised the new teaching methods I had learned at Nazareth.

Fridays were the most fun because I summed up the week with Arithmetic bees on the blackboard. Contestants shook with excitement as they ran to the front of the room. Holy Cards were the prizes. Spelling tests were funny because I liked to give silly sentences for the word examples, even using their names in the wording when possible. The one I used for the word liver was; "Lively Laurie loves to eat liver in the living room." That elicited a lot of "ooohs" from the class. It was fun to crack jokes with them, these boys and girls laughed without going wild. They knew when a joke was over and immediately settled back into their work.

My being only twenty meant that my students were half my age, and I was almost as energetic as they were. Joining them, I played kickball and chased them in Fox 'n Geese and Red Rover, Red Rover. We sent the losers through the "Greasy Barrel." Many of the kids challenged me to foot-races, and with my long legs, I usually beat them. On the rainy days of November and April, we played Black Magic and Huckle, Buckle, Beanstalk in the classroom. We went out on snowy days. The kids loved throwing snowballs, building snowmen, and shoe-sliding down the icy path on the slight hill by the Rectory – so did I!

The Catholic School System allowed time in the daily schedule for the students to have two recesses, fifteen-minutes in the morning and twenty minutes after lunch. I never punished talkers during recess, wanting them to exercise off the excess energy of sitting in their desks all day. Punishment for talking in class was five minutes after school for each time their name was on the board. This was the school-wide, no-talking policy, and it seemed to work.

Being the era of Sputnik – America realized that other nations might be outpacing us. Our president, John Kennedy, encouraged elementary schools to start teaching foreign languages. Having just taken two years of French at Nazareth, I thought it was a beautiful language, and decided to teach it to my class. The Nuns loved John Kennedy, after all, he was our first Catholic president, and they were thrilled when I volunteered to do this. The other two lay teachers taught Spanish to their classes.

Catholic parents considered the Sisters excellent teachers. They were revered for their strictness and competence. We new lay teachers strived to be given the same respect. Classes were kept on their toes by giving frequent pop-quizzes. The children teased me moaning, "Oh, Miss O'Daniel, do we have to," but soon stopped complaining and got out their pencils and paper because they loved to be challenged.

The Catholic System had many check points during the year to make sure the teachers, especially the lay teachers, were doing a good job with their classes. Standard examinations from the school board were held every eight weeks. All teachers were required to report their class results to the headquarters of the Catholic School System. Supervisors came to the each school to observe new teachers three times during the year to see if you were doing a good job, and more if they thought you weren't.

At the end of the first six weeks, it was time for report cards. Report cards were serious business, so serious that the teachers were not allowed to hand them out. One of the three priests appeared at the door for that privilege – same as it was when I was in grade school.

On the first day that my reports were to be passed out to the students, Father Ed came to the door. When he handed out the card, he made personal comments to the student, such as, "You are improving from last year, Rickey" or, better stop talking so much, Bobby." The priest always ended the session by reminding the students that the grades on the left side of the card, the conduct side, were the most important part of the report card. "You can get a job if you're not the smartest person in the world, but nobody wants you if you can't behave!" he reminded them. When Father Ed turned to leave, all the students arose, stood beside their desks and spoke in unison. "Good afternoooon, Father Ed," in a sing-song-ie chant.

Every day at noon, the whole school stopped whatever they were doing, even if the class was in the cafeteria eating lunch, folded their hands and prayed when Angelus bells rang. The Angelus was a special prayer honoring the Blessed Mother. The bells rang loudly and repeatedly for about three minutes. The Sisters were very proud of them and bragged, "These bells have been ringing at this church since 1902. Can you believe that some of the new people in the neighborhood want to stop them?" they shook their heads and sighed, disappointed in the changes they saw occurring in the community around the church.

Some of the other practices at Holy Name were part of the times. As teachers, we got to eat lunch free, and the food was delicious. Our cook, Mrs. Kaelin, a mother of one of our larger parish families, had cooked for Holy Name many years. What a cook! Her fried chicken, roast beef gravy and mashed potatoes had me returning back to the line many times over. Delighted that we lay teachers loved her cooking, she always greeted us with a big smile. "Have some more?" she beamed. She wore big blue, pearl, plastic clip-on earrings and fanned out a pretty blue and white flowered handkerchief in the chest pocket of her white uniform. We only had a twenty-minute lunch break, but we young girls moved fast.

Holy Name didn't have a faculty lounge. We ate in the room with the furnace, which was located across the hall from the kitchen. Mrs. Kaelin sent food over to the convent for the Nuns who didn't have their turn to eat in the cafeteria with the children. "It's nice of the Sisters to manage the students during lunch so we can have some time to ourselves," we three lay teachers commented. We were able to learn a lot of methods from each other.

Our weekly faculty meetings and all the office equipment were both located in the basement recreation room of the convent. This was handy for the Nuns, but not so handy for us lay teachers. The equipment consisted of a typewriter, paper cutters, a mimeograph machine and the purple masters needed to use it. When I used a mimeograph master, I typed very cautiously because there was no way to correct a mistake. If a mistake was made, you had to cut it out with an exacto-knife. Masters were expensive and Sister Phillip Martha frowned if you used too many. *Like my father,* I thought, *all adults must hate waste.*

This room was so busy after school that I sometimes got in a hurry when mimeographing my tests. The purple ink easily got all over my hands. If I scratched my face, it ended up there. Most of the time I forgot to check my face before I headed home on the bus, and looked pretty silly with a purple nose. Mimeographing was such an aggravating mess that I chose to give most of my tests orally.

Dad was wrong in his assumption about the neighborhood around Holy Name. There were racetrack people in this vicinity, but ours was a proud working class parish. Many of the students attending the school were descendants of the families that had built the parish 1902. Several members of my class told me about their parents and grandparents coming here as children. It gave me a good feeling to know this. A lot of of these people were the owners of the businesses that we passed on our walks to and from the bus stop on Winkler Avenue. To me, the area was pleasant and stable.

Fundraisers made Holy Name an active parish – making money in many ways. Built on the southwest corner of the playground in the 1950s, the gym was a great moneymaker for the parish. On Wednesday and Friday nights it was used for bingo, on Saturday afternoons, it became the only local skating rink. Kids came from all over the area and paid fifteen cents for an afternoon of fun. To mothers it was a cheap form of babysitting. Saturday evenings it was rented out for dances.

I soon learned that Father Frank had his own way of doing things. One of his traditions was to give the school the whole week of Thanksgiving off. The building was then used for a two-day Thanksgiving Festival. This was the major fundraiser for the running of the school. My students helped me make some of the preparations for the festival on the Friday preceding the holiday break. Dizzy with excitement, it made them feel important to do their share in making the money needed to keep the school going.

All the classrooms and the cafeteria were used for the festival. We swept out our room and made sure the blackboards and dust ledges were carefully washed. The children unloaded their desks and took everything home. That evening, the Men's Club took the desks from all the rooms and pushed them to the ends of the halls. The rooms were used for cakewalks, bingo games, fruit baskets wheels, poker games, etc. The festival was like an indoor picnic.

The Monday of the break was scary for me because it was also Parent-Teacher Conference Day. *The parents'll find out how young I am, and they won't think I'm competent,* I feared. When Mrs. Eison asked me, "Is this your first year of teaching?" I was lucky enough to remember Sister Walter Ann's suggested answer, and said (without lying), "This is my first year of teaching here at Holy Name." Mrs. Eison was nice enough not to press me, but I'm sure she wasn't fooled. Then she told me, as most of the parents did that day, "Michael is really enjoying school this year." Many of them alluded to the fact that their child was excited to have a lay teacher.

****

The festival was extra work, but it was nice to be off school for a week and out on the farm. All the teachers returned in the evenings to work the festival booths. I really didn't like taking the dangerous bus ride back to Hikes Point late at night. The festival didn't close until around nine o'clock. Luckily, Rita – one of the other lay teachers who lived in the east end borrowed her father's car and we shared the cost of the gasoline.

My job for the festival was to count money for the cakewalk that took place in my classroom. The beautiful homemade cakes were four layers tall and made with pride. I overheard some parents make comments about how colorful my room looked. In trying to eavesdrop, I found it hard to concentrate on the money and had to start over many times. I was afraid they would then say, "Oh my, but isn't she stupid!"

The festival did much in showing me the spirit of the community surrounding Holy Name. These humble, "salt of the earth," people impressed me with their laughter and good humor. Many who came to the event didn't have kids in our school, but looked forward to the fun of the festival because it had been a neighborhood tradition since the depression era. Several parents introduced themselves to me whose kids attended Heywood School.

****

The next month, December, found my classroom a blizzard of Christmas activities. We celebrated an early snowstorm by filling the windows with hand cut snowflake doilies. Later, using our time from our Friday art classes, we decorated the rest of the room with garlands of construction paper chains, strings of popcorn and handmade ornaments. As we worked, we sang along with Mitch Miller's Christmas songs on my little record player. "Frosty the Snowman," and "Santa Claus is Coming to Town," were the children's favorite.

Before Christmas Break, Holy Name held a Christmas Recital for the parents. My students sang the French Carol, "I'lle Anne' the Divine Infant." Rita had her second graders recite a Christmas poem in Spanish. Sister Phillip Martha, Father Frank and the parents were bursting with pride. So was I. I was as happy to be here at Holy Name, as some of my other Father Pitt friends were to end up in the rich east-end parishes like St. Agnes or Holy Spirit.

Anticipation built up in my students, and myself, as Christmas drew nearer. For our Christmas party, the students had drawn names like they did every year. The cost for a gift was limited to a quarter – they bought each other yo-yos, new things called markers, sets of jacks or playing cards.

Upon entering my room that last day before Christmas break, I was surprised to see my desk piled high with gifts. The students gave me perfume and lipsticks, umbrellas, pretty bath soaps and salts, candles, scarves, mostly from Leo's Variety Store. Some of them brought in beautiful home knitted hats or mufflers. Penny Smith gave me an incredible blue and white crochet and fluted flower basket.

"My grandma likes you, and she made it for you." she said. "She told me to tell you that it has to be washed in sugar water and stretched around this ice tea glass as it drys, to get it stiff like this." Her grandmother had placed a drinking glass inside the basket, to hold it erect and so it could be used as a vase. My most wonderful gift came from Nancy Preston, whose mother was a buyer for Dolfinger's

Fine China store downtown on Fourth Street. Dolfinger's slogan said that they sold "Only the best in china and crystal." Her present was a splendid cut-glass Bavarian crystal candy dish. It reminded me of the one Aunt Ida used to have filled with chocolates on her coffee table.

Mama was amazed to see all my gifts. I shared some of the perfume and lipsticks with my sisters, Margaret Jane and Theresa. Just entering their teen years, they were delighted to have them.

I missed my students during Christmas holidays and sent each child a personal Thank-You card, telling them how much I appreciated their gift. *This will introduce them to my class on letter writing,* I thought, knowing that I would be teaching it later in the spring. I was eager to get back to work. When school started in January, several students told me it was the first time they had ever gotten anything in the mail addressed to them.

****

By this time, I had grown very tired of the long bus ride from Hikes Point – and of waiting for busses in the cold and the rain. Before Christmas Break, Sally Major had told me of her mother's 'Rooming/Boarding house across Third Street from the church. Sally was part of the group that stayed after school with me everyday. One day when the children walked me down to the bus stop at Winkler, Sally said, "Miss O'Daniel, you should move into Mama's rooming house when that L&N man moves back to the country at the end of the year." I decided to take her up on it!

In my mind I did a quick calculation. *The room cost ten dollars a week. On my $200.00 a month salary I can easily afford that,* then again, I thought. *But, Mama will miss the five dollars a week I pay her. On the other hand,* my mind went on, *I won't need daily busfare – it will even be cheaper!* My parents started charging me rent after I got a full-time job.

When I discussed this idea with Mama, she was fearful of me being in that neighborhood at night, and Dad agreed with her. After some serious complaining on my part, both of them came around to my point of view. They had to allow me to spread my wings – I reminded them that Johnny moved out last year when his aerial survey job took him out of town. However, I heard them say the words, again and again, "But, you're a girl," before they finally gave

329

in. To keep the peace, I had to agree to come home for the weekends. "That neighborhood's not safe," they said, and I couldn't convince them otherwise.

The Majors were a nice family, and seemed pleased that I was living, along with seven other people, in their rooming house. Most of the people only roomed there, which meant they fixed their own meals. One old man, named Mr. Beswic, also boarded, this meant that Mrs. Major fixed all his meals and sent them down to him via one of her children. All the tenants had separate living quarters, but shared the same bathroom and refrigerator. *This is like the movies of life in New York City,* I thought, excitedly, when Mrs. Major showed me the room that was available to rent. It was fully furnished and more than met my needs.

"Miss O'Daniel is going to live at our house," Sally chanted the afternoon I told my helpers that I had decided to move in.

This was like a home away from home for me. Mrs. Major was very motherly and had me up to their place (which was the whole upstairs floor), for dinner, frequently. Sally had an older brother named Carl, who was a son from Mrs. Major's former marriage. He was twenty-four, good looking and quite nice. His being divorced made Mama even more nervous about my moving in there. Mama was right, it didn't take me long to fall for the charms of Carl Tremont, but he soon moved to Orlando, Florida. Sally was disappointed because she had hoped we would get together.

My mornings were much easier, now. Fixing a cup of instant coffee on my hot plate, I dunked a peanut butter sandwich into it. At last, and with delight, I said good-bye to my morning biscuits. I didn't leave the rooming house until the church bells started ringing at 7:25. Usually, some students who lived close by were with me, carrying my materials and opening doors. I didn't need to carry a purse, anymore.

I was really glad to live in the area, and the students were happy to have me there. In those days, it was considered safe to spend time with teachers, and I became part of the life in the neighborhood. After the classroom was cleaned, John Berry and Sally walked me home across the street every day. John lived down the block, Sally, of course lived upstairs. Somedays after my schoolwork was done, we went back to the schoolyard and played kickball, or joined other students over at the Cozy Theater for a movie. Another student, Joan Hail, who lived down in the next block of Third Street, told me the neighborhood rumors about the Cozy.

"Miss O'Daniel, they pay you a dime for every rat you kill in there." We laughed. But, after seeing the place, I didn't think she was kidding. The plaster was peeling, the springs popped up through several of the chairs, and there were big holes in the dirty, matted carpet. We didn't realize that the owners were just waiting for American Air Filter located next door, to expand their property and demolish the theater.

Ronald Clark and Penny Smith lived on Fourth Street and joined us often. The kids enjoyed what ever was going on. In those days, it was a privilege just to be with the teacher. Sometimes they did nothing but chase after the tennis balls I knocked up against the tall brick wall of American Air Filter. I wanted to impress Ken, my new Bellermine boyfriend, who was also a local tennis pro, with my tennis skills – but, I needed to learn them first. By this time, Bill and I had parted ways because Bill decided to go back with a former girlfriend. In fact, they were to marry in June. I met Ken through my best friend, Mary's, boyfriend.

The kids also helped me when it was time to go to the grocery. We walked to the Kroger on Montana Avenue, about seven blocks away from the rooming house. John brought his little red wagon when he could get it from his older brother Bobby, who used it to deliver newspapers, and helped me carry things home.

During one particularly huge snowstorm, when even the Catholic schools closed, (which hardly ever happened because the Nuns lived next door to the schools), I heard John knocking on my rooming house door, enthusiastically calling out, "Miss O'Daniel, all the kids are over in the side lot by the church. We have two forts ready for a snowball fight – be on my side – pleeese..." Bundling up, I and ran out to join them. After our snow battle, Sally's mother called us upstairs to their apartment for hot chocolate and marshmallows.

For Valentines Day, the students surprised me by chipping in and delighting me with a large red velvet heart-shaped box of chocolates. Their faces beamed when they saw the big smile on my face. They were even more thrilled when I passed most of the candy back to them. It was more fun for me to watch them enjoy it.

Each child had a shoebox covered in red construction paper sitting on their desk lid. We had used the art class from the Friday before to decorate them. My little record player spun out the rhythms of "Peter and the Wolf" as all of us walked stealthily around the room putting Valentines into the boxes. I gave every child a valentine and a little package of Valentine "Conversation Hearts" candy treats that I had gotten at Leo's.

Hearing a knock on my classroom door, I found out that the children had another surprise in store. Two of the mothers, Mrs. Frager, mother of my look-alike twin girls, MaryLou and Mary Beth, and Mrs. Briggs, Doreen's mother, stood there with a big smiles, plates of red heart shaped sugar-cookies, and red cherry Kool-aid for all of us.

****

The season of Easter was another special time for Holy Name. After Holy Thursday, most of the Catholic Schools got off for Good Friday. I learned not to be surprised that Father Frank had other ideas.

"Good Friday is the most important day of the Church calendar," he told us new teachers at the Tuesday faculty meeting that week. "To make it a day of significance for the children, we here at Holy Name have them come to school and spend part of this sacred day together," he continued. "In return, they get an extra day off next week. But they don't always get it off – they must earn it." When I found out what the special requirement was, I was amazed that they ever got it off.

After Mass on Good Friday morning, the whole student body walked across the playground in complete silence. Once in the classrooms, they were required to be totally quiet for the next three hours. This was to honor the three hours that Christ spent hanging on the cross. As my students entered the room, they went straight to their desks, folded their hands in front of them on the tops of their desks, and looked at them with down cast eyes. They were to spend this time in prayer for a holy Easter. Every fifteen minutes I rang the chime-bell on my desk. The students raised their heads and looked at the blackboard where I had written a special religious question for them to ponder. Most of these pertained to the seriousness of Lent and the journey Jesus made carrying the heavy cross. Teachers were not allowed to talk, either. Fathers Bob and Ed, and Sister Phillip Martha walked up and down the halls of all the floors to make sure that silence was indeed being maintained.

The week before, the students and I had hung colorful construction-paper Easter eggs from the long florescent ceiling lights. They had also colored a ditto of the "Paschal Lamb" as we sang along with Nancy Preston's record, *Here Comes Peter Cottontail,* and *In Your Easter Bonnet.* Most of the class had given up candy for Lent, and they were longing for their Easter baskets.

At eleven o'clock that morning, the whole student body gathered in the church on that Good Friday morning, to say the "Sorrowful mysteries of the Rosary, and the "Stations of the Cross." As in my childhood at St. Bartholomew's, all the statues and paintings in the church were covered all during Lent in purple Lenten cloth. "The Stations of the Cross" were located above the wainscoting on both sides of the church. Each of the twelve scenes was done in expensive "del arobia" style of painted plaster and depicted Jesus' path toward the crucifixion (*more sacrificing done by the original church members who built Holy Name*), I thought. The Stations were almost as pretty as the stained glass windows above them, and were not covered in the purple cloth.

I could feel eagerness in the air for Father Frank's announcement about the extra holiday when the solemn rituals were finished. He must have been satisfied with our silence because after the prayers, with Father Ed's help, he unsteadily climbed the steps to the pulpit, looked out over us, and said, "Students, I am sure God is pleased with your efforts today," his voice wavered. "Have a blessed Easter, and you may have Easter Monday, Tuesday and *Wednesday* off."

****

After Easter break, I got a new student named George Spencer. He was a smart-mouthed little guy, whose dad was involved with the racetrack. This *was* the kind of kid Dad had feared for me. His father was a stable groom, and he brought his family up here temporarily from Florida. They were only to be in town until the Kentucky Derby was over. That would be during the first week of May.

George was quite a flirt and sent little Doreen Briggs wild. He harassed and teased my sweet little class. Unhappily, I noticed some of my students laughing at his unruly behavior. My corrections didn't seem to have much effect. More disappointing to me, some of my students became involved with his antics – even acting out. No doubt about it – George's influence was bad! I found him hard to manage and wished I could still call on Bill for discipline tips.

While watching George's clowning around in the cafeteria one Friday, Sister Phillip Martha pulled me aside and said, "You better rein him in Miss O'Daniel – it only takes one bad apple to spoil the barrel." Her comment disappointed me because I had hoped she would have a solution. His parents couldn't be reached because they didn't have a telephone. Sister Phillip Martha didn't accept that as an excuse and told me stiffly, "Well, then you'll need to make a home visit. Holy Name won't tolerate this type of behavior."

****

Suddenly, that Monday morning, he didn't appear for school. I was happy to have a "George-free" day, and joyfully relaxed into my schedule. At lunch, Sister Phillip Martha pulled me aside again. This time she had big news.

"That new boy in your class, that George, was caught smoking on the playground on Saturday during the skating party. Plus, *and worse*, he tried to talk Doreen Briggs and Betty Brown into taking off their blouses for him." Sister Phillip Martha's eyes narrowed in displeasure as her details went on, "Father Bob caught them just in the 'nick of time.' They were hiding behind the gym. The children were at the skating party and both Father Ed and Father Bob were watching the skaters. When Father Bob noticed those three had disappeared, he went to find them. Of course, Father Frank immediately expelled George, and called the girl's mothers. Were they ever upset!"

Yay! I thought, *George is history.* However, I felt sorry for this street-wise kid and the kind of future that must lie before him. But, I was delighted to have my lovable little class back again. Luckily, George was not there long enough to cause any permanent damage and they settled back into being their wonderful selves.

Soon spring came. My spirits were high as I watched the days lengthen and new green come to the old trees. Sounds of spring filled the neighborhood, the noises of hammers and saws joined the returning migrant bird calls, as homeowners entered their old homes into the annual springtime "paint-up, fix-up" period. My heart always lightened in the spring, to me it was the season of hope and rebirth. I started daydreaming of summer vacation soon to come. But, my heart grew heavy when I realized that my sweet group was about ready to move on to the fifth grade.

Mother's Day came and each child pleased their mother with handmade cards listing chores they promised to do without complaint. Those that could afford it also added a pretty handkerchief from Leo's Variety Store to their card, they cost twenty-five cents.

The heat of May almost drove us out of our ancient building. I opened the large windows for the breeze that whisked between Third and Fourth streets. Wasps, whose nests were high up in the building's box gutters, helped themselves to my classroom. The students cheered as I chased them around the room and smashed them with my broom. Concentration on lessons was hard for the children to do until I succeeded. Some days one of the parents sacrificed a fan for us – I didn't own one. Due to the heat, the last two weeks of school were like the first two in September, half-days with no lunches.

Two weeks before school was out my class and I were done with our lessons. We waited for the examinations that would be sent in from the Catholic School Board, and filled in the time with spelling bees and several art projects. Always enjoying work at the blackboard, the students ran up for arithmetic races and hangman games. They brought in new records for Sing-along with the record player.

On "Sports-Day" the whole school went outside for competitions. My class competed in jumping contests and played kickball against the other fourth grade. We won several contests, but, of course, not everything. The eighth graders were in charge of the rotation of the classes, the refereeing, and the prizes. They were good leaders and I could tell that they felt important. Sister Phillip Martha and Father Frank were proud of them.

With special permission from Sister Phillip Martha, I took my reading classes outside with their thirty-two year-old textbooks. We read them under the shady maple trees on the Heywood side of the church where some of the students and I had held our snowball fight back during January. From here, we could look into the windows of the Brothers' Fish Fry Restaurant on the corner. It belonged to my student, Tommy's family.

The end of the year meant scrubbing down the furniture, wrapping the bookcases in newspaper, stripping all the bulletin boards and cleaning the blackboards. We carefully dusted off and rolled up my teaching flip-charts and the ABC Cards. I put my room number and name on everything. The floors of all the rooms were to be shellacked over the summer. I would be getting this same room again next year, and was glad.

In order to pass to the fifth grade, the students had to master the difficult standard examinations that were sent out by the Catholic School System. Failure to do this meant being held back, no matter how well the student did during year. As fearful as the students, I knew this would really show if I could teach or not. I breathed a sigh of relief when all my students, even Bobby Skaggs (the cut-up) and Teddy Beckman (the former non-reader), passed. Yes, reading finally clicked in for Teddy. A beaming smile replaced his former fearful grimace.

On the last day the students didn't have to wear uniforms. They looked so much more grownup than they did in September, which was the last time they were out of uniform. *They're moving on,* I contemplated. I was very pleased with them. Father Frank passed out the report cards for the three lay teacher's classes. His voice shook as he made individual comments on each child's progress for the year. I admired the way the children revered him – not a snicker was made about any of the stumbling or quivering he did. *How can he remember the progress of all 475 children in this school?* I wondered, and then I realized that he knew each child because he had known the families for so long. It was obvious that Father Frank considered this school to be as precious to him as a child of his own would be. He came to the three lay teachers' classes because he wanted to be sure how well we had done this year.

Letting the children chatter until the dismissal bell after Father Frank left, we talked of summer plans as we waited. Again, just like the day before Christmas Break, my desk was filled with small gifts. There were apples, freshly picked spring flowers wrapped in wet newspaper, or home baked cupcakes or cookies.

When we parted, several of the children had tears in their eyes as they said, "You're my favorite teacher, ever." I enjoyed their comments but knew that I was their first lay teacher, so I didn't let these remarks go to my head. Grateful for getting to be part of this unique window in the history of Catholic School education, I realized that in a few years, lay teachers would feel ordinary to them.

The charm of this class would always be with me. In those days, actions between teachers and students were so formal that I couldn't imagine hugging my students good-bye. I stood at the door and they each shook my hand as they left the room. "Good-bye, Miss O'Daniel, Good-bye, Miss O'Daniel, I heard them say as they lined up in the hall, and readied to go back into their world for the summer. We wished each other a happy summer. Upon the sound of the dismissal bell, we marched in line to the corner of Fourth and Heywood like any other day.

My usual group of helpers followed me back to stay after school and chat for the last time. We really didn't have any work to do, as we had already done it. So today, we were much more informal. I could tell they felt naughty in singing this, because of the sheepish grins I noticed on their faces. They gathered around my desk and chanted the same end of the year rhyme that the kids back at St. Barth's sang when I was in school – though certainly not to the Nuns!

"School's out, schools out
The teacher let the monkeys out,"
They really got a little blushed when they said the last line;
"One went east and one went west,
One went up the teacher's dress."

They held their mouths and giggled, with their eyes rolled up to check my face. I smiled, on the outside, to my faithful little group of helpers, and on the inside, to me for being blessed enough to have gotten to work with this wonderful group of children.

Turning in my keys in at the office, I left Holy Name to begin my summer. John Berry and Sally Major walked with me back across Third Street to my room at the rooming house. Mrs. Major brought down a pitcher of lemonade and baloney sandwiches. She took a break from her chores to help the children and me get things packed up in my tiny room. I caught the bus back to Hikes Point that afternoon. My time in this neighborhood was over for the next three months. Tomorrow, Mama and my brother Jimmy and I would arrive in the family station wagon. We would move my stuff back to the farm at Hikes Point for the summer.

Actually, even better than that, I was ready for my next adventure. In two weeks, I would be leaving Louisville on the Greyhound bus to spend my summer in Madison, Wisconsin. Because of the night classes I had taken this year, I only needed twenty-seven more college hours to graduate, and I would take some of these requirements at the University of Wisconsin. This trip was suggested to me by Tom, a friend of the Major's family. Tom was University of Louisville law student. He lived in the neighborhood, next door to the Cozy Theater, and had gone to high school with Mrs. Major's son, Carl.

On one of the evenings when the Majors invited me up for dinner, Tom was also there, and seemed to have an answer for my empty summer. I told him I wanted a "big college" experience, instead of what I had been used to at Nazareth, a small girls' school. He assured me that this "Big Ten" school would more than answer my wishes. Tom had attended there during one of his undergrad summers. Most of the campus was located between two lakes – Lake Mendota and Lake Monona.

Tom bragged, "In the summer sessions, the fraternities throw kegs of beer in Lake Mendota before morning classes. They pull them out after lunch for afternoon swimming parties. Everyday!" he emphasized. I didn't even like beer, but this sounded like a lot more fun than Nazareth, "The toughest girl's school in the south."

Chapter 19:

"Where is Pat?"

Mama was so excited that she danced through every day since she got the great news. We were moving to the city – the family was finally leaving Hikes Point! It was 1964. Ours was just about the last farm left there. The chairman of the town council told Dad, "The people in the new subdivisions don't like the smell of your pigs. You have to get rid of them." Dad knew his days were numbered when Stiedenberger's farm across the road from us was sold the year before to become "Hikes Point Plaza."

"If I can't raise my hogs, we're moving to the city!" Dad shouted to the family when the man left.

Mama's life-long dream had *always* been to live in the city. "I've never been grateful for those filthy hogs until now." She laughed as she told me of her good fortune. I was home for a weekend visit from my rooming house across the street from Holy Name School.

My brother John had stopped by Louisville during the week before, taking a few days off from his aerial survey job. Together, he and Mama looked through the home sales booklets. Almost breathlessly, Mama showed me the picture of the house they agreed would be worth checking out from the sales booklet. It was near Cherokee Park in the Highlands area of town.

Morris decided to check it out the next night when he took his girlfriend, Judy, home to the Highlands. As Morris passed by the large arts and crafts style home on Alta Avenue near Cherokee Park, he knew it was for us.

"Mama's gonna love this place," he told Judy. Noticing the house was vacant; they got out of Morris' car and stumbled around the yard of the huge empty building in the dark. He liked the yellow brick, and the big screened front porch. Because the house was so massive, it had been sitting on the market for over a year. Dad knew this meant they would be ready to negotiate a good deal. There were twelve large rooms, eight of them bedrooms. Best of all for my family, the house had five bathrooms, this meant no more fights in the bathroom line!

When he saw it, Dad was satisfied, too. "I like this place because the extra side lot is big enough for the little kids to play in, and for me ta' raise a vegetable garden. Plus, I can store my tools in the three-car-garage." I'd never seen Dad this excited about anything before. Too big for most people, this house was a perfect size for our family of thirteen. He sold off part of our cornfield and paid cash for the house.

As for me, I was delighted about the move, even though I already lived away from home, my fiancé, Ken and I would be getting married in August. The Catholic rules at that time dictated that marriages take place in the girl's parish. St. James, built in 1904, was our new parish, and a lot prettier than St. Barnabas, in Hikes Point. As I had done the three summers before this, I would be leaving the rooming house as soon as school was done, and return home for the summer. This time, I would live in our new house on Alta Avenue until my marriage to Ken in August. I was thrilled, too. Now Theresa and I would share a much larger room, with a large walk-in closet and bright sunny windows. No more time stuffed under the eves!

When I went back to Holy Name the following Monday, I got Sister Phillip Martha's permission to call John at his aerial survey office in Oklahoma. She led me into the private area of the convent where there was a special phone connected to a "Watts-Line."It was a line that discounted long distance calls. I was eager to tell him that the house worked out for the family. Mama refused to waste money on such a call. "It's not an emergency," she had said when she insisted that I put the phone down at home. "You know Dad will get mad if we make an unnecessary long-distance call! I can write him a letter."

John was delighted to hear the good news, "So, we're finally getting out of Hikes Point," he said. "It's really not the same place as it was when we grew up," he continued. "It's sad to come home now, with the farms all gone. It's not pretty anymore, and there's no safe place for the little kids (Phil, Bill and Pat), to play like we used to have with the creeks and the woods."

I agreed, "Hikes Point is nothing now but shopping centers, apartment buildings and subdivisions. Even Dad's not happy out there now. I'm sure the little kids will enjoy playing in Cherokee Park, if the side lot gets too small for them."

After we hung up I thought, *John's great to talk to now that we've grown up.* I had noticed that about Morris, too, the last time I was home for the weekend. He was so busy, I hardly got to see him anymore.

Dad bought the house in March, but didn't plan to move the family in until school finished for the kids in May. Besides, the place was dusty and dank after sitting vacant so long, and Mama had her dreams of how she wanted it to look when the family arrived. Spring was moving along fast, and a lot of work still had to be done before school was out.

****

Dad dropped Mama and my youngest brother Pat, age five, off at the house every day on his way to work at Wideman's Beer, close by, on Baxter Avenue, near Broadway. This was about five minutes away from Alta Avenue. Every day they brought over boxes of stuff and lots of cleaning supplies. They worked from eight o'clock in the morning to four thirty in the afternoon, when Dad picked them up on his way back home to Hunsinger Lane.

****

On one particular day in April, Mama was excited about a big plan to start working on the floors. She and Pat had already scrubbed out all the cabinets, mopped the floors, and dusted down the walls.

"Today, I'm gonna shellac the parquet in the living room and dining room," she announced, grinning ear to ear, as the boys, Jimmy, Tony and Morris, filled our turquoise Chevy Kingswood station wagon with buckets of shellac, varnish, turpentine and brushes to add to the other supplies they already had stored at Alta.

"Josephine, you tell those boys to hurry up and get that stuff packed. I don't want to be late for work again!" Dad yelled out the back door of the kitchen as Mama supervised the loading of the station wagon. Inside the house, Margaret Jane finished the breakfast dishes as Theresa and Mary Ann got Billy and Phillip ready for the

St. Barnabas school bus. It would arrive at seven-thirty. With our new parish, the bus now came by the house.

Even though she was 50 years old, the adventure of the move had Mama giggling like a teenager. When they got to the new house on Alta, she and Pat quickly unloaded the supplies from the station wagon before Dad, who was always in a hurry, sped off to Weidman's.

Soon, Pat had everything that Mama didn't need to do the floors hauled down into the basement. He took down jars of canned goods, boxes of empty canning jars, and more cleaning supplies. He was strong for a five- year-old, but farm kids start doing hard work early in their life.

"Stack all that stuff on those shelves down there," Mama yelled down the steps to him, "and then come back up here and sweep the front porch and the walk." She poured a bucket of water to damp-mop the floors and get them ready for shellacking. Pat finished his job in the basement, and then did the sweeping out on the front porch and walks. He knew that Mama wanted the neighbors to think we were going to be good people for this nice neighborhood.

After the sweeping, he helped her get all the doors and windows open. Then he placed the oscillating fans where she wanted them. While Pat took a break, Mama damp-mopped all the wood floors downstairs, the living room, the dining room, two bedrooms, the den and a long parquet hall.

"They'll be dry enough for me to start shellacking 'em after we eat our lunch," Mama said as she pulled their fried baloney sandwiches and homemade cottage cheese from the picnic cooler. She was thankful that we no longer had the cumbersome army cooler. They sat on wooden benches that were attached to the knotty pine walls in the breakfast nook by the kitchen. The best thing about lunch for Pat was that he got to have a whole six-ounce Coke as a reward for the extra work he was doing at the new house. Back home, he had to split his Coke with Phillip and Billy. Soft-drinks were one of the unnecessary foods that Dad called 'monkey-food,' his word for junk food. Our family handed Cokes out quite judiciously.

Lunch was over and Mama had nothing for Pat to do for awhile, "I'm gonna' play ball outside," he said, starting for the side lot.

"Maybe some of the kids in those apartments next door will come out and play with me, like they did on Saturday."

"But Pat, today's a school day." she reminded him, "there may not be any kids there. When you get tired, come up the kitchen steps and take a nap in the back bedroom. And, don't come out of there until I come get you. I don't want you stepping on my wet shellac."

He watched Mama kneel down and tuck her work dress between her knees. She put a scarf over her dark hair to keep it from flying in her face with all the fans blowing across the room. Humming, she started working at the front corner of the living room floor. The strong smell of shellac hung in the air.

Pat bounced his ball loudly down the back steps from the screen porch behind the kitchen and on out into the lot. He avoided the prickly thorns of the rose bush by the gate, and made as much noise as he could, banging the ball on each dribble and slamming the gate. He didn't like to be alone. As the baby of the family, Pat was used to others being around, usually Phillip, age nine and Billy, age seven.

Despite the noisy racket he made, no other kids came out to join him. To kill some time, Pat ran up and down the lot and climbed some of the smaller trees in the fence line by the alley. After awhile, he bored of playing alone. Coming up the back steps, he heard Mama whistling and singing as she watched the parquet regain its shine. He peeked down the hall from the kitchen and saw her kneeling in the middle of the living room floor. She wiped the sweat off her brow with the back of her hand, as she moved back and forth over the wood. The hard work didn't bother her at all, even though the fans were not able to remove all strong fumes of the shellac from the house.

Not wanting to disturb Mama's mood, Pat climbed into the twin bed in the back bedroom. This bed was the only piece of furniture Dad had moved into the house because there was so much work to be done on the floors and the walls. Mama's singing lulled Pat off to sleep.

*****

In no time it was after four o'clock and time for Dad to arrive from Wideman's. Mama heard the car's horn honking loudly from the driveway by the side kitchen door. "Well, I'll swan! If that don't beat all! Why's he always in such a hurry?" she declared, as she slowly pulled herself up from the floor in the hall. Mama stretched to ease the crick in her back and then stared admiringly at her work. Exhausted, and a little bit groggy from the shellac fumes, but still thrilled, she was eager to tell Dad about her accomplishments of the day. The living room floor was done, as was the dining room, and part of the long hall.

"Hurry up, Josephine," Dad yelled out the window of the station wagon, "I want to beat the afternoon traffic."

In sort of a daze, perhaps from the overpowering fumes of the shellac, Mama grabbed her purse, the picnic cooler and some dirty rags to wash and ran outside where she lifted the back door and piled them into the rear of the station wagon. Before she opened the front door to get in, she stopped short, "Wait," she said, her mind obviously scattered, she ran back toward the house, "I got to put the paint brush in turpentine." The words flew over her shoulder as she unlocked and opened the basement door to find the turpentine bucket.

Locking the door behind her as she left, she thought, *living in the city is gonna' be different. Can the kids get used to lockin' doors, now?*

"Come on Josephine," Dad prodded her, interrupting her thoughts again. Her concentration scrambled, she hurriedly jumped into the car and they drove away.

On the way home they talked about what they needed to pack up that night, and what the kids should do to help get ready for the big move. At this point, my family had lived on Hunsinger Lane for seventeen years. My parents had been farming all of their twenty-five year marriage. A lot of work was involved in moving to the city. The animals and farm equipment had to be sold or given away because neither would be needed, anymore. In many ways, this saddened Dad – but not Mama.

Dad had already sold his big tractor and most of the hog-killing tools to a farmer in Jeffersontown. Now, he had to finish selling the animals. "I'll call on Blanton's Farm tonight, and see if they'll buy Calfie," he said reluctantly, as they drove along. "I don't want to sell her to Bourbon Stock Yards. Maybe Larney will take the chickens. He told me he found somebody to buy the hogs."

"But, I'm not selling my hog-killin' knives, though," he went on. "They belonged to my father, he said they'd been in our family since the O'Daniels came to Kentucky over two hundred years ago." Dad rambled on, remembering the night before when he had shown off the knives to Jimmy. Unwinding their silken cords, he taken them out of their flannel wrappings and stroked their ivory handles. Jimmy had stopped packing the tools in the shed where he had been working next to Dad, and moved over to get a better look at them. He could feel Dad's pride as he saw the glint on the blades reflected by the tool house light. They looked at each other, grimacing, as the realization of the new life in the city was beginning to sink in. On Alta, these knives would lose the place of prominence they had held in our family for over two hundred years, and become just plain knives.

Quiet for a while, my parents soon picked up their busy chat as they left Cherokee Park and turned left in front of Bowman Field Airport, for the last leg of the trip back to Hikes Point. Daddy cleared his throat as he listened to Mama's progress with the beautiful hardwoods. The excitement of their new adventure was bringing them closer together. It almost seemed like they were setting up their first household. They knew they'd be up working late into the night, but they didn't care.

****

Long after Dad and Mama had left Alta Avenue, Pat was awakened by the lights shining in the bedroom window from the apartment building next door. Darkness surrounded him. *How come we're here so late?* He wondered, and rubbed the sleep from his eyes. *Daddy must a' forgot us.*

Climbing out of bed, he called, "Mama, Mama, where are you?" The words echoed back from the large, empty rooms. Still groggy from his long nap, he stumbled into the kitchen. The house looked ghostly, with the streetlight from the alley shining through the large tulip poplar tree by the kitchen window, and casting long shadows across the linoleum floor. Starting to go out to the screened-in back porch behind the kitchen, he stopped himself, remembering, *Mama won't let me go out in the dark.* He was afraid to walk around the scary house alone, and besides, he didn't want to track on Mama's newly shellacked floors.

Suddenly, he realized what had happened. *Daddy must ta'come, picked up Mama and they forgot about me.* Unconcerned, he assured himself, *they'll be back and get me soon.* Pat ignored his hunger and went back to sleep while he waited.

****

Meanwhile back at the farm, Mary Ann thought she missed seeing Pat at supper. "Where's Pat?" she asked Mama.

Still distracted with all her busyness, Mama said, "Oh, he must be out in the pasture field playing with Billy. Now, you go on into the living room and finish packing those up those boxes in there with Theresa. Then she turned her attention to Margaret Jane, and said, "Go upstairs and help Tony pack up the drawers in the back of the attic." Preoccupied, she talked as she continued to stare around the room at everything at once.

After supper, Dad had left to talk with the men at Blanton's Farm down on Six Mile Lane about buying Calfie, and of course, he shared a few beers with them. Morris was at work at Woolworth's Five and Dime across Hunsinger Lane in the new Hikes Point Plaza Shopping Center.

As darkness came on, the kids began to form the line for our one bathroom, as they got ready to go to bed. "Wow, we're gonna have five bathrooms, no more standing in line," they laughed and elbowed each other, high in anticipation for the new life they would soon be leading. In my parents' bedroom, Mama knelt beside her bed saying her nightly rosary. She thanked God again for the new house, and tonight she begged Him to let the Blantons buy Calfie. None of us wanted to see our wonderful cow go to the slaughterhouse.

****

On Alta Avenue, morning finally came, streaking the dawning sun across the empty room, shining on Pat's blond head and waking him. Hunger pulled him out of bed as his little stomach growled. When he realized where he was, his eyes opened wide as he stared at the empty rooms. Swallowing hard, he realized that he had spent the whole night alone in this gigantic house. He wanted to cry, but he didn't. Now that it was daylight, he could go outside. Having watched Dad drive from Hikes Point to Alta Avenue for months now, he was sure he knew how to get home.

His thirst drove him to the kitchen, but Mama had taken all the dishes home to wash the night before. Being too short to reach the kitchen sink, he went to the bathroom and leaned in to take a drink from the faucet on the bathtub. *Time to start my long journey home,* he thought.

Just a block down the road, he reached Cherokee Park and turned right. The chilly morning air made his little tennis shoes fly down that hill and up the next. When he reached the convergence of Spring, Speed and Cherokee Park Road, he wasn't sure which way to turn. Sitting down on the curb by the sidewalk, he began to cry as the awesome fear of his situation began to settle in.

After a while, a man in a long, black Packard, pulled up beside him. Rolling down his window and turning off the morning news, the man leaned out and asked, "Young man, what are you doing out here on the road all by yourself so early in the morning?"

"I'm lost," Pat whimpered. "My Mama left me at our new house and went back to our old house. I'm trying to get home." He continued sobbing.

Obviously a family man himself, the man pushed back his hat and scratched his forehead, then asked, "Well, son, do you know how to get back to your old house?"

Pat cocked his little blond head to the left and said, "Daddy drives through the park, and I don't know how to get through the park. It's a really big park," Pat stretched his hands apart to emphasize its size as he went on, "but after that, you go past the airport, and I know how to get home from there."

Pat forgot to tell the man the name of Hikes Point, which would have helped greatly. "Well, that's not far!" the man said, thinking Pat was talking about Dutchmans Lane, on the other side of the park. That street was just only a couple of miles away. "Get in son; I'll have you home in no time!"

Living in Hikes Point, a community where we always accepted rides from neighbors, due to the lack of availability of very many busses, Pat didn't think anything about accepting this ride from a total stranger. Even though he seemed like a nice man, he was still just a stranger to my little brother. Pat's tears dried as this helpful man reached over and pushed open the passenger door. The aroma of the rich leather upholstery escaped as Pat climbed into the shiny black Packard.

****

Meanwhile, back at Hunsinger Lane, Mama got breakfast ready with the help of my sisters, Margaret Jane, Theresa and Mary Ann. The long line formed for the morning use of the bathroom, as the family got ready for school. Dad was drinking his second cup of coffee and giving his daily orders on the chores he wanted each kid to do that day as he did everyday.

"Josephine, when you get to Alta, today, tell Pat to sweep off the basement shelves back in the tool room. I want to start moving my hand tools over there."

Looking around, Mama shook her head and said, "Pat's not up yet. Who does he think he is, sleeping so late with all we got ta' do?" without stopping, she continued, "Billy, go upstairs and get him up."

Billy's answer surprised her, "But Mama, he's not in his bed. I didn't see him when I got up. I thought he was already down here in the kitchen."

Previously nervous about Pat, Mary Ann ran to the front of the bathroom line and pounded on the door, "Who's in there?" she demanded, hoping Pat would be the one to answer.

"Hey, wait your own turn," Morris yelled out through the door at her.

Mama's face went white as she realized the situation, "JH, do you remember Pat getting into the car at Alta yesterday?" she asked Dad, her voice trembling as she spoke.

Dad's coffee spilled all over the place when his fist hit the table. "You mean that kid's been in that empty house all night by himself!" he shouted. It didn't occur to him that his rushing had anything to do with Mama forgetting about Pat in the first place.

"Get Morris outta' that bathroom and make him drive you over there and get that kid. I'm late now; I gotta' get ta' work!" Jumping up from the table, he left as Jimmy brought in the bucket of Calfie's morning milk. Setting the bucket on the cabinet, Jimmy helped Tony get Mama out to Morris' old, black Chevy. She was shaking so much she could hardly walk.

All the brothers and sisters worked to finish breakfast, pack the lunches and get ready for the school bus. They were too scared about Mama and Pat to do their usual morning mischief.

Morris pushed the "pedal to the metal," and drove his temperamental jalopy as fast as he dared. "Oh Lordy! What have I done? Pray, Morris, pray!' Mama pleaded. "I just hope Pat didn't wander off and get lost in the park. If he did, we'll never find him!' Sobbing, she continued, "Oh God, how could I have done such a stupid thing as to forget my own child?" It didn't occur to her that Dad *also* forgot him.

Morris, seeing how upset Mama was, tried his best to soothe the situation. "Now, Mama, you know God watches out for us, just like you've always said." Morris's words sounded sweet, but Mama was too distraught to hear them. He turned from Taylorsville Road at Bowman Field and entered the Seneca portion of Cherokee Park.

****

The car with Pat in it arrived at Bowman Field, missing Morris' old jalopy by only a few minutes. "Which way, now?" the man asked. Pat's lip trembled and he started crying again. He was too scared to think. The man pulled the car over in front of Air Devil's Inn, across from Bowman Field Airport, and turned it around.

Looking at his watch, the man said, "Son, I'm sure your Mama and Daddy are going crazy looking for you. You know they had to miss you when you didn't come down for breakfast. I bet they'll go back to your new house to find you. Since that's where they left you, I'm taking you back there." The man rubbed Pat's head again as he spoke. Starting to smile, Pat's tears dried, as he thought of seeing Mama soon.

Pulling his Packard back out on Taylorsville Road, the man and Pat went back into the Seneca Park portion of Cherokee Park as they took a right turn by the airport. Soon they found themselves on Cherokee Road again, where the man had picked Pat up a few minutes earlier.

All of a sudden, Pat jumped up from his seat. Leaning forward, with one hand on the dashboard, he used the other one to point out the front window, as he shouted, "There's my brother's car!"

Surprisingly, Morris' old black Chevy was right in front of them. Without knowing it, they had followed Morris and Mama through the park and then up Cherokee Road. Presently, Morris arrived at the turn off for Alta Avenue and slung his hand out of the window to make a left-hand turn signal. The man followed Morris' old jalopy down Alta as he turned into the driveway at 2324. The man pulled his Packard up in front of the house.

"Mama, Mama!" Pat screamed, jumping out of the car and into Mama's surprised, but anxious arms.

"We tried to get to your house, but your son lost the way," the man explained to the Mama and Morris, leaning out the window of his car.

"We appreciate you helping us out, Mister," Morris said, reaching into the car to shake the man's hand.

"God bless you, sir," Mama sniffled. The man tipped his hat to her. Men didn't shake women's hands in those days without their husbands being present. Straightening his tie, he said, "My name's John Moore. I live a few blocks away from here down on Bonnycastle. I'm glad to be of help. I'm a father myself, and I just couldn't let the poor little fella' sit there crying on the curb. I'm sure somebody would do the same thing for one of my kids if they ever got lost. My wife and I have seven, and we may just leave one of 'em somewhere tomorrow," he laughed. Mama and Morris joined him in nervous laughter, releasing some of the anxiety that had built up that morning.

"Be sure to thank the nice man for helping you out, Pat," Mama said, reminding Pat of his manners. Then she said, "I'm glad to know we will have such nice neighbors, Mr. Moore. We'll be leavin' good neighbors in Hikes Point – what's left of 'em." Her voice trailed off. It was the first time she realized that she was going to miss anything from the farm.

"Thank you for helping me, Mister," Pat mumbled from behind Mama's skirts. Mr. Moore chuckled again and drove off to work. "Gotta' get downtown," he said, his words flying out the window as his car left the curb.

Looking into Mama's face, Pat said, "I was real scared." As he relived the memory, he started to cry again. "Thank God you're all right," Mama started crying, too. She picked him up and carried him to Morris' old car with tears of joy rolling down her cheeks.

"I'm glad you're back," Morris said, rubbing Pat's head.

Settling into the front seat with Pat on her lap, Mama pulled up straight and sucked in her breath, "No matter how much I wan' ta' move inta' that house, it wouldn't be worth it to lose my baby," she said through her tears. "Today, we're gonna' stay at Hikes Point and just pack up some stuff there. I'm not going to be in such a big hurry any more. I declare, I learned my lesson!" she said, a sigh of relief bringing a smile to her face.

Not wasting this opportunity, Pat looked up at Mama as his blue eyes widened and asked, "Can I have an extra Coke today?"

They all shared a good laugh, and the anxious morning disappeared.

Daddy's Expectations

Success for my father was
eleven healthy children
raised by hard work,
good food and shared
sacrifice.

His values molded
our young lives into the adults
he desired to carry
his 'good name,'
his integrity
out into the world.

His demands:
-Always use good grammar
-Never leave the house with
dirt on your shoes
-Stand up straight
-Pay attention!
shaped our lives.

-Never expect anything
you don't work for,
-Know what you want
-Don't give me excuses!
-Have strong self-discipline,"
were the phrases that
formed character
in his children.

He shared with us his love
for God, the land, the gifts of
nature, woods, fields, and
all the creatures living there.

He loved the throb of downtown,
the joys of Fountain Ferry Park.
Black dirt, good neighbors, and
the quiet at the end
of the day.

He reminded us of
our responsibilities to:
-Take care of our body,
-Rotate the crops,
-Pamper the cow,
-Give Sunday to God, and
give the Lord His due.

He guided our
appreciation of the
finer things we didn't have
because of his love for them:

His appreciation of the past
influenced our value of history,
His admiration of old buildings
and beautiful architecture, lead
us to work in preservation.

His ideals were guided by
the country ways that
comforted his parents,
and molded him as
he grew up on his
childhood farm.

His hands never rested,
never wasted...
His mind always busy
creating, problem solving,
making life better for us.

He was quite a Dad!

Epilogue

Dear Reader,

Thank you for reading the account of our family's transition from the O'Daniel Farm in Gethsemane in Nelson County, Kentucky to our life in the active Highlands Area of Louisville. It was always my mother's fondest dream to live in the city. I hope you have enjoyed this trip backwards, and the review of life details as many people lived them during the mid-part of the Twentieth Century.

Even though I have completed the documentation of this part of my family's life, I thought you, the Reader, might be interested in a synopsis concerning the outcome of my family members, and a brief word about my childhood experience.

My family owned the wonderful home on Alta Avenue for almost forty years. Several of the large oak and maple trees were toppled in the extra lot by the 1974 tornado. Always a consummate farmer, this delighted my father, as it allowed him to grow even more vegetables there. This garden was the envy of all the neighbors who walked by it. My parents continued to can and freeze crops until my father passed in 1990, at age 79. Mom passed away in 2001 at the age of 87. We hated to see the house go, but we had to sell it in order to settle the estate. As I stated in the story, Dad was able to negotiate a good deal on that house and lot when he bought the property in 1964 because he paid for it in cash. The house alone recently resold, for over twenty-seven times the amount he paid for both the house and the lot in 1964. The extra lot is now occupied by a separate large federal-style home.

The saddest event that happened to the family was the death of my sixth brother, Phillip, born in 1955, at the age of 18 in a car accident, in 1974. To date all the rest of my siblings are alive and happy, with nine of the remaining ten still living in Louisville. John and his family settled in Texas.

On my Dad's side of the family: Aunt Bertha died in 1968 at the age of 88. Uncle Mac, Dad's brother, died in 1972, at age 66. Aunt Gen died in 2003; she was in her late 80's. My cousins, Pat and Alice are now living in upstate New York.

As for my mother's side: Aunt Aurelia and Uncle Earl moved back to Howardstown in 1952 to help my Grandfather, Emanuel to manage the Boone Brothers Farm. They stayed to raise four boys, Rick, Frank, Alvin, and Danny. Emanuel died in 1969, not long after Great Grandma Sudie. Great Grandma lived to be 102 years old, and enjoyed receiving letters form the Lyndon Johnson, the president of the United States, and Pope John 23rd at her centurion celebration. She kept her sense of humor right up to the end. Uncle Bud, Aunt Lena, Mary Jane and Hugh died in the ninety's. the rest of the cousins are alive and doing well.

Sadly, Uncle Earl died in 2004, but with the help of three of her sons who live nearby, Aunt Aurelia still manages the farm. Always a welcoming and generous hostess, she stops her chores immediately upon the arrival of any guests, and makes them the center her of attention. The farm is host to several family reunions and campouts every year. At this writing, four of Mama's siblings are still alive, Garland, Mary Cora, Aurelia, and Saloma. Uncle Ed's wife, Aunt Lila and Uncle Garland's wife, Aunt Mary, are still with us, as well. Aunt Aurelia declares that the Boone Brother's Farm will always be a working farm. We hope that she will have her wish.

Because the Gethsemane house in which I was born on the former O'Daniel farm is now being used as a retreat house, Mama, Jim, and I stayed there one weekend. Laughing, Mama said, "It sure feels good to come here and sit down in this dining room and have somebody wait on *me*, for a change." Continuing to recall the days when we lived there, she declared, "And, I don't have to carry any water up that hill from that spring, anymore, either." Along with the other retreatants, we enjoyed good cooking and the peacefulness of the countryside.

****

As for the outcome of myself and my other siblings: My husband Ken and I were married for fifteen years and had two children, a girl, Leah, and a boy, Jason. They are now both adults. Leah and her husband Matthew have a son named, Gavin. Jason has an incredible job that has him traveling worldwide. I taught school for over thirty years in both the public and private school systems, and enjoyed it immensely. I am now a health counselor and find that very satisfying work, as well.

My brother John, a retired college professor, has two children, Andrea and Ward, and lives with his wife, Marilyn, in Austin, Texas. Andrea and her husband, Eric have have a son, named Taylor.

Morris (Marcellus) has two children, Christie and Robert, both still in collage. Morris has owned a very successful hair salon in Louisville for several years.

Jim has been an important part of the community as the collector of all state and property taxes for Louisville and Jefferson County, for the past several years. He and his wife, Linda (also called Nickie), have a daughter, Angela and two grandsons. Angela, her husband Rick and the two boys, Christopher and Thomas live in Cincinnati, Ohio.

Margaret Jane (Marty) is retired from the insurance industry and lives in Louisville. Her son Phillip, his wife Patti and son Nick live in a suburb not far away.

Theresa and her husband, Jamie have two children: Karen and her husband Ken, and Trey and his wife Farrah. Both couples live in Louisville. Theresa still enjoys working in an Attorney's office.

Tony, a Vietnam Veteran is retired, lives in Louisville and enjoys working with mechanics.

Mary Ann (Annie) and her husband, Terry, live in Louisville. They have two children, Tara, and Tim. Tara and her husband, Jimmy, have two daughters, Addison and Molly. She, Jimmy and their family live in the Cincinnati area. Tim also has a daughter, named Paige. Mary Ann is a dental hygienist and loves her work.

Bill and his wife Angela live in Louisville. He is a manager for the parks department. Angela is an Ex-ray technician.

Pat has two boys, Matthew and Josh, who are both still in college. Pat lives in Louisville and works in construction.

****

It would take many pages to describe what I learned from the busy childhood I was fortunate enough to have. Valuable lessons don't come easily; you have to search through the shaft to get to the kernel. But, in short, I think one word accurately sums up my experience. That word is integrity. My parents used its themes as the guide to mold our lives: self responsibility through hard work, strong character through honesty, appreciation of quality, thrift, and thoughtful use of all things, care about your neighbor's welfare and respectful use of the land.

Dad would say, "Know what you stand for and live that way." But what Mama said always strengthened me more, "Have strong faith and work hard, then God will give you all you need." The most important thing I learned from Mama was the importance of civility and how to be a peacemaker. As a child, I fought like the rest of my siblings. I did not recognize this trait until I was an adult, and out on my own. She used a common cliché to sum up this characteristic, "You can catch more flies with sugar, than you can with vinegar."

About the Author

Deanna O'Daniel considers herself fortunate to have grown up after World War II, during America's greatest period of prosperity for the middle class. This was also the period of America's greatest migration – from farm to city life. O'Daniel's father, being a consummate farmer, desired to have it both ways: a farm on the edge of Louisville, Kentucky. This made for an interesting and busy life for his children, particularly, Deanna, as the oldest daughter.

Spending many hours alone doing monotonous farm chores lead her to become reflective and creative. Reading, and exploring the countryside that she loved at Hikes Point, then a rural area dotted with farms, were her greatest joys. She started a hobby of writing and illustrating her own novels as early as the fourth grade. However, life interfered, and she did not return to writing until after her mother died in 2001.

Born in 1941, and being a few years older than the Baby Boomer Generation, Deanna was able to take advantage of a scholarship program offered to college students in order to help handle the huge population explosion that the Boomers put on the classrooms. After just two years in college, Deanna started teaching when only twenty years old. She taught for almost thirty years between 1961 and 1997.

Although, she loved teaching, she tried her hand at other careers, in order to explore more of the world. She became a bank teller, an accounts payable clerk, a real estate agent, a motivational therapist, and is now a counselor in mind and body therapies.

She owns a Company called, *SelfSeek Spiritual Center*. In this company, she works to help people better their lives in areas of stress management through leading retreats, yoga, and meditation. She also counsels clients to release addictive behaviors such as smoking, etc.

CPSIA information can be obtained at www.ICGtesting.com
Printed in the USA
270177BV00002B/100/P

9 781452 041780